LIONS IN WINTER

Chrys Goyens   Allan Turowetz

Prentice-Hall Canada, Inc., Scarborough, Ontario

Canadian Cataloguing in Publication Data

Goyens, Chrys.
  Lions in winter

ISBN 0-13-537457-X

1. Montreal Canadiens (Hockey team)—History.
I. Turowetz, Allan, 1948-   . II. Title.

GV848.M65G69 1986   796.96'26   C86-094262-7

Prentice-Hall Inc., Englewood Cliffs, *New Jersey*
Prentice-Hall International Inc., *London*
Prentice-Hall of Australia, Pty., Ltd., *Sydney*
Prentice-Hall of India Pvt., Ltd., *New Delhi*
Prentice-Hall of Japan Inc., *Tokyo*
Prentice-Hall of Southeast Asia (Pte.) Ltd., *Singapore*
Editora Prentice-Hall do Brasil Ltda., *Rio de Janeiro*
Prentice-Hall Hispanoamericana, S.A., *Mexico*
Whitehall Books Ltd., Wellington, *New Zealand*

ISBN 0-13-537457-X

Production Editor: Sharyn Rosart
Design: Bruce Bond
Cover Photograph: Bob Fisher
Manufacturing Buyer: Don Blair
Composition: CompuScreen Typesetting Ltd.

Printed and Bound in Canada by John Deyell Company

1 2 3 4 5 JD 90 89 88 87 86

CONTENTS

To my late father Jacob and to my wonderful wife Gail—the two guiding forces in my life.

A.T.

To my Mom and Dad and the Eaton's catalogue people who got two Montreal Canadiens sweaters to Kitimat, B.C., in time for Christmas, 1955.

C.G.

Introduction

Images.

Stills. Sepia-toned pictures freezing the time and place of an outdoor rink in the winter of 1931, and young men like Sylvio Mantha, Aurele Joliat, Howie Morenz and Nick Wasnie who will never grow old. In the manner of professional athletes across the generations, they stare defiantly at the camera, daring the clock to move. The fabled *bleu-blanc-rouge* is many shades of brown.

Stillness. The eerie silence that greets sportswriter Andy O'Brien on that March day in 1937 when he enters the Forum and finds it crammed full with fifteen thousand people. In a coffin at centre ice lies Howie Morenz, a scant six years removed from that day in 1931 when he and his teammates dared the second-hand to continue its sweep.

Still. Elmer Lach and Maurice Richard embracing in mid-air on an April night in 1953, their sticks high after an overtime goal, and Boston captain Milt Schmidt sitting on the ice knowing that the Stanley Cup has eluded him one more time. Or an April night the year before with the Rocket, blood streaming down his face, shaking hands with Bruins' goalie Sugar Jim Henry moments after shrugging off a concussion and the entire Boston team to score the goal that eliminated Beantown yet again.

Moving. The earliest televised black-and-white images of the fabled warriors of the 1950s—Jean Beliveau, Dickie Moore, Henri Richard, Boom Boom Geoffrion, Doug Harvey and Jacques Plante—steamrolling the opposition en route to five straight Stanley Cups.

Slow motion. Frank Mahovlich dropping a pass to Phil Roberto, and then *his* drop pass to Beliveau, who sweeps in on Minnesota goaltender Gilles Gilbert and leaves him in a confusion of green-and-gold as goal number 500 slides into the far corner.

Colour. Ken Dryden leaning on his goalie stick, watching the action 160 feet away where players such as Guy Lafleur, Bob Gainey, Steve Shutt, Larry Robinson, Serge Savard and Guy Lapointe mount a ferocious red, white and blue assault.

Splash. A young kid named Patrick Roy talking to his goalposts while the Madison Square mob hoots in derision. Three hours later "Roo-Ah" and seven rookie teammates have the last laugh. Two weeks later they complete their defiance of the odds and common sense to add *their* own silver to the biggest trophy case in North American professional sport.

Tradition.

That ugly word that hangs like a life sentence over any player who wears the *bleu-blanc-rouge* because it means that when he takes to the Forum ice, he faces not only the other team but also the bronze busts in the Forum lobby.

Tradition is images, evocations of other times and other successes that bend the time/space continuum. Tradition is commitment to those images and the people who inspired them.

Many athletes prove that they can play with pressure. Few can play with tradition.

Tradition is commitment to *la Sainte Flanelle* . . . the Holy Cloth. Whether it be the Yankee pinstripe and those monuments in deepest centre field that recall a sports stadium in the Bronx and decades of pre-eminence in baseball, or perhaps the Kelly green with white trim of the Boston Celtics and memories of players with names like Jones, Cousy, Russell . . . there is something instantly recognizable about the uniform colours of a special team in a particular sport. Few will argue that Yankee pinstripes represent baseball at its finest over the twentieth century. The same glory is attached to the Boston green and white in professional basketball.

In professional ice hockey, it is *la Sainte Flanelle* ... the red-white-and-blue and the distinctive CH of the *Club de Hockey Canadien*. As much as Harold Ballard might demur, attempting to raise the tattered standard of the Toronto Maple Leafs, that Agincourt was fought—and won— long ago.

The Montreal Canadiens and their celebrated road uniform are instantly recognized anywhere in North America—even in places where hockey is not popular. Indeed, that is probably the greatest test of a dynastic organization—the recognition factor of its colours by people with little interest in the sport.

Most of all, though, *la Sainte Flanelle* means organization. The Montreal Canadiens have become the signature team in their sport because of organization: the behind-the-scenes arranging that led to the on-ice heroics of the young men in the still and moving pictures.

But images are all foreground.

* * * * *

This book will attempt to meld those images with the background: the organizational theory and the production of results on the ice. The authors firmly believe that the Montreal Canadiens never would have attained their full status without a strategic edge over the competition. Nor would they ever have enjoyed such an edge on the ice without a clearly articulated off-ice organizational policy.

We look at the names and try to convey what they meant then, and still mean today. Maurice Richard, the city boy, and his country cousins, Jean Beliveau and Guy Lafleur, were a lot more than mere hockey players.

They stood for something special, the pride and aspirations of a people that had enjoyed too few heroes in modern times. As a result, and no matter how hard they try, the Rocket, Gros Bill and the Flower will never be average people in the eyes and hearts of their contemporaries.

We look at the Grey Eminences who stood behind them, men with names like Dandurand, Gorman, Raymond, Selke, Pollock.

We endeavour to explain the folklore by applying sociological and organizational terms and theories to the apparatus that provided the foundation for the on-ice magic.

No one, however, can truly explain the magic. And we would be fools to try.

An Anecdote

The year: 1983. The place: Moscow.

Serge Savard, the recently appointed Managing Director of the Montreal Canadiens, is making the almost obligatory introduction tour of the hockey hotbeds of Europe and the Soviet Union.

This is the real world of National Hockey League executives. In the best American Express tradition, no NHL General Manager should be without at least one trip to the USSR. However, NHL self-image being what it is, the club Public Relations people tell the media Savard is on a "western" scouting tour: they don't say just how far west.

Savard has been here before, with Team Canada in 1972, during that most emotional of series. That was a time of adversaries, when the Soviets would pull little tricks like constantly ringing the room telephones of Team Canada players in the middle of the night to disturb their sleep. Frank Mahovlich was a particular target.

These, however, are enlightened times. The Soviets have since won their share of games with the NHL pros, and vice versa. Hockey hegemony now is recognized to be a fleeting thing, resting on the talents of one or two superior players who define the vintage. Grudging respect is given and taken.

After the protocol is dispensed with, the vodka comes out and the hair is let down (as much as it can be under the circumstances).

Savard finds himself making small talk at a not-so-official official reception, along with a great many dignitaries.

Across the room, a grey-haired gentleman painfully makes his way toward the Canadian visitor. His progress is impeded equally by advanced age and infirmity and the presence of a fawning group of sycophantic functionaries.

The Red Sea of people parts in front of a curious Montrealer.

"Tell me, Mr. Savard," says the Grey Eminence, "what is happening with our Canadiens? I can hardly hold my head up in the Kremlin these days."

"We're having our ups and downs, as you may have noticed," Savard replies, equally curious and surprised.

"Yes, I know the feeling." Several minor officials, looking terribly anxious to please, press around. Eventually, the man is introduced; he is Mikhail Suslov*, member of the Politburo and the Secretariat of the CPSU Central Committee. He is known in the highest circles of international politics as the Kremlin Ideologue, the man who defined communism as it is practised in the Soviet Union.

Officials of all kinds beam benignly as the hockey man and the politician discuss matters far removed from SALT II and the Helsinki Agreement. It turns out that Mr. Suslov is a fan of Bob Gainey, Guy Lafleur and his favourite player, Larry Robinson.

His curiosity piqued, Savard wonders aloud where the elderly gentleman picked up his information.

"We in the Old Guard have been Canadiens' fans for many, many years," he smiles. "I have long been a supporter of your illustrious team and great hockey players like Maurice Richard, Jean Beliveau, Jacques Plante and others. . .

"For the longest time the Canadiens were very popular with the Old Guard in the Politburo, but now the younger men are switching. They seem to have a preference for Mr. Gretzky and the Edmonton Oilers but we have a name for them. . ."

Savard bites.

"What's that?"

"Defectors."

*Mikhail Suslov has since passed away.

Prologue

ANNOUNCER: *For years, fans like you have provided that special "Go Habs, Go!" enthusiasm that has contributed so much to the success of the Montreal Canadiens. That's why the Montreal Forum invites all you true red-white-and-blue fans to come cheer on the Canadiens in the coming Stanley Cup playoffs. There are still plenty of great seats left and, if you act quickly, you could be right there in the heat of the action, encouraging your Habs on to victory! The entire team is counting on you for your vocal support to spur them on, as they begin their quest for the Stanley Cup. Remember, the Canadiens and the playoffs have been a Montreal tradition for the players and you fans for years! And now you can play your part in this hockey history by picking up your playoff tickets at the Forum box office from Monday to Saturday—or at any TICKETRON outlet. The Canadiens' first playoff game will be at 8 p.m., April 7th at the Forum. Be there to add your voice to the roar of the crowd, as the Canadiens' Stanley Cup playoff tradition continues . . . it's "Go Habs, Go!"**

Radio commercials for the Canadiens? Vulgar advertisements and blandishments to get the public to fill the Forum for playoff action! *Sacré bleu-blanc-rouge, ce n'est pas possible!* Has the world turned over?

It was not so long ago that the entire marketing program for the *Club de Hockey Canadien*, the proudest dynasty in professional ice hockey history, comprised one bold conceptual stroke: ensuring that the wallet-sized folding Canadiens' schedules and the October-to-April Molson's

---

*Radio commercial, late March, 1984.

calendars were in the taverns of Quebec before the last week of September.

This was an era that predated "demographics", "positioning" and "hustling the product". All the marketing necessary for the product was done where it counted. On the ice. The players took care of product control. There was no such thing as buying radio spots or newspaper space. Sports public relations people and marketing experts will let you have this one for free: "Nothing succeeds like success."

The Canadiens would win, win, win. With style. With panache. With élan. They would skate faster than the other guys, score more (and more exciting) goals and play flashy, crowd-pleasing hockey. Marketing and public relations were superfluous. After all, Buckingham Palace does not soil its regal hands with common currency. Neither did the Canadiens.

Any suggestion of vulgar commercialization emanated from outside, from people who were only too happy to function as subservient "suppliers to" and "sponsors of" the Habs. The people within the organization were free to concentrate on hockey. What spilled over would be handled by someone else, usually a Molson's marketing man, who saw each goal scored in liquid measurement.

But that was another time. This is Mr. Orwell's 1984. Monday, April 2, 1984, to be exact. If Big Brother isn't watching you directly, you know he could if he so chose. 1984 is a marketer's world. Image is everything, and it's right up there in omnipresent video. Of all the times for the team to lose its identity, its soul.

It is a beautiful, early spring day. The sun is shining strongly on St. Catherine Street on this peaceful Monday afternoon. But it is fraudulent; the ten degree Celsius (fifty degrees Fahrenheit) weather is bolstered by a sun that is more light than heat. Within minutes of sunset, the chilly reminders that winter is still around will be there for all to feel. Still, sunset is hours away.

The city has gone on a diet. Everywhere you look, people have shed their winter parkas, balloon-like outer garments filled to bursting with expensive down or less costly synthetics. Slimmer, lighter overcoats prevail. Here and there, Quebec's version of California's beach people dare sports coats and sweaters. The afternoon announcers on the radio, French and English, announce the Nicest Day in Creation. Forgive them all their trespasses, Oh Lord, for they have survived yet another Montreal Winter. Cabin fever *reductio ad absurdum.*

The streets are still wet from an early morning rain. The sun is bright, but it's not strong enough to dry them yet. Very little snow can be seen within the city limits. And there is still enough wind to keep people moving briskly.

About two blocks east of the Forum on St. Catherine, the picture window of a cigar store-newsstand has a foldout from a local newspaper. Thirty or so Montreal professional athletes are grinning toothsomely at passersby. Their faces are Florida-baked. The sign says "Good Luck in '84 Expos—*Bonne Chance en '84!"* These are the perennial bridesmaids of the National League's East Division. Judicious dealing in the off-season has brought some bullpen relief to the pitching staff. For yet another year, most baseball pundits (more in the U.S. than in Canada) are picking the Expos to win the division and even the National League pennant. The sports talk shows on radio are full of baseball fans looking forward to the warmth of summer and the year ahead. They wax optimistically in both official languages. This will be the year. The "wait 'til next year" of the beloved Brooklyn Bums is about to come true. The Good Guys are finally going to do it. The Expos open in Houston on Tuesday.

An afternoon sports talk show is interrupted by a black cloud. Occasionally, a caller refers back to the previous year. His sport is hockey. The host sighs audibly. "Go ahead, caller," he says heavily. You can almost see him slump in his seat, shoulders down. Or reach for another cigarette, automatically, listlessly.

The fans have been venting their spleen all winter but remain pained and constipated.

The Montreal Canadiens, pride of the great white north, are launching their playoff season on Wednesday night, in the bandbox Boston Garden, home of the Bruins, winners of the regular season of the Adams Division. Nobody waxes optimistic. The word "wax" does come up, usually in descriptions of the surface upon which the home team seems to have played its last season.

As in, "What did they do, wax the ice? The way those bums kept falling down on their rear ends all year...."It has been the worst of years for professional ice hockey's most prolific team. The feeling at home is *"sacré bleu-blanc-rouge, what a disappointment!"*

And, of course, the Canadiens could not even be good at being bad. What has frustrated the fans most in this, their worst year in 33 seasons, is that the team would often rise up and smite some of the top pretenders in the National Hockey League. They waltzed into New York and handcuffed the Rangers, beat up on the Bruins 7-2 in Boston, handled the Flyers in Philadelphia, the Flames in Calgary, the Nordiques in Quebec. Just when you were expecting them to settle into a pattern of hopeless mediocrity and really lose everything, they'd revert to the team that has awed generations of ice hockey players. Every time you wanted to laugh at them, a safe emotional release, they'd force you to take them seriously. It was slapstick at its best ... just when you would figure the seltzer bottle was empty, or the pie would never get thrown... POW, right in the mush.

The hotline frustration is not in the least cathartic. The fans are emotionally spent. The sports talk program host has heard nothing but bad hockey analogies (the analogies were good, the hockey was bad) for six months. Screw the playoffs. Bring on the baseball team. At least *they* haven't choked since last September. Don't bother us with the Canadiens. We don't want to know.

The team faithful are so down that they don't see the silver lining in the cloud. It showed a glimmer just last night, when the Boston Bruins surged ahead of the Buffalo Sabres on the last night of the dreadful 1983-84 season, to win the Adams Division. That means Montreal at Boston, Quebec at Buffalo in Wednesday's playoff opener. Buffalo owned the Canadiens all year; against Boston the Habs played better.

That almost means new life for the home team, if rookie coach Jacques Lemaire can come up with a game plan that will negate the Bruins' one offensive line (Middleton, Pederson and a fill-in). That strategy could prevent the omnipresent defenceman Raymond Bourque from ever skating in a straight line—then Lemaire's task will be to encourage his team to score first and throw a checking blanket over the Bruins' lunchpail brigade.

The local fans are so down that they can't even look up the road to Quebec, where the organized pandemonium that is Michel Bergeron's Nordiques' offence is the ideal antidote to the precision game that Scotty Bowman's Sabres have used to destroy the Canadiens.

Montreal versus Quebec in a best of seven, *un quatre de sept?* Get serious. It will be Buffalo-Boston in the Division Final. Nobody is in a mood to even dare dream; even when the talk show host wearily trots out The Playoffs Cliché.

"You never know," he intones, "it always seems that someone comes out of nowhere in the playoffs to be the hero. The Canadiens may have some player who is going to surprise everybody this year...." He never gets to finish the sentence.

"Like who?" The caller's voice is scathing and dripping with sarcasm. The winter was cold. The snow was deep. The hockey was terrible. "Steve Penney?"

Having delivered that devastating riposte, the caller abruptly ends the conversation. The talk show host smoothly manoeuvres the conversation back to baseball. He's had enough grief for the winter; the ratings period is almost over. Maybe seven days down south somewhere in two or three weeks, get a headstart on the summer tan. Get the cold out of the bones. The hockey season will be over by Saturday, Sunday at the latest, if the Habs get a little feisty and squeak one out against the Bruins.

"We'll break for these messages and be right back," he sighs.

* * * * *

It is in this atmosphere that François-Xavier Seigneur must work. It is perhaps the best example of the curious time warp that affects professional sport that thirty-four year old "F.X." is known as an up-and-coming young man while thirty-two year old hockey player Guy Lafleur is perceived as only weeks away from his pension cheque.

Guy Lafleur is the old Canadiens, getting older. F.X. Seigneur, vice-president of marketing for the *Club de Hockey Canadien*, is the new Canadiens, a glimpse at the team's future.

The former is downstairs practising with his team-mates for the playoffs. His scope is limited to the next game, the next opponent, the next shift. He lives in neatly segmented 20-minute slices. He also lives in the limelight; it has shone kindly on him in the past but is merciless in this, his longest season.

F.X. can be found upstairs, in a functional office along Executive Row. Apart from the special wall-hanging with the stylized CH which greets you in the anteroom (something recent that they never had when the Canadiens were winning, you can't help but wonder why; now, they "buzz" you in after quadruple-checking your bona fides with other sentries), there are few indications that you are in the Forum.

It could be any one of thousands of corporate offices downtown—all muted ecrus, beiges and browns. Understatement belies success, they say. In the Canadiens' scheme of things, success certainly has been understated recently, and that's what's hurting the team. Very few Canadiens fans have ever heard of F.X. Seigneur, or most of the people who work upstairs.

The greetings dealt with and discarded, we get straight to the meat:

"How do you market a loser?"

No double takes, no injured look, no excuses.

"The same way you market a winner," Seigneur replies.

"Nobody in marketing consciously sets out to market a

loser or a bad product, or one for whichever reason hasn't made an impact in the marketplace," he explains calmly.

"We didn't set out to market a bad hockey team, and we don't think we have marketed a bad hockey team either. Yes, we have had what is for us a bad season on the ice. The Montreal Canadiens have not played under .500 hockey since I was in diapers. But the marketing program for this team was drawn up a year ago. It did not take the team's fortunes into consideration because any marketing man will tell you that can't be done."

The man is a breath of fresh air. Short, precise answers to questions at a time when sportswriters all over the city are speculating that wrists are being slashed all over the building and honoured (and dearly departed) heroes of the *bleu-blanc-rouge* are turning over in their graves. To be frank, we were expecting evasion.

"The secret to successful sports marketing, in hockey, baseball, football, whatever . . . is to devise a plan that will be in effect despite winning or losing on the field or on the ice. That's why you market a team," Seigneur continues.

Let's get serious here! We are talking about an institution in the sports world. We are talking about a team with few peers in the annals of sports. We are also talking about a tradition of winning that allowed the club to sneer at such devices as public relations, marketing, and advertising . . . until very recently. Does this mean that the team on the ice has become secondary to the team in the executive suite? Or that hockey is less of a game than winning the "beer wars" (Molson's Canadiens *vs* O'Keefe's Nordiques)?

"We are also talking about the 1980s," comes the reply. "We are talking about television, mass communications, more competition not only for the sports dollar, but also for the loyalty of the fans. We are talking about competing for space in the media with much more competition than we ever faced before. The Montreal Canadiens do not just compete against the other teams in their Division or Conference or even the League."

Seigneur does not raise his voice. He responds calmly, much like a fellow student or student adviser at a college seminar.

"Today, we compete against the Nordiques, the Montreal Expos, to a lesser extent the Montreal Concordes (CFL), tennis, jogging, racquetball, squash, the movies, television, video, Hulk Hogan, rock concerts . . . whatever you can think of in the entertainment world. The Canadiens fans may be as loyal as ever before, but they have many more interests than ever before; many more ways of spending their money. So we have to take into account all of these factors when we sell the hockey team.

"I know a lot of hockey purists in this town might be upset to think of the Canadiens as just another product, but we have to look at it in this way when it is time to plan for the next year. Just like we did last year, looking ahead to this year."

For staunch Canadiens supporters, the marketing battle was a revelation. Shortly before the season started, the team published an insert in the daily newspapers. An expensive, four-colour production, its glitzy sales message took a lot of people by surprise. So well done was the artwork that it ended up on the bedroom walls of many young Habs fans.

The Canadiens, whose fans usually passed season's tickets down through the generations in probate court, were marketing "mini-packages" of middle-range tickets. Fans could select ten-game "mini-schedules", and reserve their tickets for games they really wanted to see, at prices that real hockey fans could pay.

No more taking out a second mortgage to finance two tickets in the Reds, times forty games. No more trying to foist Pittsburgh or Los Angeles tickets on friends and acquaintances.

No more tradition . . . where the faces in a section of Reds or Whites would not change in a decade . . . and the fans in that familiar spot were as close and as much a part of the team as the mercenaries who wore the uniform on the ice (and longer-lived, too!).

Visions of the Apocalypse danced before the moist eyes of the regulars, even those regulars who were never closer to the team than the radio or television set but took perverse pride in the club's lording it over mere mortals. There is little snobbery on this planet that can match that of the fans of a true sports dynasty; whether they worship at the altar or via long distance, the club reaches out and touches them.

At the beginning of the big marketing year, there was optimism in the product, in the plan. At the end of the year, the product was not anywhere near up to standard, but attendance was up. The marketing plan worked, even if the season did not.

"We've had a bad year on the ice, nobody in these offices is going to deny that," says Seigneur. "But attendance has been up four percent over last year. We've managed to smooth out the peaks and the valleys of the season."

But what about the imperious Canadiens, Lords of the Ice, the club that never had to advertise? That disdained public relations as something forced on lesser beings? What about tradition?

"My greatest ally," says Seigneur.

"We're going to be seventy-five years old this coming fall. We have just had a bad season. But tradition doesn't go down the drain just like that. The banners with all the Stanley Cups indicated on them are not going to be torn down because we've had our first losing season in thirty-one years. They'll stay up and remind our fans about exactly what the Forum and the Canadiens are.

"During the summer, many fans will think more about the first seventy-three years than just last season. We are still very popular. In a poll of sports fans across Canada last year, we were Number One in hockey with twenty-one percent popularity. Toronto Maple Leafs, who haven't won a Stanley Cup in almost two decades, were Number Two with eleven percent. Does that tell you something about old loyalties? The New York Yankees went through hard times in the late '60s and early '70s before they came back strong. But they still were the New York Yankees and still the most recognizable baseball team anywhere.

"The product still is good, gentlemen," he concludes

with a flourish, "and, should we have a good playoff series . . . it will all be back in our laps. You see, in sports, with its instant success or failure situation, you never know when it will turn sour or unbelievably good. It is that fragile and immediate."

F.X. Seigneur, former COJO (Montreal Olympic Committee) cadre member, former executive assistant to a federal government minister, a pinstriped-suit type, perhaps is the most representative example of the new direction in organization taken by the *Club de Hockey Canadien.*

In recent years, the club featured a structured hierarchy, but the lion's share of power remained at the top, usually in the hands of one man.

The club was fortunate in that Frank Selke, the innovator, and Sam Pollock, his successor, were grassroots geniuses who understood that they were only as good as their organization and surrounded themselves with very competent help. Still, at the top was the lone decision maker. The underlings, many of whom who would seed the NHL in managerial talent (Cliff Fletcher, Al MacNeil *et al*), could only pass up recommendations and await decisions.

The Canadiens owe most of their early success to the fact that they were run this way before any other club, and that their decision makers listened to their advisers closely, placing a lot of trust in their expertise. Yet the Boss had his finger in every pie.

Today, the Canadiens are run like any other business. The new Canadiens' hierarchy features a standard organizational chart. Five vice-presidents work under President Ronald Corey. Their tasks and responsibilities are clearly defined. There is little overlapping. There are Monday morning management meetings every week.

"There have been lots of changes in the way business is done in the last ten years," says Seigneur.

"We are striving very hard to be as professional upstairs as we have always been downstairs. Mr. Corey is very clear on this. He says he has surrounded himself with an all-star management team and expects us to perform like the professionals he knows we are."

Seigneur has produced results. In a battle with the Nordiques and the dreaded other brewery (from whose bosom Ronald Corey was plucked) for market share in Quebec, which was for generations the sole fief of the Canadiens, the club has begun to reclaim lost ground. Since the entry of the Nordiques into the NHL in 1979, the Canadiens have been on their heels.

After all, everyone loves an underdog, and the Canadiens were seen to be a little too high-handed in their dismissal of their country bumpkin cousins, especially since they could not back it up with any measure of finality on the ice. As well, the Nordiques and Carling O'Keefe Breweries actively sought out the Quebec hockey fan, working hard both within the club and the brewery to sell, sell, sell, all over the province, and that included Montreal.

Most unfortunately for the Canadiens, the Nordiques benefited in their early days from some subtle racism, becoming Quebec's French team while the Canadiens and their "anglo-dominated" front office were seen as Quebec's English team. At the time of the referendum, when sovereignty-association emotionalism reached a fever pitch in the province, too much of this silliness found its way onto the sports pages.

For a while, especially in the French-language newspapers, hockey writers and columnists were openly cheering for the Nordiques. That, like the other outward signs of Quebec nationalism, died down with time, but not before there were unfortunate incidents; during the Nordiques-Canadiens playoff in 1980-81, General Manager Irving Grundman and his wife were spat upon and called "dirty Jews" at Quebec's Colisée, and the Canadiens entourage had to demand extra security from the Nordiques. (None of this untoward behaviour would be in evidence during the 1983-84 playoffs as fans in both cities would be models of decorum during the High Anxiety of '84.)

While nothing excuses that kind of behaviour at any level of society, the point was that the Canadiens were particularly ungracious towards the Quebec team when they entered the league (once refusing an exhibition game in Chicoutimi that would have made a lot of fans in the province's hinterland very happy) and spent some years paying for it. Of course, the Quebec nationalism that served the Nordiques so well in early years, especially when they changed the team uniform to look very much like a Quebec flag, would come back and bite them too. Nobody can estimate how many fans they lost when Premier René Levesque, whose Parti Québécois was setting new lows in the opinion polls, came out with a statement that the Nordiques were more representative of Quebec than their Montreal cousins. The people who run the show at Atwater and St. Catherine must have breathed a sigh of relief upon hearing those words.

"Does the Premier mean to say that we are not as Québécois as the Stastnys?" Seigneur can't resist the barb, delivered with a little smile.

"You'll note that the Nordiques walked away from that nationalism stuff a couple years ago. It was a risky business and they knew it. Neither of our teams have to bother with any of this. The product on the ice is good enough so that it is unnecessary."

But as the saying goes, all that has passed is prologue. The Canadiens have rebounded in the hearts of fans, even though the season has tried their patience. F.X. Seigneur's "mini-packages" have done very well. The club had expected to sell a thousand of them. They frantically called a halt to the program after the first three thousand were sold.

"This used to be a very conservative organization," Seigneur says, "and some of those early mistakes were probably those of people who were too careful, rather than those of people who were snobs, or trying to put down others. Do you want to know how conservative they were? We just had our first computer put in two months ago."

Welcome to reality. Today, as distasteful as it sounds to the purists of yore, it is a very different world. The trends have changed, and the markets and audiences have also changed.

"Ronald Corey started out as a marketing guy, he knows what it's all about. No matter what the team does on the ice, we have to be there ahead of them, actively working to sell the product. And if that means running a radio commercial to sell playoff tickets, that's all part of the deal. And all of this doesn't mean to say that the team on the ice means nothing because that isn't true either. If we have three or four very bad seasons, all the best marketing strategies in the world aren't going to help.

"And, you know, we're not far apart from those people who complain about the tradition of the *bleu-blanc-rouge*. We certainly want to perpetuate tradition because it is the strongest marketing tool we have. We are in a privileged position with the Canadiens, in that their history can be part of the marketing plan.

"We don't want to build on the past though ... we want to try to use the past to build on the future," he says, as we leave his office.

We'll be back in a couple years to pick up the conversation with F.X. Many things will have happened in the interim.

1

Setting the Stage

"Time is but a stream I go fishing in."
Henry David Thoreau

The Forum, ice hockey's Holy Place, is quite unlike most shrines or churches in Montreal. One who is not familiar with the city but who has grown up on the legend of the Canadiens and has seen the inside of the Forum hundreds of times through the eyes of television will no doubt be disappointed. The Forum should be more like the Montreal churches that Mark Twain wrote about: overpowering, imposing, opulent, classic. The Forum should be as representative of hockey history as were those churches of Quebec's once pervasive Roman Catholicism.

Yet unlike the teams that have made the Forum great, the building itself is squat and functional. The only concessions to architectural élan are the escalators on the St. Catherine Street side of the building. The sides of the escalators feature fluorescent panels. Viewed from outside, at night, the image is of crossed hockey sticks.

Inside, the Forum is just another hockey rink at first glance. If you've visited any arena of size in the National Hockey League, the impression here will be one of overwhelming sameness. The team colours prevail—red, white and blue in ascending order of seats ringing the ice surface. But for those colours, you reason, it could be the Forum in Inglewood, California, or the Capital Center in the middle of nowhere between Baltimore and Washington. Second glance will uncover a series of visual clues that indicate the familiar and the fabled.

The stylized CH at centre ice will be the first reminder of what this building has meant to the sport. But that isn't the key to the Forum either. There must be something else that reveals the true Forum, home of the Flying Frenchmen, birthplace of firewagon hockey, one of the most famous sports gathering places anywhere in the world, known from Kitimat, B.C. to Antigonish, N.S.; from Atlanta, Georgia, U.S.A., to Tiflis, Georgia, U.S.S.R.

Where is the real Forum? Look up. Straight above your head, in the rafters. There you'll find the real Forum. There, high above the ice, they hang silently. To call them just pieces of cloth is like describing an Arras tapestry as just another wallhanging. They reveal what the Forum has meant to ice hockey, and the reason why this rink can be like no other. Only the Forum holds twenty-three separate white panels on which these words are written in blue with red trim: "Montreal Canadiens, Stanley Cup Champions".

No other rink can present players, referees, journalists and spectators with such an imposing view. Even the Russians look up and take notice when they visit. And they are psyched, because this has to be the most intimidating view in the game.

Ice hockey's dynasty of dynasties hangs high. Unequivocally *the* club team of the sport, the Canadiens are also the team that has come to epitomize the sport, the Soviet national team included. A paean to enlightened management techniques and specialized know-how; a certain way of doing things since time immemorial. A red, white and blue strategy. Hockey history cut from whole cloth. But, as the Bard wrote: "There's the rub."

Looking up at those banners you become instantly conscious of how history can lie, how the trappings of a dynasty present a picture that is larger than life ever was or ever could be, and how myths are perpetuated.

Look up at the banners hanging silently in their glory and you can see the incomparable Howie Morenz stick-handling fluidly at centre ice. Look at those that end 1956-57 or 1958-59 and picture Rocket Richard steaming in on Glenn Hall or Terry Sawchuk, his eyes blazing like the single light on an overnight freight. Look up at the Forum and see Jean Beliveau, a *seigneur* of the twentieth century, a true aristocrat on ice. See Doug Harvey single-handedly controlling the entire game for minutes on end, or Guy Lafleur, blond hair streaming behind him, sweeping down the right wing and firing a laser blast into the far corner, ankle high to the goalie's right. Remember Ken Dryden, all 75 inches of him, leaning forward on his goalstick in his characteristically pensive pose while his teammates swarm all over the opposition 180 feet away.

Look at the banners and fall into history's trap. Communications consultants have spent their careers building this folklore of the Montreal Canadiens.

Today's researchers and analytical hockey insiders, who are far more familiar with the infrastructures of the modern corporations that most professional ice hockey teams have become, would work up a quite different kind of perspective on the club's glory than that of the common fan. They would identify acute insight, long-term strategic planning, an integrated and systematic recruitment program and an intense commitment to the hockey organization as a family as the elements which have contributed to an important and highly visible tradition.

George Kendall, Leo Dandurand, Joe Cattarinich, Louis Letourneau, Tom Gorman and even to some extent Frank Selke could not explicitly envision the *Club de Hockey Canadien* as a multi-level corporation, yet they managed it along corporate lines. The introduction of solid business principles and an all-encompassing work ethic helped to shape the organization's direction and guaranteed its growth and continuity.

The average hockey fan had trouble separating the hockey club from the business organization for a lot of reasons, most of which would keep a phalanx of sociologists publishing until the end of this century and well into the next: the common man (read working stiff) identifying with a winning tradition that helped ease the drudgery of his everyday life; the French Canadian's association with a winning collectivity, especially at a time when he might have felt insecure in a province dominated by an English-speaking economic elite, and many others.

How does a sports organization come to be perceived as a viable business arrangement? More significantly, how does a sports organization sustain its standards of excellence over time, while others remain unsuccessful or mired in mediocrity?

The answer to the first question is that the organization develops constancy—a consistent presence and image. Secondly, it faithfully maintains that constancy with its fans. In other words, the organization enters into a social contract with its followers.

It would be futile to delve into the mystique, history and impact of the Montreal Canadiens without pausing to look at the team from a fan's viewpoint. Over the years, there have been many celebrated team followers, among them Jockey Fleming, Dutchy, and Kid Mercury.

In our minds, the most irrepressible was Harry Brown. He is our Common Fan and he has a way of putting history in its place. To look at Harry and his world is to put the impact of the Canadiens into context.

If you had ever met Harry Brown, or happened to be discussing him with friends today, the first remarks might be something like: "It's a good thing Harry isn't alive to see this." "This" being the sportsworld of the 1980s—the world of agents, hockey players who have shopping centres written into their contracts, hair dryers in the dressing room—the sports world of the Information Age.

Harry was a product of another Information Age, a time of cigar-chomping journalists who imparted their bon mots from Olympian press boxes to sports fans who related to life in black and white. He became known as the Great Prognosticator because he started work as a messenger "pushin' a bike" up and down Montreal's celebrated city core—"where downtown is *really* downtown" —delivering for the telegraph people. He later moved inside where he would see all the copy the journalists and newspapers would send to each other. Like many wire operators, he became good at picking horses by accident. Because he punched out the pre-race programs and post-race results so often, some names were subconsciously filed away—only to re-emerge when Harry discovered the tracks. Hence the Great Prognosticator.

Today, years after his passing, there are those who will swear that he was Leo Gorcey, that he had lifted the accent of the Bowery Boys and carried it home to Montreal. Others, amateur philologists perhaps, would have recognized Montrealese—a curious patois spoken in this city's blue collar English community. It is a hybrid of cross-cultural communications with the other side—English kids who grew up scrapping and playing with French-speaking neighbours in Point St. Charles, Notre-Dame-de-Grace and Rosemont all speak it.

Harry was street people, a celebrated mooch, and downtown Montreal was his turf.

If you were a writer and connected with sports in even the most remote way, or fancied yourself a part of the *centreville* tableau, you would occasionally find yourself talking with, and trying to escape from, the Great Prognosticator.

He was the city's most indefatigable purveyor of the facts—pronounced "facks". In his early eighties, he also was without a doubt the most bowlegged man to ever live: "You jam a leather bicycle seat up your ass every day for twenty years and see where it gets ya, sonny," he would tell all and sundry from his perennial perch at the Montreal Press Club. Harry sidled along at about a mile a year like a fiddler crab, but even the fleetest of foot could not escape his inexorable approach.

Harry ran the Press Club. Oh, the regular journalists with pretensions of professional association would actually go through the trouble of holding nominations and electing one of their own every second year or so, but Harry ran the Press Club.

And there he would be at four in the morning, starting a fight in the poker game ("ya sunnuvabitchin' sandbagging tomatacan, ya held out on me!") and there would be a horrific crash as Harry tossed his cane at the sliding doors of the poker room. Seconds later, his walking stick recovered, Harry would sidle out of the room, throw some travelling profanity over his shoulder, and head for the men's room.

About thirty minutes later, one of the more daring souls in the club, noting the protracted absence, would timorously venture into the WC and invariably discover Harry asleep on his feet like an egret against a urinal, his cane wedged against a partition for balance.

He was in his element in early May. The Run for the Roses was on the horizon in Louisville and the Canadiens were involved in their annual Run for the Silverware.

The Montreal Men's (changed after a major league feminist furor in 1971) Press Club at the Mount Royal Hotel was the unofficial Stanley Cup headquarters. Harry was the unofficial NHL host. The wee hours usually found him and NHL veterans like Red Sullivan and Milt Schmidt at the club's dilapidated piano singing Broadway show tunes from the forties. If any member of the NHL chorus forgot a lyric, or challenged Harry on one, the Great Prognosticator would silence them with an embarrassing tidbit from the transgressor's career like, "How'd ya ever get into the Hall of Fame, Schmidt? Go out into the front hall. There's a picture of tha Rocket scoring a Stanley Cup winner and you sittin' on ya ass like a baby." You sang the songs Harry's way.

Before he passed away in the early 1970s, he loved expounding on Montreal's sports teams. What he called the Alouettes is a sound that cannot be repeated in any manner, including phonetically. What he thought of the Expos, then a struggling expansion team, was not much. He would start talking about the denizens of Jarry Park, would make a connection with this name or that name and you'd find yourself back in the glory days of the 1940s, talking about the Royals, Jackie Robinson, the

Duke and Delormier Downs. But mention the Canadiens and the philosopher-cum-historian would be in his element.

"The facks is," he would begin, gently hooking you by the elbow with his cane, (after all, he was going to hit you for a drink as payment when the consultation was over), "tha Habs are tha best team in the history of tha game. They *are* tha history of tha game and I don't care if Conn Smythe croaks when I say it. All you gotta do is go down ta tha Forum and look up. Tha facks are there for all to see."

The Great Prognosticator was a notorious bottom line man—"tha horse comes in, or it don't. It makes all the difference in the world, tomatacan"—and "facks" were his stock in trade. To Harry, history was finite and absolute, and measured in terms of win, place and show.

To most hockey fans, history is finite and absolute. But, while hindsight may afford one an unimpeded view of things, its perspective is very poor when you're a betting man. Harry bought the pennants hanging in the Forum rafters because they were common currency— just like winning tickets in your hands on your way to the pay window at the track. His long years had taught him that the past is the only thing you can take to the bank. No matter how good you were at handicapping the horse, the deposit you made wasn't always the one you thought you did.

Although Harry Brown was old enough to have been there when the Canadiens began and to follow the team through more than fifty years of history, even his eyewitness history could blur with the passing decades.

Harry's history was a little off; but his buying into the Canadiens' mystique was not. At the outset, the Montreal Canadiens were neither a dynasty nor a major force in hockey. They eventually emerged as both because Tommy Gorman instilled a business ethic and then Frank Selke provided the meticulous planning and direction that would make them a business first, a hockey team second.

Perhaps the most accurate gauge of Selke's political and social astuteness was that although he built a business dominated by English-speaking managers, he purposely played down the business aspects of the organization and played up its most acceptable side: the hockey team. It was no accident that management kept a low profile in those days.

Sports franchises become successful when the members of the sports audience in a given area become committed supporters of that organization and buy into its future (by accepting its past and supporting its present). Selke knew this instinctively and worked at obscuring the roles of the people who wore suits to work and kept the organization running smoothly.

Everything depended on a carefully cultivated image. Public relations and marketing directors are very aware of how to trade on such a commodity, no matter how superficial it may appear. In the Canadiens' early days, the social and cultural attachments seemed more visceral as an entire class took the club's daily doings to heart. These attachments long pre-dated the relatively young sciences of public relations and marketing.

In a detailed and systematic fashion, the hockey club became a part of the community's everyday activity. Defeats were taken personally while successes were honoured and recognized regularly.

The hockey club managed to build an Ivory Tower, complete with imaginary drawbridge, which was occasionally lowered to allow the fans to visit—quite unlike other barriers in certain areas of Montreal which remained forever raised, cutting off a large part of the population from the city's riches and beauties.

The team crest or logo became a symbol for Montreal and Quebec fans. The players who bore the crest bravely on their chests were charged with a meaningful set of responsibilities, for they were perceived as advocates of the community, rather than just simple representatives of a hockey team. In a sense then, the *Club de Hockey Canadien* was undergoing an institutionalization process, one which was external to the individual and beyond his control.

One does not have to study institutional power for a long time to understand its significance. Not only do institutions exist, they are perceived as having the moral right to exist. The Canadiens' mystique and credibility were nurtured within the context of these institutional arrangements. A sense of honour came to be associated with the opportunity to perform within the club's ranks. A special feeling of overwhelming servitude and enthusiasm engulfed the novice.

This deep-rooted commitment embraced the neophyte, the hockey rookie, so that the need to motivate him was diminished. For generations young hockey players have said, "Playing for the Montreal Canadiens is more than enough motivation," and they believed it. That feeling would become very evident during the 1986 Stanley Cup playoffs. In the sports world, this kind of hyper-commitment is a luxury afforded few teams.

It was achieved primarily by Selke and embellished by Sam Pollock. Selke orchestrated the situation in such a way that the novice actually believed the club was doing him a favour by permitting his participation in the team. How many millions of dollars have corporations spent in trying to exhort new recruits to believe in an enterprise's potential and to share in the long-term commitment to its success? For the Canadiens, external motivation came from the community, which had adopted the presumed success potential of the team. Internal motivation derived from the players' shared-belief system, which was gently introduced throughout the organization.

If a youthful hockey player comes to believe in the expected success of a franchise, he is more likely than not to set his sights on playing for that franchise. That was certainly the case in Montreal and Quebec before the National Hockey League introduced the universal draft; family, friends and acquaintances would find a way of letting the Canadiens know when and how well a young prospect was developing. Thus, the organization's recruitment process was facilitated wherever hockey was played. The young player believed that he would acquire all of the necessary knowledge and skills as a consequence of his involvement with those seasoned veterans who had been injected with the ten cc.'s of commitment and ten more of both expertise and personal discipline.

The process of transmitting the knowledge and skills was further enhanced by the rich oral history which emphasized the importance of winning . . . and how it came to be expected.

Simply put, these are the sociological reasons why the people embraced the myths. People bought the tradition and the rich cultural tapestry which was being woven because in doing so they became part of it all.

History dwells on the rise of the Roman Empire, but it comes close to ignoring the fall. Lots of famous people, some historians, some not, have said that about the historical process. The consensus is that your history is only as good as the club public relations man who will write it many years later. And the people who were there and will go along with it. There is no problem finding folks to fit into this latter category. We all want to say we were there, and that includes the 415,000 people who saw Bobby Thompson hit his "shot heard around the world" in person at the Polo Grounds back in 1951.

"History is something that never happened, written by a man who wasn't there," is one of the most famous quotes about the subject. History teachers generally start new semesters with it. A lovely pithy statement, it is snickered at politely.

History, Montreal Canadiens' version, certainly happened. It just didn't happen quite the way you've been led to believe. The "facks"—those twenty-three ghostly shrouds hanging above the Forum ice—attest to the consistently best professional hockey team the world has known. And, with twenty-three Stanley Cup championships, and a remarkable twenty-seven final series appearances, they pay tribute to a sports organization whose exploits are the sport of ice hockey.

However, permit us a historical asterisk. The facts can, and do, lie.

There can be no doubt that with the advent of the new millenium, when the historians and anybody else with the ability to put a few words down begin chronicling the superlatives of the hundred years past, Montreal Canadiens will be known as the ice hockey team of the twentieth century. Even if the Habs don't win another Stanley Cup in the next fourteen years. Even if another team goes on a prolonged winning streak. That much is in the bank.

Yet the glory they will reap is recent glory. Yes, Montreal Canadiens, seventy-six years old in 1986, have defined professional hockey in North America. Yes, they have provided much of the sport's romance, especially south of the border in the Flying Frenchmen era.

It wasn't always that way. In the team's first forty years, 1909-10 to 1949-50, they won six Stanley Cups. Since then, however, the team has won seventeen NHL championships in convincing fashion. Many fans easily recall the "five straight" team of the late 1950s and the "four straight" team of the 1970s. In fact, many forget that only a Toronto upset in 1967, the last year of the six-team NHL, prevented another "five straight" team from 1965 to 1969.

With that kind of recent glory, especially in the television age, it is no wonder that the red, white and blue is compared with the New York Yankees.

There was a time, however, in the 1920s and 1930s, when the Canadiens not only failed to capture the imagination of the hockey world, they couldn't even win over the fans in Montreal. Things got so bad during the Depression era that there was even talk one year of transferring the franchise to (horror of horrors) Cleveland. In these days of revisionist and instant history, the myth obscures the reality.

The *Club de Hockey Canadien* was born at a time when Montreal was one of several hockey hotbeds. The pre-First World War era was busy for Canada. The country was literally pulling itself up by the bootstraps and fortunes were to be made in "that there wilderness". Canada was definitely a hewer of wood and drawer of water, as well as a miner of silver, gold and most of the valuable minerals upon which old-time fortunes were made.

Teams with names like the Kenora Thistles, the Renfrew Millionaires, and the Dawson City Klondikers all would challenge for the Stanley Cup and, in the case of Kenora, actually win it, in 1906-07. Towns like Cobalt and Haileybury challenged Renfrew in northern Ontario for highest concentration of silver millionaires and best "store-bought" hockey teams. As Trent Frayne writes in *The Mad Men of Hockey*:

> In the spring of 1909 the silver magnates brought the Ottawa Senators and the Montreal Wanderers to the north country for an exhibition series. When the teams returned home, half the players stayed behind to cash in on the bonanza. The whole area was hockey crazy.
>
> Tens of thousands of dollars were bet on each game; often thousands changed hands on a single goal. Miners in the crowds fought in the rinks during games and up and down the streets after them, and during that wild period the best hockey players in the world were performing in this backwoods league formed to take advantage of the silver discovery.

Up to and during this era, the enduring hockey power was a team from Montreal called the Wanderers. It won the Stanley Cup four times between 1905-06 and 1909-10, after breaking the Ottawa Silver Seven's string of three straight Cups. The Wanderers were the pride of the Eastern Canadian Hockey Association and brought glory to their league in years when champions of various leagues challenged for the Cup. At one point in 1910, there were twenty-five professional ice hockey teams in Canada alone, including the fledgling *Club de Hockey Canadien* of the new National Hockey Association. Montreal was home to five such teams: the Canadiens, Shamrocks, Nationals, Wanderers and Victorias. The Canadiens' beginnings were singularly inauspicious as they finished the first NHA season with two wins in twelve games. Year two was quite different, mainly because a different team wore the Canadiens' name. In 1909-10, the NHA team called the Canadiens was owned by J. Ambrose O'Brien and T.C. Hare of Cobalt.

The league, well aware that ethnicity was box office gold, granted the two men a franchise to ice an "all French Canadian team," which they did, hiring the celebrated Jack Laviolette as coach and manager.

In 1910-11, a challenge to the team name and right of franchise was forwarded by George Kendall, owner of the *Club Athlétique Canadien*, a very popular French-speaking sports club in the city. He told the National Hockey Association board of directors that he owned the rights to the *Club Canadien* name and would undertake very expensive and time-consuming litigation if a franchise was not forthcoming. League management quickly saw his argument, and also understood that the popularity of the *Club Athlétique Canadien* would almost ensure a successful fan base for the team, and Kendall (also known as Kennedy) received his franchise. With Georges "the Chicoutimi Cucumber" Vezina in goal and stars like Didier Pitre and Jack Laviolette, Kennedy-Kendall's Canadiens won their first Stanley Cup in 1916.

For the team's first three seasons, it was Montreal's French team, by NHA rules and constitution. In 1912-13, the league relented and allowed the Canadiens to dress two English-speaking players while the other teams could sign as many as two French-speaking players each. The Kennedy-Kendall era ended five years later, when the popular Montreal sportsman died in the influenza pandemic (1918 to 1920) that killed more people around the world than the First World War.

Thus began the first modern era of the Montreal Canadiens. The team was purchased for $11,000 by three Montreal businessmen-sportsmen, Leo Dandurand, Joseph Cattarinich and Louis Letourneau. It became part of the brand new National Hockey League, intending to make a big impact south of the border.

In 1924, a Boston franchise was added, and teams from New York and Pittsburgh followed a year later. Chicago

Black Hawks and Detroit Cougars were next, in 1926, and the early foundations of the NHL were set.

Teams would come and go in the 1920s and '30s— among them the Ottawa Senators, Pittsburgh Pirates, Philadelphia Quakers, New York Americans and Montreal Maroons—but the Original Six (as they would become known) were in place: the Canadiens, Toronto St. Pats (later Maple Leafs), Cougars (later Red Wings), Bruins, Rangers and Black Hawks. The Canadiens, still very much the Flying Frenchmen of the old NHA days, became popular gate attractions around the league and especially tough rivals of the Quebec Bulldogs, Maroons and Senators. The team, which featured a collection of stars with names like Newsy Lalonde, Aurele Joliat, Howie Morenz, Joe Malone, Sylvio Mantha and the infamous Cleghorn brothers, Sprague and Odie, won three Cups between 1923 and 1931.

It also set about developing its historical character. Yet the *Club de Hockey Canadien* did not immediately stand the NHL or the sports world on its ears. The fabulous Flying Frenchmen were just one of many teams, no more, no less. But they were an organization that would eventually develop what sociologists call an "occupational culture" which was to foster a winning tradition by stressing the importance of success.

One would assume that most work organizations naturally generate such strong beliefs and commitments among their employees. The truth is that these qualities take years to cultivate.

In the case of the Canadiens, those athletes and administrators not willing to commit themselves to the degree considered necessary for success were selectively eliminated from within the organization.

Can you imagine how successful most corporations would be if their potential recruits were straining at the leash to work for them?

In the corporate world, IBM (Big Blue to Montreal's Red, White and Blue) fostered a parallel belief system. Preaching loyalty, dedication, hard work and integrity as core variables, Thomas Watson Jr. combined history with culture to create a sense of belonging to a winning tradition within his organization. Like Frank Selke with the Canadiens, Watson was a grand master in the area of strategic long-term planning and systematic recruiting. He was acutely aware of the importance of human resource development and was highly selective when choosing a plan for growth and development of what we now call corporate synergy.

Just as Selke would expose new recruits to legendary tales of the great superstars and their accomplishments, by the simple expedient of turning their everyday dressing room into a museum, so did Watson dwell on IBM's early days when his highly motivated workforce, supported by brilliant Research and Development people, began to make inroads in the marketplace.

Sociologist Orrin Klapp calls this an identity voyage, a fantasy ride that allows new recruits to identify with the legends and folk heroes of their particular organization. One reason why Detroit Red Wings have been so feeble in recent years is that only the city's hockey fans identify with Gordie Howe, Ted Lindsay, Sid Abel and Alex Delvecchio; the players cannot and do not.

Imagine the uproar in Montreal if Maurice Richard were allied with another hockey team, as is Gordie Howe (with Hartford). The close identification of present players with the team's legends helps to build camaraderie and generates cohesion from within.

Ken Reardon, Sam Pollock and Toe Blake were experts at the task of transmitting the central components of the occupational culture. When Irvin, charged with the same responsibility, failed to keep his superstar Maurice Richard sufficiently motivated to rank individual urges below the importance of team activity (the 1955 outbreak which led to his suspension and the notorious Richard Riots), he was quickly replaced by Selke, a close friend. The lessons of commitment are followed by all, at all levels of the organization.

In April, 1986, forty-nine years after Howie Morenz died, the latest version of the Montreal Canadiens are skating through a strenuous workout and preparing to meet the Hartford Whalers in the Adams Division final. Head coach Jean Perron and his assistant Jacques Laperriere put their charges through their paces for ninety minutes.

High in the east-end reds, the decades meet. Toe Blake, who as a junior was scouted by Morenz and who played with Joliat, sits quietly watching the colourful swirl on the ice. He chats with Ronald Corey, Jean Beliveau, Serge Savard, Doug Harvey, André Boudrias, Jacques Lemaire and Carol Vadnais. Except for team president Corey, all have played for Montreal at one time or another and sport Stanley Cup rings.

Down on the ice, the players occasionally glance up and notice the cabal. They know what those people represent and they possess the drive to achieve some of that glory.

Five weeks later, rookie Brian Skrudland wipes champagne from his eyes in a Calgary dressing room, hugs the Stanley Cup and says:

"This is what Larry Robinson, Bob Gainey and Toe Blake meant."

History, whether purely factual or that wonderful synthetic thread woven into a folkloric tapestry, is an integral part of this hockey team.

2

Assembling the Cast

"We will now discuss in a little more detail the struggle for existence."
Charles Darwin

One thing that has distinguished the Montreal Canadiens throughout the team's history has been the almost unbroken succession of superstars who have epitomized the team.

While most have been true Flying Frenchmen, handing the torch down from generation to generation (Richard to Beliveau to Cournoyer to Lafleur), the first was a Swiss-Canadian from small-town Ontario.

Howie Morenz, the Stratford Streak, was the catalyst and the superstar whose name first defined the Montreal Canadiens in their true beginnings, the 1920s and 1930s. Teamed up with colourful characters like Aurele Joliat, Billy Boucher, Armand Mondou, and Sylvio Mantha, Morenz was arguably the best player to don skates in his era.

That is quite a claim, when it is considered that athletes bearing surnames like Patrick, Boucher, Conacher and Shore played in the same period. Perhaps the best way to make the case for Morenz is to step outside the sport for a moment.

The 1920s, as most observers will tell you, was the beginning of the golden age of sport. That is largely because most avid sports fans would rarely, if ever, actually see their sports heroes in action. It was the era of the re-created sports event—when radio announcers, improvising sound effects, would take play-by-play off the wires and re-create sports contests such as baseball games, championship boxing matches, or great track-and-field matches.

It was a time when "spectators" were found at home, straining to hear the descriptions of fevered action emanating from a Motorola or Philco crystal set and letting their imaginations envision the scene.

On the playing fields were herculean characters like Babe Ruth in baseball, Red Grange in football, Bill Tilden in tennis, Bobby Jones in golf. In the ring were incomparable champions like Jack Dempsey and Gene Tunney. Olympic swimmers like Johnny Weismuller and Buster Crabbe went right from the Olympic Pool to Hollywood. Women's sports were also well represented, with names like Helen Wills and Gertrude Ederle in tennis and golfer Babe Didrikson.

Even the supporting casts were full of people larger than life—baseball managers like McGraw, McCarthy, Huggins and Ott; coaches like Rockne; promoters like Tex Rickard and writers like Grantland Rice, Ring Lardner and Damon Runyon.

What the fans never really saw, and never really heard, was re-created and reproduced for them by these titans. A Grantland Rice story would instantly elevate the pedestrian to Olympian heights. It was vicarious hero worship three times removed.

Into this world slipped the fledgling National Hockey League. Not only did the league, its teams and its players have to compete with other sports for the sports dollar, always the case in any era, it had to find someone who would make the American sportswriters sit up and take notice.

And it had to be someone who could join Ruth, Dempsey, Jones *et al* in the pantheon of the golden greats. Someone whose very presence would actually coax an adjective or two from a kingmaking scribe and who would be written up as an honest-to-goodness legend.

That person was Howarth W. Morenz, and the man who found him was Canadiens' owner Leo Dandurand, a man who loved the horses and was fully light years ahead of his peers in his understanding of the value of public relations and promotions in an era built on them.

Mere mention of Morenz to his contemporaries still gets results a half-century later. Eyes glaze over and memories play on a private video recorder of the mind. The superlatives flow easily.

"Howie Morenz was in a class by himself, the greatest player I ever saw." Heady praise. The source is Frank (King) Clancy, a man who has spent almost seventy years in and around the National Hockey League as a player with Ottawa Senators and Toronto Maple Leafs, referee, coach and executive. Today he is right-hand man to Toronto owner Harold Ballard.

"He was the best in his day, the best I played against and the best I've ever seen. He could get to top speed in one stride, he was a threat to go from end to end through an entire team at any time and he shot the puck as hard as any man who ever played."

Clancy the executive takes over from Clancy the player, coach or referee. He begins to discuss the real value of Morenz in the 1920s. The Roaring Twenties. The Golden Age of Sport.

"He sold one hell of a lot of tickets at a time when hockey really needed somebody who could pull in the fans.

"If you went to a baseball game and saw Babe Ruth powder one over the fence, you didn't need to know first base from the ass of your pants to realize that you had seen something special. It was the same thing with Morenz. You didn't need to know the difference between a hockey puck and your belly-button to know that when you had watched Morenz play the game, you had seen something special."

Of the Three Musketeers who owned the Canadiens at the time, Dandurand was the man with the street smarts, the man who knew that the product was the thing that mattered, and that it was competing against other products that were well established. When he plucked the flashy Morenz out of the wilds of Ontario, he knew that the introverted player would have to become the super-hero of the sport, if it was going to stand a chance of survival.

In Morenz's first professional season—1923-24—the league was struggling to survive with three solid clubs: the Ottawa Senators, Toronto St. Pats and the Montreal Canadiens, plus an anemic Hamilton Tigers franchise. On Canada's West Coast, the Pacific Coast Hockey Association was flirting with financial ruin, reduced to three teams which were losing large amounts of money.

Three years later, in 1926-27, the NHL was a ten-team league, with six of those franchises in the United States, where the money was. The arrival of the Boston Bruins in 1924, Pittsburgh Pirates and New York Americans in 1925, and the New York Rangers, Chicago Black Hawks and Detroit Cougars in 1926 moved the game to the United States in a big way. Dandurand flogged Howie Morenz and the Flying Frenchmen like Colonel Ruppert sold the Sultan of Swat and Murderers' Row. The league went along for the ride.

"When the Canadiens and Howie Morenz came to town, the American teams beat the drums hard about the games," Dandurand said. "That attracted the casual fan who went to see hockey out of curiosity. But they only had to watch Morenz play the way he did and the Canadiens' approach to the game and they were hooked.

"There was only one Morenz and there has been none like him since," Dandurand wrote in *The Hockey Book* (edited by Wilfrid Victor "Bill" Roche) in 1953.

"Full speed going both ways—giving his brilliant all—all of the time. The game has changed considerably since his days and I doubt there will ever be another like him."

Hyperbole certainly, because people like Eddie Shore, Bun and Bill Cook, the Patricks and the Bouchers more than did their jobs for their respective franchises. Yet the Canadiens had that something extra which made them special. They were the Flying Frenchmen, romantic foreigners from the Far North who spoke of a romantic North American tradition—Radisson, Marquette, the *coureurs de bois*, colourful fur traders.

Dandurand understood the promotional punch of golden boys and foreign myths. He merged the two successfully in Morenz and the Canadiens. Thousands of American hockey fans grew up believing that Morenz was a famous French Canadian name in Quebec. *Mais oui* —sell, sell, sell! Even when Morenz would do a very rare radio interview south of the border, the fans would strain to hear his peculiar French accent. Howie Morenz could have been exactly the same superstar with the Toronto St. Pats, later the Maple Leafs. But the impact would never have been the same in the United States. He needed the Canadiens and their mythic potential as much as the team needed him and his prolific on-ice exploits. One wonders if Morenz and the NHL could have survived his playing for another team. That almost happened.

Morenz shone at hockey at an early age, starring for four years with the Stratford Midgets, a perennial junior hockey power in southwestern Ontario in the post-First World War era. Morenz played on a line with Roter Roth and Frank Carson, the latter a future star with the Montreal Maroons of the NHL. Stratford also had a senior team playing in the Ontario Hockey Association and this team would often call up Carson and Morenz to bolster their lineup.

Although the teams in the fledgling National Hockey League sent scouts to beat the bushes for talent, quality young players did not automatically gravitate towards the upper echelons of the sport once they had finished their junior years. Such was the case with Morenz, who took a job as an apprentice machinist in the Stratford railway shops.

Larger companies in those days sponsored sports organizations for their employees, and a few judiciously selected ringers. The railways were famous for this. After all, who could better assure transportation for tournament-bound players? It was at such a tournament in Montreal that Morenz was spotted. Morenz scored nine goals for the Stratford CNR team against Montreal's Point St. Charles machine shop team at the old Mount Royal Arena (where the Montreal Canadiens first played) on a warm Saturday afternoon in the spring of 1922.

The referee for that contest was Ernest Sauvé, a former player with Cecil Hart's All-Stars, a collection of hockey players that was one of the best amateur teams in Canada in 1913. After the game, he got on the telephone to his former coach, and Dandurand dispatched Hart to Stratford to sign him.

It was a long summer, however, and local pressure was applied to force Morenz to remain in Ontario, if not with the local Stratford seniors, then with Toronto in the NHL. Just before training camp, Montreal received a wire from the young centreman stating that he had changed his mind about playing for the Canadiens and could Mr. Dandurand please tear up the contract?

No dice, said Dandurand. Morenz was to play professional hockey. Despite Morenz's doubts, this was an entirely good idea, since the young man was as terrible with his personal finances as he was good with his stickhandling on the ice and had run up a few debts back home to the tune of $800. (In those days that sum could buy one a new car and still leave enough left over to pay a couple of months' rent.)

The telegram didn't work, so Morenz sent Dandurand a letter:

> "Dear Sir;
>
> I am enclosing a cheque and contract to play hockey with your club.
>
> Owing to several reasons, of which family and work are the most to consider, I find it impossible to leave Stratford.
>
> I am sorry if I caused you expense and inconvenience, and trust you will accept the returned contract in a sportsman-like way.
>
> Yours truly,
> Howarth Morenz"

"Monsieur Leo" hadn't acquired his impressive reputation by falling for every line handed to him, no matter how genuine it seemed. He described the incident in *The Hockey Book.*

> The letter was written on August 10, but the postmark on the envelope shows that it did not reach Montreal until August 23. Howie had evidently carried it around and thought about it before he finally put it in the mail. I promptly phoned Morenz at Stratford, told him there would be a railway ticket for him at the stationmaster's office in Stratford, and asked him to get on an evening train and come to Montreal for a personal conference with me. Howie agreed to meet me at my office the next day.
>
> He arrived on time, too. But he was adamant in his refusal to turn pro, declaring that he would never report to the Canadiens or any other NHL club. During our conversation, Morenz insisted that with his job in the Stratford car shops and with what he was 'getting on the side' to play OHA intermediate hockey, he would be better off to finish his shop apprenticeship and stay out of professional hockey.
>
> Then I told him as kindly as possible that business was business, and he would have to comply with the terms of the contract he had signed.
>
> Morenz broke down and wept. With tears running down his cheeks, he declared: 'I don't believe I'm good enough to make a place on your team, and you will be everlastingly sorry you forced me into pro hockey. You'll have to take the responsibility of depriving me of my livelihood and my amateur standing.'

At that, Dandurand was sorely tempted to call the deal off, but he remained steadfast.

Within a week of training camp, and a tough week it was, because rookies were severely tested by veteran incumbents, Georges Vezina and Sprague Cleghorn were convinced that the introverted young hockey player would be a great one. They were absolutely right.

Morenz on the ice, Dandurand upstairs. It was the first in a series of famous upstairs, downstairs Canadiens' couples that would make this a hockey franchise like no other.

Aurele Joliat remembered both well.

Joliat came to the Canadiens in 1922, in a controversial trade for Newsy Lalonde, the Habs' most popular player at the time, but well past his prime. The trade made Dandurand so unpopular in Montreal that he had to have his phone disconnected. Lalonde, the spirit of the Canadiens in their first decade, did not complain. Dandurand had negotiated a new contract for him worth more than double what he was getting in Montreal.

Joliat, an Ottawa native, had a French name, but he was the son of a Swiss Protestant and he was the first to tell you his French was lousy.

"Still, it was easier for Dandurand to trade Lalonde for me than for a Dick Smith."

At trade time, he was playing for the Saskatoon Sheiks and barely weighed 135 pounds soaking wet. Still, he was a fast-skating, smart left winger and scored twice in his first Montreal game, finishing his rookie season with a very respectable 13 goals.

"Dandurand stuck his neck out for me and I had to deliver."

Montreal would finish in second place that year and would be edged out in playoff action by a tough Ottawa team. The next summer would see Dandurand at his best, and two rookies named Mantha and Morenz join the team.

Joliat has his own private little joke for those who must ask the obvious question: "What was it like playing with Morenz?"

"I never played with Morenz," is a response guaranteed to send the questioner right into the archives.

"Wait a minute. It says right here that you guys were on the same team, hell, the same forward line, for more than a decade."

Joliat pauses, letting the full impact of his little joke build up.

"I'll tell you . . . I played with him, but not exactly with him, if you get what I mean. I was always in front of him or behind him. I could never stay even with him, that's

for sure. Jesus Christ, could he go! End to end rushes . . .
none of this back and forth passing to get there. . . ."
Joliat doesn't notice it, but he is speaking much faster
now, in short, clipped phrases, his words bunched together, and with that faraway look in his eyes . . . "He
went straight from end to end."

Morenz on the ice, Dandurand and his people like Cecil
Hart upstairs: it was a combination that produced
legends.

Leo Dandurand was something of a celebrity in Montreal in the 1920s. Without a man like him, the Canadiens
might never have made it. He was the ideal man to take
over after the death of Kendall-Kennedy and keep the
dream of the *Club Athlétique Canadien* alive.

> Hockey always has been a game of weight and power, and a
> small man needed a great deal of skill to make it as a pro. I
> believe that speed and skill are the best ingredients of the
> game. I view the Canadiens as playing a very fast, slick game
> but not being bullied by anyone. I don't want hoodlums, but
> I do want he-man hockey talent to meet all and any situa-
> tions, to be able to win by whatever means are needed.

That was Leo Dandurand's hockey philosophy all
wrapped up in a neat quotation uttered the day he
masterminded the purchase of the Canadiens. From his
remarks it would seem that the team he was buying into
was a collectivity of listless, less-than-spectacular journeymen who simply weren't effective when the going
got rough. With names like Laviolette, Vezina, Pitre and
Lalonde on the honour role, that obviously was not the
case.

Still, Dandurand was the consummate showman and
he wanted to start selling an image right away. The
image would be "Firewagon Hockey"—something that
the Flying Frenchmen could market very well south of
the border. Dandurand, who knew "south of the border"
very well—it was his backyard—got on the job right
away.

Dandurand, Joseph Cattarinich and Louis Letourneau
were Montrealers who had been around. They were

popularly referred to locally as the "Three Musketeers". Dandurand, who traded on his name as a native-born French-Canadian, actually was born in Bourbonnais, Illinois and moved to Canada at the age of sixteen, in 1905.

He was thoroughly outgoing, known for his flamboyant lifestyle and pluck. His fame in Montreal was sufficiently widespread that he was referred to simply as "Monsieur Leo". Dandurand had a broad interest and involvement in sports and was a promoter *par excellence*, whose executive ability matched his imagination and congeniality.

He carefully nurtured the myth that he was the "man with the Midas Touch" and maintained a reputation of always backing winning ventures. Of course, his successes depended on wisdom, shrewdness, promotional ability and good research—but he wasn't the man to give a successful formula away.

His interest in sports was not always in the wings. He began as a founding father of the Canadian Amateur Hockey Association and even refereed in the old National Hockey Association, where he had several celebrated run-ins with Kennedy, the man he would succeed at the helm of the Canadiens.

Joe Cattarinich also started out on the ice—as goalie for the Canadiens in the club's inaugural 1909-10 season. Cattarinich was such a team man that he suggested the club woo Georges Vezina, the man who was to replace him between the pipes. When the time came to purchase the Canadiens, he was a successful Montreal businessman who had done well in other ventures on both sides of the border with Dandurand.

Of the three, Louis Letourneau was the most carefree, a well-to-do amateur sportsman and partner with the other two in various undertakings, including ownership of a thoroughbred race track in Cleveland. When word came down that the Canadiens would be sold at auction, all three men were busy with the summer meeting in the Ohio city. Dandurand sent word to an acquaintance, Cecil Hart, to function as his agent at the auction and go as high as necessary to buy the team. Two other groups were interested—Tom Duggan, representing the Mount Royal Arena Company; and NHL president Frank Calder, speaking for Ottawa interests. Bidding opened at $8,000 and Hart immediately bumped it to $8,500. Calder then stepped in and asked for time to consult his backers.

The auction resumed a week later and this time Duggan dramatically laid ten $1,000 bills on the table.

The theatrics were wasted, however—Dandurand had picked his man well. Hart calmly got on the phone to Cleveland, described what had happened, and was told to do whatever was required. He offered $11,000, the other two potential buyers backed off, and the Three Musketeers had a hockey team.

Dandurand later offered his memorable quote about the kind of hockey player he envisaged wearing the *bleu, blanc, rouge*. He immediately set about living up to it. His first acquisition bespoke a man who had spent years in horse racing. He went for bloodlines when he acquired Billy Boucher, a slick Ottawa native and member of the family that would eventually provide four NHL players, including older brother Frank, a future Hall of Fame member. Despite Dandurand's claim that he would never brook the presence of hoodlums on his team, he next sought the services of hockey's premier enforcer—a Montrealer with the colourful name of Sprague Cleghorn.

You might go up to Sprague Cleghorn or his brother Odie and jokingly mention that his name sounds like a root fungus. You would do it exactly once, and you would never do it again. Along with Cleghorn, in a trade with Hamilton, came Billy Couture (often known as Coutu) a former Canadien with a penchant for ash surgery, who as a Boston Bruin in 1927 would be banned for life from hockey for attacking a referee.

With Coutu and the Cleghorns on the team, the fleeter skaters and playmakers could operate with relative impunity—in those days that meant the opposition wouldn't attempt to rearrange your facial features more than once or twice a game.

After a celebrated rift with Lalonde in the new management's rookie season, Dandurand gave Sprague Cleghorn the job of team leader, the equivalent of team captain. He never regretted it. Cleghorn's tenure gave all appearances of being a short one, however.

In a game at Ottawa, February 1, 1922, Cleghorn decided to get even with his former team for trading him. His single-game savagery would probably net him a life sentence in today's much more civilized game. The best description of the on-ice mayhem is to say he simply excised the opposition's top three players from the game.

He began with star defenceman Eddie Gerard, who was dispatched with a five-stitch gash just above an eye. Scoring ace Frank Nighbor followed, smashed to the ice with a vicious check that injured an elbow. A butt end to Cy Denneny's face opened up cuts on the nose and over the eye and had the first aid people scrambling for medical supplies.

The punishment for all this? A match penalty and the recommendation by referee Lou Marsh that he be banned from the sport. Ottawa strongly protested Cleghorn's behaviour and asked for a life sentence, but Toronto and Hamilton refused to go along with the suggestion. Since unanimous approval was necessary, Cleghorn dodged a bullet.

The tough Montrealer, quite a dandy off the ice (players on his team often joked that he and Odie spent as much time in front of mirrors checking out the latest additions to their wardrobe as they did playing—but never to their faces) was never repentant. In later years he would admit to purposely injuring the three Senators and claim proud participation in "more than fifty stretcher-case fights" during his career.

If King Clancy can rhapsodize about the ephemeral hockey talents of Morenz, his description of Sprague Cleghorn is in more down-to-earth language.

"Sprague was just tough and mean, the best at using the butt-end of his stick that I ever saw," Clancy recalls. Rather than the faraway look elicited by his recollections of Morenz, you get the feeling he's looking over his shoulder as he recounts this tale.

"He also wouldn't hesitate to give you a hook in the face or cross-check you in the back of the head."

In Trent Frayne's excellent book, *The Mad Men of Hockey*, Clancy describes the following incident.

> He was just a terrible man to have to play against, a terrific stick-handler, a master with the butt-end, and tough, holy Jesus he was tough. One night he broke loose with the puck and sped towards our goal. There was just one man between him and it. I came rushing back and as Sprague neared the last man I tapped my stick on the ice a couple of times like you do when you want the puck, and I yelled: 'Over here, Sprague.' Well, he naturally thought it was a teammate and he slid me the puck without looking, and I sped the other way with it. So when the period was over I was feeling pretty good as I walked to our dressing room and the fans were applauding me and just as I was going in the room, I heard this friendly voice, 'King', and I turned around to see who it was. Well, I want to tell you, my friend, did I ever get a sweet whallop in the kisser. It was Sprague all right, just quietly turning off my lights. Jesus, did he hit me a beauty.

Cleghorn was not all muscle, though. He scored 17 goals, high for league defencemen in that era, and "only" had 63 minutes in penalties. The Canadiens finished the Three Musketeers' first season with a 13-11 record and Dandurand pledged to continue improving his club.

That summer, he met George Boucher, Billy's brother, at the racetrack (where else?) and the Ottawa star mentioned a player in Saskatchewan who might be a star. Not long afterward, Aurele Joliat was on his way to Montreal.

A year later, of course, Morenz would join him. The subtle blend of superstar forward (Morenz), skilled muscle (Cleghorn) and front office know-how (Dandurand) was coming together for the first time in Canadiens' history. It would be repeated over and over again in the next sixty years.

Yet, although the Canadiens were assembling their on-ice team, little was being done about developing the front office team. To be sure, Dandurand was nobody's fool and as good a sports entrepreneur as there was at the time. And for all of his braggadocio, his "Midas Touch" and the "Monsieur Leo" all over Montreal, Dandurand showed a lot of common sense when he hired the quiet Cecil Hart to run his team.

Nevertheless, there were few efforts to build a front office organization that would ensure the on-ice product would never be diluted. A major reason was that, although the Canadiens constituted a high-profile sports and business venture, they were not Dandurand's main business interest. In those days, ice hockey was at best a four- or five-month endeavour while horse racing—harness and thoroughbreds—was a year-round preoccupation, especially with Dandurand's interests south of the border.

There was very little work done to develop a minor-league or feeder system of teams, or a network of scouts who would eventually beat some of Canada's most isolated bushes in search of young men who could play the game.

Marketing and promotion were practically unheard of. Management would trade on the names of their star players, as is done today, but would go little further. Endorsement contracts and third-party promotions were rare. Selling the team usually involved only the simple act of publishing schedules.

As for a comparison of the Montreal Canadiens' nuclear family of the modern era with the teams of the 1920s, there is none to be made. The players then were as close as today's because success was directly linked to on-ice cohesion. But that was as far as it went. As Mrs. Georges Mantha reminisces:

"While there was a certain status in having a family member on the team, the city was not yet the Montreal Canadiens hotbed it would become later. There was little in the way of facilities for wives and relatives; if you wanted your wife to be there, you bought a ticket. As for physical facilities, forget it! The wives of the players had an unofficial lounge, a restroom on the second floor. There were some pretty good fights in there, let me tell you!" It seems that Mesdames Morenz and Joliat, who enjoyed their status as the *grandes dames* of the Montreal Canadiens, would brook no challenges to their authority.

Conversely, today's Canadiens family is an extended one and includes spouses, girlfriends, parents and children of the players. Everything is done to make these people feel comfortable at a game—whether they are related to a ten-year veteran or a youngster just called up from Sherbrooke (AHL) or a junior team. If you are going to demand loyalty from your employees, Frank Selke reasoned, you must show them respect and fair treatment.

Today's front office follows that dictum to the letter.

The Three Musketeers, Dandurand, Cattarinich and Letourneau, were in the hockey business to make money, or at the very least to gain a little public respect that might help overcome the taint of their involvement in horse racing. Wasting a lot of time or energy coddling the friends and families of their players was not on their agenda.

They were businessmen of their time, operating on handshakes and personal relationships that would be anachronistic in this day and age. One example of that closeness took place in 1926, when the New York Rangers were being assembled by Conn Smythe, and later the Patrick family. Leo Dandurand helped the Patricks negotiate their way through a variety of player deals after they sold the Pacific Coast and Western Canada leagues and moved east to join the NHL.

The names involved in the deals read like a list from the Hockey Hall of Fame: Eddie Shore, Ching Johnson, Taffy Abel, the Cooks, Frank Boucher and Red Dutton. After the wheeling and dealing had ended, Dandurand invited the Patricks over for dinner at his home.

"How about Herb Gardiner?" he asked. The fine defenceman had not yet been included in any transaction.

"He's yours if you want him," Lester Patrick replied.

"How much?"

"One dollar."

"Done."

Gardiner was a mainstay of the defence that played in front of George Hainsworth in 1928-29, when the little goalie allowed only 43 goals in 44 games and compiled 22 shutouts.

Business was up close and personal in that era and a tad less scientific than in today's corporate world.

All of that notwithstanding, Dandurand and his fellow Musketeers put together a team that won the Stanley Cup in Howie Morenz's first year, 1923-24, and two more in 1930 and 1931.

"We almost lost the Cup after the first one," Dandurand wrote.

The team was invited to the Université de Montreal after they downed Ottawa, Vancouver and Calgary in the playoffs. (It was only after 1927 that the Cup would become an exclusive NHL trophy.) The Stanley Cup was presented to the Canadiens during a special ceremony and all of the players headed to Dandurand's home in the high-rent district. In Montreal, they don't exaggerate when they say high-rent district. Dandurand's home was high atop Mount Royal in Westmount.

After the game, several players, including Sprague Cleghorn, Sylvio Mantha and Vezina, piled into the boss's Model T for the trip. Things were going fine until the car encountered Côte St. Antoine Road, a sight that would gladden the heart of many an Alpine downhiller. Cleghorn had been carrying the Cup on his lap when all three players piled out to give Monsieur Leo and his Tin Lizzy a push up the hill.

The rough defenceman gently set the Cup down on the curb, and the car was pushed to the crest of the slope. About two hours later, Mrs. Dandurand was ladling out refills of her famous punch when she chanced to remark: "By the way, where *is* this famous Cup you've all been talking about?"

Cleghorn, never at a loss for words, replied: "Uh-oh!"

Dandurand and Cleghorn sped back down Côte St. Antoine to the spot where the Model T had originally stalled. The Cup was still sitting there.

Several years before he passed away, Dandurand was asked about the business side of hockey in his day.

"Let's just say it was a less complicated time," he replied.

In 1932, the Montreal Canadiens were barely a framework for the modern-day business organization. Frank Selke was fourteen years away. And a good part of those fourteen years would represent the worst period in the club's history.

3

The Darkness Descends

Nowhere can the myth of the invincibility of the Montreal Canadiens be shattered more easily than in the Depression Era.

Those who might today purposely or unconsciously manipulate history to say that the Canadiens were always the best, always at the top of the heap, forever the Flying Frenchmen, might be very surprised to discover how bad the team was in the 1930s and '40s. And those who believe that the team never trades its top superstars, such as Richard, Beliveau and Lafleur, may be stunned to learn that Howie Morenz was dealt away to Chicago in 1934.

If you can look beyond popular mythology to the facts, you will find them very revealing. The Dandurand-Morenz Era peaked in 1929-30 and 1930-31 with consecutive Stanley Cups. The next time the Montreal Canadiens would win Lord Stanley's prized hardware would be in 1943-44. That thirteen year drought was the longest in the club's history. During that period, Detroit won three times (1935-36, '36-37, '42-43), and Toronto (1931-32, '41-42), the New York Rangers (1932-33, '39-40), the Chicago Black Hawks (1933-34, '37-38) and the Boston Bruins (1938-39, '40-41) all won twice. The city of Montreal's drought was not as long as the Canadiens' because their arch-rivals, the Maroons, managed a Cup of their own in 1934-35. Not only were the Canadiens not winning, it seemed that everybody else was. Some dynasty.

The troubles did not descend on the team all at once. As the saying goes, they were long in coming, and even longer in staying. They began shortly after the 1930-31 Stanley Cup win, off the ice. The nucleus of the Stanley Cup winners, George Hainsworth, Sylvio and Georges Mantha, Marty Burke, Aurele Joliat, Morenz, Pit Lepine and Johnny Gagnon, remained intact for the next two years. The changes took place in the front office. Dandurand, Cattarinich and Letourneau had done the team proud since its purchase in 1921. They had hired qualified management, which in turn put together competitive and exciting teams on the ice. They stayed on top of all developments in hockey in the city, including wresting the Forum away from the Maroons.

A frequent topic of conversation in Montreal in the early 1930s was: "Which team will move?" The Canadiens and Maroons, arch-rivals on the ice, were even more competitive off the ice, as everyone involved realized that only one team could survive in the long run. Talk of merger was heard occasionally, with fans openly fantasizing about the powerhouse that would result from such a benevolent matrimony. Merger discussions were often heard in higher financial circles, and discreet feelers would go out from one camp to the other at almost regular intervals.

The partnership continued for two more years but it was doomed to failure; the principals had too many other interests making demands on their time and effort. Insiders say that Dandurand, always on the lookout for excitement, had gotten bored. Enter "Tay Pay" (from the French pronunciation of T.P.) Gorman.

To better understand what was happening, it is necessary to take a sidetrip via Ottawa and Chicago. Ottawa was the hometown of sports entrepreneur Thomas Patrick Gorman. For all of those modern-day sportswriters who firmly believe they know better than the sports managers they cover, Tommy Gorman is an inspiration. He not only said so as sports editor of *The Ottawa Citizen* in the pre-War era, but when he was given the opportunity he went out and proved it with the three Cups his Ottawa Senators captured in 1920, 1921 and 1923.

"The Great Gorman" was the title of the March 1, 1946 article in *Maclean's*. Sportswriter Jim Coleman wrote:

> Mr. Gorman combines some of the characteristics of P.T. Barnum, Shirley Temple and a very shrewd banker. His hockey antagonists frequently regard him with chagrin, but Mr. Gorman can afford to chuckle at this discomfiture—he is the only surviving member of the four men who originally formed the National Hockey League.
>
> Also, even if he has no other claim to fame, he would go down in history as the only former police reporter who had a chance to make a million dollars from a thoroughbred horse. However, he was the victim of a fate which can befall only an Irishman or a newspaperman—the horse thoughtlessly took ill and died!

Tommy Gorman's first job was as a page boy in the House of Commons and his energy was such that he attracted the attention of Charlie Bishop, a reporter with *The Ottawa Citizen*. Bishop got Gorman a job at the newspaper and his boundless energy served the young Irishman well; he advanced through the ranks from copyboy to police reporter to sports editor in jig time.

"Tommy soon realized that you couldn't do what he liked to do best—make money—working for a newspaper, so he left in 1917 to become publicity man for L.N. Bate, the owner of the Ottawa hockey club," Coleman reminisces.

Within a year, Gorman and Ted Day, owner of the Ottawa Arena, purchased the Ottawa club for $2,500 and Gorman was sitting at the table in Montreal's Windsor Hotel forming the four-team National Hockey League with Frank Calder, Mike Quinn of Quebec and George Kendall of Montreal. Within five years, the Ottawa Senators had won three Stanley Cups.

You couldn't keep Gorman in one place for any length of time. In 1925, he sold his share of the Ottawa Senators to Frank Ahearn for $35,000 and all of the latter's stock in Connaught Race Park outside Ottawa. Two days later, he joined Tex Rickard with the New York Americans. The Gorman family owns the Connaught track to this day.

Tex Rickard and friends were big money boys; they liked to make it and spend it, and even to spend it while making it. Gorman was in his element and it took him only a few days to convince Rickard to buy the Hamilton Tigers, lock, stock and hockey sticks, for $75,000.

It was a fast crowd in New York, sometimes too fast, and Gorman was a veteran of the police desk. He realized that some of his bosses might be using their speed to stay a step ahead of the law. Gorman's intuition never failed him. The club's owner shortly thereafter found himself in the Atlanta federal penitentiary in a one-way dispute with the U.S. Internal Revenue Service, *à la* Al Capone.

In 1928, Gorman left hockey and joined his friend Jim Crofton, a.k.a. Sunny Jim Coffroth, at the new Agua Caliente racetrack just outside Tijuana, Mexico. The track was an immediate success, the finest facility in the southern California area at a time when the sport of kings was banned in that state. Messrs. Crofton and Gorman were in the chips and a wonderful business opportunity galloped into view in 1932.

A large gelding from Down Under with the improbable name of Phar Lap was setting the racing world on its ear, winning races with ridiculous ease. The horse's ownership and entourage consisted entirely of "horse people" who had lucked into a moneymaker but whose lack of business acumen was severely reducing their earning potential. Phar Lap won the Agua Caliente Handicap without difficulty, and Gorman convinced the Australians to let him arrange a series of races across North America, culminating "back East", where all the money was.

Disaster struck quickly. Phar Lap died under mysterious circumstances and his handlers were convinced that he had been poisoned. Then legislators in Sacramento decided that horse racing in California was not a bad thing at all, and Hollywood's finest no longer had to travel to Agua Caliente to bet on the thoroughbreds.

Hockey beckoned anew.

You'll draw a smile from his son, Joe Gorman, when

the stories turn to his dad, a handsome Irishman whose eye for the ladies was well-known. Tommy had a gift of the blarney, but he also was a workaholic, who never feared putting in an eighteen-hour day.

"Dad was involved in hockey, horses and baseball in Ottawa and Montreal and was a good friend and business acquaintance of Dandurand and Cattarinich. Dad was on his way back to California in 1932 when they pulled him off the train. They had $50,000 invested in the Chicago Black Hawks who were owned by Major McLaughlin and they wanted him to keep an eye on their investment. So they made a deal with McLaughlin that Dad take over coaching the team."

In the language of that era, Major Frederic McLaughlin was a "beaut." Reports indicate that Major Hoople might have been closer to the truth. The rich son of a man who had made his fortune in coffee importation, he was a tall, movie star type who affected a clipped moustache and bow ties. He played polo and was a prime mover in the social whirl of the City With Big Shoulders. The Black Hawks were named after the famous 85th Black Hawk Division of the U.S. Army, to which the Major had belonged during the First World War. The Major must have felt he had never left the trenches and his machine-gun battalion behind, because he ran his team accordingly.

Four years before he created the Chicago franchise, the Major married movie star Irene Castle, of the famous Castle and Castle dancing team, and he really began putting on the ritz.

Tommy Gorman appeared on the scene in 1932, when the fortunes of the Black Hawks had definitely begun to wane. Up until that time, Chicago had finished third, last, last, second, second and second in the NHL's American Division. Every time the Hawks threatened to bust out into a good team, McLaughlin dumped another coach.

In six-plus seasons, Pete Muldoon, Barney Stanley, Hugh Lehman, Herb Gardiner, Tom Shaughnessy, Bill Tobin, Dick Irvin, Godfrey Matheson and Emil Iverson had stood behind the Chicago bench. Consistent with the Major's idiosyncratic behaviour was his hiring of Matheson. They met aboard a train in the U.S. Midwest and struck up a conversation. Matheson mentioned that he was a Winnipegger and the Major's eyes lit up. If this man was from Canada, the Major reasoned, he must know quite a bit about hockey. When the train arrived in Chicago, Matheson was the new coach of the Black Hawks.

That kind of sublime silliness put the team into financial hot water. Chicagoans loved the sport, but they were not going to stand still for a second-rate team. Their attitude and a bad frost in Brazil had the Major scrambling for working capital. Enter Dandurand and Cattarinich.

"Dad had orders to improve the team so that Dandurand and Cattarinich could get their money back, and that's what he did," says Joe Gorman.

Gorman picked up the coaching reins in the 1932-33 season and the Hawks finished dead last. The following year, Gorman made a few judicious player moves and the Hawks finished second in their division and third overall in the league. A veteran crew which included Taffy Abel, Lou Trudel, Lionel Conacher, Paul Thompson, Leroy Goldsworthy, Johnny Gottselig, Mush March and Chuck Gardiner wreaked havoc in the playoffs, sweeping Detroit in a four-game final to win the Stanley Cup.

In Major McLaughlin territory, that could be both good and bad news for the coach. McLaughlin had been feuding with the Norris family, who owned the cavernous Chicago Stadium, ever since 1928, when he refused approval for a second NHL franchise in Chicago.

In response, the Norrises founded the Chicago Shamrocks of the American Association in 1928, and they played before larger crowds in the Stadium. When that league went belly-up in 1931, McLaughlin signed a three-year contract with the Stadium and was happy for a while, until the Stadium began to lose money and was bailed out by the Norris family.

"The Norris and the Wirtz families owned Detroit and New York and they wanted Chicago and the Stadium. Wirtz and my father discussed the Chicago-Detroit series, and at that point, my father knew he was finished. He knew he was going to get the squeeze and he did not want to finish there on an unsatisfactory note. Whatever his impression of what Wirtz was trying to say to him about the series, my father told me that he wanted no part of any discussion about games, and that was that. They won against Detroit (1-0) that night and my father, who was living at the Sherman Hotel, packed up all of his belongings and left them in his car, which he parked about five blocks from the Stadium. When the game was over and the celebrations quieted down, he went out to the car and started to drive home to Canada."

Gorman had been away for a while and discovered to his dismay that Stanley Cups won in Chicago did not endear him to all Canadians. Crossing the border at Windsor, he was stopped for expired licence plates and tossed into the hoosegow for an overnight stay. Canadians awoke to pictures in their morning dailies of the Stanley Cup-winning GM en route to jail.

That didn't faze him and he continued on to Montreal for a meeting with Dandurand.

"At the time, the Canadian Arena Company owned the Maroons and they were having all sorts of problems with them at the Forum. The building was mortgaged to the skies and there was serious talk of turning the Forum into a streetcar barn to serve the west end of the city. Joe and Leo got their money back but they were still in trouble financially."

Dandurand and Cattarinich recommended to Senator Donat Raymond, co-owner and chairman of the Canadian Arena Company, that a job be found for Gorman, a top-notch hockey manager and businessman. He was appointed manager of the Maroons.

"My father brought in Lionel Conacher as coach, and players like Alex Connell and Allan Shields to go along with guys like Toe Blake, Cy Wentworth, Jimmy Ward,

Hooley Smith, Bob Gracie and Herbie Cain and the Maroons finished second in their division and won the Stanley Cup."

No book on the Canadiens of this era would be complete without a look at the Maroons, Montreal's other team. In fact, many oldtimers will tell you that it was the Canadiens who were the other team. The Maroons-Canadiens rivalry was one of the few things that could get cash-strapped Depression era hockey fans into a rink in the '30s, especially since the English-French animosity was built in right from the start.

In 1924, Dandurand, the consummate showman, sold one-half of his territorial rights to Jimmy Strachan, a Montreal businessman and owner of the Canadian Arena Company. Sold might be too strong a word; he almost gave them away for $15,000.

A seasoned horse player, Dandurand was taking a calculated risk. The thing that has made Montreal hum for centuries, any politician or sociologist could tell you, has been the finely calibrated cultural tension between the English and French communities.

If anyone was tuned into this cultural phenomenon it was Dandurand—a French Canadian who had spent the first sixteen years of his life in the United States. His impeccable English and French allowed him to circulate freely in the two communities. His inherent sense of showmanship told him these were the things of which great rivalries, and profits, were made.

In *The Hockey Book*, edited by Wilfrid Victor (Bill) Roche, Dandurand explained his reasoning.

Allowing the Maroons to get into the Montreal hockey picture was no big-hearted gesture on my part. I saw in them an important and lucrative local rivalry, as well as a fine addition to the league and to hockey in general.

I let Maroons in for only $15,000, which was considered, even by the Maroons directors, to be very reasonable. It was understood among the other three member clubs of the NHL that year—Toronto St. Pats, Ottawa Senators and

Hamilton Tigers—that the $15,000 was to go to the Canadiens.

That price, incidentally, established a precedent for the submission fee of franchises of Boston (1924), Pittsburgh and New York Americans (1925) and New York Rangers (1926). However, the $15,000 caused an NHL rumpus. Toronto, Ottawa and Hamilton began to think they ought to share equally with the Canadiens in the money which Maroons paid to enter the league. That didn't suit me because it had been privately agreed that the cash would go to Canadiens. The rub was that there was no written record of any such agreement, nothing in the minutes of the league.

The Canadiens finally did get all of the money, and from then on a stenographer was present to take the minutes of every NHL meeting. Dandurand insisted on it.

Dandurand's estimates of the rivalry were proved right the very first time the teams faced off in their Forum. When the *bleu-blanc-rouge* took to the ice against the maroon-and-tan, anything could happen on the ice and in the stands. Both teams were epitomized by one player or a specific line. For the Canadiens it was Morenz, Joliat, Black Cat Gagnon and their go-go speed. For the Maroons, it was slower-paced, hardnosed hockey as personified by the Three "S" Line of Nels Stewart, Babe Siebert and Hooley Smith.

"Hooley was just about the meanest guy you ever saw," is the standard quotation from any Maroons or Canadiens fan from that era. Legendary tough guys like the Cleghorn brothers had long retired but the Canadiens had the likes of the Mantha brothers, Georges and Sylvio, Albert "Battleship" Leduc, Pit Lepine and Joliat.

How bitter was the Canadiens-Maroons rivalry? The answer best comes from Maroons defenceman Red Dutton, a western cowboy who would also star with the New York Americans, and serve six years as NHL president. Getting antsy before a game while the referee hunted for three ounces of black, vulcanized rubber, Dutton offered the famous line: "Never mind the goddamned puck, let's start the game!"

Even Dandurand had no immunity from the rivalry: in one game he got involved in a fight between Smith and Newsy Lalonde!

"They were bigger than us and they played that way," Joliat reminisces. "But we couldn't back down. We had nowhere to hide, we were playing all of our games against them in our own city and everybody knew that each game we played meant a lot more than others. Especially in the mid-'30s when nobody knew which team was going to survive in the city. By the time we got there, it was like we were playing to be the team that deserved to stay. Man, I'd say they were tough . . . I can't remember anybody who was tougher than Hooley Smith. There were guys like Eddie Shore who would never back down from anybody, but Hooley took care of him. Battleship had a couple good scraps with those guys, too. I have to laugh when today's hockey fans cry about the Big Bad Bruins or the Philadelphia Flyers because they have a fight or two during a game. In those days, these guys were surgeons with their sticks. When a fight started on the ice, it might end up in the seats or under the stands, and everybody was in it."

The Maroons entered the league in 1924. They won their first Stanley Cup two years later. In 1927 and 1928, the Maroons-Canadiens rivalry was set in stone, with the Habs nipping their crosstown foes in a best-of-three series the first year, and the Maroons returning the favour the next.

In 1928, the Maroons extended the New York Rangers to five games, losing the deciding game on home ice in a game that could be charitably described as poorly refereed. The fans weren't in such a charitable mood; they tried to penalize the unfortunate official, who needed a police escort out of the building.

The Maroons were nothing if unpredictable, dropping into fifth place in the Canadian Division in 1929, then storming back the very next year to win the division and lose to the Bruins in the playoffs. And while the Canadiens may have been unhappy at losing the regular-season championship to their hometown foes, they took solace in the Stanley Cup championship, their first of two.

After the consecutive championships, it was the Maroons who captured the hockey headlines in the city. They took the much favoured Toronto Maple Leafs into overtime before succumbing in the 1932 playoffs and were eliminated by the Detroit Red Wings and Chicago Black Hawks respectively the next two years. In 1935, however, their time came as they squared off again with the vaunted offensive machine of the Maple Leafs' "Kid Line"—Charlie Conacher, Joe Primeau and Busher Jackson. Playing tough in the corners, gang defence and relying on the red-hot Alex Connell in goal, the Maroons won the Stanley Cup—the last that would be awarded a Montreal representative until 1944.

Almost as soon as it had started, it was all over for the Maroons. Both teams had financial problems in the Depression Era, but it was the Canadiens who were in the direst straits. A bad, almost directionless team, the Canadiens were getting used to playing before crowds of 2,000 and less and were losing a lot of money. The nadir for Montreal hockey fans came in 1937, the year that Howie Morenz returned to the Canadiens and died; a year when almost every description of the teams started with "financially strapped."

On September 17, 1935, it appeared that the merger rumours would be borne out, when the team was sold to Ernest Savard, Louis Gelinas and Colonel Maurice Forget. The three had formed a syndicate and were linked indirectly with the Canadian Arena Company. The latter had two main properties, the Forum and the Montreal Maroons.

"Montreal had to become a one-team arrangement and that was part of the deal that was kept quiet. The team was purchased and the plan was to move the franchise to St. Louis, but Conn Smythe, that man of wonderful vision, scotched that," said Gorman.

"At that time my father was out of it, because the Senator turned the hockey operations over to Ernie Savard, a drinking buddy. He might have done that because, once again, Dad was too successful and won the Cup that first season. It isn't easy to fold a Stanley Cup winner to keep a seventh-place team (the Canadiens). That kind of move would have been dynamite, French majority or no French majority."

The 1935 Cup champions maintained their momentum by winning the Canadian Division in 1936, but lost in the first round of the playoffs. The next year, they finished second in the regular season and went into the playoff semi-finals. In 1937-38, the once haughty Maroons expired with nary a whimper, failing to make the playoffs with 12 wins, 30 losses and 6 ties in the 48-game regular-season schedule. On August 25, before the next season would start, the Maroons ceased operations. It had been decided in the boardroom that if any team would survive in Montreal it would be the Canadiens; after all, the population base for the city was seventy percent French-speaking and the Canadiens were their team.

Nobody gloated. The Maroons had won the respect of their adversaries in their brief lifetime; winning two regular season championships and two Stanley Cups in a scant fourteen years. And the fans who had packed the Forum for Habs-Maroons games knew that they would miss the special "family feud" that those two teams represented. There were a lot of distraught Maroons fans, too, who felt that they could never support a team they had loathed so long and with so much passion. In time, however, most came round to support the Canadiens.

"The saddest thing is, that once the Maroons were folded, Savard messed up completely. Instead of moving the Maroons to St. Louis and rebuilding the Canadiens, they amalgamated the two teams. But they gave away most of the good players, like Gracie, Cain and Dave Kerr and kept Wentworth and Stu Evans, who were both on their last legs."

Gorman was still very much a part of the Canadian Arena Company and his job as business manager was to fill the big building on as many nights as possible.

"My father quietly began building up the Quebec Senior Hockey League. They had several teams from the Montreal area and also from Valleyfield, Shawinigan, Ottawa and Sherbrooke, and they used to play Sunday doubleheaders at the Forum. The QSHL was a winner and it happened at the Forum. How do you keep a building going?"

The answer would do Hulk Hogan, Nikolai Volkoff and Andre the Giant proud. Gorman "discovered" professional wrestling, which was becoming popular all over the United States.

Eddie Quinn was the big Montreal promoter and a yet-unknown French Canadian named Yvon Robert was about to become a bigger draw than the Canadiens.

"Dad was into everything in those days, and the Forum was starting to look a whole lot better, profit-wise. Wrestling took up a lot of summer and fall dates, and ice shows helped fill the quiet nights in the winter and spring."

The Canadiens were still alive, although not kicking very much. In 1938-39, they finished sixth in a seven-team league and in 1939-40 they dropped to dead last with 25 points on 10 wins, 33 losses and 5 ties in 48 games. Something had to be done, and Senator Raymond stepped in.

William Northey now was running the show and a deal was made with Lester Patrick in New York to have some of the Rangers move to the Canadiens and to bring in Frank Patrick to manage the club. This was not a particularly bad idea. The Rangers had finished second twice in a row during the regular season, and sparked by the goaltending of Dave Kerr (remember him?) and the play of Phil Watson, the Colvilles, the Patricks (Lynn and Muzz), Babe Pratt and Bryan Hextall, had skated away with the Stanley Cup in 1939-40.

The Patricks had a superb hockey reputation and it was hoped that Frank would help pump new life into the Canadiens. He started by suggesting former New York great Bun Cook as coach.

Northey went to Toronto to consummate the deal and

interview his new coach. There was a knock at his hotel room door. When Northey opened it, Bun Cook literally fell through, dead drunk. The interview ended on the threshhold, so to speak.

Tommy Gorman then was dispatched to the Big Apple to discover what was going on. After all, the 1940-41 season was rapidly approaching.

"Lester Patrick hemmed and hawed and my Dad said: 'Listen, I don't have a lot of time to fool around. Training camp opens in a couple weeks. Lay it on the line.'

"Lester cleared his throat and said: 'The directors won't go for the deal.' Dad got back on the train to Montreal. What else could he do? Now he had to report back that the Canadiens essentially didn't have much of a team."

Gorman was not completely helpless. He knew where he could find a top-notch coach in a hurry because Toronto sportswriter Andy Little had tipped him off to the fact that Dick Irvin was through in Toronto and would soon be replaced by Hap Day.

Joe Gorman, who by now was his father's "gofer", accompanying him everywhere, was sent to the Mount Royal Hotel to meet Irvin and drive him to Ste. Adèle, about forty-five miles north of Montreal, in the Laurentians.

"Dad gave Dick the lowdown, he wanted him to know exactly what he was getting himself in for. We did not have a hockey team and we were going to have to start from scratch to put one together."

That kind of assessment made no friends with the hierarchy, especially Senator Raymond, who resented Gorman's implied criticism of his friend Ernest Savard. Senator Raymond also knew that the indomitable Irishman thought little of his bona fides, too.

If French-speaking Quebec thought Senator Raymond was a top society man and politico, the treasurer to the Quebec Liberal Party and power behind the scenes, what with his genteel cattle and horse breeding farm in Vaudreuil and his connections in the Quebec legislature and

House of Commons, Tommy Gorman and his buddy Maurice Duplessis, the Union Nationale leader who would be Quebec Premier for more than twenty years, contemptuously dismissed Senator Raymond as little more than a Liberal party bagman.

Their hostility remained unspoken because both men recognized that they needed each other. Gorman's business acumen had begun to show dividends for the Forum. He was actually making a profit, something totally alien to the Old-Boys-Club style of management that had existed before.

"When Dad returned to Montreal, he found out that these idiots had signed away everything . . . the concessions, advertising, the game program . . . to all of their friends. He put a stop to that in a hurry and made recovering these things his first priority."

Gorman made his point to Raymond and other disbelievers about the collective worth of the Canadiens in the most graphic way possible. He put the entire team on waivers, with the exception of Toe Blake. There were no takers. Dick Irvin heard the real story during that meeting in Ste. Adèle.

"Dick got something like $4,500 or $5,000, which was pretty good money in those days. The whole dressing room had to be cleaned out and he had to do it."

Frank Patrick was still in the picture, the remaining evidence of Senator Raymond's pique, but not for long.

"Frank was a nice man, from a good hockey family, but there had to be a reason Lester let him come to Montreal. He was totally off the wall. He kept talking about taking the team to train in Sun Valley, Idaho, and making a movie about it. My father kept asking what team he was talking about. What they had in Montreal was a complete disaster."

Gorman and Irvin eventually began to build a team and slowly put together the elements of a winner. Toe Blake was the one-man nucleus, but he was joined that year by a raw defenceman from Winnipeg named Ken Reardon. He picked up former Canadiens defenceman

Jack Portland from Chicago, and Elmer Lach, a rookie centre from Saskatchewan, also joined the team that year.

Another member of that team would achieve notoriety in a completely different fashion. Antonio "Tony" Demers was a smooth-skating right winger with a devastating wrist shot who scored 13 goals and assisted on 10 others in 46 games in 1940-41. Nine years later, the season after he was voted the most gentlemanly player in the Quebec Senior Hockey League, he became the first and only former Montreal Canadien ever to be accused of murder. He was later convicted of manslaughter in the beating death of his girlfriend, and sentenced to fifteen years in prison. He served half of that sentence at St. Vincent de Paul penitentiary before being paroled.

The patchwork quilt Canadiens finished sixth in 1941 and 1942 but were showing signs of developing into a team, especially after such promising young newcomers as Buddy O'Connor (1941), goalie Paul-Emile Bibeault (1941), Butch Bouchard (1941), Maurice Richard (1942), Glen Harmon (1942), Mike McMahon (1943) and Bill Durnan (1943) came aboard. The 1942-43 team moved up two places in the standings, ending a four-year playoff drought for the Canadiens.

A year later, everything came together at once. The Canadiens, led by the Punch Line of Blake, Lach and Richard, the rock-ribbed defence of Reardon, McMahon, Frank Eddolls and Bouchard and the goaltending of Durnan, set a regular season points record—83—on an unbelievable 38 wins, 5 losses and 7 ties in a 50-game season. Detroit finished second with 58 points. It was the first of four straight Prince of Wales championships for the Canadiens.

The Habs topped off their greatest season with a 4-0 icing of the Chicago Black Hawks in the final round. Dick Irvin and Tommy Gorman had done the job.

More importantly, Quebec senior hockey, which Gorman had actively cultivated, was beginning to pay dividends. Montreal was acquiring a number of quality players, many of them French Canadians, who graduated from junior ranks and preferred to play senior closer to home rather than moving to the United States or Western Canada for seasoning in the minor pros.

The Canadiens did not win the Stanley Cup in 1944-45, but came back with a vengeance the following year to cop another. Everything was going well, on the surface. However, beneath the surface, the Gorman-Raymond feud was raging.

"In 1946, my father had about all he could take from Raymond. He had done his job and the Forum was in great shape. They were debt free and showing some profit because of ice shows and wrestling. The Canadiens were packing them in and the Senior Hockey was still drawing big crowds too. The company had about $600,000 in the bank."

Tommy Gorman had a network that fanned across the province. One fine summer day, defenceman Mike McMahon came into his office and told the general manager that he had found the Canadiens' next goalie. About two weeks later, McMahon walked into Gorman's office with a fifteen year-old from Quebec City, named Gerry McNeil. McNeil, at the ripe old age of sixteen, wound up with the Montreal Royals seniors.

"That was the whole point to the network that was feeding my father at the Forum," Joe adds. "McNeil cost the Canadiens nothing; neither did the entire line of Blake, Lach and Richard. Blake came when the Maroons folded, Richard came up through Quebec hockey and Lach came to Montreal after a tryout with the Rangers. They cut him and he passed through Montreal on his way back out west, staying at the Queen's Hotel. Gordie Cannon drove him out to our training camp in St. Hyacinthe for a look-see and that was that."

A Toronto referee named Bert Hedge tipped off Gorman on a young player named Ted (Teeder) Kennedy, and the general manager added him to the Canadiens negotiations list. Kennedy was traded to Toronto two years later, for Frank Eddolls and Joe Benoit, two players who would be important cogs in the Canadiens team of the 1940s.

Gorman received a lot of criticism for that trade, because Teeder Kennedy became one of the very best players in the NHL and the inspiration for a Toronto team that won four Stanley Cups in five years between 1947 and 1952.

"What most of these people didn't know was that when Teeder was eighteen, he and his father came to Montreal and met with my dad. Mr. Kennedy explained that his son was Toronto born and bred and that he had only one desire in life: to play with the Maple Leafs. My dad could have insisted that he play in Montreal but he respected what the young man and his father were saying. So he traded him to Toronto."

It worked out for both teams. Gorman's connections reached even further than the boondocks of Quebec or Saskatchewan. He was an Ottawa boy, and in that civil service town, that meant he grew up with more than a simple nodding acquaintance of some government VIPs.

When the Second World War got under way, the question was whether or not the National Hockey League and other professional sports organizations would be able to maintain operations. A long debate in Congress finally decided that major league baseball and other sports could continue in the United States, and Canadian sports entrepreneurs lobbied for a similar decision north of the border.

Here, however, they ran into a stone wall in the person of James Layton Ralston, a staunch Maritimer and Minister of Defence in the Liberal cabinet of Prime Minister Mackenzie King. Senator Raymond, for all of his connections, had no say with the Minister because the men were on opposite sides of the Conscription issue. French Canada voted almost ninety percent against a draft that would send their young men to fight in what was considered a British war; English Canada voted the opposite way in almost the same proportion.

King walked a political tightrope when he compromised: young Canadians could be conscripted for service in the armed forces but they could not be sent overseas. Ralston was outspokenly against that decision; he favoured overseas conscription. He also was dead set against business as usual for professional sports and said so.

Other well-connected NHL representatives, like Conn Smythe and league president Red Dutton, tried to dissuade Ralston but to no avail. Without conferring with Cabinet, he unilaterally decreed that all sports were over and that Canadians had to engage in the war effort as a total activity.

"My Dad had grown up with the three Lynch girls, as they were known in Ottawa. One married into the Labatt family, and another married D.C. Coleman of Toronto, a member of the Canadiens' board of directors and father of sportswriter Jim Coleman. More importantly though, when she was a young woman, she was pursued by two men, Mr. Coleman and Mackenzie King, and it turned out that she had been the love of the Prime Minister's life and he still had a soft spot for her.

"She telephoned the Prime Minister and arranged an appointment with Mackenzie King for my father, Mr. Dutton and one of the Norrises, in King's office. When they got there, the Prime Minister took them down the hall, ushered them into Mr. Ralston's office and said something like, 'Take care of these gentlemen.' The message was clear: Mr. King wanted professional sports to continue and Mr. Ralston should pay serious attention to that fact."

Ralston's objections were also tempered by the fact that Dutton, a decorated war hero in the First World War, was petitioning that hockey continue even though he had recently had two sons killed in action, a week apart.

That incident was a coup which raised Gorman's worth around the league. Nonetheless, by the war's end, the Gorman-Raymond acrimony meant that the partnership was destined to end. And when Tommy Gorman was in the Senator's bad books, he couldn't win for losing.

"I remember an incident where Senator Raymond's wife wanted to go up to the country house in the

Laurentians. The Senator was out of town and besides, he had put up his car for the winter. My father suggested that Gordie Cannon drive Mrs. Raymond and their four children up there, which he did. When Raymond found out, he raised holy hell."

The last straw was Atwater Park, a long-time baseball field across Atwater Street from the Forum where Babe Ruth had once played a game, many years before, on a barnstorming tour. Gorman, ever alert to potential revenue, suggested that the Canadian Arena Company purchase the park and use it for parking in the short term, while keeping a sharp eye on the long-term real estate development possibilities.

"Dad knew they could get it for $125,000 and the parking revenues in one season would take care of the purchase price. As well, the team was planning to raise ticket prices and Dad figured that the parking facility would allow the club to cancel the ticket increase. By this time, however, Senator Raymond was against everything my dad suggested. What the Senator did was take all the profit out of the company. My dad was a businessman with an eye to the long term and he wanted to plough all the profits back into the company. He couldn't stay under those circumstances."

There are always two sides to a story, of course. The other side in this case was a gentle hint from the Forum that Tommy Gorman was actually let go for reasons relating to alleged irregularities involving ticket sales. It seemed that some famous Montreal scalpers, Jockey Fleming among them, were getting choice seats to sell "off market", and suspicion fell on the general manager. None of this was ever proven, and Joe Gorman vehemently denies the allegations.

This chapter essentially has been Tommy Gorman's chapter, and with good reason. His contribution was virtually expunged from the Canadiens' historical record over the years as the Selke-Pollock story grew. Whether Frank Selke did it on purpose or not, the impression is that Selke came to Montreal to a franchise that was in utter disarray.

Nothing could be further from the truth.

Frank Selke walked into an operation that for the most part was thriving. The Canadiens had won the Stanley Cup April 9, 1946, with a 6-3 win over Boston at the Forum. The team line-up had names like Lach, Blake, Richard, Mosdell, O'Connor, Bouchard, Reardon, Eddolls and Durnan. It was coached by the redoubtable Dick Irvin.

The time had come for the Senator and "Tay Pay" to part company. The clincher was a replay of Chicago, 1934.

The Gorman family still talks about a telephone call Irvin received before the fourth game of the final series in Boston, with the Canadiens leading the series 3-0. It came from someone high up in the Canadiens organization and it contained instructions to bench Toe Blake. If Boston won that night, the teams would return to Montreal for the fifth game. The story goes that Irvin was fit to be tied when he came away from the telephone.

"What do I do?" he asked aloud.

For Gorman, it was a case of *déjà vu*.

"My dad confronted Dick and said he didn't much care what happened but Blake was going to play, even if he and Irvin would be out of a job the next day. The Canadiens lost that game legitimately that night, and won the Cup back home in Montreal."

A short time later, Tommy Gorman was gone, for all intents and purposes, a non-person in the Canadiens' history.

He returned to Ottawa and the Ottawa Auditorium, which he owned in addition to the Ottawa Senators senior hockey team. He enjoyed a healthy, happy career with his baseball, hockey and horse racing interests until he died in 1961.

Phar Lap may not have delivered the goods for him but a lovely young girl named Barbara Ann Scott did. After she won the 1948 world figure skating championship, the rising young star was frozen out of the lucrative U.S. ice show market by some short-sighted and chauvinistic American promoters. T.P. stepped in and personally set up a tour of Canadian cities and rinks that made both skater and promoter a respectable profit.

Perhaps the reason for his faint appearance in the archives of the *Club de Hockey Canadien* can be traced to one very revealing comment Frank Selke made to us many, many years later.

Senator Raymond was the director of a Toronto bank and attended that institution's Annual Meeting in May, 1946. While in Toronto, he called Selke, who had already left Smythe and the Maple Leafs.

"I told him I couldn't work for Mr. Gorman. Mr. Raymond told me they were going to retire him at the end of their business year, the first of July. So I came down."

Why couldn't Selke work for Gorman?

"He was an odd person. Tommy was the kind of guy— I don't mean this wrong—if the truth served better, he would still tell you a lie. Tommy was a wonderful guy in many ways. Did a lot of things. But he was a peculiar person. And he had gotten himself in wrong and they had gotten rid of him."

To paraphrase the proverb, the truth will always belong to the last historian.

4

Maurice Richard
The Lion Rampant

The New York Yankees had Babe Ruth. He was the star of the dynasty that gave birth to Yankee tradition. That is why Yankee Stadium in the Bronx is called The House that Ruth Built. The legitimization of baseball, especially after the Black Sox scandal of 1919, rests on Ruth's shoulders. He gave the sport character, notoriety and definition. Before Ruth, baseball had been perceived, like most other professional sports, as something tawdry, a jock *demi-monde* inhabited by barely literate farm boys, greasy hucksters and colourful characters; in the 1920s, it became respectable and joined the mainstream of North American life.

"He launched baseball . . . he had the largest following in the history of the game—no doubt about it," said Branch Rickey in *The Old Game*.

"In the 1920s, baseball needed a revival of faith and Babe Ruth was exactly that. He was a necessary focal point for public adulation." Ruth's astonishing 59 home runs in 1921, and his 60 homers in 1927, captured the imagination of a post-War generation like few other sports feats. Everything about the Babe was genuinely heroic.

Which is not to say that the Sultan of Swat was Caspar Milquetoast. On the contrary, he was true to his origins

—a saloon and orphanage in Baltimore. He, and others including Ty Cobb, Walter Johnson, Pie Traynor, Lou Gehrig and Connie Mack, gave America what it wanted: believable heroes, a Pantheon of Homeric figures untainted by scandal. Boxing, horse racing and hockey strove valiantly to join baseball on this Doric pedestal, but with little success for many years to come.

Boxing and the horses made great movies because they contained the stuff of life, all the elements of the human condition wrapped up in a sports contest. They pitted shining Good Guys against villainous Bad Guys and characters of all the shades of grey in between. The trouble was, too often those sports were featured outside the sports pages, as this week's petty gambler, or last week's mob figure confronted a Grand Jury to explain the mechanics of the Big Fix.

Apart from the Black Sox scandal, baseball was remarkably free of such taint. Football, having taken the college route of academic respectability, would eventually join baseball in the ranks of mass popularity sports that were above suspicion, but that wouldn't happen until the 1950s. Basketball also did not achieve universal popularity until later. Hockey, especially in Canada, would also receive its benediction in the 1950s.

Any cursory examination of sports history will be misleading because it cannot accurately paint the whole picture. To clearly understand the mood and feelings of an era, one has to emerge from the sports pages and do a time line study of the period. Scouring the microfilm library of a newspaper, or viewing the fragile kinescopes and film of the 1930s and '40s, paints a distorted canvas. The sports reporters and recorders of the time were consummate professionals and the honoured ancestors of today's media professionals. Like today's counterparts, they sold sports with magnificent reporting of events and stars. But a simple search of the sports section of the day could not tell us what was inside the heads of the people who sat in the seats.

Were sports heroes then comparable in stature to the media superstars of today? Was Jack Dempsey as big as

Muhammad Ali? Could the Manassa Mauler almost single-handedly stop a generation of young people from going to war as Ali did ("I ain't got no quarrel with the Viet Cong") with the youth of the 1960s? Did athletes get involved in politics? Were they big in advertising and commercials? When they spoke, did anyone listen? What did the fan in the stands feel about his sports heroes? What did he feel about his social condition? What kind of a day did he have prior to attending the sports contest? How did he respond to the media coverage of sports?

All of those questions, and especially their answers, would be essential to anyone attempting to gauge the true impact of a sport or an athlete within his social context.

No picture of the era would be complete without a basic comprehension of where the athletes stood with the public when they were away from the playing fields and locker rooms. The verdict was far from unanimous but the majority opinion was that most professional athletes were "rubes", dumb hayseeds scant weeks removed from isolated farms, barely literate and unable to function in civilized society. Those men who rose to lofty heights on the playing field, whose exploits were legend in the sports pages, were forgotten souls when the contest was over.

To say that a majority inhabited a special jock *demi-monde* is no exaggeration. They were not the solid suburban citizens today's athletes have become, commonly perusing the stock market tables and addressing the monthly luncheon of the Advertising and Sales Club, when they aren't calling up their agent to complain that they have been benched because the manager doesn't understand them, not because of their .244 batting average.

In the 1920s, Ring Lardner's comic strip "You Know Me, Al" was quality satire, a sensitive and knowledgeable send-up of Jack Keefe, a fictional hayseed Chicago White Sox pitcher, writing home about his exploits to boyhood buddy Al Blanchard in Bedford, Indiana. The White Sox, of course, were a terrible team, decimated three years earlier by the Black Sox scandal when eight starters were banished for life for throwing the World Series to the Cincinnati Reds. The best teams of the time were the New York Giants and Yankees. One thing all the clubs had in common, whether good or bad, was that the ballplayers were depicted as boorish oafs, with few redeeming qualities beyond those necessary for making a living at the game. "You Know Me, Al" was popular satire because it was thinly veiled truth, or accepted as such, anyway.

A sample of Jack Keefe's letters home:

> Dallas, Tex., March 31 Well friends I never would have loose this game to the giants only for Schalk and when Young come up in the 8 innings I wanted to give him a curve ball but Schalk insisted on a fast one and Young hits it out of the ball pk. and if that is getting any help out of your catcher I am nuty and the next time you can bet that I wont pay no tension to a catcher just because they got a reputation.

While the good burghers of the middle class paid as willingly for their athletic thrills as they did for other kinds of entertainment, the people employed in these industries did not enjoy the upscale images of today's athletes. A professional athlete in most sports during that era was just above bank robber and con artist on the social scale. Yes, he was a colourful character; but usually because he was so uncouth that every third word was profane. He spent his entire salary on cheap booze and women and was headed for the junkpile the moment his athletic skills deserted him. The young son in a middle class household might announce to his parents that he wanted to be a pro athlete when he grew up, and receive the same amused response as if he had decided to be a cowboy, but as he matured he would receive a subtle message: this is no kind of life for an honest citizen. And if you think that attitude was ridiculous or self-righteous, think about this question: How many of today's enlightened parents in the middle class would react favourably to a son's announcement that he would like to become a professional boxer?

If it seems that we are belabouring the issue, there is a reason. It establishes the true context for what Ruth and a few others accomplished. It also illustrates just how tough it was to attain respectability for professional ice hockey.

If other sports and their athletes were considered beneath the pale, that was especially true for hockey. The men who played the game most often were under-educated farm boys, or city kids who had dropped out of school to pursue it, a situation which continued well into the 1970s until the arrival of the U.S. college players and the Europeans. The players of hockey's first decades were mercenaries, pure and simple, and let loose the dogs of war on each ice rink where they played. They were mostly hard-drinking (those train rides could be wild) gambling womanizers who reacted with scorn to the alarms of the bourgeoisie.

On the ice, they routinely knocked each other's teeth out, carved intricate designs on each other's faces and generally comported themselves in a manner that would get them thrown in the slammer should any of their mayhem stray off ice. Quite often it did—a hockey crowd was no place for the faint-hearted in the 1930s and '40s.

While people like Morenz, Taylor, Shore, Joliat, Lalonde, the Cooks and the Patricks laid the game's foundations, the sport simply did not enjoy the respectability of baseball. For that, a Babe Ruth was needed, someone whose skills were sublime, someone whose name would fill the rinks with all ranks of society. A superstar. Someone who could, as Branch Rickey said, "launch" the sport.

They found him. His name was Joseph Henri Maurice Richard.

Born August 4, 1921, Maurice was the eldest son of Onesime and Alice Richard, who were part of the post-War exodus to the cities by young francophones all over Quebec. Onesime and Alice left their native Gaspé and settled in Montreal, where he went to work as a carpenter for Canadian Pacific Limited. After a short time spent in the Plateau Mont-Royal area, they moved to the isolated Nouveau Bordeaux district, north of the city and across the Rivières des Prairies from Laval. It was on that river, and in the schoolyards of the Bois-de-Boulogne and Laval that Maurice Richard developed his formidable talents.

Like a great many young hockey players of talent, Maurice Richard would play six or seven days a week during the season, as a member of a school team, a parks or recreation league team and perhaps a third sports association team. He began to attract the attention of hockey people all over the city, but there was no specific meeting with a hockey scout who would pronounce the fateful words: "Maurice, how would you like to play for the Canadiens?"

"It never happened that way," Richard says. "It might have a couple years later, but then the Canadiens did not have the kind of organization Mr. Selke built. They owned four or five junior teams and controlled senior hockey too, but it was run like a bad orchard. They waited until the wind would blow the apples out of the trees.

"If you were any good, you would eventually work your way up and they would notice you. It was nothing like today's Junior Leagues and articles in the newspapers for ten year olds."

In his teens, Richard came under the tutelage of Paul Stuart, who despite his name, was a French-speaking Montrealer who did his best to ensure that young francophones would get a fair shake in the pros. He was in charge of the almost forty hockey teams that played in the midtown Parc Lafontaine area, and mentor to hundreds of boys. Richard was introduced to him at the juvenile level and Stuart immediately saw in him something special. He also knew that a rising young French-speaking star in the NHL would have to learn to take care of himself, and enrolled the thin, fragile youth in boxing lessons with Harry Hurst, a Montreal prizefighter. Not just content with attaining a level of pugilistic proficiency that would stand him in good stead in any hockey rink, Richard entered the Golden Gloves competition and acquitted himself well.

"But I was a hockey player, first and foremost," he says. "I really enjoyed boxing as a one-on-one competition, but hockey was my game. I will say that my ability to take care of myself with my fists around the NHL allowed me to play hockey a lot more. In those days, nobody gave you anything in hockey—if an opponent sensed a weakness, he would be on you every game."

The establishment, and some observers of the time, would argue that the absence of a process of natural selection in Montreal could easily have cost the Canadiens the services of Maurice Richard. The only factor militating in the club's favour was that the other teams in the league were even shorter in organizational talent. Montreal was a hotbed of hockey and a prominent nursery of talent, but most of the other teams stayed away, giving the Canadiens free rein.

The clubs did have territorial agreements, and the Montreal Canadiens generally had *carte blanche* to proceed as they saw fit with hockey talent in Quebec. The other teams were by no means barred from searching for talent in the city and environs. Most of the time, they just did not bother.

Stuart and Paul-Emile Paquette, who ran his own juvenile team, saw the raw talent of Maurice Richard and tried to tell the Canadiens. Yet in those days, Flying Frenchmen or not, the club was not about to chase after every talented young French Canadian who came along. With the demise of the Maroons, and the transfer of former Maroons like Toe Blake, Herb Cain, Jimmy Ward, Bill MacKenzie, Cy Wentworth, Stew Evans and Babe Siebert, the club had a decided "anglo" tint. That carried on into management, where Tom Gorman, who had managed the 1933-34 Chicago Black Hawks and the 1934-35 Maroons to Stanley Cup victories, now was general manager of the *bleu, blanc, rouge.* Cecil Hart, Pit Lepine and Dick Irvin were his coaches, Lepine only as a fill-in in 1939-40 after the death of Siebert.

Irvin was fresh from Toronto, where he had coached the Maple Leafs for a decade. Hart, who coached the Canadiens for ten seasons, seven in the late 1920s, and three more in the 1930s after a five-year hiatus, was a

well-respected hockey man as well. But neither had connections in the French-speaking community.

"So don't be so surprised that these people didn't come
after me when I was younger," Richard cautions. "The
amateur leagues received some media coverage in those
days. But it was nothing like the attention Bobby Orr,
Guy Lafleur and Wayne Gretzky received when they
were young. Those guys were ten, twelve or fourteen
years old and they were in the newspapers and on television a lot. Not in our days."

Stuart was a very talented hockey man and was offered an opportunity to coach the Canadiens' top feeder
team—the Canadiens Seniors. He accepted on one condition—the club would favour the development of French
Canadian talent. The Forum demurred and Stuart stayed
in Parc Lafontaine. Both Paquette and Stuart realized
that someone would have to pay attention to their protégé so they went to see Arthur Therrien, coach of the
Verdun Juniors, one of the Canadiens' five junior teams
in the metropolitan area. The message was simple:
"Come and see this kid, you will not waste the trip."
Therrien could not help but be impressed. Richard, then
a left-winger, was averaging six goals a game and typi-
cally would score a couple at the end of rink-long rushes.
Along with 125 other hockey players, he was invited to
Verdun's training camp, but no promises were made.

"Quite a few of the other players there were the stars
of their juvenile or midget teams from all over the province too," he recalls. "Just being invited to camp at that
level meant something special in those days." Richard
impressed during his first scrimmage with two goals that
involved through-the-opposition manoeuvering. He
made the team, but not as a regular.

"I spent some time on the bench early in the season
and I would play on the third or fourth line a lot. But as
the schedule went on, and I got more confidence, I
started playing better and better and pretty soon was
playing on the first or second line. That was when I knew
that I would one day get a chance to try out profession-
ally. The top juniors always got a tryout and that year I
led the league in scoring during the playoffs."

The next step up came very quickly, when Richard was invited to the Canadiens Seniors training camp the following September. He played well, made the team and had already scored two goals when the teams went into the third period of the Canadiens Seniors first regular-season game. Richard picked up the puck just outside his own blueline and steamed up-ice. Just inside the opposition zone, he was knocked off balance and slammed into the corner boards. His skate caught in a rut at the base of the boards, his body's momentum swung him back towards the ice, and his ankle snapped. Season over.

In 1941, he returned to the Canadiens Seniors where he was converted to a right winger and played well for the first twenty games of the year ... until a broken wrist in the twenty-first game sidelined him for the rest of the regular season. He came back to score six goals in four playoff games and was considered a shoo-in for a post on the parent club's 1942-43 edition. That summer, Maurice Richard worked hard as a machinist and married his childhood sweetheart, Lucille Norchet. He also tried to enlist in the Canadian army but was turned away because of his ankle injury in 1940. (Richard would try again in 1943, with the same result).

Training camp came and went and Richard's participation could be wrapped up in one sentence uttered by coach Irvin: "The kid is a natural."

The kid might have been a natural but Irvin wasn't going to tell him that personally. That wasn't his or the Canadiens' way. Jacques Plante, who would join the Canadiens ten years after Maurice Richard, tells of the Rocket's earliest beginnings and an apocryphal story which would be used to prove a point to all Habs rookies down through the years.

"When Rocket first came up in 1942, to show you what kind of guy he was, he was a rookie at the same time as Bobby Fillion of Thetford Mines. Dick Irvin was coach and he played them off against each other. Both players would skate in the pre-game warm-up but they didn't know until after the warm-up which one would be playing. After it was over Irvin would tell them who was playing and who would have to get undressed. One day

Rocket was told to go to the room and he just kicked the door right through, he put his foot right through the door, and then went in to shower. He was twenty-one years old, a rookie, and to do that to Dick Irvin showed that he had a lot of character. This was the type of guy Irvin was looking for. Irvin would love a good fight on the ice during practice. He would instigate things, people would blow off steam, and then laugh about it afterwards."

Dick Irvin's blasting cap to Rocket Richard's dynamite stick was an ideal combination as the Canadiens began to rebuild. However, thirteen years later, the combination would have devastating side effects.

General manager Gorman agreed with Irvin's assessment of the rookie after that initial training camp, and Richard graduated to the big club, signing his first professional contract (two years) two days before Hallowe'en. Less than a month later, he would begin amassing Ruthian headlines such as "The New York Rangers beat Maurice Richard 5-3." Things went well for the first six weeks of the season as Richard began proving his worth in every rink in the league. Two days after Christmas, in a game against the Bruins, he took a hard check in the third period, fell awkwardly, and fractured his right ankle this time. Later that evening, Irvin wondered aloud to the press: "Richard may just be too brittle to play in the National Hockey League."

"Three major injuries in three years—I wondered too," Richard says. "I knew I was a lot stronger than they gave me credit for and that I could play against anybody in that league but I was going to have to prove it. It is hard to fight against the other teams and your own coaches, management and team-mates. Getting a reputation that you are injury-prone is something very hard to get rid of. I also knew that if I hurt myself again in the next season or two, the Canadiens might ship me just about anywhere."

It was indicative of the management practices of the age that no one would discuss these issues with Richard himself. It was also the beginning of his disenchantment with the people in the front office, a bitterness that lingers even today.

"What bothered me the most was that nobody would come up to you and talk about such things, man-to-man, face-to-face," he says. "That is not pride or egotism . . . it is honesty and respect to treat someone this way. I was a very young man starting out in hockey and, so far, very unlucky. Instead of recognizing that, the club worried publicly about whether I would be able to last in this league. Tommy Gorman never said this to me but he did talk about it to the papers. I did not appreciate that but I was young and he was the boss . . . I could say nothing."

Compounding the troubles with Richard were the on-going problems that the club experienced in the era: the Canadiens had been down for so long that few fans remained to support the team.

"When I was playing senior hockey, quite often we would fill the Forum while the Canadiens played to a half-full Forum," Richard recalls. "Most of that was because they had been such a bad hockey team for so long. But a large part was because they had few recognizable French Canadian stars. Maybe that is why they were so nervous about me making the team. If I could be successful, and a few others like Butch Bouchard and Fernand Majeau, we could get the people back."

The Canadiens and Maurice Richard would be most successful, far beyond their wildest dreams, in 1943-44. They would post one of the best records in the history of the NHL, 38 wins, 5 losses and 7 ties in 50 games; Richard would score 32 goals, 23 of them in the last 22 games of the season—after missing a large part of the early season with yet another injury, this time a dislocated shoulder. The season started with Richard receiving permission to switch uniform numbers to 9 from 15. He was a happy man and proved it with two goals in each of his first two games as he played alongside two new linemates—Toe Blake and Elmer Lach. His bad shoulder put the brakes to his scoring but the New Year came in with a bang. Richard, fully recovered from the injury, scored his first hat trick Dec. 30, 1943 (against Jimmy

Franks of Detroit), and went on a tear. By season's end he was only the fourth member of the Canadiens (Joe Malone with the league record of 44 in 22 games, Newsy Lalonde and Howie Morenz) to score 30 or more goals in a season.

Richard's value to the team was without question as the playoffs beckoned.... The Canadiens, with essentially the same lineup, had finished in fourth place the year before. With the additions of goaltender Bill Durnan and Richard, they catapulted into first, and awaited the post-season tournament with optimism and some newfound cockiness. That was quickly drummed out of them in a 3-1 loss to Toronto. Bob Davidson, the Bob Gainey of the era, threw a checking blanket over Richard and the Forum crowd went home muttering to itself.

"I remember going up to their goalie Paul Bibeault near the end of the third period and telling him things would be different in the next game," Richard says. "I didn't know how right I would be ..."

Like most great athletes, Richard can recall his greatest moments in the most minute detail, recounting events as if they were happening in the present. Also like most great athletes, he is at a loss to explain why those moments came about. He cannot analyze them now and never could.

In this case, most National Hockey League veterans agree, the superstar was born. The date: March 23, 1944. The place: the Forum.

"We went through the first period scoreless," recalls Ray Getliffe, the Montreal centre who had nicknamed Richard "Rocket" earlier in the season, "and it looked like they were going to shut Maurice down forever. But he had other plans."

The breakthrough came in the second period, when Richard finally shook off Davidson and scored three times.

"He was on another planet, in another world," said Getliffe. "He had that look in his eyes; like the other players against him weren't even there ... like he was all by himself on the ice. I played with him, and sometimes when I was on the ice with him, and I saw him coming in my direction with that look on his face, I wanted to jump right over the boards out of his way. Can you imagine what the opposition felt?"

On that March day, it would not be hard to imagine how the Leafs felt: Richard added two more goals in the third period, and the final score read: Richard 5, Toronto 1. No other hockey player had ever scored five goals in a playoff game. The Richard legend was born.

Ten days later it was Richard 3, Chicago 1. The Canadiens swept the Black Hawks in four games and Richard scored 12 goals in 9 playoff games. After thirteen very long years, the Stanley Cup returned home with the Canadiens. The drought was over and a new age beckoned.

In 1927, as the Bambino pursued his sixtieth home run, the event was of such significance that the press coverage moved from the sports pages to the front page. In 1944-45, Maurice Richard muscled aside the Second World War and earned his way to page one. Germany was collapsing on all fronts in February and March, 1945, and the same could be said of opposition defences and netminders in the National Hockey League. Richard was on the trail of the elusive scoring record of 44 goals held by Joe Malone.

His pursuit of the record was about as easy as the Allied mop-up operations in Europe; everywhere Richard turned he found an adversary poised to use any tactic necessary to stop him. One such hired thug was Bob "Killer" Dill, a player who had been banned from the American League and the nephew of two famous prizefighters, Mike and Tommy Gibbons, from whom he had acquired a certain pugilistic prowess. Richard was scoring at an unbelievable rate of a goal a game and the challenges were mounting. Before he would go into an enemy rink two questions were bandied about liberally in the papers. How many goals would he score that night? And who was the designated hitman for the opposition?

The Canadiens were scheduled for a Madison Square Garden contest against the Rangers a week before

Christmas and every hockey writer from miles around was speculating on the "inevitable" Richard-Dill confrontation. In those days, the sportswriters were not under pressure from crunchy granola publishers to clean up the game and downplay hockey violence. They knew the fans loved it, as they do today, and played it up. Some pre-game stories were "Tale of the Tape" boxing-style pieces. The rather unique Garden fans were fairly slavering over the prospects of their man stopping the Rocket in more ways than one. The puck was dropped to start the game and Dill immediately made his presence known, ramming Lach into the boards. Throughout the first period, the Rangers player did everything he could to goad Richard into a fight, but with no success.

In the second, he got his wish. Dill and Chuck Scherza began a scrap behind the Rangers net with Lach and Blake, two men who could take care of themselves. It appeared that the referee had sorted things out and players were milling about when Dill manoeuvered near Richard and said something to the effect of: "Is the frog scared?"

Richard scored a one-punch knockout, a right hook that lifted Dill off his feet and left him in a crumpled heap on the ice. The belligerents repaired to the penalty box area where a somewhat revived and chagrined Dill began vociferously planning his revenge. Before entering the penalty box, the players came together a second time.

The headline in the New York *Daily Mirror* summed it up best: "Dill Pickled." Richard caught the Ranger with a series of punches, the most devastating being a right to Dill's left eye, which opened a large cut. After serving his double majors, Richard scored the game-tying goal, his 19th in 19 games. After the game, Rangers' coach Frank Boucher ranted: "If he doesn't learn to control his temper, that crazy Richard will kill somebody one of these days."

As for Dill, he met Richard after the game on 49th Street, smiled broadly as he told the Montreal star it was the hardest anyone had ever hit him, and accepted Richard's dinner invitation! And so it went in Richard's ascension to superstardom.

Three days after Christmas, Richard showed up in the Canadiens' dressing room at the Forum and headed straight for the trainer's table. Sprawling on it, and looking exhausted, he announced that he had been moving house all day with his brother and could hardly move. "You'll have to do it without me tonight," he concluded.

Three hours later, Richard was in the same dressing room, trying to explain to reporters how he had scored five goals and added three assists in a 9-1 dismantling of Detroit. He couldn't, but that bothered no one. Most of the reporters admitted they just wanted to get close to greatness, even if the quotes were starvation rations.

Seven weeks later, he scored twice against the same Red Wings in a 5-2 victory; his 42nd and 43rd goals of the season, tying Cooney Weiland for second-highest goal total in NHL history. What was so astounding was that the Rocket scored the 43 goals in 38 games. In Toronto the next week, he tied the Malone record of 44 and received a standing ovation from the normally reserved Maple Leaf Gardens crowd, even when the P.A. announcer refused to acknowledge the record-tying feat.

A week later, the same teams were at the Forum and the Leafs were determined that Richard would not set the record against them. Everywhere Richard went that night, two, three and four white-and-blue shirts faced him. Nick Metz and Davidson, top defensive wingers, shadowed him mercilessly and the tension grew as the first two periods went by. The tension on the ice was palpable—at the slightest provocation, Canadiens and Leafs players would drop the gloves and go at it. With such attention paid Richard, his team-mates found themselves with open ice and led Toronto 4-2 midway through the third.

Almost 14,000 fans jumped out of their seats when Richard picked up a loose puck, shook off two checkers and bore down on Toronto's Frank McCool. McCool held his ground and made the save and 14,000 disappointed fans sighed, and sat down as one. There were about four minutes remaining in the contest when Blake hit Richard with a little flip pass in the Toronto zone. The Montreal winger never hesitated, even though he was at a bad angle out near the faceoff circle. The puck hit his stick and he let it go simultaneously ... into the net past a startled McCool.

There was a sudden hush. And then the Forum exploded. The Canadiens streamed out onto the ice, Blake made straight for the net to retrieve the puck, which later would be presented to Richard by Malone. The game would not resume for another fifteen minutes.

And so it went. The magic 44 eclipsed, people began speculating whether Richard could score 50 goals in 50 games, an unheard-of feat, easily the match of Ruth's 60 circuit blasts. With eight games remaining, could Richard score five more goals?

When would Richard score his fiftieth? Where would he score it? The tension mounted as the season wore down to its conclusion. The Canadiens played against Chicago Black Hawks in their home ice finale and Richard was a man possessed that night. He had 49 goals to his credit and appeared ready to sell his soul to the devil to score number 50 at home. Late in the third period (like the preceding Toronto game) a magnificent opportunity presented itself with Richard all alone in front of the Chicago goalie. A sprawling defenceman tripped him at the last minute and a penalty shot was awarded. It was not to be. Richard missed and scored his fiftieth in Boston.

50 goals in 50 games. In a six-team league. In an era where just about every hockey player thought it was his sacred trust to separate an opponent's head from his shoulders if the latter had the audacity to attempt to score against the former. It was a momentous feat and set the Richard legend in stone. Hockey was well on its way to respectability and acceptance ... on the streaming shirt-tails of Maurice "Rocket" Richard.

After 1944-45, Maurice Richard's stardom was assured, even with the ascension of Gordie Howe of Detroit. If anything, Howe was Gehrig to Richard's Ruth; a quiet farm boy with prodigious hockey skills, who would eventually rewrite the record books in a career whose longevity still baffles experts. (Howe would play against both Richard and Gretzky, which is a little like playing baseball against both Ruth and Aaron). You can still start a fist fight in certain drinking establishments in the old six cities by simply stating that Richard was vastly superior to Howe, or vice versa.

It would be easy to continue the recitation of Richardian anecdotes and facts. The pages would quickly melt away and a thick tome would emerge. However, this work concerns itself with the Montreal Canadiens, the birth of their legend, and the organization that learned to make that special status work for the team. Without giving Maurice Richard's career short shrift, suffice it to say that he was the superstar who truly launched the on-ice dynasty. His was the most special Canadiens legend, eclipsing even that of the fabled Howie Morenz, who once had lain in state at centre ice of the Forum.

If there was any doubt what Richard meant to hockey, especially in French Canada, that doubt was erased on St. Patrick's Day in 1955. The Canadiens were defending Stanley Cup champions that March and were winding down another season in fine style. Unlike the teams of the late 1940s, of which French Canadians formed a definite minority, the '54-55 Canadiens overflowed with French Canadian players of all-star quality: among them Bernard "Boom Boom" Geoffrion and the regal Jean Beliveau. Coming down to the last four games, Richard, Beliveau and Geoffrion were 1-2-3 in the NHL scoring race and Richard was fighting for his first-ever Art Ross Trophy and the $1,000 in prize money that accompanied it.

On March 13th, against Boston, Richard and Hal Laycoe hooked up in a brutal stick-swinging incident that saw the Canadiens forward go berserk after Laycoe (a former team-mate) cut him for stitches on top of the head. Richard attacked Laycoe and decked him; then picked up his stick and hit the Bruins player with it three times, all the while fighting off linesman Cliff Thompson, who was trying to separate the two.

"At this point, it was almost like he discovered the existence of the linesman," said coach Dick Irvin the next day. "I still don't know whether or not Maurice recognized who he was."

That will remain a moot point. Even Richard can't or won't say for sure, almost thirty years later. His personal Official Secrets Act has not yet reached its statute of limitations.

What happened next was that Richard turned on Thompson and hit him twice in the face. He was immediately assessed a match misconduct and NHL president Clarence Campbell was called in to investigate the incident. Earlier in the season, after a fight with Toronto's Bob Bailey, Richard had taken a swipe at linesman George Hayes and was given a match penalty for his efforts.

To this day, many people believe there was a movement to "get" Richard, and that its main proponents were at the highest levels of the league . . . the owners of the other five franchises.

"Even today, I have not shaken the feeling that certain people felt it was time to punish Richard for the way he acted on the ice," said Frank Selke in 1983. "Although I hoped for the best, I expected the worst when Campbell announced his decision."

Richard, Kenny Reardon and coach Irvin were summoned to Campbell's office in Montreal's Sun Life building. The verdict was harsh—Richard was suspended for the rest of the season and the Stanley Cup playoffs as well.

Clarence Campbell, a pillar of White Anglo-Saxon Protestant rectitude, had spoken. Until his last day, he maintained that he took the correct action. Until that very same day, a lot of people in the know swore that he sold out to the other owners and that his action was a calculated slap at the Canadiens, Richard, and French Canadians in particular. He would receive evidence of the popularity of such sentiments very soon.

Richard insisted, also until Campbell's last day, that the suspension had been a mistake. Pressed by a journalist for his thoughts on the former NHL president at Campbell's Montreal funeral in 1984, Richard stated simply: "He was wrong."

The day after handing down his decision, Campbell and his fiancée took their seats at the Forum for a game between the Richard-less Canadiens and Detroit, Campbell proving once again that he was totally out of touch with the French-speaking majority of the city in which he lived. He simply did not realize that the hardheaded attitude he had demonstrated was nothing short of an incitation to riot. Earlier that day, the Montreal police and City Hall both had contacted the NHL president and asked him to stay away from the Forum. They had received all sorts of threats of violence against him, as did his own office. Several callers were emphatic: if Campbell walked into the Forum, he would be carried out.

Campbell entered the Forum that night in spite of the warnings, and, inevitably, the fans' anger erupted.

Shortly before the game got under way, a large crowd formed outside the Forum, at St. Catherine and Atwater. Many had tickets and would enter the building shortly before the 8 p.m. start. Many others, however, had no tickets, but were there to express their displeasure in the Richard sentence. Many carried placards and signs depicting Campbell in the rudest fashion. Inside the building, a "he'll show, he won't show" guessing game was going on in the stands. The game started and Campbell's two reserved seats remained empty. Scattered throughout the building were as many as 150 special policemen hired for the occasion.

About halfway through the period, Campbell and his fiancée took their seats. What seemed to compound matters was the fact that the Canadiens did not appear to have their minds on the game. After the league president's arrival, Detroit scored three quick goals and led 4-1. The crowd began yelling, *"On veut Richard—à bas Campbell"* (We want Richard—down with Campbell) and the NHL executive sat stoically through the verbal onslaught. By the end of the period, the hostilities were no longer merely verbal; fans began throwing everything in reach ... fruit, hot dogs, rubbers, and programs ... at Campbell, as people in his vicinity scrambled for cover. He maintained his stiff upper lip until a young man attacked him physically and was pulled away by Forum security at the last moment. Then it really hit the fan. A tear gas canister went off just a few feet from Campbell, and the fans who had toughed it out thus far abandoned ship, tears streaming down their faces. The Forum was ordered evacuated by Montreal fire marshals and the game was forfeited to the Red Wings. Nobody knows to this day whether the canister was thrown by a policeman or a disgruntled fan—a later investigation proved that it was the kind sold to the Montreal police by the manufacturer.

The people inside the Forum stormed outside and were joined by hundreds of angry fans who had been unable to attend the game. The rioting began.

From the surge of spectators exiting the Forum, many of them with tears streaming down their faces because of the tear gas, those waiting outside received their signal. Anything that could be thrown was hurled in the direction of the Forum and the sound of breaking glass filled the air. The barrage was so concentrated that police supervising the evacuation inside had to turn several thousand spectators around and escort them out via the side exits. Cars, taxis and buses on St. Catherine and Atwater became moving targets and drivers and passengers alike had to hit the floor to avoid a shower of glass as windshields and side windows exploded. The wail of sirens joined the street music and was followed by the sound of running feet as rioters scattered in all directions, trashing storefronts all along St. Catherine. Newspaper kiosks were overturned and set ablaze as police arrived in force. But they, too, had to advance carefully, as they came under bombardment from the agitated crowd. Several police cars were heavily damaged and more than once a policeman who had arrested wrongdoers and was preparing to take them away had to surrender his prisoners when surrounded by crowds of rioters.

Dozens were arrested, and St. Catherine Street was a river of glass all the way to University (about two miles east of Atwater) before the outburst was tempered around midnight. The newspapers had a field day on March 18, with French and English dailies taking opposite sides. The Canadian Press wire agency described the uprising as the "worst seen in Montreal since the anti-conscription riots which marked the last War."

Thirty years later, historians and sportswriters alike look at the Richard Riots as a watershed in the development of Quebec society. Rejean Tremblay of *La Presse*, a sports columnist who started out as a Latin and Greek teacher, says:

"If, at the time, many anglophones were unwilling to acknowledge that the Campbell-Richard confrontation had political consequences, I don't think that is the case today. Too many people say Quebec's Quiet Revolution did not begin in 1960 with the arrival of Jean Lesage and the Liberals, but with the Richard Riots. That told us that this backhanded attitude of the English establishment would no longer be tolerated." Maurice Richard was not just a hockey player; he was the French Canadian incarnate.

Sociologist Orrin Klapp has written that hero worship is a yearning relationship in which the individual escapes his own frustrations or inadequacies by wishing or imagining himself to be like someone whom he admires. The profound impact of Maurice Richard can best be explored through analysis of the ways in which local fans made deep commitments to him.

Ever since humanity's earliest societies, heroes have been used by the masses for what sociologists now call individual dream realizations—to supply a type of psychic mobility for those who cannot make it on their own initiative. This generally is most prevalent in an adolescent population, for it is here that idealization is freshest and most impetuous—part of the process of parental control giving way to the influences of peer group pressures and the need to embrace a fairly precise and all-encompassing belief system.

For the French Canadian of the 1950s (and they were still called French Canadians then), the identification with the Montreal Canadiens and the success of the team's French Canadian stars was particularly overpowering. In fact, it was so pervasive that Frank Selke worked extremely hard to downplay the huge contribution of the primarily all-English front office. At a time when thousands of francophone Montrealers chafed under an anglophone bit in the workplace, Selke felt, quite rightly, that the players should and would get all the attention.

And no one wore the *Sainte Flanelle* with more pride and character than Maurice Richard. Three decades later, Richard himself is very aware of the symbolism of St. Patrick's Day, 1955.

"Yes, I realize I was important to a lot of people as a symbol, but I could not look at the politics of it," he says. "Even discussing it along these lines makes me feel a little funny. How would you feel to be discussed by historians like this? I was a hockey player; I have always been a hockey player ... it was my *métier*. When you talk about the politics, you talk about people manipulating things that happened, a long time after they happened."

Yet there could be no doubts about the influence of Richard. That was recognized the night of the riot, when Selke called him and asked him to come back to the Forum and personally ask the crowd to disperse.

"I told him that would only make the situation worse," Richard says. "They would have probably carried me down St. Catherine on their shoulders and started something worse."

Montreal was in turmoil the next day, a Friday. Mayor Jean Drapeau, who had experienced uprisings during the anti-conscription riots as a member of the Bloc Populaire, laid the blame squarely on the shoulders of Campbell. The mayor said that Campbell's attendance at the Forum was overt provocation, and that nothing untoward had happened during the first ten minutes of the game prior to his arrival. A war of words began between the two, with Campbell expressing his concern that the first magistrate of the city of Montreal would take him to task because he refused to acknowledge the threats and warnings of "several hoodlums" to stay away from the game.

Campbell himself spent the day answering telephone

calls from journalists all over the world and had to deny a rumour that he was about to resign as league president. "Me resign?" he scoffed. "The league governors have all called me and congratulated me for attending last night's game," he replied, once again proving in the minds of the suspicious that something more than a simple hockey fight was behind the Richard suspension.

Richard was receiving telephone calls too, many from influential friends who were worried about a replay of the previous evening's festivities.

Later that evening, a sombre Richard, impeccably dressed in a grey suit, sat in the Canadiens dressing room at a small table. On it was a veritable forest of microphones, bearing the flashes of Montreal's radio stations and the French and English networks of the Canadian Broadcasting Corporation. At 7:15, the hockey player began to speak, in French and in English. Richard began by admitting his disappointment over the severity of the sentence, and how he would miss not being with his team-mates in the playoffs. He spoke quietly, in a very subdued manner, but his words carried immense weight. There was to be no more talk of riots and revenge. Maurice had spoken.

And on this, the most traumatic evening of his career, Maurice Richard was confirmed as the quintessential superstar of the game ... the Babe Ruth of professional hockey. His influence transcended the mere 200 feet by 85 feet enclosure on which he plied his trade.

Yet oddly enough, it also was the beginning of his eclipse as team leader as well. Maurice Richard would return to the Canadiens and captain his team-mates to an unprecedented and unmatched five straight Stanley Cups. He would end his career with 544 regular-season goals, another 82 in the playoffs. He would have seasons of 38 and 33 goals the next two years, but would tail off to 15, 17 and 19 goals in 111 injury-plagued games between 1957 and his retirement in 1960.

That does not mean he did not contribute. Far from it. Ralph Backstrom, a soft-spoken native of Kirkland Lake,

Ontario, and the best third-string centre in hockey at the time, became a regular in the 1957-60 period when Rocket's star was on the wane.

"I was in awe of Rocket. I did not know what to say to him so I sat in the dressing room in a catatonic stupor during the first few weeks I saw him as a team-mate. The man hated to lose. If the team suffered a defeat, he would stalk around the dressing room glaring at people. He wasn't chastising any particular individual but was generally aggressive and visibly upset. It was important for me to watch him that way. He was communicating some significant values and I realized at that point that if he wasn't satisfied with the performance on the ice, I could never be content either. But the hockey tradition, the one that Mr. Selke fashioned, was really carried on by the Pocket Rocket, Maurice's brother Henri. He was my role model throughout my playing career."

The Rocket, the Lion Rampant, could only snarl his frustration at his own shortcomings in his latter years. He could inspire, but he was not the leader his brother Henri would be, nor that Jean Beliveau was, for that matter.

Still, he was pure competitor. Jacques Plante played with Rocket throughout his professional career, but his most vivid images of the Rocket are from Richard's early retirement years.

"In his playing days, Rocket was not the greatest skater or the most efficient playmaker, but he had the biggest heart in the league. They can tell all the stories they want about Gordie Howe but the Rocket played with fire in his eyes. He would do anything to win the game. The most fascinating thing about him was that he was no different in practice. The closer he came to the net, the faster he moved. Then all that you could see were those big black eyes staring you down. It was like being mesmerized by a cobra; he had a hypnotic ability about him.

"The irony, of course, is that he did not change his style even after his career came to an end. We used to practice every Saturday afternoon from one to three at St. Vincent de Paul arena—we called ourselves the Saturday Gang— and since I was the better of two goalies, I always played against Maurice. The guy still had contempt for his opponent and if I stopped him during a rush, he would become incensed at me and come at me again—it was almost as if we were competing in an important match. That's where you could see Rocket's true character. Even then, he was constantly looking for the edge and that is exactly what Frank Selke was looking for when he recruited him."

Although he was still ferocious in his declining years, the Lion could always find time for novices. Rod Gilbert, a handsome French Canadian winger who, along with Jean Ratelle, escaped the Canadiens' recruiting dragnet and went on to star with the New York Rangers, has a more pleasant memory of the Rocket in his last season.

"I was a rookie just up with the Rangers from junior and I spotted him in a coffee shop at a hotel near Madison Square Garden one day late in the season. I was really nervous about approaching him, but I did and I asked him if he had any tips to give someone who was just coming up. He really surprised me when he told me he knew who I was and had read good things about me. He said something like, 'Sure kid,' and agreed to meet me at Madison Square after both teams had practised. He told me to bring my skates and stick."

Gilbert, a little timidly, showed up at the appointed time and Richard skated out onto the ice carrying his stick in one hand, a bucket of pucks in the other.

"He dumped the pucks all over the ice in one end and spread them out all over the ice surface," Gilbert recollects. "And then he just started wheeling and shooting them into the goal from every angle—backhand, forehand, wrist shots, slapshots—and just about every one of them went in.

"I must have stood there with my jaw hanging down when he skated up to me and said: 'If you want to play in this league, kid, you have to know where the net is.' He then just skated off the ice."

No one knew better than the Rocket where the net was.

The Campbell suspension robbed him of his only chance to ever win the league scoring championship. He would never get another; even on the Canadiens he was to be eclipsed by players with names like Beliveau, Moore, Geoffrion and his brother, Henri Richard.

To this day, there are Montreal fans who curse Campbell in his grave.

5

Father Frank's Masterplan

The Canadiens' dynasty began August 1, 1946, when a short, bespectacled man in a crew cut, a dead ringer for comedian George Gobel, strolled into the Forum.

The first two words of French that Frank Selke had learned were *carte blanche*. That was what he had been given days before by Senator Donat Raymond.

"Mr. Selke, do what you must do to make the Montreal Canadiens the most impressive team and organization in professional hockey," Senator Raymond told the native of Berlin (Kitchener), Ontario. "You are in complete charge of the team. What you say, goes."

Frank Selke smiled, remembering the celebrated feud with Conn Smythe that had driven him to Montreal, and went to work. Using the third word of the French language that he had learned, he issued his first order, the prime dictum that was to launch one of the proudest teams in club sports.

"Clean the toilets: this place stinks like a *pissoir!*" It was a beginning that lacked the romance and impact of a jeroboam of champagne swinging in a high arc to splinter against the bow of a new ocean liner. Yet from this mundane christening, a championship team was born.

The little man in a baggy business suit who took over the fortunes of the Canadiens that sweltering August day looked like a shy, retiring bookkeeper. As with many famous leaders, however, Selke's small stature (5 feet 2 inches and 150 pounds) hid a giant intellect and mastery of details. At fifty-three, he had already been involved in ice hockey management for thirty-nine years, starting at the precocious age of fourteen in his hometown of Berlin, which would change its name to Kitchener during the First World War.

The son of a Polish immigrant farmer, Selke turned to organizing and coaching in his early teens and put together his first good team—a juvenile aggregation with the improbable name of Berlin Union Jacks—when he was nineteen. Although they formed a younger and smaller team than most in Ontario, the rough and tumble Polish and German kids from a working-class neighbourhood stunned observers by not losing a single game en route to the 1913-14 provincial championship.

"We were the kids from across the tracks and everybody looked down on us," Selke reminisced. "It seemed we always had to fight just to stick together and play, so we turned into a team of real scrappers. We owned the corners and we were proud of it."

The following year, the Union Jacks were accepted into the Ontario Hockey Association junior league and were handed the raw end of the scheduling stick by the resident teams. They need not have bothered: Father Frank's boys won the league title anyway, only to lose in the championship playoffs to the pedigreed Toronto Varsity Juniors, captained by a man named Conn Smythe.

The First World War barely interfered with Frank Selke's budding hockey career. He joined the Canadian army for a three-year stint and, while awaiting his posting overseas, was asked to organize recreation for the troops. Selke put together a quality team that played at the intermediate level and, to raise money to support it, he even organized a variety show that sold out the auditorium of St. Jerome's College in Kitchener.

Well before the war, Selke had left school at a young age and, in 1911, began an apprenticeship as an electrician. He resumed that trade in 1917 when he received a medical discharge from the army and also took up where he had left off as an organizer of hockey teams.

It was in the latter capacity that he stopped off in New Hamburg, Ontario one winter to scout a young goaltender named Schmidt, one of three brothers who played between the pipes. He found his goalie, and also the goalie's sister, Mary. Frank married Mary shortly after receiving his army discharge.

After the war, there was an exodus of Canadians from the countryside to the big cities. The Selkes headed for Toronto, where Frank went to work for the University of Toronto as an electrician and coached the University of Toronto Schools team to the Ontario junior hockey title in 1918.

He left UTS after that season and coached several other teams in the Toronto area before taking the reins of the Toronto Marlboros in 1924. The Marlboros' junior and senior teams were to become the prime feeder clubs for the soon-to-be organized Toronto Maple Leafs and Selke was only a few short years away from a career in professional hockey, leaving the life of an electrician behind forever.

The Selkes' attention to the family aspect of hockey stood Frank in good stead with the higher amateur leagues and, eventually, the pros, because family friends would turn out to be stars when they grew up. Mrs. Selke had seven of her own children, but she was also den mother to countless others. As she told a Montreal newspaper in 1964:

> I'd have to say that Toronto's Kid Line of Harvey (Busher) Jackson, Joe Primeau and Charlie Conacher were my earliest pets. I'd been the family chauffeur for years. Many a winter I packed six or seven boys like Harvey and Charlie into our old Reo and took them to games around Ontario.
> One boy I remember as well as any . . . was Red Horner. He was our grocery boy. He loved to pause in our kitchen for a glass of milk and homemade biscuits.

The Selke family knew well the value of minor league clubs to supply the big team. Frank put together a powerhouse Marlboro team with those very same boys: the three members of the Kid Line, Horner and Alex Levinsky on defence and another forward named Bob Gracie.

At this time, a familiar name surfaced in Selke circles, that of Conn Smythe, the old Toronto Varsity captain whose team had beat out the Union Jacks for the OHA junior crown in 1913-14.

While Selke was building his hockey career, Smythe was also making a name for himself as a hockey manager in Toronto with the Varsity Blues and, later, the Varsity Grads.

So good were Smythe's teams (Varsity won the Canadian intercollegiate championship at a time when Canadian college hockey really meant something and then went to the final of the Allan Cup) that his fame spread southward. In 1924, the National Hockey League opted to expand to the United States and, after the auspicious beginning of the New York Americans, management at Madison Square Garden decided that a second team in the Big Apple would also draw well. In March, 1926, the New York Rangers were born and Colonel John Hammond was placed in charge. The timing was right, merging with Smythe's Varsity successes, and when Conn's name was suggested, Colonel Hammond sent for him.

Smythe was signed to a three-year contract and charged with putting together, and then managing, the Rangers. One of the first players Smythe signed was a tall and taciturn goalie named Lorne Chabot, the very man whose acrobatics had carried his Port Huron team past the Varsity in the Allan Cup final. The old Western League was folding and Smythe went hunting for talent. He picked up Winnipeg's Ching Johnson and Taffy Abel, both talented defencemen. Then he heard that two Saskatoon players, Bill and Bun Cook, were being courted by James Strachan of the Montreal Maroons and were on their way east to sign with that team. The ever-resourceful Smythe waylaid the brothers in Winnipeg and $5,000 in bonuses turned them into Rangers. Bill Cook recommended a centre who had played for Vancouver and Frank Boucher was signed as well.

When Smythe was done, the New York Rangers had spent $32,000 and the Big Apple had its second professional hockey team. The irascible Smythe had done it his way and the results would be visible to all when the team took to the ice. However, before the Rangers could skate out for their first game, Connie was gone.

Smythe did not intend to move to New York, a major mistake for anyone hired by a New York sports organization, and began setting up the Rangers' training camp in Toronto. His premature departure centred on the non-signing of former NHL great Babe Dye, who had been offered to the Rangers. Smythe refused to sign Dye, even after several telephone calls from Colonel Hammond, whose ears were being bent by local experts in the Big Apple. Hammond went to Toronto to bring his team home and brought a replacement manager, Lester Patrick, with him. Smythe met them at the railway station and was told about the managerial change. He was so upset that he allowed Hammond to buy him out for $7,500.

That year, the expansion Rangers finished first in their division and third overall in the National Hockey League. A year later they were the Stanley Cup champions. On the Stanley Cup it says Lester Patrick, manager. A few people, Madison Square Garden president Tex Rickard among them, knew that this was Smythe's team, although everyone acknowledged that Patrick was a first-rate coach.

Among those who recognized Smythe's contribution was Jack Bickell, one of the top men with the hapless Toronto St. Pats franchise. The club was so bad that halfway through the 1926-27 season, half of the team's owners wanted out. An offer to buy and transfer the team to Philadelphia was being seriously entertained when Bickell contacted Smythe.

Would he take over the team? Not if it moves to Philadelphia, replied the staunch Torontonian. If Smythe could match the Philadelphia offer of $200,000, Bickell replied, the team could stay in Toronto. Smythe threw in $10,000 of his own money and began pounding on every door in sight. He convinced Bickell to keep his $40,000 interest in the club and found investors with another $75,000. With that money in his pocket, and a promise to pay the remaining $75,000 within thirty days, Smythe killed the St. Pats. On Feb. 15, 1927, they were reborn as the Toronto Maple Leafs.

Smythe, ever ungracious in victory, would spend the rest of his days taking credit for the Maple Leafs. A single-minded, tough-talking, straight-shooting (most of the time) egocentric who flirted with megalomania, Smythe was the very antithesis to Selke. Yet this was the man for whom Selke soon would go to work.

The ensuing feud became an NHL legend. Smythe described some of its high points in *Conn Smythe, If You Can't Beat Them in the Alley,* written with Scott Young:

> My loss of faith in W.A. Hewitt didn't take long, but I really didn't get onto Frank Selke for many years, probably because he was a good hockey man and a hard worker, even if some of his hard work turned out to be against me. When I first hired him before the Gardens was built, I paid him out of what I was getting. I thought that was fair; he was doing some of my work, so there was no reason for the Gardens to pay me for that work, and pay him too. A sportswriter at the *Globe*, Ralph Allen, later nicknamed him Little Rollo. I'm not sure exactly what that means, but Selke tended to be sanctimonious in his dealings with other people. Years later in an interview in the *New Yorker*, Selke described me as a brilliant but sometimes impossibly egotistical man, which might be true, but to my mind it's better than being the way he was. I like things to be out in the open, seen, and understood. He worked another way. As this is written, it is more than fifty years since I first hired Selke. I think he did well from being my assistant, but when the crunch came it was plain that he had no loyalty to me. Because of his hockey knowledge, hard work, and sobriety he was a good man up to a point, but then he was a minor leaguer, as far as I was concerned.

A psychiatrist reading those lines might draw some very interesting conclusions about Conn Smythe. The truth of the matter was that Smythe did resurrect the Toronto NHL franchise, but it was Selke who delivered the players that allowed the Maple Leafs to win their first Stanley Cup. Before Selke was hired, Smythe was struggling with a bad team that invariably failed to make the playoffs. One day he called in Selke and Bill Christie, coach of the senior Toronto Marlboros, to ask, "How in the world are the Maple Leafs ever going to take the Stanley Cup away from the Montreal Maroons?"

Selke, the man whom Smythe would call duplicitous, underhanded and disloyal, answered in character: "I'll tell you how. Just fire the old men you have playing with your team now. Replace them with these young bucks I have with me on the Marlboros."

Always gracious with the free advice of others, Smythe retorted: "There are times when I think there's something wrong with your head," and a wonderful working relationship was born. Two years later, when the Leafs moved into the brand new Maple Leaf Gardens, and celebrated with the club's first Stanley Cup, the players who delivered the silverware were Frank's boys—Charlie Conacher, Joe Primeau, Busher Jackson, Alex Levinsky, Red Horner and Bob Gracie.

They had been moulded into a fine hockey club by a new coach found by Smythe, a hockey innovator from Saskatchewan named Dick Irvin.

Even before the team won the Stanley Cup, there was the matter of building the Maple Leaf Gardens, a project that became a monument to Smythe's persistence and drive. Smythe was everywhere in the Queen City while the Gardens were being built: one moment on the construction site, another hustling Garden shares, and the next sweet-talking worried bankers and investors. He put everything he had into the project, but even here Selke quietly helped him out. While Frank was assistant manager of the Leafs—a job description that included such esoteric tasks as publicity man, advertising salesman, game program editor and hockey scout—he managed to put his old electrician's background to good use, having retained his union card as an honorary business manager of the International Brotherhood of Electrical Workers.

As hard as Smythe had driven himself, it appeared that the sale of stock in the Gardens would fall short of the amount necessary to start construction. Selke went to his union connections and asked the electricians if they could convince the other workers in the building trades to take twenty percent of their pay in Gardens stock. They agreed and Smythe was able to coax a similar agreement out of the banks. Smythe, of course, took credit for the entire plan.

Smythe and Selke set about building a strong franchise in Toronto and the Leafs won two more Stanley Cups by 1946. In 1939, with the Second World War under way, a middle-aged Smythe was one of the first Canadians to volunteer for active service. He was called up in 1942 and the team essentially passed into Selke's control.

Smythe formed a battery which became part of the Seventh Toronto Regiment, Royal Canadian Artillery. He put all of his prodigious energy into the task and was given the rank of active Major and named Commanding Officer of the Thirtieth Battery. While Smythe dedicated most of his time to preparations for war, Selke was at home taking care of the store. After the 1940 season, Smythe did take the time to engineer a move to Montreal for Dick Irvin because, "I didn't think he was tough enough, without me backing him up, to do what needed to be done." He hired Hap Day to coach the Leafs, then went into the army and spent the year at Camp Petawawa, training to go overseas.

In September, 1942, Smythe moved to England. Two years later he was wounded in action. Smythe returned to Canada, where he promptly became embroiled in a major army scandal. He came home on a hospital ship, and with characteristic honesty told the *Globe and Mail* that Canadian soldiers were not being adequately reinforced in the European theatre of operations. The real scandal was that the Mackenzie King government was going to have Smythe court-martialed until the federal Minister visited the ETO and confirmed everything that Smythe had said.

Even though Conn Smythe returned home from Europe in September, 1944, and soon would be discharged from the army, he was in no condition to return to the Leafs. He would not see his first hockey game in three years until February 1, 1945, and it was a Chicago-Montreal contest at the Forum which Smythe attended because he was in Montreal for a meeting of the NHL Board of Governors.

Nevertheless, a little more than a year later—May, 1946—Smythe had returned to Maple Leaf Gardens with a vengeance and forced Frank Selke to resign. Nearly all of the main players have since passed away, including the two principals, and chances are that we will never know the real reasons why Selke was fired.

Years later, both men were still taking their shots.

"I think he respected my worth as a hockey manager but he could never admit that my ability for identifying hockey talent and moulding a team were far ahead of his," Selke said.

"That rankled. It really bothered Conn to have to overhear other NHL governors and managers dropping the little lines like: 'Yeah, but he's got that Selke doing all of that for him.' It drove him crazy. I remember some incredible messages he would send me from his overseas office. How in God's name can you run a team from France? Besides, winning the Stanley Cup in his absence did not mean a thing: he still had me down as the publicity man and Conn took all of the credit."

One version of the story relates that the situation came to a head over a trade engineered by Selke in 1943. A young defenceman, Frankie Eddolls, was moved to Montreal in return for a centreman named Ted Kennedy. The substance of the trade did not upset Smythe; the fact that it was consummated without his stamp of approval did.

"That bothered Conn and he let me know it in no uncertain terms in a note from Europe," Selke recollected. "Time has surely proved we were right in our estimation of Kennedy. Kennedy had no equals in taking face-offs, or in coming up with the winning plays in the clutch games."

Of course, the Selke and Smythe versions diverge.

"Frank Selke always said for public consumption that he and I parted company because of a trade he made without my permission, while I was overseas. This is not true but probably sounds better, which is why Selke would say it. Certainly I was furious about not even being consulted. Eddolls had joined the Air Force soon after signing with us and I thought trading him was a stinking trick to play on a man who was going overseas. But if that was to be the end of Selke with the Leafs, why did I wait three years before telling him to walk the plank? And why didn't I fire Hap Day, too? Hap had a bigger voice than Selke in deciding on the trade."

Smythe explained that Selke was out because he sided with the wrong people (Ed Bickle and Bill MacBrien) in a Maple Leaf Gardens power struggle which was eventually won by himself. Both versions probably contained more than a kernel of truth. In the end, the two lifelong antagonists parted company.

Why so much information on the inner workings of the fledgling Toronto Maple Leafs in a book about the Montreal Canadiens?

With Selke en route to Montreal, Smythe finally could boast that he had an undisputed hand in building an NHL dynasty. The catch was that the dynasty would turn out to be the Montreal Canadiens, not the Toronto Maple Leafs. Had Smythe and Selke been able to work together, the odds are great that the Toronto Maple Leafs would be acknowledged as professional hockey's dynasty. But the true dynasty did not start until that humid August day in 1946, when Frank Selke followed his nose into the lobby of the Montreal Forum.

Some thirty-seven years later, on Canada Day in 1983, Father Frank welcomed us to his Rigaud farm and spoke about the big moment. "I'll never forget that first afternoon at the Montreal Forum. The place was filthy and the stench of poorly managed urinals knocked you down when you opened the front door. I had come from the working class and I would not stand for sloppiness at any level."

Hockey always had been a family oriented activity for the Selkes and Frank's first responsibility was to the fan who bought tickets to the games. "The local fan deserved to sit in comfort and enjoy a high quality of entertainment, so my first task was to invest more than $100,000 in a new plumbing system and undertake major renovations in the building." His hockey family's *raison d'être* was to welcome other families into its home, the Forum, and so this home had to be maintained with pride.

A hockey rink was a respectable place, with no room for rowdyism from fans or poor manners from staff. If you could remember those simple rules you would always be in Father Frank's good books.

Yet his order to renovate was more than a mere device to clear the air at the Forum. It was also Frank Selke's first totally independent decision in professional hockey; he now had the autonomy to build the kind of hockey organization he always had wanted.

"I'll never forget that day, August first," says Camil DesRoches, who had begun working part-time for the Canadiens in 1938. "Mr. Selke walked into the Forum and very quietly let everyone know that he was the boss and would be the boss for a very long time to come. He did something that impressed me very much; he went around the whole building and introduced himself to everyone, ushers, carpenters, plumbers, ticket people. And from that day on, he always would have a hello and nice words for his people, no matter where they worked in the Forum." To DesRoches, who became the club's publicity director in 1947 and is still with the Canadiens, Selke was a second father: "I called him Daddy and he treated me like one of his sons."

Everywhere in DesRoches' office on the second floor of the Forum are reminders of the Canadiens' storied past: over here a colour picture of the three Flying Frenchmen—Richard, Beliveau and Lafleur—over there a black and white shot of Camil at centre ice with Toe Blake and Frank Selke; beside his desk a signed picture of Prime Minister Brian Mulroney and Mrs. Mulroney. The most important picture is directly across from DesRoches' desk—it is the picture of the 1959-60 Montreal Canadiens, the team that was to win its record-setting fifth straight Stanley Cup later that season.

"That was Frank Selke's team all the way," says Des-Roches. "He built it from the bottom up."

To appreciate properly what Father Frank had wrought, one must return to 1946 and Selke's arrival at the Forum. It would be wrong to suggest that the Montreal Canadiens were a poor team prior to Selke's arrival. After all, the 1943-44 Canadiens had lost only five games —an all-time league record—en route to the Stanley Cup, and would repeat that success with a Cup victory in 1946. But they were far from the Flying Frenchmen of sports lore: both teams had only five French Canadians— Maurice Richard, Butch Bouchard, Fernand Majeau, Robert Fillion and Leo Lamoureux in 1943-44 and the same group, with Gerry Plamondon replacing Majeau, in 1945-46.

"One thing we had instilled in Toronto was a certain way of doing things, right throughout the organization," Selke recalled, "and I felt that the only way to guarantee long-term success for the Canadiens would be to do the same. But we had to do two things; build an organization which on one hand could recruit the very best talent available right across Canada, and at the same time develop the pool of players in our backyard, Quebec."

A young man from Montreal's West End named Sam Pollock, and defenceman Kenny Reardon, who retired from the Canadiens after the 1949-50 season, were given the task of running the sprawling minor league system with Selke. The Selke tentacles reached everywhere, with Montreal-sponsored teams in British Columbia, Saskatchewan, Manitoba, Ontario and Quebec feeding young players into the various levels of the professional leagues, in which many more Montreal teams were set up.

Selke, who in later years would become a recognized breeder of thoroughbred horses and prize chickens, likened the burgeoning system to farming. "I've always been a gentleman or *ad lib* farmer, always doing something around the house like landscaping or fixing things that needed it. I operated those clubs like a farmer, nurturing good potential players like plants and helping them come up and ripen in the system until they were good enough to join the big club."

The Selke farm system was vast. "We helped teams everywhere in hockey. We had ten teams in the Winnipeg area and we paid for the whole amateur system in Regina. And at one point, we were paying $300,000 a year in amateur development in Edmonton." Those kinds of expenses deterred other NHL managers, but not Selke. He ran his system as a farm and each year harvested a crop.

"We never interfered with the teams at the local levels. All we were interested in was developing good players and that we did. It paid for itself because we were able to sell about a quarter million dollars worth of quality players every season." They were sold to the other five clubs, of course, sales which would benefit the Canadiens in the years ahead.

"It was very convenient for some of the other organizations to save their seed money and they came to depend on us to beat the bushes for quality players for them," Selke smiled. "That meant, of course, that they bought players who were a level below our best, and that we knew everything there was to know about those players. This would eventually work out to our advantage."

When Selke rolled up his sleeves and went to work in 1946 he was dismayed to learn that he had come up against a formidable foe—himself—when the season got under way. The Canadiens lost the Stanley Cup final that year to the Maple Leafs, the team that Frank had built. Teeder Kennedy would lead Toronto to three straight Cups, lose one to Detroit, and win a fourth in 1950-51 on Bill Barilko's overtime goal against Montreal.

No matter that Selke could not win a Stanley Cup during his first six years at the Forum; he was building a system that would deliver championships like clockwork once the apparatus was wound. In 1947-48, a raw rookie from west-end Montreal named Doug Harvey took over Frankie Eddolls' Number 2; a year later a young Winnipegger named Tommy Johnson joined the club during the playoffs. In 1949-50, kids with proud French-Canadian names like Bernard Geoffrion, Dollard St. Laurent and Jean Beliveau had tryouts with the team, and in 1951-52 Dickie Moore and Don Marshall surfaced.

The Quebec junior system, with teams like the Canadiens Juniors, Royals, Nationals, the Verdun Maple Leafs and Quebec Citadelles, delivered an astonishing number of top-quality players. Selke's investment was paying off.

Yet it was not merely the simple expediency of buying an extensive farm system or paying for a Quebec Junior league that would make the Canadiens something special. Any other team with a similar idea could duplicate those feats. Selke also instituted a particular Canadiens' way of doing things at all levels of the organization.

The feeder hockey systems were full of bright-eyed, talented young hockey players with a dream. They all flashed their stuff and, if their talent was sufficient, they moved up a level approximately every other season. To the outsider, this was a glamorous lifestyle, holding the promise of much greater riches at the top. Many young boys became very conscious that they were the objects of constant observation and assessment, and they learned that the whole dream could end abruptly, cruelly. Most teams preyed on the positive side of the promise, and lost many young talents along the way because they failed to realize that the occupational or job culture they had created also contained a negative side. Selke, who had been telling hockey players that they just weren't good enough since he was fourteen, recognized both sides of the coin and saw to it that his players did too.

He knew that hockey's occupational culture locked the individual into a situation which left him with less than a magnificent set of alternatives. In Selke's eyes, young hockey players were vulnerable and easily influenced. They could be directed, but it had to be a gradual process. The *Club de Hockey Canadien* adopted a particular set of strategies which underscored the significance of the minor leagues as a training ground for the all-stars who were preparing to enter the higher professional ranks.

As the young players progressed through the various levels of expertise, they underwent a socialization process during which the cultural values of winning were stressed more and more. Other factors which came into play were the influence of the media, the selection of current Canadiens' stars as role models and the formal and generalized system of coaching throughout the system.

The Montreal Junior Canadiens, Quebec Citadelles or the Regina Pats player shifted in focus from play to work, a shift that was characterized by a changing lifestyle which further integrated the life of the potential professional into the occupational culture. As a result, the Canadiens' juniors tended to be a little more serious, a little more mature than their counterparts in other organizations. While this could never be a substitute for pure hockey talent, when it came down to two players of equal on-ice skills, the Canadien usually would show more character. As a result, many young players who laboured long in the Canadiens' system only to fall short at the very last stage, still found employment as valued NHL players on the other five teams.

Selke had identified four stages in a young player's recognition of the professionalization process. They were: 1) the awakening of interest in a pro career; 2) the crystalization (resolve) of this interest; 3) the consolidation and commitment to that career, and 4) a review of that commitment. Most young hockey players who advanced to the junior ranks usually found themselves forced to move to a small town and were systematically cut off from family and friends. A large portion of a young player's life and energy would then revolve about practice, games, equipment preparation, meetings with management, and travel. Educational pursuits had been left behind, usually at a very young age, and the players were forced into a regimented way of life governed by the schedule and team curfew. The team scouts were always around, watching games and trying to assess the intangibles. As cruel as it sounds, the survivors were generally hockey players of character.

Floyd Curry, who came up to Montreal for the first time in 1947-48, and to stay two seasons later, described the process. "Junior hockey was more helter-skelter; [some good] players didn't play their positions quite as well [as they could have] while others looked much better than they really were. As we progressed, the speed increased, the guys became a good deal tougher and the demands of the hockey club became more acute. It really wasn't all that different because we were still playing hockey, but the sweater and the pride associated with this organization made matters much more complex."

Some twenty years later, when Ken Dryden moved into the NHL, the Selke message had spread to players at all levels of hockey. "I saw few differences in the transition from university to the professional club, since I always thought of myself as a professional. The necessary preparations for winning the contest were paramount in my mind and that commitment never left me. There were few differences in drills, practices or approach to the game; curfews were observed judiciously and the camaraderie flourished as always within the ranks of the team. I suspect that the most significant difference rested in the fact that you were playing against guys who were generally better than you."

Selke looked for three essentials in his players: a strong hockey background; a deep commitment to winning or an equally strong aversion to losing; and the sense of self-confidence, self-direction and self-motivation necessary in a player who would be asked to accept the team's regimentation. He wanted his players to adopt a shared perspective, rather than just an individual one. Personal expectations, attitudes and motives had to become team expectations, team attitudes and team motives.

Those players who made it received all the support in the world; they became part of the Canadiens family team and were protected and organized to ensure maximum performance. Frank Selke treated the Forum carpenters, telephone receptionists, publicists and ice makers as part of his family, and the men who wore the club uniform were expected to respond in the same way. Supportive communication and interaction were encouraged at all levels among team members.

As Jean Beliveau recalls: "It was much easier to be involved in a family experience in those early days because we travelled by train. During the trip, most of the guys, especially the veterans, would review the evening's contest and you learned a great deal just by listening to them. With air travel, these kinds of discussions do not take place, so that if the coach doesn't offer a strategy for success, the guys never get to talk about their mistakes."

Another centre, Ralph Backstrom, echoes Beliveau's sentiments. "We were very close to one another, but I think that winning was the most important thing that we had going for us. When things were not going well, we were frank with one another. Doug Harvey would call a team meeting and we would all show up early at some local bar to have it out. Sometimes we deliberated for hours during the long train rides between cities, but in the final analysis, we policed ourselves. Our coaches gave 110 percent but it was really the players whose pride and deep feelings of commitment sustained the family entity."

In one way Beliveau was wrong: the demise of train travel did not diminish the Canadiens' habit of socializing as a team, especially on the road. If that custom was a strong point of the powerhouse team of the 1950s, its 1970s counterpart also socialized in much the same manner, even though the train travel, a natural mixer, was no longer available. The major difference of the 1970s was that the players had to work a little harder at maintaining the sense of togetherness.

"We were always able to go out as a group, to a bar or someplace when we were on the road, and talk things out when we were not doing well," says Steve Shutt. "Players may have had best buddies and all that, but when the team went out, the *team* went out and if there were any problems to hash out, we did it then and there." This system worked, even though it may have caused difficulties for the coach who was used to taking the leadership role in problem-solving. Scotty Bowman experienced occasional problems with team unity and the club's committee of veterans for the very good reason that the process of developing team unity depended on the players coaching themselves to some degree.

"This was pointed out in funny ways, sometimes," laughs Shutt. "I remember that we were out in Oakland one night and had one of our meetings and the boys all crawled back to the hotel very, very late, way past Scotty's curfew. Was he ever steamed, and he even felt worse when the Seals took a 2-0 lead on us in the first period! Now when Scotty got really pissed at us, he could scream and rant with the best of them. This time was different, he was almost subdued and some of us were going 'uh-oh' when he came into the room between periods. 'All right, that's it, you guys. If you don't want to play, I'll be damned if I'm going to coach you,' he said in the softest voice, and then he stomped out of the room. He wasn't kidding. He didn't say a damned thing for the next two periods so we coached ourselves, took care of all the line changes and played the game. We won, 6-2." Frank Selke had been gone for eight years when Shutt was drafted by the Canadiens from the Toronto Marlboros, but his legacy remained. The players in the '70s could occasionally get along without their coach, or father figure, because they were a tight familial unit.

There were never unclear lines of authority with Selke. Clear, concise coaching and leadership were important to Selke, and for many years he was happy with Dick Irvin, who had preceded him to Montreal by six years and won two Stanley Cups in the interim. Whether Selke's coach had a smooth disposition or was as abrasive as a brick wall did not matter. The coach had to be able to spell out the rules, set standards of performance, and call the plays. He was required to be a disciplinarian and stern taskmaster, and he had to believe in the product and remain highly committed to the task at hand. As a clever decision maker, Selke fervently hoped that his coaches would have enough personal strength to forego popularity.

Dick Irvin qualified for that job description, even though Selke admitted that Irvin gave him fits during key games.

"I remember the playoff series with Toronto in 1947. Richard had been suspended for two games and we had fallen behind. I was convinced that we would not come back, but in the sixth game we had them on the run. With thirty seconds left in that game, they pulled their goalkeeper for a sixth attacker and won the right to face off in our end. What does Irvin do? He pulls Curry, Mosdell and Mackay off the ice in favour of Rocket and Lach. I was so upset that I jumped up out of my chair to get Irvin's attention. Why would he choose to put the goal scorers on the ice when we were in desperate need of defence? Senator Raymond told me to relax and sat in his chair smugly, convinced that we had the game in the bag."

Selke's voice, thirty-six years later, still contains the exasperation he felt that night. "Kennedy won the draw and passed the puck to Smith. Before I could turn my head, the light went on. I rebuffed Senator Raymond for interfering with my plan. But that was Dick's record all along. He could never win the big one. He wasn't Toe in the clutch."

That might not be a fair observation; after all, Irvin had won the Cup with the fledgling Leafs, and then twice with Montreal before Selke arrived there and would win it once more in 1952-53 with the Habs. If Selke had his doubts about Irvin, he took his time in expressing them because Irvin remained coach of the team until the aftermath of the Richard Riots in 1954-55, taking his team to seven games in the final against the Red Wings that year despite the suspension of Maurice Richard. But Selke was firmly convinced that Irvin had exacerbated the

Richard situation and that the times called for a coach
who could cool down the tempestuous superstar when
the situation called for it.

Another problem was Selke's close friendship with
Irvin. Both men were fanciers of fine specially bred chick-
ens and pigeons. As Selke wrote in his autobiography,
Behind the Cheering, in 1962:

> I am sure that some of the best days of my life were those
> spent with Dick and the fancy chickens and pigeons we used
> to keep out at Gordon Green's farm near Ste. Thérèse.
> Since 1956, I have had a lovely farm of my own near Rigaud;
> and as I putter about the assortment of good birds I keep
> there, I cannot help but think of how wonderful it would be
> if Dick could just come down the lane some day, with a
> carload of the birds he loved so well, and dump them in the
> barnyard. Our disagreements about the finer points of
> hockey were sometimes bitter; but we always enjoyed the
> arguments we had about fine feathers.

Selke told Irvin that he could no longer coach the
Canadiens, but that there would be a position for him
elsewhere in the Canadiens' organization if he wanted it.
The Canadiens' general manager also knew that Irvin
had an out, that he had been talking quietly with Chicago
during the season about a return there. Given the alternative, Irvin chose Chicago.

"What none of us knew at the time was that, all that
year, Dick had been suffering from a form of bone can-
cer. It was to culminate in his untimely death two years
later. So he had reason enough to be restless and miserable. But, to this day, I miss this lovable, truculent Irishman who never learned the meaning of the word 'quit' in
a hockey game."

If Irvin, the innovator of hockey coaches in the 1930s
and 1940s, was going to Chicago, where could Selke find
a quality replacement?

What better man than quiet Hector "Toe" Blake, the
classy left winger who for years had been Richard's partner (along with centre Elmer Lach) on the celebrated
Punch line? But hiring Toe Blake was not as easy as it

seemed and at one point during that summer, Selke began to regret having forced Dick Irvin to move to Chicago.

"The board of directors and the French Canadian players wanted a French coach, while I supported Blake. I could sympathize with these people; French Canada was supplying so many wonderful hockey players and yet no one was giving jobs to French Canadian coaches, who were as good as anybody around.

"If Montreal Canadiens didn't hire French Canadian coaches, who would? I found that to be pretty sound reasoning, but I was personally committed to Blake. I thought he was the ideal man to keep Maurice in line and take our young veterans to the Stanley Cup. I thought a good deal about our former captain, Butch Bouchard, but I didn't think he had the knack or patience to become the team coach." Selke stuck to his guns, subtly reminding Senator Raymond of the *carte blanche* he had received nine years before, and Blake became the new coach of the Montreal Canadiens. It proved to be the right decision in the long run, but Selke made sure that it was cleared by Richard, during a long meeting arranged to receive the Rocket's blessing.

There is, however, another version to the Blake hiring which differs considerably from the Selke story. After Toe retired, he spent some time coaching in the Quebec Senior League with Valleyfield, and then moved on to the Canadiens' AHL club in Buffalo. Blake then left the club in mid-season, and Selke reputedly had said he would never again coach in the Montreal organization.

"I got the story from several sources," said Joe Gorman, "that Frank Selke was all set to hire Billy Reay as the coach when Maurice Richard came to my father and said he would quit. The press conference announcing it was to be held the very next day."

According to Gorman, his father suggested that Richard call writer Marcel Desjardins and give him the scoop that the players all wanted Blake to coach them.

Doug Harvey, who now works for Joe Gorman at

Connaught Raceway, across the Ottawa River from the Canadian capital, said he had confirmation of the Gorman version from another source.

Whatever the circumstances of his hiring, and the Gorman-Selke feud that reaches beyond the grave, Blake proved to be one of the best-ever professional coaches, in any sport. Said Jacques Plante: "The guy knew how to prime you for a game; he knew what button to push to get the most out of guys because he always wanted to maintain the edge. Even if it was a so-called nothing game near the end of the season, he would always be saying things like, 'We might see this team in the playoffs so don't let up. If they give you a good run tonight, we'll have them believing that they can beat us and then we're in real trouble.' Toe kept us alert and always prepared."

Blake's reputation is sterling from all angles, on-ice and off. Hockey referee Red Storey: "Toe was the strongest guy behind the bench that I've ever seen. For me a good coach is the guy who can get the most out of his players, push them to the limit, discipline them when necessary but consistently retain their respect and admiration. That was Blake. He was loyal to both the team and the organization.

"I remember that he would close the dressing room door after a bad game and raise the roof in there. But when that door opened to the media, you never heard a bad word from him about any of his players. That kind of class will keep you in white shirts for a long time."

Blake took the Canadiens, now definitely the team that Father Frank built, to five straight Stanley Cups, from 1956 to 1960. After a three-year domination by Toronto Maple Leafs in the early 1960s, Blake coached Montreal to three more championships before stepping down after the 1968 season, having accumulated eight cups in thirteen years of coaching.

Once Frank Selke's machine was assembled, it hummed smoothly over the next few years, and even the sale of the Montreal Canadiens in 1957 did little to affect it. Senator Raymond, by then seventy-five years of age, wanted to slow down, but he would not sell his Canadiens to just anybody. He settled on a fellow Senator, Hartland de M. Molson, scion of a prominent Quebec brewing family with long roots in the province. Senator Molson and his brother Tom took over the *Club de Hockey Canadien* and the Canadian Arena Company in late September.

Little changed. Frank Selke continued as managing director and talented younger men like Pollock and Bowman moved from square to square on the organizational chart in places like Peterborough, Hull-Ottawa and Houston, Texas. In 1963, Father Frank celebrated his seventieth birthday and some gentle pressure was exerted to persuade him to retire and enjoy his later years, secure in the knowledge that he had been the architect of the best hockey team ever, a feat which he knew would stick in the craw of his perpetual antagonist, Connie Smythe.

Yet like many very active people, Frank Selke was the last man who wanted to retire. He just couldn't see the sense of turning away a sharp, experienced mind, only to replace it with someone new whose experience was still to come.

"Senator Molson asked me to retire. He said Molson's had a mandatory retirement policy at age seventy and my time had come. I told him to put me up against any man near my age and he'd see. He agreed with me but kept pressing and this distressed me. My skills had not diminished, like those of a hockey player physically past his prime. I knew full well that I could continue to run the team for many years to come."

It was not to be. Waiting in the wings was Sam Pollock, a man who had learned the ABCs of hockey management at Selke's knee and who would prove every bit as astute and influential as his mentor. "I can only guess that there was a very real fear at the board of directors level that if a place wasn't made soon for Sam Pollock, he would leave the organization and go to another team, or into the business world," Camil DesRoches recollects.

"As far as I can recall, Sam never even hinted at such a thing, but these people were pretty smart businessmen and they didn't want to take any chances. And when you think of what Mr. Pollock would accomplish for the Canadiens over the next fourteen years, you can understand why the board was nervous."

Senator Molson negotiated a compromise; Pollock would become the new Managing Director in 1964 and Frank Selke would, in that most famous corporate euphemism, "move upstairs" as a special adviser.

"So they set me up in a beautiful office, and nobody bothered to come and see me," Selke complained. "I was a vice-president and member of the board but it meant nothing. I was never invited to attend board meetings." Selke stayed active in parts of the hockey world, remaining as chairman of the selection committee for the Hockey Hall of Fame, an organization he had practically invented a year after joining the Canadiens.

He dedicated himself to his family and the full-time pursuit of activities that had previously been hobbies. Selke purchased a 220-acre farm near Rigaud, Quebec, about forty miles west of Montreal, where he raised prize chickens and thoroughbreds, as well as Galloway cattle. Only the latter turned a profit for Rolling Range Farm, but that did not matter.

Father Frank had a place for his family, as the spread contained three homes (two married daughters and their families lived there) and a guest house. He lived there for more than twenty years before he passed away at age ninety-two on July 3, 1985. Throughout the last two decades of his life, he was a Forum regular in Box 2, Seat 10, where he watched his team, now Sam's boys, roar into the television age and expansion. Occasionally the television cameras would flick over to that spot, as if silently imploring Father Frank to give his blessing to the events taking place before him. Whether he knew the cameras were on him or not, he appeared to sit there with a small smile at the edge of his mouth as the *bleu, blanc, rouge* swirled all over the ice, usually against inferior opposition. It was a smile of proprietorship, the same look his wife Mary must have seen when he stood behind the bench of the Berlin Union Jacks in 30-below temperatures at the outdoor rinks of southern Ontario some sixty years before. Sometimes, with the camera still on him, Frank Selke appeared to be looking across the rink, where his old adversary Conn Smythe might have been standing and glaring at him. Well over a century of hockey antagonism had passed between these two old war horses.

"The funny thing is," Camil DesRoches recalls, "that the Smythe-Selke feud seemed to be more for public and media consumption than anything else. I always wondered if both men were afraid of admitting to the other the kind of respect they felt for each other. All I know is that I worked with Frank Selke for many, many years in Montreal and many times when I had to go to Toronto on team or Forum business, he would give me a note and say, 'When you get there, go see Connie and tell him you're there for me, he'll fix you up.' Both of them were involved in thoroughbred horses, Selke breeding them and Smythe racing them, and [they] would occasionally get together in the hockey off-season. Smythe, "the enemy", died in November, 1980.

On July 4, 1985, Father Frank paid his last visit to the lobby of the Montreal Forum. There he lay in state, arrangements of funeral flowers tastefully arrayed about him. The place smelled a lot fresher and a whole lot more successful than it had on that faraway August afternoon in 1946. And you did not have to approach the casket to know that Frank Selke had that quiet little smile on his face.

6

Jean Beliveau
The Lion Regal

It is a surprisingly brisk August day in 1976, a reminder that the warm afterglow of the recently extinguished Olympic Flame too soon will be replaced by the glacial Arctic winds that sweep down from the north and across the St. Lawrence lowlands every winter. Jean Beliveau is well-protected against the gusts in a three-piece pin-striped wool suit. The navy suit is moulded to his large frame and sets off his silver hair. He stands six feet, three inches tall and carries 215 pounds on a very large frame, "about five to ten pounds over my playing weight," but he looks even larger than he is. When he first rose to prominence in hockey he was a skinny 170 pounds and disarmingly handsome.

Thirty years later, his face would be described as interesting, from his aquiline nose to the high cheekbones and eyes sheltered by a prominent, chiselled forehead. He has the aristocratic features you might find in a portrait of some long-lamented *sieur* hanging among those of several generations lining a hallway in a French chateau, or with that nose, in profile on a Roman coin. He has a presence that makes heads turn, even in places where they have never heard of ice hockey.

The chill wind is refreshing for the vice-president of corporate communications of the *Club de Hockey Canadien*.

It was a long trip from Frobisher Bay the night before. He was asked by an administrator of an orphanage in that Arctic settlement if he could deliver a short speech. Forewarned by meteorological forecasts that the weather would be uncertain at best, Beliveau went anyway. "I made a commitment," he sighed gently, remembering the turbulence on the return flight.

Beliveau got home late but was at the office early. He had an appointment with a journalist, and his general rule applies to all situations. After the interview, we leave the Texan Restaurant, across Closse from the Forum, and head east down St. Catherine Street, the main downtown thoroughfare. A voracious reader, Beliveau is on his way to a nearby bookshop to pick up another text. Unlike many young hockey players who came out of junior ranks in his day, Gros Bill had finished his high school studies. He refused to leave it there, however, and sometimes during his playing days more energetic teammates anxious to go out and take the edge off would chide him for having his nose buried in yet another book. "I looked forward to having much more time to read when I retired. . ." He lets the statement trail off with a smile of resignation. Today, with his Canadiens job, his Foundation and several corporate directorships, he has even less time for his beloved books. Yet it seems that every day he still finds himself in a downtown bookstore somewhere, poring over the titles in French and English, oblivious to the stares and pointing fingers of other bibliophiles.

At Fort and St. Catherine Streets, still several blocks west of Beliveau's destination, an obviously inebriated citizen of the streets cuts across our path. Standing directly in front of us, with that curious list to one side that identifies winos everywhere, he sports a tattered suit and long, multi-coloured beard.

"*Ah, le Gros Bill,*" he says, his eyes alive with recognition. "I will never forget the goal against Boston in '71". Jean smiles gently, and you could see the mental wheels turning quietly as he asks himself, "Which one?"

The drunk demonstrates prodigious recall. "The second game when they had you down 5-2 after two periods. Early in the third period, you and Ferguson took the wind out of their sails with early goals. Do you remember?"

"*Ah, oui,*" Beliveau replies, his voice surprisingly soft. And two hockey fans spend ten full minutes happily discussing The Seven Games That Broke Boston's Heart. Dozens of pedestrians step gingerly around them, their faces a curious mix of contempt for the wino and starstruck awe for Number 4.

Time is fleeting, there are several appointments on the afternoon agenda. "I must go now," Beliveau announces quietly.

"Thank you, Jean," says the wino, perhaps wondering if this encounter has really happened. "You're welcome," Beliveau smiles quietly, and shakes the hockey fan's hand.

In 1125 regular-season games over 18 full seasons (plus two amateur tryouts) and another 162 playoff games, not one negative word has been uttered about the man who wore Number 4 for the Montreal Canadiens. Harry Sinden, a ferocious competitor and innovative hockey mind, said it for everyone: "It would be like desecrating a monument."

If Maurice Richard, despite the competition from the great Gordie Howe, trailblazed for the modern era of professional hockey, Jean Beliveau consolidated the sport's acceptance into the entertainment mainstream of North America. Richard was Ruth to Howe's Gehrig, and Beliveau was hockey's Joe DiMaggio. As to relative importance with the Canadiens, it might be best to say that Richard epitomized the back of the sweater, the celebrated Number 9, while Gros Bill perhaps best described the front of the sweater, the legendary CH. No one ever has or ever will wear the *bleu-blanc-rouge* with more distinction than Jean Beliveau. The scope of that statement can only be truly understood when one takes a moment to pause and recall the greats who wore it with pride over the decades and now reside in the Hall of Fame.

As well, no one has ever worn a "C" on his hockey sweater with more impact, on any NHL team. Jean Beliveau was leadership personified.

In many ways, his childhood bordered on a small-town Depression-era Quebec cliché. He was born August 31, 1931 in Trois-Rivières, the eldest of seven children, five boys and two girls (a third girl died in infancy). His birthplace is significant, located as it is about halfway between Quebec City and Montreal. It is, perhaps, an omen of the celebrated tug-of-war that would come two decades hence.

The Beliveau family did not remain in Jean's birthplace long. Arthur Beliveau, a lineman with Shawinigan Power, moved his brood to Plessisville and then on to Victoriaville when Jean was three. Here he grew up and first came to the attention of the hockey world.

"I grew up right next door to a church, and as was the case with many young French Canadian boys of that time, I became an altar boy. You would have a lot of early Masses in those days and when the other boys couldn't make it on time because of weather conditions, there would be a knock at our door. As it turned out, I was on the altar nearly every morning."

After Sunday Mass at Les Saints-Martyrs Canadiens church, Jean would exchange his censer for a well-taped hockey stick and join the couple of dozen boys playing hockey on the rink Arthur Beliveau constructed every winter in the family's spacious backyard.

"The deal was almost a Quebec tradition," Jean smiles. "My dad would put up the rink and flood it; we had to shovel it clean before our games. If you get six or seven boys with shovels and the rest with their hockey sticks, the rink gets cleaned pretty fast. We would play all morning until it was time for Sunday dinner. Most of the Quebec-born players I played with on the Canadiens remembered starting out this way ... if it wasn't on a homemade backyard rink, it was on a frozen lake or river."

There was one rule in the Beliveau Backyard League: every man for himself.

"That's where the really good NHL stickhandlers started out. There were few rules and the teams changed every five minutes, this kid switching to that team, those two coming over to this one. It was a scrimmage and you tried to hold on to the puck as long as you could. The bigger boys would stickhandle and keep the puck away from the little guys, who would start out by learning to check. As the little guys grew up, they became the boys who manipulated the puck. We didn't have organized leagues or teams with sweaters and all that; we really didn't even have rinks but we all learned to play and play well. The first real rink I would play on would be that of the Sacred Heart Brothers."

Jean played for teams at his first two schools, the Académie de Saint-Louis de Gonzague and the Collège Sacré-Coeur. He began to show his talents at an early age. It was while he was a student at the College studying technical education (electricity, in case he decided to follow his father to Shawinigan Power) that local hockey people began noticing him.

Maurice Richard was making waves in the NHL when the Victoriaville stringbean began to show his stuff in ice hockey. The Second World War was over and Jean was sixteen when he began to play intermediate hockey, perhaps the best-named league of them all. In the mid-40s, Quebec hockey revolved about the powerful Senior semi-pro league and a handful of smaller, less important junior leagues. (All of this would change within months as Frank Selke and the Canadiens began reforming the junior hockey picture).

Both the Senior and Junior leagues were for players with a future or, in the case of the Seniors, for old pros who still enjoyed the game and might seek to pick up a few dollars close to home.

Intermediate, or in-between hockey, was comprised of teams stocked with players of all ages who might not be quite good enough to play Senior or, in Jean's case, did not have a junior franchise nearby. These teams would be a mix of young talents like Beliveau and players in their twenties and even thirties who might be a step too slow or a mite short in overall ability to play Senior. Suffice it to say that junior-age hotshots were considered fair game and that this was probably the toughest league in which Jean Beliveau ever was to play.

"I played for the Victoriaville Panthers and we were owned and run by two local businessmen, Mr. Robitaille, who owned an auto parts store and Mr. Buteau, who acted as our coach. The coaching then was not very scientific and we spent most of our practices in full scrimmages. These were tough enough but the games were something else." Beliveau was so good that he often played the whole game, skating at centre until he tired and then dropping back to defence for a rest. By the midway point in the season, he had scored 47 goals and was attracting a lot of interest around the province.

In 1948-49, Victoriaville was awarded a franchise in the Quebec Junior Hockey League, which Frank Selke was trying to buttress with more funds, expanding what had been a four-team league to eleven teams. The new team's management came looking for the tall young centreman who had shown his ability in intermediate hockey.

"We would like to sign Jean to play for us," they told Arthur Beliveau.

"There is one condition," Beliveau replied. "Jean retains his own rights." Knowing full well that Beliveau and another local boy, Paul Alain, were their best players, the owners agreed.

"My Dad was looking out for my interests. He knew that I could go far in hockey and that if I committed to one team, one management, that it might not do me any good. He was right, of course, the Victoriaville team lasted one year in the league and then folded."

That one season with the Victoriaville Tigers launched Beliveau. The Tigers' gold-and-black uniforms with a tiger's head superimposed on a large black "V" impressed the people of Victoriaville but few others. Playing with strictly homebrew talent, they were easy prey for powerful teams from the Quebec City and Montreal areas. Still, Beliveau, then already six-feet, three-inches tall and weighing 170 pounds, scored 48 goals and added another 27 assists in a 48-game season for a club that finished out of the playoffs.

"The most important thing about that season was the coaching. Roland Hebert was the man who coached me and he believed in giving me as much ice time as I needed to develop. He felt it was the only way I would learn and I believed him. Hockey is a game where ice time is very important; the more you play, the better you will get. Practice time is nice and so are drills but game action is what creates the best players."

Professional scouts now were sitting in the stands, scrutinizing the tall skinny kid who was playing for his hometown team. There was a lot to see; Beliveau was on the ice forty minutes a game, and although the Tigers were not a winning team, he showed enough talent during that year to impress everyone. The Quebec Citadelles formed one of the league's powerhouse teams that season, and when they met the Tigers at home, they were confident that they would easily extend their 16-game undefeated streak. The late Jacques Plante tells the story.

"In those days, if teams were tied after regulation, you played overtime and not sudden death either. Jean was playing his usually great game and kept his team in against us—I think he scored the goal that tied the game in the third period—and then assisted when Victoriaville scored to take the lead. That did not bother us all that much because we had pulled out of several games like that already so we pressed to the attack. Our guys were in their zone when our defenceman took a shot that hit the post. One of their defencemen just swung at it, it hit the boards and I look up and there is Jean skating for all he is worth trying to catch up with it over our blueline. I had no choice. I rushed out at the puck because it was closer to me and I was just about to hit it away when he reached out with those tentacles of his and poked it past me. So there I was lying on my stomach halfway out to the blueline and Jean had an empty net and the puck. He didn't miss and we lost."

Performances like that excited the scouts. After a single season at home the Victoriaville franchise folded, and Jean became the most sought-after player in the junior league.

"They had a trophy they gave to what they called the best professional prospect and I won it. After the Victoriaville team folded, I was a free agent and able to sign with anyone I wanted. Montreal and Quebec both wanted me and I could choose, which was my father's idea all along. It was a tough decision to make because both teams were exceptionally strong and had excellent players. There were people like Bernard Geoffrion, Dickie Moore and Dollard St. Laurent playing for some of the Montreal-area teams and others like Jacques Plante in Quebec."

The Montreal-based teams played out of the Forum or the Verdun and Palestre Nationale rinks. They were powerhouses: the Junior Canadiens, the Montreal Royals, the Verdun Maple Leafs and the Nationals. They all wanted Beliveau.

"A representative of the Forum came to Victoriaville offering me all kinds of contracts to play with Junior Canadiens, and Quebec was after me, too."

Roland Mercier, who later would serve as president of the Canadian Amateur Hockey Association, and also would be instrumental in securing Guy Lafleur for another Quebec City junior team, was general manager of the Citadelles. The owner was Frank Byrne, an important figure in the pulp and paper industry. They were relentless.

In the end, geography and urban sprawl were the deciding factors. Victoriaville was closer to Quebec City than Montreal. As well, the smaller, more comfortable Quebec City would provide less culture shock to a former altar boy from Les Saint-Martyrs Canadiens.

The Montreal-Quebec bidding war and his performance with Victoriaville during the previous season led to bigger and better headlines during the off-season. A third factor also was involved. The old Colisée had burned down during the spring and construction was proceeding apace during that summer to ensure that the new building would be ready for the hockey season. That explained Mercier's and Byrne's anxiety as far as the tall centre was concerned. Both men were convinced that Beliveau was the attraction who would fill the new rink, and help pay off the mortgage. They were proven right on all counts.

There was someone in Montreal who was not terribly upset by the Quebec City decision. Frank Selke already had his mitts on the junior and the way he discovered him showed just how small the world of ice hockey really is.

"Rollie Hebert, his coach at Victoriaville, attended the wedding of my daughter to Paul Bibeault, the goalie. He came up to me at the wedding and said: 'Mr. Selke, I have a player who plays for me in Victoriaville that you should sign. He is a big, strong fellow and he will be an excellent professional one day.' So I went down to Victoriaville and talked to him and his father. I had an interpreter for his father and me. I signed him to what we called a Form B, which gave us an option on his services if he decided to turn professional, provided we could satisfy him financially. There was no way of forcing him to take a bad salary then. The terms had to be entirely satisfactory to him."

Arthur Beliveau's shrewdness had paid off yet again, as Frank Selke was to realize two years later. Unlike most other hockey players signed to the universal "C Form", which made them chattels of the team in question, Beliveau had independence of movement. If he was still good enough after his junior hockey days, the Canadiens would have to come after him with something a little more substantial than a "for show" signing bonus and the NHL minimum salary.

At that moment, however, it was up to Beliveau to prove that his performance in Victoriaville meant more than just the easy goals of a talented local boy scoring big without any pressure on him. From now on Beliveau would be playing on a team in the thick of a championship race and the opposition would be gunning for him.

The tall centreman, who seemed to add about ten pounds a year to his large frame, lit up the junior league. He came up against some superb hockey players, among them his nemesis, Dickie Moore, with the Sam Pollock-coached Juniors, and Skippy Burchell and Geoffrion with the Nationals. Joining Beliveau on the Citadelles was Camille Henry, a diminutive winger who would star with the New York Rangers for many seasons during the 1950s and early '60s.

The new Coliseum was unfinished as the season began, so the Citadelles played the early part of their 1949-50 home schedule in Victoriaville, a nice treat for their star centre.

"We held our training camp in Victoriaville because the Colisée was not ready and then ended up playing our home games there until December. In reality, I didn't leave home for the first time until the Colisée was ready, just before Christmas 1949. And ready is not quite the word; we had to dress in the older rink about 300 yards away, and carry our skates to the new Colisée in December, January and February."

Those who wondered if the Citadelles' new centre would fill the rink had their questions answered early. Tradesmen were still hard at work finishing the building when the first crowd of 10,000 showed up and the Citadelles were on their way. For the rest of the season and the next, 10,000-plus crowds were the rule in the Colisée.

"We set records in the Colisée that they couldn't break today because of the way the rink was renovated six years ago. Back then we had a playoff crowd of 16,800 or so against Barrie Flyers but now the stadium capacity is only 15,400. There is no standing room there now and that's what made the difference with the big crowds."

The big crowds also came out in Montreal to fantasize about the "Class of '31"—Beliveau, Moore and Geoffrion —who one day might graduate to the big team and help the Canadiens become *une équipe extraordinaire*. Beliveau and Geoffrion battled for the league scoring lead all season long with Moore a half-length behind. Better still, the fans' fantasies were stoked by the fact that the three players complemented each other, with Beliveau playing centre, Moore at left and Geoffrion at right wing!

Three years before Jean Beliveau became a Canadien, Montreal sportswriters were regularly indulging themselves in "What If?" pieces. The entire province sighed in anticipation of the blessed event, with the only vote of dissension registered by the solid citizens of *La Vieille Capitale*, who would do anything to keep Jean "home" in Quebec City. Everywhere else in the National Hockey League, scouts who had covered Quebec, and noted the coming of Beliveau *et al* were drawing a gloomy picture for their medium- and long-term team fortunes.

Everywhere else, perhaps, but Toronto, where that noted talent man Conn Smythe held sway. Tommy Gorman, no longer with the Canadiens but still very much involved with the Quebec hockey and horse racing scenes, was passing through Toronto with his son Joe when he decided to pay a courtesy call on Smythe. They were joined by Toronto coach Hap Day and spent parts of an agreeable spring afternoon swapping tall tales.

"At one point," said Joe, "Connie asked my Dad if he had any good hockey players for him in Quebec."

"Sure thing. There's a kid who can't miss called Beliveau from Victoriaville playing with Quebec City."

"Conn and Hap started laughing like they were going to split a gut."

"Beliveau? He will never amount to anything!" roared Smythe. "We saw him play against Barrie Flyers in the Memorial Cup and they put him in their back pocket."

The senior Gorman looked at the Toronto Twosome with stupefaction. "You're going to lay all of this off on one game?"

"We saw what we had to," was the gruff reply. "And in any case, we have this kid called Eric Nesterenko who is going to make everybody forget about this Beliveau."

The Gormans later discovered why Beliveau and his team-mates were blown out 8-3 in the Barrie game. Flying was still an adventure in the early '50s and the

Citadelles had spent twelve hours sitting around airports during the day of the game, finally flying into Toronto just before game time.

Joe Gorman confides, "Dad really respected Smythe's hockey know-how after that."

Jean played two superb years in junior hockey, despite the fact that he was the rope in a protracted tug-of-war between Frank Byrne and Frank Selke during that entire time. The top junior players who had signed B or C forms were invited to the Montreal Canadiens' September training camp every year and Beliveau was no exception. Gros Bill, Geoffrion, Moore, Dollard St. Laurent and Don Marshall were among the young players who showed up and impressed management.

Beliveau was the jewel, however, and his value increased every October when he would politely, but firmly, turn down Frank Selke's offers and return to Quebec City. The pressure was really turned on after both Moore and Geoffrion signed right out of junior. These two talented kids cried out for a centre! The whole team cried out for a centre! Elmer Lach was on his last legs.

But Beliveau felt he had commitments in Quebec City and could not make the move until all of these were met. In his last year of junior hockey, the team and Quebec fans bought him a 1951 Nash and it bore the special licence plate "9 B" for his number 9. Jean had signed an endorsement agreement with a dairy and the senior Aces were talking of offering him anything the Canadiens might, just to keep him in that city.

"I was paid very well in Quebec City; Frank Selke could not give me more money because then I would be getting more than people like Maurice Richard and he could not have that on his team. For three years I came to the Canadiens' training camp and they were kind of scared. In those days they put players who signed the B Form on a special negotiating list and they could only keep two or three players on it. When they signed or released a player, then they could protect someone else."

Like many of the teams in the senior league, the Quebec Aces were a company team, owned lock, stock and barrel by Anglo-Canadian Pulp and Paper. Money was no object, especially since Beliveau would be responsible for three or four thousand extra patrons during every home game.

How popular was Jean Beliveau back then?

In October, 1952, the Dean of (English) Canadian hockey writers of the day, Andy O'Brien, was despatched to Quebec City by *Weekend Magazine* to discover what the fuss was all about. Jean Beliveau was to be the subject of a full-colour cover story headlined: "He's Hockey's Most-Wanted."

He writes:

> We drove from the auditorium in a swank, cream-coloured convertible, the second car presented to the twenty-one-year-old whiz by his admiring fans (the first had been presented at age nineteen). It bore a special Quebec licence plate with the number '2 B'; the then Quebec Premier, Maurice Duplessis, has '1 B'.
>
> Jean parked his convertible directly in front of the main entrance of the famed Château Frontenac Hotel and we went up to my room. He poured himself a beer and was in the act of lighting up a cigar when there came a knock on the door. I opened it and in walked a Quebec City policeman. Taking off his fur cap, the cop said in French:
>
> 'If you let me have your key, Jean, I'll park your car.'
>
> Without interrupting his discussion, Jean threw the cop his keys. The cop backed out of the room apologetically. Frankly, I was awed—but I shouldn't have been.

Jean Beliveau, the Anointed. Guy Lafleur would tell of a similar incident twenty years later when he and his family drove into Montreal to attend the NHL draft that would make him a Canadien. They were lost downtown and desperately searching for the Queen Elizabeth Hotel. When they found it, there was still a problem: the Lafleur family car was on the wrong side of the six-lane Dorchester Boulevard heading west and there wasn't a left turn in sight to bring them back to the hotel. At a red light, a local cop recognized Guy and helped him make an illegal U-turn across five lanes of traffic so that he could have his meeting with destiny. Clearly, rules were for mere mortals.

In 1950-51, while still a junior, Jean Beliveau served up *un petit apéritif* to Montreal hockey fans when he scored a goal and an assist against Chicago in the second game of a two-game trial. At the end of that junior season, it appeared that he would head to Montreal. He could sign with the Canadiens or find a job and play Senior hockey.

After long deliberation, and yet another Canadiens' fall training camp session that left Montreal's management drooling, Beliveau returned to Quebec, this time to play for Punch Imlach and the Aces. He now was a strapping 190-pounder and ready to play with the big boys. But how could he accept money to play with the Aces when the Canadiens owned his professional rights, acquired when he signed the B Form? Quite simply, the Quebec Senior Hockey League was classified semi-professional, even though all players in it were paid. A few, like Beliveau, were paid salaries that matched those received by pros, but that was just quibbling.

The Aces were as strong as many very good American Hockey League teams and included such players as Dick Gamble, who would later play for Toronto and Montreal; Marcel Bonin, fresh out of junior and a future Red Wing and Canadien; Ludger Tremblay, the older brother of Gilles Tremblay, and former Leaf Gaye Stewart. After a slow start, Beliveau caught fire and won the league scoring championship with 45 goals and 83 points. He was Rookie of the Year, centre on the First All-Star team, and best pro prospect in the league and the Aces' team MVP.

He was, as Punch Imlach invariably replies when asked the inevitable question, "The best player I have ever coached."

He was also a rapidly maturing hockey player coveted not just for his prodigious on-ice talents but also for his leadership qualities.

"I think one thing that has always struck people, apart from his tremendous talent, is Jean's leadership," says Imlach. "At the beginning, he would lead by example through what he did on the ice—making passes, checking, scoring goals. Later, especially in his second year, he would take over the leadership of the team. It seemed a natural thing to happen. He did not go looking for it; it went looking for him."

The 1952-53 season in the Quebec Senior Hockey League was combination ice hockey and soap opera. Beliveau filled the rinks all over the circuit, often drawing crowds of 15,000 to the Forum and the Colisée. But was it really Beliveau by himself? Absolutely. If Gros Bill was injured, the arena was half-full; if he played, it was standing room only.

The soap opera could have been called "An Act of Faith". Most QSHL fans went to see Beliveau play fully convinced that each game would be his last, that the Canadiens could not afford to leave him in semi-pro hockey as they fought their way to the Stanley Cup. It was well known that Gros Bill had made a commitment to Frank Byrne and Roland Mercier. It was equally well known that Frank Selke wanted him and Selke usually got what he wanted.

Punch Imlach threw out the challenge to the rest of the hockey world: "The NHL certainly must know by now that my boy rates only with Gordie Howe and Rocket Richard in their league," he told the newspapers.

The challenge was picked up ... by Beliveau. He was called up for a three-game trial, the maximum allowable under NHL rules, and wearing Dickie Moore's Number 12, scored five goals, three against the New York Rangers. This time it was no junior who faced the NHL defencemen.

Beliveau was fully grown at six-feet, three-inches and 205 pounds, a monster to opposing defencemen who were, on the average, five inches shorter and twenty pounds lighter. He was a deceptively smooth skater and possessed a very heavy half-windup slapshot that could tear a goalie's catching glove from his hand. The most dangerous part of his game was his formidable wingspan, a long reach that got him to pucks even when he arrived simultaneously with opposition players. Beliveau bearing down on a defenceman was a frightening sight: "Will he shoot? Will he take my best check and bounce off? Will he fool me with his speed? Or will he just simply make me look sick with a couple of moves and go around me like I'm not even there?" Some coaches and general managers in the league scoffed at Imlach's brave proclamation. All of the best players in the world were in the NHL, they boasted.

"Not yet," retorted those players who went up against the Quebec Aces star, "not yet!"

It was a very tough time for Beliveau, and it was not helped by the legend he was forging in the senior league.

"Just like Guy Lafleur many years later, I found myself caught in a vise, with the media pushing me to break all records the first night I hit the ice. Of course, that was impossible and it made life very, very difficult for me." Beliveau bore this with characteristic stoicism, preferring to dwell on its positive side.

"Of course, when it came to negotiating my first contract, I had an ace in the hole."

After the three-day trial, driven by an almost hysterical media onslaught, Selke went to the Victoriaville native with a new offer. The total package would be $53,000, broken down into a $20,000 signing bonus, and a three-year contract at $10,000, $11,000 and $12,000 a year. The only player close to making that money in Montreal was a little-known winger named Richard.

Beliveau turned it down.

Word came down from the President's office: "Mr. Selke, I know you have been given *carte blanche* to run the hockey operations any way you wish and I am not to interfere, but we must have Mr. Beliveau," was the message delivered by Senator Raymond. The reply was quick and uncharacteristically submissive from a Managing Director who was generally ruthless in repelling all attacks, real and imagined, on his hockey hegemony: "You're right!"

That summer, the toast of Quebec City married *une belle de la vieille capitale* and hundreds of well-wishers waved them off on their honeymoon.

Three months later, another longstanding courtship was sealed with an unusual dowry. Frank Selke, tired of being spurned by a man some called the best hockey player in Quebec, Rocket Richard or no Rocket Richard, found the solution to all of his problems.

If Jean Beliveau's B Form stipulated that his professional rights were owned by Montreal Canadiens, and everyone knew Beliveau was being paid as much as Richard by the Aces, it was time to establish that the Quebec Senior Hockey League really was a professional league. That could be done in one of two ways. The Canadiens could take the entire league to court and argue that it was professional and, therefore, Beliveau belonged to them. That would be costly and could take a long time.

The second solution might be just as expensive but a real timesaver: buy the league. Selke chose the second solution, and the Quebec Senior Hockey League became the Quebec Senior Professional Hockey League.

In October, 1953, with the television and film cameras rolling, and flashbulbs popping, Jean Beliveau signed a $110,000 contract which contained a sizable bonus, a five-year guarantee and a raft of bonus clauses. As Beliveau signed, Dick Irvin, who was standing behind him, put up a V for Victory sign and Frank Selke cracked a rare smile. Moments later, in one of his first TV interviews, Selke was asked how the Canadiens finally convinced the Aces star to sign.

"It was really simple," he replied, in his best why-didn't-we-think-of-this-earlier tone. "All I did was open the Forum vault and say, 'Help yourself, Jean.'" There was an air of levity, but Selke was not joking.

In the 1980s, it is much easier to remember the hoopla that surrounded the arrival of Guy Lafleur to the Canadiens, and the subsequent letdown as the rookie appeared to struggle in his first several seasons. Lafleur's start, in all ways, mirrored that of his idol.

Both players joined a Stanley Cup winner: Beliveau after second-place Montreal defeated Chicago and Boston to win the Cup in 1952-53; Lafleur after the Canadiens downed Boston, Minnesota and Chicago to win in 1970-71. In both cases, Montreal fans foresaw an uninterrupted string of championships and immediate individual glory for the former Quebec City heroes. In both cases they were wrong.

Beliveau disappointed those fans who felt he would win the scoring title in his first year. Plagued by injuries, he played only 44 of 70 regular-season games in 1953-54 and finished 26th in scoring with 13 goals and 21 assists for 34 points. He showed his mettle in 10 playoff games, however, with two goals and eight assists, and veteran hockey observers were often quoted as saying that the eruption was imminent.

In the second year, Beliveau moved well up in the standings, scoring 37 goals and 36 assists for 73 points in 70 full games and added 13 more points in 12 playoff games. The 73 points were sufficient for third place in the scoring championship, two points behind Geoffrion and one after the Rocket, who lost his bid to win his first-ever title in the famous suspension that followed after he slugged a linesman in Boston.

"The most disappointing thing for me was that we didn't win the Stanley Cup those first two years. Both times we could have, losing to Detroit in seven games twice and with Rocket suspended in 1955. When we came to training camp in 1955, we all knew we were going to do something."

United with all of his adversaries from junior days—Moore, Talbot, Plante, Geoffrion, St. Laurent and Marshall—and a young kid named Henri Richard who had joined his older brother with the *bleu-blanc-rouge*, Beliveau was the star of the Canadiens' youth movement that would pay dividends for the decade to come.

It was during the 1955-56 season that Beliveau bloomed and proved to the entire hockey world that he was a player of star quality. Doug Harvey describes it as "the year Jean got tough."

"In his first two years, Beliveau showed everyone he could play the game but he took an awful lot of punishment. They went after him every chance they got and

Jean rarely retaliated. I got on him all the time, and so did Dickie Moore and the Rocket. That third year in training camp I told him that if anything started, go for the guy and we'd all be right there."

In his first two seasons, Beliveau had 22 and 58 penalty minutes respectively. In 1955-56, he was nearly leading the league with 143. The following two years he had 105 and 93 minutes and after that he was left alone. The newly aggressive Canadien crunched all comers until there were no more challengers. Whenever the rough-housing threatened to spill over, well-respected fighters like Moore, Olmstead, Richard and friends covered the flanks.

When the season ended, Beliveau had won the league scoring title with 47 goals and 88 total points, nine better than Gordie Howe. Along with the title came the Art Ross Trophy, the Hart Trophy for league MVP and selection to the First All-Star team.

The best prize was yet to come. Beliveau's 12 goals and 7 assists for 19 points in 10 playoff games were highest in the league and led the Canadiens to the Stanley Cup, the first of five straight. In the 80 games he played that year, Beliveau scored 59 goals and 48 assists for 107 points, a post-expansion era scoring performance in the days of the Original Six. The hockey player had arrived, and the great leader was in full development.

How did Jean Beliveau come to assume the latter role? Why was it not assumed by someone else, a teammate like Bernard Geoffrion, Doug Harvey or Dickie Moore?

Veteran referee Red Storey traces the turnaround to the pivotal third season.

"Jean Beliveau was a man with great class and ability. I remember when he came to the league; he was very talented but also very timid. He was a gentleman, he played like a gentleman, he never retaliated. As such, everybody used to take a shot at him and somewhere during that first summer, between seasons, I think the proper people contacted him and told him how to handle himself with respect to the stick, the elbow and the body. A year later he had the respect of the players on the other team and he didn't have to play that way any more."

The recipient of special dispensation from the game of the trenches, Beliveau towered head and shoulders above the rest, playing a hurly-burly sport with an almost aristocratic sense of tradition and dignity that rendered simple statistics next to meaningless.

"You could see his effect on this team, this team that featured such great veterans as Rocket Richard and Harvey. You could see that the Rocket, who never was a great oral communicator with his teammates, was almost glad that someone like Beliveau was there to handle that. Jean spoke to all that surrounded him, he educated and coached his peers, he trained the young kids and worked diligently for the Canadiens from the day he first arrived to the present day.

"As far as I'm concerned, Beliveau represents what hockey is all about or should be about. Guys his age, like Moore and Geoffrion, did not seem to resent his leadership ability. They listened just as hard as the other guys."

Floyd Curry was one of several veterans who greeted the arrival of this very mature rookie without the slightest rancour. This was not the kind of rookie you could haze or shave bald in first-season high jinks. Jean escaped the rites of passage inflicted on his peers.

"It goes beyond class when you speak about Beliveau. I know him now as a businessman and his efforts transcend the hockey world with respect to the kinds of things that he does and how he does them. Jean is loved by everybody, even people who don't know him. All that you have to do is take one look and you feel this enormous presence."

Beliveau's leadership role became more pronounced as the years went by, but it was not until the 1961 season, after Doug Harvey was traded to New York, that he was named team captain. Curry felt that Beliveau's role was more inspirational than confrontational.

"There never was one guy on the team or in the dressing room who was singled out as the leader beyond all question. The team always had six or seven leaders and the rest of us were followers. That tradition of the 'committee of veterans' is still in force today, thirty years later."

Gump Worsley, who came to Montreal in the 1963 trade that sent Jacques Plante to New York, saw the practical side of leadership.

"The coach is the team psychiatrist, who has to be able to make twenty egos work for the team good. The captain keeps everybody together. It is his job to keep the room calm, to keep bickering down between players or their wives. That can be a big problem. When two wives pair off and get into an argument, soon enough the two players aren't talking anymore and that can lead to all sorts of dissension on the team."

The off-ice inspiration could not work without on-ice performance, especially at times when the chips were down. Despite a career that had obvious peaks and valleys, 18 goals in 1961-62 and 1962-63, a mere 12 in 1966-67, Beliveau always seemed to rise to the occasion. His toughness and grace under fire became the Canadiens' toughness and grace under fire. When he was injured and not present on the team bench, the resultant void was a chasm.

His kind of leadership helped Montreal deprive two great teams, the Chicago Black Hawks of the 1960s and the Boston Bruins of the late '60s and early '70s, of their proper due. The Black Hawks, with such stars as Bobby and Dennis Hull, Glenn Hall, Stan Mikita and Pierre Pilote, should have won more Stanley Cups in the 1960s than they did. After breaking the Canadiens' string of five in the 1960–61 semi-finals, the Hawks beat New York to capture their first Stanley Cup since the Tommy Gorman days. It turned out to be their last.

First it was Punch Imlach's defensive Maple Leafs that stopped the Hawks in a six-game final in 1961-62 to launch a string of three straight Cups for Toronto. Three years later, the Toronto streak over, Montreal and Chicago went to a seventh game at the Forum to decide the title.

In most sports, the home advantage disappears when the championship hinges on one game. Montreal fans were well aware of this, and they knew that Glenn Hall was the type of goaltender who could turn back the Johnstown Flood for sixty minutes, even if he had the disconcerting habit of throwing up before every big game.

They need not have worried. Gros Bill put the puck into the net at the 14-second mark of the game, the earliest Cup-winning goal ever in Stanley Cup history. The Habs added another three tallies before the first period was over and smothered the Hawks under a suffocating checking blanket for the rest of the evening. It was delicious irony that Jean Beliveau was awarded the first-ever trophy given to the best playoff performer— the Conn Smythe award. During the presentation, Smythe was not laughing as he had that day twenty years before when Tommy Gorman came to visit Maple Leaf Gardens.

Six years later, the Big Bad Bruins of the Esposito-Orr era were well on their way to eliminating the Canadiens, having finished 24 points ahead of the Habs during the regular season. Boston won the first game of their best-of-seven quarterfinal 3-1 and was coasting 5-1 midway through the second period of the second game. Beantown's Leatherlung Brigade sat back happily enjoying the slaughter ... the game, and the series, were in the bag. No matter what Montreal did at the Forum, they would not be able to overcome the methodical Big Bad Bruins and their scoring machine.

So there were little more than a few murmurs in Boston Garden at 15:33 of the middle frame when Henri Richard stole the puck from Bobby Orr and beat Eddie Johnston to put the game within reach. A moribund Montreal offence began to shake off the cobwebs during the remaining four minutes of the middle frame but Johnston, stung by the Richard goal, was vigilant, stopping everything that came his way for the rest of the period.

Few Bostonians or Montrealers will ever forget what happened after intermission.

Beliveau had assisted on the game's opening goal by right winger Yvan Cournoyer in the first period before Boston roared back with five straight. At 2:17 of the third, referee Art Skov sent off Phil Esposito for cross-checking and the Beliveau-Cournoyer-John Ferguson line (finesse, speed and pure menace) went to work. With Cournoyer flitting all over the Boston zone like a water bug and Ferguson cruising the slot like a Panzer, the puck was worked around the points and in front of the net. Ferguson shot, the rebound came to Beliveau at the side and it was 5-3 Boston.

Still two goals behind, the Canadiens seemed to be surging while the Bruins sagged noticeably. On his line's very next shift, Beliveau struck again, converting passes from Cournoyer and Ferguson at 4:22 and the Boston Garden was deathly quiet. From high up in the galleries came a plaintive wail: "Come onnnnnnn, Brooooons!" The smell of impending doom, a tangible electrical scent, invaded the Garden.

At 8:34, Frank Mahovlich and Wayne Cashman traded high sticks and with the teams playing five aside, Jacques Lemaire pounced on an errant puck at the Boston blueline and blistered a vicious drive just under the crossbar one second shy of the halfway mark.

Impending doom was replaced by a pall of inevitability. When the Beliveau-Cournoyer-Ferguson line skated onto the ice with five minutes remaining in regulation time, there was a buzz in the crowd. At the other end, a lanky rookie named Dryden had just stoned Esposito on a shot in the slot and a rebound. Espo sat on his bench looking haggard.

Jean Beliveau, four months shy of his fortieth birthday, should have been gasping for breath on his bench while the Young Turks fought it out in the trenches. Instead it was the younger players on the Bruins who had their heads down. With five minutes left he skated out for yet another shift. The teams lined up for the faceoff, Beliveau looking intent, Cournoyer impatient and Ferguson homicidal. At 15:23, Number 4 slipped the puck to Number 22 for the game winner. Three minutes later, Frank Mahovlich added an insurance goal. Montreal 7, Boston 5. Series tied.

At 19:14, almost as an afterthought, Boston's "Young Turk", Derek Sanderson, slashed Beliveau and Gros Bill repaid the compliment. There was a tiny smile on his face when he skated to the penalty box for a well-earned rest with his thoroughly defeated, twenty-three year old tormentor. Jean finished the game with two goals and two assists and would add but three assists over the next five games as Montreal upset the Bruins in seven games, with two wins in Boston.

Frank Mahovlich won the playoff scoring title with 27 points that spring as the Canadiens went on to defeat Minnesota and Chicago to win the Cup. Beliveau's 22 points on 6 goals and 16 assists, and his inspirational leadership, were major contributions in his last playoff series.

That inspirational leadership was spotted early by Frank Selke and it was channelled toward off-ice efforts by both Selke and Sam Pollock. The master altar boy, with his early maturity, fierce dedication to the work ethic and almost saintly demeanour, was to be developed into a goodwill ambassador *extraordinaire* for the Canadiens, and by extension, for the National Hockey League.

As Beliveau was winding down his career, the world of hockey was changing its face. New needs had emerged with respect to marketing, organizational planning and public relations. No longer could an ex-All Star, who had put in fifteen or so years of stellar on-ice performance, assume a high-profile post in the front office or behind the bench without the appropriate human resource training, for himself and his employers.

Great stars like Gordie Howe and Bobby Orr suffered when they "moved up", not because they were not prepared for it, but because the organization was not prepared for their arrival. Where to place them? What to do with them? Often the team administration was at sea, and as Howe said of his short-lived stint in the Detroit front office, before he returned as a player: "They were content to keep me in the closet growing mushrooms, opening the door to throw in fertilizer once in a while."

It was the Maurice Richard syndrome all over again; take the aging star out of uniform and have him show up at every sports banquet in sight to sign autographs and hand out beer coasters. It was an insult to the intelligence of astute people like Richard, Howe and Orr and all three rebelled.

In Beliveau's case, there never was any thought of hiring an autograph machine to represent the Canadiens; his demeanour and his statesmanship precluded any thoughts of taking the low road. He had established early his awareness and understanding of organizational needs and had a highly developed sense of fair play, which made him capable of perceiving the core of most issues.

Jean Beliveau's major attraction for the Forum front office was that even while he wore the hockey uniform, he thought like a member of the corporate entity on the second floor. He acted purposefully and confidently in both uncertain and structured situations. He was a most effective communicator, expressing himself unequivocably and directly in all situations, yet presenting himself as a most responsive listener, open at all times to the attitudes, needs and ideas of others.

Many of his teammates have said often that Beliveau left very little doubt in their minds what he thought or how he felt about important issues. If you asked Jean Beliveau for a favour, if you wanted him to integrate information from diverse sources in order to provide a coherent picture, or if you asked him to try and analyze or anticipate long-range consequences and to evaluate existing talent, you received a comprehensive response that combined insight and simplicity.

These qualities made Beliveau not only a great captain of a storied hockey team, but also a valued corporate executive. The movement from young newcomer to valued veteran to team leader took about eight years.

"I was especially fortunate in that I joined the team at a time when train travel was still the big thing. We spent a lot of time together on trains, in hotel lobbies and in restaurants and this helped promote team unity. There was always something to talk about and something to share."

In Beliveau's case, these conversations were conducted quietly, out of the limelight. More often than not, they were short affairs. Sometimes, however, Jean might spend an hour or two trying to convince a rookie to do certain things that would raise his contribution to the team.

"I remember an evening during my seventh or eighth year. Butch Bouchard was gone, so was Elmer Lach, and the team was really changing. Henri Richard arrived in 1955 and new young players seemed to be joining us at a rate of one a year. It suddenly came to me that I had a new set of responsibilities. I was one of the veterans being counted upon to head the team. A year later I was elected captain and I was surprised a bit, because I had not even been an alternate. Now I had a bigger commitment to the team." Yet another of Beliveau's special talents was an ability to read his teammates.

"Everybody is tense before a game ... hockey players are up-and-down people. I believe that even the most confident of us feel nervous inside. People used to say that Doug Harvey wouldn't get excited if lightning struck right beside him, but I'm not sure about that. Some players liked to give you an impression of composure while they were churning inside."

Craig Ramsay, a coach with Buffalo Sabres and a premier defensive forward in the NHL for fourteen years, agreed with Beliveau's sentiments.

"I wish that as a hockey player I could have experienced something other than the constant highs and lows, bouncing back and forth from pillar to post. Whatever happened to plain old mediocrity?"

In the cases of Beliveau and the Canadiens, mediocrity was anathema; the pressure was always intense and expectations were always overwhelming. The latter were shared, not only by management, coach and players, but also by the fans in Montreal who bought the tickets to watch Jean Beliveau perform. The opposition, of course, did everything they could to ensure that the performance was less than brilliant.

"I played against Dave Keon for years, so he must have been a good match for my particular style. But we all did that, didn't we? While someone was trying to impede my performance, I was doing the same to them. I played against Frank Mahovlich for years, especially when he was with Toronto, and I had my own book on him. The trick was to check him in his own end, whenever possible, because once he really got moving, he could build a real head of steam." His ability to understand the true nature of competition, to elevate it to a higher plane than simple war-on-ice, made Beliveau a better player and a classic leader.

In the end, Jean managed his non-playing career just as he had his playing years. In 1969, a year before he was to retire, he incorporated himself to take advantage of the many non-hockey opportunities which had come his way. At the end of the 1969-70 season, Beliveau visited with Sam Pollock. He had scored 19 goals and added 30 assists for 49 points, his worst season in years. The captain in him noted the lesser contribution, analyzed it, and sought to implement a solution.

"It's time to retire. I'd like to call it quits now and move on with my career."

The Canadiens were in transition. A solid nucleus of veterans, among them Ferguson, Terry Harper, Jacques Laperriere and Yvan Cournoyer were paired with a plethora of raw rookies and the team chemistry left a lot to be desired. As well, Sam Pollock had assembled a formidable collection of young professionals who would become the Montreal Voyageurs that fall. Pollock asked a favour.

"Please stay another year. We have a number of good young players on the team and we're in transition. I want you around for the kids—we need somebody in the older crowd who is able to relate to them and whom they will trust. I'm not worried about your point production, you'll get your share." Pollock was prophetic—Beliveau turned in 25 goals and 51 assists for 76 points in his last regular season and led the generation gap Canadiens to yet another championship. Then came the playoff success and Beliveau's tenth Stanley Cup.

The extra year paved the way for a milestone, Beliveau's 500th career goal. As usual, the great event was accomplished with that special Beliveau touch.

Going into the February 11 game with Minnesota North Stars, Beliveau had 15 goals for the season, and 497 for his regular-season career. At 5:55 of the first period, scant seconds after John Ferguson had returned from serving a minor penalty, Gros Bill teamed up with the "Twin Beanpoles," Terry Harper and Jacques Laperriere, to give Montreal a 1-0 lead. It was opportunism at its best, Beliveau racing onto the ice as the extra attacker during a delayed penalty.

Two shifts later, at 8:39, Beliveau beat Minnesota's Gilles Gilbert on deke, stealing the puck at the faceoff circle and walking in unmolested. The crowd went wild. With 51 minutes left in the game, Beliveau had a tremendous opportunity to score goal 500 and a hat trick at the same time! The crowd smelled an opportunity to witness history, as Beliveau would be joining exalted company in the NHL 500 Club; the Rocket, Gordie Howe and Bobby Hull.

Beliveau skated through four more shifts that period with few opportunities in the opposition zone. The second period was six and a half minutes old when Frank Mahovlich picked up the puck near his own blueline and glided over the Minnesota line. There he dropped a pass to the hard-charging Phil Roberto (replacing an injured Yvan Cournoyer) who veered off toward the right wing and left the puck at the top of the faceoff circle, taking a defenceman with him. Coming up behind Roberto, Beliveau had a clear path to the goal. He skated in on Gilbert and tucked the puck behind the goalie on a backhand. Mahovlich was on the lip of the crease and the puck came tantalizingly close to his stick. Would it go wide? Could he afford not to tip it in in a 2-1 hockey game?

Big M had assisted on Gordie Howe's 700th goal in Detroit and recognized history when it stared him in the face. He pulled his stick away from the path of the puck, it nicked the inside of the goalpost and lodged inside the cage. Number 500 for Number 4! The 16,158 fans did not stop cheering for five minutes.

Six weeks later, Rollie Hebert, Punch Imlach and Toe Blake stood at centre ice and joined in a special tribute to *le Capitaine*, who was joined by his parents, Mrs. Beliveau and fourteen year old daughter Hélène in gracefully accepting the accolades.

The club held the tribute night for their superstar, but only after they met his conditions.

"Jean refused to allow us to give him anything like a car or a cheque," said Sam Pollock. "So the Jean Beliveau Foundation was established and he was able to donate $155,000 to the start-up fund on that night." The Canadiens' sense of occasion paid off yet again in a 5-3 win over Philadelphia the same night. The only low point came when Beliveau returned home to find that burglars had stolen some jewellery and other valuables.

Thus Beliveau's extra season also allowed the Canadiens to close off his career the same way it had begun, with class. The year gave them time to prepare for his departure and their transition, just as both had prepared eighteen years ago for his playing career.

His personal preparations for re-entry into the off-ice working world were totally unnecessary. While Jean Beliveau played hockey for the Canadiens, he had also worked full-time for Molson's brewery, even during the season.

"We used to practice at ten o'clock and it would be over by noon. Whenever we were in Montreal, I would go to the brewery, have lunch with the employees in the cafeteria, and go to work. I had a small office there and one winter I would specialize, working and reading all the material they had on marketing. The next winter I might study production and another winter, transportation. By the end of my hockey career, I also had eighteen years at Molson."

Maurice Richard suffered when the time came for transition. For Jean Beliveau there was no transition.

"I think the only transition there would be was that I would not be going downstairs to put on the sweater. I just started to add new things to the job, mainly because there were no more ten o'clock practices and road trips in the way."

When it came time to retire, Jean left gracefully, with the applause of his peers ringing in his ears. On June 9, 1971, the day before the Canadiens drafted Guy Lafleur, Jean Beliveau delivered an emotional retirement speech to a standing-room-only crowd of hockey people and reporters in the Grand Ballroom of the Queen Elizabeth Hotel.

The Stanley Cup was home and it was time to quit, said the thirty-nine year old veteran, flanked by Sam Pollock and Canadiens' president J. David Molson. The club president then took the podium.

"It gives me a great deal of pleasure to announce that Jean Beliveau has accepted an executive position with the club. Effective immediately, he will be the new vice-president and director of corporate relations. In addition to being an executive officer of the club, he will be responsible for the development of corporate relations with particular emphasis directed towards the press, radio and television media. In effect, he will become the official spokesman of the *Club de Hockey Canadien*."

Molson's announcement was about ten years late. Beliveau had been the club's official spokesman in all but name for a decade already.

Two summers later, someone in Quebec City had a better idea. The World Hockey Association's Nordiques were desperate for recognition. They played in a hugely inferior league in a small city far from the beaten paths of North America's media outlets. Jean Beliveau would give them instant respectability, if only he could return to the ice. The offer was in the neighbourhood of one million dollars. Quebec and the Colisée wanted Gros Bill back and they were willing to pay.

Jean deliberated for well over a week, knowing full well in his heart that he loved his front office job, and that his sixteen year old daughter now enjoyed the presence, albeit belated, of a full-time father.

"I knew I was happy, but a million dollars is not something that goes out of your mind very easily. They wanted me to play because they needed me on the ice to sell tickets. I kept saying no to myself and the dollar signs kept popping up. Finally, I said no for sure and told them that."

On an early August afternoon in 1985, Jean Beliveau sits in his comfortable office and reminisces about his career. He is making plans for a long trip; he has been selected as Honorary Captain of the Canadian team at the Maccabiah Games in Israel and leaves two days hence. A week ago, he eulogized Frank Selke at the latter's funeral.

It turns out that some 6,000 miles away from the Forum, the Beliveau magic still dazzles. Almost fifteen years retired, Gros Bill is the biggest attraction in the camp of the Canadian contingent and the willing target of a large number of autograph hounds in Tel Aviv. He is surrounded not only by young members of the Canadian delegation, many too young to remember how he played, but also by many Israelis who were born and raised in Montreal a generation ago and who go home for a few, brief moments with Gros Bill.

7

The Fabulous Fifties

Camil DesRoches, who has been with the Montreal Canadiens in both official and semi-official capacities since 1938, becomes animated when the subject turns to the Fabulous Fifties and the real Flying Frenchmen.

"We have had many great teams in Montreal but I think none of them comes close to the 1959-60 team," he declares with the conviction of one who has wrestled long and hard with the question.

A diminutive man with a ready smile, DesRoches is very protective of his boys. You don't get word one from him without a detailed explanation of what, exactly, this book will be about. If others in the Canadiens' hierarchy might be lambasted for their shortsightedness, not so DesRoches. He has been around the organization for forty-eight years and has seen all sorts of bosses come and go. Moreover, the young men staring ahead confidently in the hockey photos that span generations are not just legends of the sport; they are his friends. Once convinced of your *bona fides*, however, he becomes a veritable fount of knowledge.

Camil's office may be a lot smaller than most on the Rue Lambert Closse side of the Forum but it makes up for that in the memorabilia it contains. All four walls are covered with meticulously cared-for pictures of the greats and near-greats. The conversation gets around to the Big Question: which edition was the best?

Camil gets up from his chair and walks around his desk to the wall facing it. There, just to the left of his office door, the last thing he sees every night when he turns off his office light is a vivid red, white and blue photograph of the Canadiens. Every office on the second floor at the Forum has such a picture, so one doesn't bother to look closely anymore. Camil makes you look and then you realize that the picture coming into focus isn't the standard photo of the current edition team—in fact, many members of the current team were not even born when this picture was taken.

"You want to know what made the five Stanley Cups so special?" He jabs a finger at the players on the 1959-60 team as he moves up and down the rows.

"Junior Langlois, Marcel Bonin, Phil Goyette, Henri, Jean Beliveau, Dickie Moore, Donnie Marshall, André Pronovost, Claude Provost, Jean-Guy Talbot, Boom Boom, Doug Harvey, the Rocket, Jacques Plante, Charlie Hodge . . . they were all Montreal boys."

Well not exactly, one interjects, Plante was born in Mont Carmel and grew up in Shawinigan, Pronovost in Shawinigan Falls, Langlois in Magog . . .

"Makes no difference. Once a Quebec boy found himself in Montreal, he was a Montrealer. These guys all made their homes here. There was no question of going home for the summer when the season was over. They were proud to live here. They were proud of what they meant to the community and they got involved. When it came time to play hockey, they had more at stake than players on a lot of the other teams."

The team of the '50s was Frank Selke's through and through and showed how well his minor league sponsorships were progressing. Practically shut out of Ontario, the Canadiens went to the talent-rich Prairies. The Montreal boys smiling at the photographer in Camil DesRoches' picture had teammates like Ab McDonald and Tom Johnson from Winnipeg; Scepter, Saskatchewan's favourite son, Bert Olmstead, and Bill Hicke and Bob Turner of Regina. The only Ontarian, Ralph Backstrom of Kirkland Lake, was swept away from the clutches of the Toronto Maple Leafs and the Boston Bruins when he was sixteen, and played four years of junior hockey in Montreal.

The combination of what the sportswriters of the day called "Gallic flair" and "Prairie hardnose" was impossible to beat, as the other five teams discovered during that era. The best part was that the Prairie boys had some of the flair and the native-bred Montrealers loved the hardnose part of the game too.

However, by no stretch of the imagination were Montreal Canadiens alone atop the league in the 1950s.

The team that Tommy Gorman put together won the Stanley Cup in 1943-44 and 1945-46 but would not skate off with Sir Stanley's silverware for another seven years. They were in a perennial dogfight with Toronto and Detroit. The statistic that backs up this claim is startling: after the Boston Bruins won the Cup in 1940-41, it became the exclusive preserve of the Canadiens, Maple Leafs and Red Wings until 1960-61, when Chicago would triumph. And Montreal and Toronto would share it for the next eight years after that!

The team that Tommy Gorman had built was a sound one and, with a minimum of tinkering by Frank Selke in the late 1940s to replace such stalwarts as Toe Blake and Kenny Reardon, battled hard at the top of the league with the Detroit Red Wings and the Toronto Maple Leafs. Detroit won an unprecedented and unequalled seven straight Prince of Wales Trophies for the regular season championship between 1948-49 and 1954-55, a tribute to the superb craftsmanship of Jolly Jack Adams and the talents of Howe, Abel, Lindsay, Kelly, Reibel and Sawchuk. Detroit's winning margin was substantial in six of those years; the closest runner-up lagged six points behind (Toronto 101-95) in 1950-51.

However, in that same seven-year period, the Red Wings would win only (!) four Cups, losing two to Toronto and one to Montreal. Chances are they would not have won a fourth had it not been for Clarence Campbell's largesse in suspending Maurice Richard for the playoffs. As it stands, the 1954-55 Stanley Cup should have been renamed the Clarence Campbell Bowl and should forever contain an asterisk in the record books—"donated to Detroit". Campbell's draconian decision against Richard—or to place it in another context, his overly generous award to the rest of the league—had three main repercussions: Detroit was able to catch and pass the Rocketless Canadiens on the last weekend of the season for the Prince of Wales championship and home-ice advantage in the playoffs; the Rocket lost his only chance at ever winning the league scoring championship; and Detroit was taken to a seventh game (in Detroit, of course, thanks to number one) by the Rocketless Canadiens before the Red Wings triumphed.

Has an off-ice decision by a league president or commissioner ever affected so many outcomes in any major sport, before or since? Is it some kind of ironic justice that Detroit has never won another Cup?

The sad part is that the Red Wings were innocent of any wrongdoing, apart from some normal lobbying by Jack Adams at the league executive level in the wake of the Richard-Laycoe incident in Boston. Yet if any team suffers in the historical context it is Detroit because, to this day, even the Red Wings players will never know if they could have won that year had the Rocket faced off against them.

Detroit won seven straight league championships between 1948-49 and 1954-55 but during the same period Montreal appeared in five consecutive Stanley Cup finals (they would go on to make it ten straight, a record which will never be broken in a four-division set-up). After losing the 1950-51 Stanley Cup final to Toronto on Bill Barilko's overtime goal in the fifth game, Montreal deservedly fell, in four games, to a great 1951-52 Wings team which had finished 22 points ahead of them during the regular season. A year later, however, Sid Abel was in Chicago and third-place Boston bumped off the Red Wings in six tough games before succumbing to the Canadiens in five games. Detroit would save some face with Cups in the subsequent two seasons, both times in seven games. Then Montreal would take over.

The 1952-53 team was a transitional squad, half Gorman, half Selke. Gerry McNeil was the regular goalie and his understudy was Jacques Plante. Today's hockey fan might marvel at the imagined feats of such a stellar netminding duo, comparing them with today's netminders, who tend to share the load 50-50, or at worst, 70-30. That was not how it worked back then, Plante reminded us.

"Gerry was the goalie, I was in Buffalo. Each team played seventy games back then and the starting goalie was expected to go all seventy if he could. Few teams carried two goalies. The other guy would come up only if there was a major injury and the starter could not go on."

Plante played three games that season, allowing four goals for a 1.33 goals-against average. Still, he wasn't going to dislodge McNeil, the Quebec City native, who allowed 140 goals in the other 66 games, posting 10 shutouts and a 2.12 average. The Second Team All-Star added another two whitewashes in eight playoff games before he was injured, and Plante registered one shutout himself in the other four games.

Plante's statistics belied his emotional state of mind during the semi-final series against a very determined Chicago team. He was pure rookie.

"I was playing in Buffalo when they called me up during the season to replace Gerry McNeil who had been hurt. Gerry got hurt again in the playoffs. The team was behind 3-2 in games and we were playing in Chicago, of all places, with the loudest crowd in the league. We were at the LaSalle Hotel and the team was just about to leave for the rink when I came downstairs. Dick Irvin called me over and says: 'Jacques, you're playing tonight. You're going to get a shutout.' I started to shake so hard that I could hardly walk to the rink. I wasn't prepared for this kind of pressure."

As Plante dressed for the game, he ran into an unexpected snag: he was literally shaking so hard that he couldn't tie his skate laces. The sight must have been a touch disconcerting to his teammates, who were getting ready in a dressing room that was quieter than a Roman Catholic church during Good Friday services. Rocket Richard walked over to the goalie and sat down quietly beside him. Jacques had no idea what to expect, but he had been around the team long enough to know that Maurice didn't believe in long speeches.

"Don't worry about it," Rocket said softly. "There isn't a guy in this room who isn't shaking inside just like you. You'll feel better once we're on the ice."

Three minutes into the game, Pete Babando skated in alone and put the rookie goalie on his bum with a nifty deke. Plante stunned the Chicago forward and the crowd with a desperate lunge, got his skate on the puck and made the save. Some nineteen years later, another rookie goaltender named Dryden would turn a series around with a similar larceny off a winger named Pappin in the same building.

"After that save, the pressure was gone. We won 3-0 and went home to Montreal, where we won the series final 6-1. I finished the series against Chicago and played the first two games against Boston. We won the first and lost the second and Gerry McNeil returned and won the last three games for us."

Jake the Shake would become Jake the Snake, a Hall of Fame netminder. Yet Plante, the epitome of the *bleu, blanc, rouge* goalie, almost ended up playing for the hated Red Wings.

"I grew up in Shawinigan with Marcel Pronovost. We were close friends and played a lot of hockey together. I almost ended up going to Detroit with him. What happened was, a Detroit scout from Quebec City came to Shawinigan to look at four players, Marcel, the Wilson brothers, Johnny and Larry, and me. I wasn't there that night so he signed up the other three and went back home. It was lucky for me that I didn't sign with them. Their regular goalie was Harry Lumley and they had young guys like Terry Sawchuk and Glenn Hall in the system at the time and I might never have gotten a chance to play. I would have disappeared somewhere, especially in Ontario where they had their farm clubs and I didn't speak a word of English. I would have been lost. Going to Montreal, I think, was the best thing that could have happened to me."

Plante would replace McNeil over a three-season period, taking over for good in 1954-55. Other players were also moving in the transition from the team of the '40s to that of the '50s.

The 1952-53 Cup team's defence was anchored by veterans like team captain Emile "Butch" Bouchard, and Doug Harvey. They were ably seconded by young rear guards Tom Johnson and Dollard St. Laurent, who became regulars in 1950-51 and 1951-52 respectively.

Up front were oldtimers such as Elmer Lach, the Rocket, Billy Reay, Kenny Mosdell and Floyd Curry and some of the kids, Bernie Geoffrion, Dickie Moore and Bert Olmstead.

Centre was a position that desperately needed reinforcement. Reay retired after the Stanley Cup win and Lach played one more injury-plagued season, in 1953-54. They were adequately replaced, however, when Jean Beliveau finally ended the suspense and signed for the new season, and Henri Richard joined the team, in 1955-56. By then, the Selke Machine was in high gear and the steady stream of young talent from Quebec, especially, and the West, became a flood.

A quick chart paints the clearest picture of the Selke airlift. Depicted below are the years the players indicated first came up to Montreal. Many of them would have several trips to the minors before they stuck with the big team.

These were the first crops of a farm meticulously seeded and cultivated by Selke, Reardon and Pollock.

Year	Player	Position
1950-51	Bernard Geoffrion	Right wing
	Tom Johnson	Defence
	Dollard St. Laurent	Defence
	Bert Olmstead	Left wing**
	Paul Masnick	Centre
	Paul Meger	Left wing
	Jim McPherson	Defence

1951-52	Dick Gamble	Left wing
	Dickie Moore	Left wing
	John McCormack	Centre
1952-53	Jacques Plante	Goalie
1953-54	Jean Beliveau	Centre
1954-55	Charlie Hodge	Goalie
	Don Marshall	Left wing
	Jackie LeClair	Centre
1955-56	Henri Richard	Centre
	Jean-Guy Talbot	Defence
	Claude Provost	Right wing
	Bob Turner	Defence
1956-57	André Pronovost	Left wing
	Phil Goyette	Centre
1957-58	Marcel Bonin	Left wing**
	Albert Langlois	Defence
1958-59	Ab McDonald	Left wing
	Ralph Backstrom	Centre
1959-60	Bill Hicke	Right wing
	Jean-Claude Tremblay	Defence

These players were the nucleus of the Canadiens' reconstruction. The asterisks beside Bert Olmstead and Marcel Bonin indicate that these two valuable wingers were obtained in transactions: Olmstead was traded to Montreal from Chicago; Bonin, who started his NHL career with Detroit, was drafted from Boston.

The others came up through the Selke system of Quebec flash and Prairie brawn.

The majority of the superstars, Johnson, Harvey, Beliveau, Geoffrion, Moore and Henri Richard, were part of successive Quebec junior league bumper crops that were harvested in the first half of the decade.

After the two Detroit disappointments of 1953-54 and 1954-55, the team that came together for the 1955-56 training camp knew that something was going to shake loose.

"We were just too good to hold down for too long," says Doug Harvey. "Toronto and Detroit had made changes but they weren't enough. We had lost a lot of good veterans and Butch Bouchard had let us know it was going to be his last year. But we had all of these super young players and we were very hungry. On top of that, the Rocket was like a bomb ready to go off. He was jobbed out of the scoring title the year before and he was damned if he ever was going to lose anything again."

The catalyst was Richard, but not the one everybody was talking about. He proved to be a small centre, all of five feet seven inches tall and 160 pounds, named Joseph Henri Richard, fifteen years younger than Joseph Henri Maurice Richard, his big brother.

"He was up for almost a courtesy look-see," Selke recalled. "He had played very well with the Junior Canadiens the year before and was only nineteen. He was invited up with our young kids and we fully planned to ship him out for another year of junior."

One fine September day, Father Frank was busy with the paperwork when a Forum employee burst into his office.

"Mr. Selke, come quick! Richard has been knocked out!"

"Which one?"

"Both of them."

Maurice and Henri were on opposite sides in a full scrimmage when Rocket zigged and Pocket zagged. Splat.

Rocket came to in the trainer's room, to find Henri, who had grown up idolizing his older brother, anxiously peering down at him. Henri had been revived first and needed only a few stitches; his lesser height meant that he had come in under Maurice and caught him a beaut when their heads clashed.

"I think Maurice had about fifteen stitches from that one," says Henri.

Maurice shook his head three or four times to clear out the cobwebs and looked sternly at young Pocket, who still was holding smelling salts under his nose.

"Henri, you gotta watch out. You could get hurt out there."

Two weeks later, training camp was winding down and the kid who had come up for a courtesy call was still in camp. Toe Blake had no choice but to keep him up, since Henri wouldn't let anyone else have the puck. It came down to the last few cuts and Selke and Blake were at loggerheads.

"There's nothing wrong with sending him back for one more year of junior," said Selke, who liked things neat and tidy, with no surprises.

"The kid is ready now," Blake countered. The matter was left unresolved.

Montreal played their last exhibition game that year against Chicago and Henri dressed. He scored twice and assisted on three other goals. A few days later he was in Frank Selke's office with the Rocket acting as interpreter, because Henri understood very little English.

Maurice opened the discussion with a simple statement: "Henri wants to play with the Canadiens."

Selke had been through this discussion with Blake several times and he countered with his one-more-year-of-junior argument, but more for form's sake, since he had been swayed by the facts. Maurice translated and Selke watched the Pocket shake his head. No dice, in any language.

"How much money does he want?"

The Rocket translated. If an injury ended his hockey career, a job at the United Nations beckoned . . .

"The money doesn't matter, Mr. Selke. He just wants to play with the Canadiens." Maurice and Henri conferred some more before Rocket offered: "How about a $2,000 signing bonus and the rookie rate, $100 a game ($7,000)?"

Selke pulled out a contract and Henri signed it.

"We were going out the door when Mr. Selke told us to hold on a minute," Henri recalls. "He took the contract back, tore it up and increased my signing bonus to $5,000. Maurice said Mr. Selke told him that he didn't want me to think later that he took advantage of my young age. He didn't know that I was almost ready to pay him for playing with the Canadiens."

Two years later, Henri was the first team, all-star centre in the league. He would retire with 11 Stanley Cups, the most ever.

In a book which attempts to focus on the personality of the so-called Big Three French Superstars (the capitals are lifted directly from the newspaper headlines that routinely described them that way), we could not have done justice to the Canadiens if we had ignored the supporting cast.

Maurice Richard, Jean Beliveau and Guy Lafleur were not surrounded by mere "quality players". They, too, had superstars for teammates. Doug Harvey won the Norris Trophy as Best Defenceman in the league seven times between 1955 and 1962, his consecutive streak interrupted only by Tom Johnson in 1959.

Jean Beliveau, Dickie Moore and Boom Boom Geoffrion won five scoring championships among them, two each for Geoffrion and Moore. Moore's 96 points in 1958-59 was challenged in 1960-61 by Geoffrion, mostly on the strength of Boomer's 50 goals, and stood until Bobby Hull edged it out with 97 points in 1965-66.

Jacques Plante won five straight Vezina trophies as top netminder between 1956 and 1960, and won again in 1962. There were a lot of smiles on the faces of hockey veterans in 1969 when Plante, then aged forty, and Glenn Hall, also forty, of St. Louis Blues teamed up to win yet another.

From 1950 to 1960, there were 120 all-star berths available to the entire league. Montreal claimed one-third of them and these selections were divided among thirteen different Canadiens.

Montreal won six Cups, and came whisker close to three more in the 1952-61 period because players like Donnie Marshall, Phil Goyette, Ralph Backstrom, Bob Turner, André Pronovost, Dollard St. Laurent, Jean-Guy Talbot and Charlie Hodge backed up the superstars. And because the superstars had character.

"Henri Richard might have been the toughest competitor I played with," said Dickie Moore.

"Dickie Moore might have been the best of the lot," said Harry Sinden. "The guy won two scoring championships on one leg. His knees were so bashed up and yet he played a one hundred percent physical game."

"Doug Harvey was the best defenceman I ever saw because he could control a game like nobody I have ever seen," said Red Storey. "Bobby Orr could break open a game at any time and was an incredible player. But Harvey could take it over. If Montreal got a goal up on you and Harvey decided you weren't going to score, that was it. Go take your shower, the game is over."

It is common to hear similar testimonials for Plante, Beliveau, Geoffrion, the Rocket and Tom Johnson.

Camil DesRoches sits in his office. We are looking at the colour picture of the 1959-60 Canadiens. The authors are from a younger generation and favour the 1975-76 Canadiens with the Lafleur, Shutt, Mahovlich, Gainey and Lemaire front line, the Big Three on defence and Dryden in goal. But the fans agree with DesRoches.

A fan vote in 1984 picked for the all-time Montreal Canadiens team five members of the 1959-60 version: Plante, Harvey, the Rocket, Moore and Beliveau. The other player to crack the line-up was Larry Robinson. No second team was named, but imagine the battle that might have raged for the two spots on defence among Johnson, Butch Bouchard, Savard and Lapointe. Or how about the goalie vote among Dryden, McNeil and Durnan?

Would Steve Shutt, Guy Lafleur, Jacques Lemaire and Pete Mahovlich have been able to outscore Henri Richard, Boom Boom Geoffrion, Toe Blake and Elmer Lach as forwards on Team Two? Where would stars such as Yvan Cournoyer, Jacques Laperriere, Gump Worsley, Ralph Backstrom and Mats Naslund fit?

1950s *versus* 1970s. Which team was better?

No less an authority than Sam Pollock puts in a bid for a third contender, the 1960s edition, which but for an upset at the hands of a red-hot Terry Sawchuk and the Maple Leafs in 1967, would have won another five straight Cups between 1965 and 1969.

"Of all of the teams we have had, this is the one that everybody seems to forget," says Sam, a characteristic grimace of pain etched on his face.

"Beliveau, the Pocket, Backstrom, Ted Harris, Terry Harper, J.C. Tremblay, Gilles Tremblay, John Ferguson, Savard, Claude Larose, Dick Duff, Cournoyer, Gump Worsley and Rogie Vachon — that team was as strong as they came."

The longtime observers are split. Dick Irvin Jr., son of the former Canadiens' coach and the dean of current National Hockey League broadcasters, opts for the 1950s, because he says it doesn't take much stretching of the imagination to see how close the Canadiens came to an incredible eight Stanley Cups in a row in that era.

"They won in 1952-53 and the next year they went seven games against Detroit, only to lose it 2-1 on a Tony Leswick goal in overtime. And the year after, they went to seven games without the Rocket. You see how little would have had to change to make it eight in a row? And at the other end, they went to seven games against Chicago, had two overtime goals disallowed, and lost in the second overtime to end their streak in the 1960-61 semi-finals."

Montreal took the end of the streak with characteristic grace. Toe Blake hammered referee Dalton MacArthur.

The Black Hawks went on to win the Stanley Cup in 1960-61 and with good reason; five of the team members were Dollard St. Laurent, Ab McDonald, Eddie Litzenburger, Murray Balfour and Reg Fleming—all former Canadiens.

Hindsight is selective, the skeptic might argue. If Canadiens fans could change history with a deflection here, a judicious referee's ruling there, could not the same imaginary happenstance have befallen them with unfortunate results during their fabled five-year run?

Not quite. In those five years, Montreal was taken to a sixth game final only once (1957-58), winning three of the finals in five games and the other in four. That left little room for the fortuitous circumstance of a deflected puck or disallowed goal.

Last but not least, what might have happened if Jean Beliveau had joined the club a year or two before he did?

It is during this kind of delicious argument *en famille* that it dawns on you. This is what they mean by dynasty.

8

Good Trader Sam

In 1978, the Queen Elizabeth Hotel hit upon a novel way
of celebrating its twenty years in Montreal. The hotel
began a "Great Montrealers" promotion, aimed at celebrating excellence in many fields of endeavour during
those two decades. The promotion was an unequivocal
success—the Great Montrealer dinner held each year
since then has become a popular celebration of the city's
best.

In the sports category, the first selection committee
had a pantheon of local greats to pick from: Sam
Etcheverry, Hal Patterson, George Dixon, Peter Dalla
Riva and Terry Evanshen from the Canadian Football
League and the Montreal Alouettes; Maurice and Henri
Richard, Jean Beliveau, Guy Lafleur, Serge Savard, Larry
Robinson, Guy Lapointe, Yvan Cournoyer and Jacques
Lemaire from the Canadiens; Claude Raymond, Ron
Piche and Bill Stoneman from the Expos and major
league baseball, and a host of athletes in other profes-
sional and amateur sports. Everybody had a favourite
candidate and it became obvious early on that the final
choice would please few and upset many, many more.

Therefore, it was almost ironic that the man they
selected was the physical antithesis of the jock: short and
portly and resembling an armchair athlete more closely
than a sports hero. He never played a minute at the
Forum, Delormier Downs, Molson Stadium, Jarry Park,

the Autostade or Olympic Stadium. But he was the best choice by far, and not one voice was raised in complaint.

The first Great Montrealer in sports was Sam Pollock, vice-president and general manager of the *Club de Hockey Canadien Inc.* Some call him the most enlightened sports franchise administrator of his time in North America. Trader Sam, the man who took over the reins of the organization from Frank Selke and improved on everything. The man who brought the Montreal Canadiens nine Stanley Cups in his fourteen-year tenure. Only one other manager in professional sports, the Boston Celtics' guru Red Auerbach, could boast of such an accomplishment, especially considering that Pollock's team won their tenth championship in fifteen years, the season after Trader Sam retired. Sam was gone but the 1978-79 Stanley Cup champions were very much Sam's boys.

"The man was quite simply the best there was," said Lou Nanne, Minnesota North Stars GM when Pollock announced he was stepping down in 1978 to pursue other business interests.

"I think that not only Montreal, but the league, has lost a tremendous person. He was the biggest leader in the game today. I know that when I was in the Players Association we were always talking about parity. I said at the time the easiest way to do it would be to loan Pollock to each team for a year. He was never wishy-washy. He was a great innovator and a leader. His ideas and examples are something we are going to emulate. He was so successful because he was just a few steps ahead of everyone else at all times."

Heady praise, and unanimous too. While many of Pollock's associates felt on occasion that he had taken them to the cleaners in a deal, the transaction still was a learning experience. Sam Pollock would always deliver value today for future considerations and you could not fault the man because his foresight was 20/20. It was a lesson that most of hockey's executives were slow to learn. But it was a lesson that, once absorbed, improved the talent in the front offices throughout the league. For among his other bequests, Sam Pollock left the National Hockey

League with a legacy of superb business sense. Gone were the recycled old war horses in ill-fitting, three-piece suits. Sitting in their seats at draft meetings and other NHL sessions were professional hockey businessmen. Those who learned the lesson best would profit soonest, among them Bill Torrey of the New York Islanders, Cliff Fletcher of the Calgary Flames and Lou Nanne.

"When I started, front office management might have been 50 percent hockey acumen and 50 percent business skills," Pollock says.

"By the 1970s, it was 25 percent and 75 percent. Now, I think it is 15 percent hockey sense and 85 percent business skills. If you want to be successful in this business, you have to follow sound business principles. That means keeping expenses low and profits high. If you follow good business principles, you will do your financial homework.

"That usually means you'll do your hockey homework too and you'll have a competitive team. Winning is what this is all about and the best way to ensure you'll win is to do your homework, all the time. Because just like on the ice, there is a competitor out there doing his homework and waiting for you to make a mistake.

"If the guy running your organization has trouble reading a balance sheet, the organization will be in trouble. Today's sports administrators have to be first class businessmen and alert to all opportunities."

Pollock demonstrated his alertness and management skills at a very young age, joining the Canadiens when he was twenty-one. Under the tutelage of Frank Selke, he would learn his hockey and management skills from the ground up.

Sam was a product of the de-militarized zone between Snowdon and Notre-Dame-de-Grace, west-end city districts, but it was in the latter that he made his reputation. Despite its French name, Notre-Dame-de-Grace was mostly English. "En, Dee, Gee," as it is popularly known, was a veritable cradle of athletic abilities, producing some of the best talent in hockey, football and baseball anywhere in Quebec. As a young man, Sam Pollock was a capable athlete, competing with distinction in the three major sports and playing the others in the shoulder seasons.

Nevertheless, he was much better at managing other players than at playing himself. Almost every street or park in NDG those days had a team in the three sports. If the players weren't competing in house leagues or school competitions, they would get together for semi-organized contests that were the closest thing to NDG all-star matches.

Sam Pollock, the son of a storekeeper who had parlayed shrewd business abilities into an impressive portfolio of real estate holdings, seemed to have a knack of bringing together the best talent. At seventeen, he was icing some of the best hockey teams and fielding some great baseball teams as well. He also managed to put together fastball exhibitions in which the star attractions were members of the Canadiens like Toe Blake and Bill Durnan. As a result, people in the upper echelons of sports management in Montreal began to take notice of "that kid in NDG."

After leaving high school, Pollock joined many of his peers in the work force in a popular job in Montreal at the time: junior clerk for a railway. In 1946, he was convenor for the Canadiens' minor league teams in the Montreal area. Essentially, Pollock's job was to keep track of the players in the Canadiens' system and to be alert for boundary infractions committed by his counterparts representing the other five NHL teams. He also signed on as manager of the Junior Canadiens.

He handled both positions with his characteristic panache and thoroughness and proved to be a good talent scout as well. Those qualities were the reasons why, at the ripe old age of twenty-one, Trader Sam became the youngest-ever coach of the Junior Canadiens.

"Sam Pollock got the job because he worked the hardest and was very shrewd," says Frank Selke.

"Financially, he was one of the smartest guys I ever knew. He asked for a chance to coach the Junior Canadiens and I let him. If anybody ever deserved it at that

age, Pollock did. And we built up a pretty good organization and won the Memorial Cup (junior), Allan Cup
(senior) and Stanley Cup."

When Selke received the blessing of Senator Raymond
to build a Montreal organization as he saw fit, he set
about the task immediately, and a young kid by the name
of Pollock got the opportunity of a lifetime to be in on the
action.

"We began to work hard at bringing all the pieces
together in the late 1940s," says Sam. "A lot of people
might not believe it today, knowing the history of the
club in the last three decades, but Montreal Canadiens
just were not organized until Frank Selke came over
from Toronto and began putting the system together. I
was supremely fortunate to be there at the time. I was
coaching the Junior Canadiens and handling the business
end, too.

"In those days, you just didn't have the front office
support staff you have today. A coach trained the players
like today's coach; but he also scouted them, negotiated
contracts with them, paid all the bills and made all the
arrangements when the team went on the road. The
coach represented the organization as far as the players
were concerned. It was the best possible education in
sports management you could ever get."

Pollock took full advantage of this opportunity, meld-
ing his strong business instincts with his talent for handling athletes and forming cohesive teams. Within three
years, the Junior Canadiens had won the first of two
Memorial Cups with Sam Pollock as coach. Dickie
Moore, a tough kid from Montreal's Park Extension, was
a member of that first Memorial Cup team in 1949-50
and later on would share in six Stanley Cups with the
parent Canadiens.

"What kind of man was Sam? I think in many ways he
was a very good copy of Frank Selke. But he had his own
ideas, I would think. Sam was very, very astute, very
intelligent."

However, Moore, an athlete whose play was fuelled on
emotion, refuses to buy the popular belief that Pollock

was a cool-headed, cold-hearted business robot who was fixated on balance sheets and bottom line considerations.

"I think that was part of Sam's act; he learned very early on that you don't get too close to a hockey player whom you might have to trade tomorrow," says Moore.

"So he often would stay in the background, away from the limelight, but I think that was because he was basically shy and a very private person. But he cared about his players and his teams and if he could help you out when you needed it, he would. I once saw Sam on a TV show saying that running a hockey team was like running a chicken farm. He said it was all business, forget emotion, it was all business. I just think that a lot of this was a front put on by a very astute man who saw the necessity of keeping his distance."

This is not to say that Sam could not get emotional. One of the images that remains with Guy Lafleur is that of a distraught Pollock agonizing in the dressing room during or after a bad game by the Canadiens.

"You always knew things were happening when Sam would get to nervously wringing his handkerchief in his hands," Lafleur laughs. "The veterans who knew better would be checking out his coat pockets to see if an airline ticket to someplace like Oakland was sticking out."

"Absolutely right," chimes in Steve Shutt. "Our joke was 'How do you spell Relief? A-I-R-C-A-N-A-D-A.' Over and out. It wasn't hard to stay motivated with Sam running the show, emotion or no emotion."

In 1951, Frank Selke had completed phase one of his rebuilding project. The Canadiens now had a network of amateur teams all over Quebec and across Canada and were building a solid professional farm system on both sides of the border. They also had the parent team, which had moved into the league's upper echelons and was constantly fighting Detroit Red Wings and Toronto Maple Leafs for the Stanley Cup. The second phase of the plan commenced.

That year, Selke began devoting most of his attention to the NHL team, and divided the Canadiens' elaborate farm system between Pollock and Ken Reardon, the former Canadiens' all-star defenceman who was also son-in-law of Senator Raymond. Pollock and Reardon got right down to work, solidifying weak franchises, stocking them with talent discovered by an increased scouting staff. If there was a talented player anywhere in Canada, he was either playing in the Canadiens organization or being thoroughly analyzed by Canadiens talent scouts. Rare was the new player who graduated to an NHL foe without an updated file sitting in Forum headquarters.

"People have asked me many times how someone goes about building the kind of tradition the Canadiens have enjoyed for so long," Pollock says. "It is really quite simple. You build a top-notch organization manned by the best people at all levels. You get each man doing his job on the ice and off the ice and all of a sudden, you're a winner."

Believe it or not, that's the easy part. Where most sports organizations go wrong is in letting up once they have reached, or are near, the top of their sport.

"Once you're a winner, you keep improving on perfection. You keep making the trades and changes that will strengthen the team, even if they aren't popular at the time. You go about your business. That is where we might have been different from other franchises. Once we started winning, we worked even harder to continue winning. Too many organizations relax at this point."

Frank Selke and Sam Pollock managed to instill traditional values into the organization. Many are preached with near-evangelical zeal even today.

Did they set out to build tradition?

"You can never set out to build tradition," replies Pollock. "You start out to build a winner. If you can perpetuate that winner, you might end up with tradition. But tradition is a by-product. It can only be measured after the fact. But the obvious fact, too, is that success breeds tradition. In the case of the Canadiens, the oldest team in professional hockey, they have been blessed through the years with one or two superstars; they've always had the Hall of Fame players. That and the fact that tradition will build up when you're winning because when you are talking about a championship team, there is a lot more stability than you will have in a losing club. Winning clubs don't change players, coaches or management as often as losing clubs. That's where tradition is built up."

No matter how far a proud franchise might stray from its days of heady success, it will always have something to return to quickly if it begins to win again, Pollock believes.

We discuss the New York Yankees, and especially the teams of the Yankee Stadium drought from 1965-1974. For a decade, that team stumbled and lurched through dismal seasons and yet, when the Thurman Munsons, Lou Piniellas and Reggie Jacksons ignited the pyrotechnics of the late 1970s, it was as if the Yankees had never been away. A decade of bad memories had been wiped from the slate.

In the dismal season of 1983-84, the Canadiens mirrored the Yankee situation. After turning in the club's first sub-.500 season in forty-three years, the Canadiens lit up during the playoffs and it was as if the regular season had never happened.

"I can't say exactly why but I think I know why that is," says Pollock. "People will always recall the good memories and today's good times will reinforce that. Once you have had something, accomplished something or shared something, you can go back to it. It's an intangible but you can use it. Everybody who has ever been in the organization shares in it. That is why the Yankees, Celtics and Canadiens are so intimidating. They have history on their side."

After coaching the Junior Canadiens, and while he was managing one-half of the farm system, Pollock took charge of the Hull-Ottawa Canadiens, and built a strong team in the shadow of Canada's Parliament Buildings, winning two championships in the Eastern Professional Hockey League. He moved on to the Central Hockey League, and two more titles at Omaha, and sent a steady stream of quality players to Montreal.

He held that position at the end of the 1963-64 season when Frank Selke was asked to retire by Molson's, the owners of the Canadiens who had bought out Senator Raymond and his partners in 1957. Their policy was mandatory retirement at age seventy. Selke was seventy-two when he stepped down.

Suddenly, a very shy organization man who was one of the best-kept secrets of the hockey world found himself sitting at the biggest desk in the Forum, running the most celebrated franchise in professional ice hockey. Gone was The Old Man, who in seventeen years had moulded the Canadiens into a powerhouse while quietly cutting a major slice of the glory. The Canadiens were very definitely Selke's team.

In his place was a still quieter businessman who would spend his fourteen years at the helm shunning the limelight with even more vigour. Sam Pollock had arrived. The National Hockey League would never be the same again. (Just reading those two sentences would make Sam blush a deep Canadiens red and start to fidget.)

After the long years of Selke rule, the Canadiens were left with one of the top sports franchises in the world, although the team had been eliminated in the first round of playoffs four years straight. It would have been very easy for Selke's successor to coast, to bask in the reflected glory and play it safe. Pollock took a different route, turning up the throttle, and adding his own work ethic and prodigious skills to the task at hand. If the Canadiens had grown good under Selke, they were to become great under Pollock.

"Sammy Pollock took over an empire and I'd say he did a hell of a job when he took over," says Red Storey, former NHL referee and member of the Hockey Hall of Fame.

"Sam Pollock had a tremendous secret that put him far ahead of his opposition. He was very, very dedicated and worked eighteen and twenty hours a day while the other managers were working eight or ten. He not only worked harder, he was smarter, and a guy who can put those two together is going to be more successful, don't you think?"

More importantly for Storey, who had seen the best and worst of managers come and go in his decades in the game, Pollock's character was his strongest advantage. "I liked him a lot because he was down-to-earth, he had no delusions of grandeur. I think his biggest reward was being successful at what he was doing. He did not need anything else."

When this observation is repeated to the subject himself, the reaction is vintage Pollock. He squirms in his chair, his feet out straight from his body. He crosses them this way, then that. And then, naturally, he tries to deflect the question.

"Well, I never thought personality entered into it," he says, reddening visibly. "If I could accomplish the job, it wouldn't really matter if I chose to stay in the background or spent a lot of time in front of the media, would it? All that would matter would be that someone was taking care of business and that we were winning."

But someone who spent a lot of time grandstanding for the media or entertaining them and playing up to fragile egos in the press would be mismanaging valuable time better spent doing the club's work, right Sam? The response is a "you-got-me" wounded look.

"There could only be one boss, one person in charge of where the team and the organization were going to go," he declares. "Responding to the media, or playing to the media, or listening to the fans is the quickest way to start losing. The fans are great, but the thing they respect the most is a winner.

"The thing they know the least is managing a sports franchise. They have their favourites and strong emotional attachments with them. A sports administrator who wants to be successful can never think that way."

That kind of rationale and business pragmatism helped Pollock outwait Ken Dryden when the rangy goaltender-lawyer insisted on a renegotiated deal in mid-contract; and trade away popular favourites like Ralph Backstrom, Peter Mahovlich and Ted Harris when he felt he could make deals that would strengthen the franchise in the longer term.

Pollock served the Canadiens best in the decade of 1966-1975. Two major upheavals struck the microcosm of the National Hockey League during that period: the 1967 Expansion and the formation of the World Hockey Association five years later.

In the latter case, Pollock was one of the few NHL bosses who held firm against the onslaught of the WHA in the mid-1970s. While other teams panicked and began signing all-star and journeyman alike to guaranteed long-term deals, Pollock let people like Frank Mahovlich, Jean-Claude Tremblay, Marc Tardif and Rejean Houle go to the new league. No player, no matter what his past contribution, was better than the team itself in the organizational scheme of things. A player may be more valuable to his team than a teammate, but he could never be more valuable than the team. One policy covered every man who donned the red, white and blue, be he superstar or plumber.

Ken Dryden learned that lesson when he spent 1973-74 articling for a Toronto law firm at $135 a week. The other burgeoning superstars on the team—Guy Lafleur, Larry Robinson, Guy Lapointe, Serge Savard, Jacques Lemaire, Peter Mahovlich and Steve Shutt—went to school on Dryden. If Pollock was able to stand firm against the goalie, winner of the Calder (rookie) and Vezina (best goalie) trophies in his first full season, he could certainly stand firm against an individual forward or defenceman.

The policy was simple. The players would earn their superstardom. Then they would be paid accordingly.

"I felt that a player would have to prove his worth as an individual and team member before he could be considered a superstar," Pollock explains.

"Some were quite upset to hear my definition of superstar. I felt that a superstar was a player who had produced well-above-average performance for a period of time. This definition was given a severe test during the WHA war. Teams in that league were giving journeymen $100,000-plus a year, teams in our league were following suit, and I was trying to convince our players that their paydays would come if they produced for the best hockey team in the world."

Pollock's strategy worked. All of the great young players stayed with the team, with the notable exceptions of
Tardif and Houle (although Houle would return later). In
addition, Pollock saved a lot of money by refusing to
enter the bidding wars. So respected was he by his players for the courage of his convictions that Dryden had to
sound out a few intermediaries before he could approach
Pollock about a possible return. "Will he talk to me?"
Dryden asked.

Hurt by Dryden's defection, Pollock nonetheless was
still the consummate businessman. Dryden was welcomed with open arms and, after a spotty performance in
his first few months, would backstop Montreal to another four Stanley Cups.

Even today, many years after the fact, the Dryden
episode rankles. The year that the goalie sat out was the
first of two in which the Canadiens found themselves
out of the Stanley Cup final. Two good young goalies,
Wayne Thomas and Michel "Bunny" Laroque played
well; but neither was a Dryden.

What also hurt at the time was that two former Canadiens, Tony Esposito and Rogatien Vachon, were dazzling
the league with their acrobatics between the pipes.

And if there was a player on the team who would best
understand where Sam Pollock was coming from, it had
to be Dryden, the articulate and intelligent Cornell grad
who was combining law studies at McGill University
with his job as Montreal Canadiens' top goaltender.

"We had an honest difference of opinion," Pollock says
wistfully.

"That's what it was," agrees Dryden, an individualist
who guards his privacy as fiercely as Pollock. Both refuse
to discuss the matter any further.

The Canadiens' GM was not upset with the reinforced
bargaining position now held by the best players.

"The worst thing at the time wasn't what the WHA
was paying top players," he says, "it was how the whole
scale was thrown off. All of a sudden, career minor
leaguers and unproven rookies were getting all sorts of
money they didn't deserve. You can't pay a prospect

$50,000 a year when he's only worth $25,000. A lot of people in the league argued that $25,000 at a time when we were controlling million-dollar budgets wasn't all that much difference. I said, multiply it by ten and you're talking a quarter of a million dollars." Pollock's parsimony not only saved money, of course, it made money. It also made him the envy of his peers in both leagues, if peer means counterpart, and not equal.

Nevertheless, one must quickly dispel any impression that Pollock was a fiscal Simon Legree, keeping his slaves in line with starvation rations. He had to find the middle way between the no-responsibility, no-incentive fat contracts that turned some hockey players into non-producers, and those that represented modern-day indenture, not recognizing the realities of the current-day market. A stolid insistence on value paid for value received would have hurt the team eventually, no matter how efficient the Canadiens' farm system.

The answer was simple: bilateral contracts that would provide both security and incentive to hockey players. Guy Lafleur signed such a contract in 1975, a ten-year deal with a veritable staircase of raises that would maintain him as one of the best-paid athletes in the game, especially if he performed as one of the best. If, at any time, either party was dissatisfied with the arrangement, they could sit down and discuss the matter rationally and with the most amicable relations.

"I learned at this time that long-term contracts were useless unless they had a reasonable form of renegotiation built in," Pollock says. "You had to build in flexibility because you could predict that somewhere down the road, one side or the other was bound to be unhappy over something." This pragmatism was respected by his athletes and freed them to concentrate on their performances. Pollock established the rules early in the game and then lived by them.

If Pollock was not overly generous with his players' salaries, neither did he underpay them. When Lafleur was drafted in 1971, he immediately became the highest-paid rookie ever to play with Montreal. He received a

$55,000 signing bonus and $25,000 a year for the 1971-72 and 1972-73 seasons, for a total of $105,000. Built into the contract were bonus clauses worth between $1,000 and $5,000.

Did this special treatment upset team veterans?

"Not at all," Pollock replies. "They, better than anyone, knew the value system on the team and the emphasis placed on performance. Lafleur had been recompensed for his performance in the junior ranks and the fact that he was the first draft choice overall. His salary was not out of line with the club's salary structure and his play as a team member would be rewarded by bonuses." Instead of opening the bank vault and inviting his players in, Pollock hit on the novel strategy of opening the door and giving them a quick glimpse, nothing more, before closing it on their noses.

This rational approach to financial motivation seemed to escape most of his counterparts in the other NHL front offices who blithely signed twenty-two year olds to large long-term contracts with few incentives but to show up and put on the uniform and skates.

Silent Sam preferred that his charges make their money the old-fashioned way: by earning it. The bonus system was the great equalizer in Montreal, and many of the bonuses were team-oriented.

"The bonus system was in effect for about twenty years by the time we signed Lafleur and we had had a great deal of experience with it. However, I must point out that if you are discussing basic salary, that's another story. No young player, no matter what he has accomplished in junior hockey, commands a higher salary than that given to an established veteran and Guy Lafleur was no exception. He could not possibly expect to receive more basic salary than an established star."

This even-handed approach was respected by players and agents alike.

Nevertheless, even Pollock was able to come up with an imaginative stretching of his principles when Lafleur was tempted by the WHA. Nothing could be more natural than for the new Quebec franchise in the WHA to be interested in Lafleur, the young man who had starred in that city for almost six years before he moved on to the NHL.

When the Montreal Canadiens retreated to their Stanley Cup playoff hideaway in the Laurentians in April, 1973, the upstart Nordiques chose that moment to offer Lafleur a three-year contract at $90,000 a year and a $50,000 signing bonus. As heady as those numbers sounded, however, Lafleur was not impressed, because other WHA franchises had opened the vaults for people like Derek Sanderson, Bobby Hull and Gerry Cheevers. Lafleur and his agent asked for $200,000 a year, or about what Cheevers was getting from the Cleveland Crusaders.

The major stumbling block was whether or not the contract could be guaranteed, given the shaky financial status of several WHA franchises. After Lafleur's agent, Gerry Patterson, expressed his misgivings on this score, the Nordiques returned with their final offer; a $465,000 three-year package which included a $60,000 signing bonus and salary of $125,000, $135,000 and $145,000 over three years.

Now the ball was in Pollock's court and only some nifty footwork could get him into position to play it cleanly. Pollock knew that one player he could not afford to lose was Lafleur, not with superstardom beckoning to him. More importantly, he could not have Lafleur return to Quebec, where he might help the Nordiques to seriously challenge the Montreal Canadiens for the loyalty of hockey fans across the province. Last but not least, he did not need team harmony disrupted as the Habs entered the playoffs. It was a managerial mine field.

The pressure to have Lafleur return to Quebec was formidable. Guy had constantly filled the Colisée during his days with the Remparts and was mobbed by autograph seekers wherever he went in that city, especially after the tumultuous 1971 Memorial Cup series. *La métropole* had stolen Jean Beliveau in the 1950s and had repeated the dastardly deed two decades later with Beliveau's heir apparent. But now the WHA had given

Quebec the opportunity to repatriate Lafleur. The fans circulated petitions and the radio talk shows stoked the fires. Even some of Quebec City's financial movers and shakers like Marius Fortier and Roger Barre involved themselves in the plans.

That is what Pollock faced when he went to the Canadiens' Board of Directors.

"This is the one young man we cannot afford to lose," he told his bosses. "He will lead us to the Stanley Cup in a couple of years, and probably more than once. If he goes to the other league, he will help them establish credibility in Quebec, something they have in only a few places, with people like Bobby Hull. We'll lose in several ways."

The board of directors expressed their faith in Trader Sam's judgment and he returned to Gerry Patterson, Lafleur's agent. The deal was a ten-year, million dollar contract, plus signing and performance bonuses. Lafleur was free to renegotiate after three and six years, in case the NHL salary scale raced ahead of his contract. Last but not least, the Montreal Canadiens took out a one million dollar life insurance policy on Lafleur.

Patterson and Lafleur both agreed; it was a tremendous deal and would make Lafleur the Canadiens' first-ever millionaire. A week later, Sam Pollock and Irving Grundman were the proud hosts at a tasteful press conference and reception at the Forum press lounge where the new contract was announced.

How important a feat did Pollock accomplish in retaining Lafleur? A month later, the Canadiens won the Stanley Cup final in six games on a goal by the other right winger, Yvan Cournoyer, against Tony Esposito in a final game 6-4 victory. A month after that, Lafleur married the daughter of Roger Barre, one of the Quebec City negotiators.

A lovely reception was held afterward for family and a few close friends at Barre's home in suburban Ste. Foy and after the toasts had died down, Barre cornered Patterson.

"You know, Gerry, time alone will tell if you have made the right decision for Guy," he said in the wounded tone of a rejected suitor. Patterson couldn't resist. "Roger, Guy makes up his own mind. I had nothing to do with his decision to marry your daughter."

By the time the NHL was involved in total war with the WHA, the Canadiens' patriarch was well established and considered the major mover in the league's upper echelons.

Pollock had arrived on the scene in 1964, just as the National Hockey League was seeking to expand its horizons. Ever mindful of the fact that television was becoming the major medium for professional sport, and that the league would never have a chance of shaking the U.S. money tree without better geographical distribution of its teams, the league studied expansion. Some teams favoured measured expansion, two teams at a time every two years over the period of a decade or so.

Pollock led the group that recommended the league immediately double in size. He and his allies were up against league conservatives who felt that the shock of such a large-scale expansion would devastate the NHL and its calibre of play for a generation. They were blind to new possibilities, among them the fact that the United States and Europe would soon be providing quality hockey players to the NHL in record number, thereby swelling the talent pool. Of course, these would be the same people who would later complain about the "foreign" incursion into the sport.

"Their approach would not have worked," reflects Pollock. "We had to immediately guarantee geographical balance. We could never hope that the U.S. networks would even consider us if we had no teams out west, for example. We had to get into some of the top markets as soon as possible."

Pollock, and a few other visionaries, pushed hard for major expansion, recommending it as a good business decision. Others, many of them purists dedicated to the quality of the game, worried about diluting the talent base.

"Diluting the talent base, or watering down the product, as quite a few people were arguing, was not the priority expansion was," Pollock recalls. "We had to get into some important markets in the west and midwest. Chicago could use the competition from Minnesota and St. Louis. New York could use the competition from Pittsburgh and Philadelphia. And we needed teams in California so we could cover the United States from coast-to-coast. Those were important considerations if ever we were to penetrate the American TV market."

Also, many hockey players who had been labouring long in the American and Pacific Coast hockey leagues were quality players, and could easily step in and play for the new NHL franchises.

The league voted for a six-team expansion and the winning applicants were Philadelphia, St. Louis, Minneapolis-St. Paul, Pittsburgh, Los Angeles and Oakland-San Francisco.

The next step was to decide on parity. How could these teams be stocked with players and become competitive in the space of one summer? Very few of the Original Six wanted to lose their top players. Many of the team GMs were also leery of losing their protected players in the organization, those young kids who were a season away from maturing.

Most important was the fact that they really didn't want to give up protected territories, such as the Canadiens' protected area (Montreal) which provided so many quality players each year.

"But a lot of these things had to be done away with," says Pollock, "or this thing would have never worked. One solution was to bring in the universal draft of amateur players, where all twelve teams would have a shot at the best juniors and college players graduating each spring and the last team in the previous NHL season would draft first."

In recognition of the original teams' junior development system, which was soon to be dismantled to provide players for the six new franchises in the new draft system, Montreal was given the right to select two French Canadian players in lieu of their first two draft choices for a five-year period in the mid-sixties. However, because of the phasing-in period, 1969 was the only year in which this special provision helped. At that time, the Canadiens selected Rejean Houle and Marc Tardif. If this system had lasted one more year, they would have been able to draft Gilbert Perreault the following year.

"I don't know how many times sportswriters have written that we maintained our strength for years because of this so-called unfair advantage," Pollock said. "It just never happened that way."

Pollock also recommended that there be a moratorium of two to five years on trading draft choices, so that the clubs could mature with these players and, although they might suffer for two or three years, would find themselves with a solid nucleus five years down the road.

The other clubs turned that suggestion down. That bout of myopia would cost them dearly, as Pollock turned out to be the best manipulator of draft choices and veteran talent ever seen in the league. Going into the expanded NHL, Pollock was sitting atop the best organized and richest franchise. Top young and veteran talent sat in places like Houston, Cleveland, Springfield and other cities. New franchises, hoping to become competitive earlier than the opposition, turned to Pollock for help. He helped them, but they paid a price.

In 1969, Montreal drafted Rejean Houle and Marc Tardif 1-2 and selected another speedster, Bobby Sheehan of St. Catharines Black Hawks, number 32. A year later, Pollock went into high gear. Goalie Ray Martiniuk of Flin Flon Bombers was picked number 5 and forward Chuck Lefley of the Canadian National team was number 6. Lower down in the order came Rick Wilson of the University of North Dakota, a player who would toil on the Montreal defence for one season and then be despatched for more draft choices.

A year later, jackpot! Guy Lafleur was selected first overall but he was not alone. Number 7 was Chuck Arnason from Flin Flon and number 11 was a tall, classic skater from the Ottawa 67s named Murray Wilson. If that wasn't enough, Pollock took a flyer on a skinny defenceman with Kitchener Rangers in the number 20 spot and Larry Robinson became a Hab. Further down in the order came players like Greg Hubick, Mike Busniuk and Peter Sullivan, all of whom would toil in the organization for several years before moving on to other organizations for more draft picks.

The Lafleur pick, of course, was the most famous product of Pollock's wheeling and dealing, exchanging value today for future considerations. In 1970, Pollock sent forward Ernie Hicke and a draft choice to Oakland in exchange for their first-round pick in the 1971 draft.

Such was Pollock's reputation by then that everybody began reading ulterior motives into virtually every transaction he made. Late in the 1970 season, the story goes, Pollock awoke to the fact that he had been too generous to the Seals, when they threatened to overtake Los Angeles Kings. Sam needed a last-place finish by the Seals, so that the inverse order of the draft would give him first selection. He quickly despatched veteran centre Ralph Backstrom to the Kings and Backstrom did his job, helping that team improve and stay ahead of Oakland.

That story has been in print for fifteen years, and one version even claims that the Canadiens secured the retransmission rights for the first Muhammad Ali-Joe Frazier fight for the Forum from Kings' owner Jack Kent Cooke.

Pollock has a one-word response: "Bunk!"

In 1972, Montreal used its accumulated picks to select Steve Shutt, Michel Larocque and Dave Gardner in the 4, 6 and 8 spots respectively. Defencemen John Van Boxmeer and Bill Nyrop were numbers 14 and 66.

And so it went. Whether or not the top choice panned out, and that wasn't always the case (for example, Cam Connor in 1974), Montreal usually found itself with an abundance of high choices and, even after the other teams started to refuse draft choice swaps, managed to find more good players in the lower echelons of the draft. In 1974, Montreal drafted Connor, Doug Risebrough, Rich Chartraw, Mario Tremblay, Gilles Lupien, Marty Howe, Jamie Hislop and Dave Lumley (number 199)—all players who would play in the NHL for a variety of teams. Three years later, it was Mark Napier, Normand Dupont, Rod Langway, Alain Côté, Gordie Roberts,

Robert Holland, Richard Sevigny, Mark Holden and Craig Laughlin.

Montreal could pick high, they could pick low. Two celebrated grinders, Canadien Chris Nilan and Boston's Louis Sleigher, were Montreal draft choices in 1978 and numbers 231 and 233 overall. Two of the current stars, Mats Naslund and Guy Carbonneau, were selected numbers 37 and 44 in 1979 and St. Louis Blues goaltender Rick Wamsley was number 58 the same year. In 1980, the Doug Wickenheiser draft year, Montreal found Craig Ludwig at 61, Mike McPhee at 124 and Steve Penney at 166.

Trader Sam traded for draft position, and he delivered quality to the expansion teams. While today's experts, taking advantage of their 20/20 hindsight, will castigate Minnesota's Wren Blair for draft choices he sent to Montreal, they will conveniently forget, of course, that players like Ted Harris, Gump Worsley, Danny Grant, Jude Drouin, Dave Balon, Andre Boudrias and Claude Larose were the backbone of the North Stars for many years and, in fact, came close to upsetting Montreal in the 1971 Stanley Cup semi-final.

The St. Louis Blues received a raft of Canadiens farmhands and found themselves in the NHL final for three straight years between 1968 and 1970. Players like Noel Picard, Jimmy Roberts, Red Berenson, Ernie Wakely, Bill McCreary, Christian Bordeleau and Fran Huck became household names in Missouri.

"Restocking the team was important to us and we quickly realized that the draft was going to be the major area of importance," Pollock says.

"That meant we had to increase our scouting staff, to ensure that we saw all of the best players available and were able to assess them. That also meant that we would draft for specific players with specific talents."

A prime example was Bob Gainey, the current captain, acknowledged by most hockey observers as the best defensive forward to ever play the game. As strange as it might sound, Montreal acquired Gainey by dropping down five positions in the draft.

"The Gainey draft developed out of a very large set of

circumstances," says Pollock. "I always tended to look at the overall or big picture, such as how many players we had, and how many players we were going to have to protect in a given year. Very seldom was my philosophy to win a championship first, especially at the expense of developing a good team, because if you worried about winning the championship in one particular year, you could make some very bad mistakes.

"Two things distinguished the 1973 draft year. First, it was probably the most competitive year between the NHL and the WHA. Second, there were more high-calibre players available that year, even though the first choice, Denis Potvin, was head and shoulders above everyone else. And there was absolutely no chance of trading up a spot for Potvin; Bill Torrey let everyone know that Potvin was a franchise player and would be an Islander for life."

Montreal traded the second pick to the Atlanta Flames for two first round picks, the number 5 pick that year and another first round pick another year. The Flames drafted Tom Lysiak, a flashy centreman whom *they* felt would be a franchise player. Not long afterward, the St. Louis Blues came calling and said they were desperate to draft a tall goaltender with Calgary Centennials named John Davidson. The Blues feared that the Boston Bruins, drafting sixth, would take Davidson, whom *they* felt was a franchise player. If Montreal would switch their number 5 choice for St. Louis's number 7, the Blues would kick in an extra first round choice at a later date.

It was a good gamble for Pollock. The Canadiens' scouting staff had the first five selections down pat and the club was gambling two new first-round picks that the Boston Bruins and Pittsburgh Penguins would not take Gainey. It worked. Boston opted for a former team-mate of Guy Lafleur, a flashy Quebec Remparts centre named André Savard, and Pittsburgh selected high-scoring winger Blaine Stoughton.

"So we got Gainey, a player who had a reputation of being a great defensive player and who had learned defence under the best, Roger Neilsen in Peterborough."

You could hear a pin drop at the Mount Royal Hotel

when the Canadiens announced their draft choice. "Bob *qui*? How many goals has he scored lately?" You had the feeling that Harry Brown would already be squawking downstairs in the Press Club.

When it came to draft futures, Montreal's so-called knowledgeable hockey fans went for the glitz, just like everyone else. Defensive forwards were anathema to them, despite the fact that people like Kenny Mosdell, Jim Roberts and Claude Provost had been protecting the rears of more gifted scorers for decades at the corner of Atwater and St. Catherine.

Pollock acknowledged the criticism, but made a strong point, one which was quietly enforced over the years. Whether the Canadiens fans were knowledgeable or not, and every cab driver in town knows he can run the Canadiens better than the current GM, Pollock ran the team.

"The fans represented the bottom line and our success would be measured in the numbers who came to the Forum and paid to see our hockey players," he said.

Nevertheless, Sam Pollock could not have the fans running the hockey team. Decisions would have to be taken with the best information at hand, and accepted. The same rule applied to the media mavens who were a step removed from their *confrères* in the cars with dome lights.

Other GMs had rabbit ears, and were a little too quick to acknowledge the howls and downturned thumbs. Sam would thoroughly plan his move, assess it and go ahead, fully expecting to be judged by history somewhere down the road. More than a dozen years later, the Gainey move clearly proved right.

"Just like in any other sport, your first-round picks are usually not defensive linemen and even if there isn't a terrific quarterback available, they usually tend to be great offensive players," says Pollock. "We were looking for a great defensive player." Ever the diplomat, Pollock returns their self-respect to Montreal cabbies and sports-writers. "Don't get me wrong, we were very conscious of our fans. But we ran the team."

After years of learning from Frank Selke, and helping

build up an organization whose tentacles reached into every corner of hockey-playing North America, Sam Pollock was the first hockey man to know when the time had come to get rid of expensive and cumbersome operations.

"We were as much a victim of the television age as was baseball and all of its minor leagues," he says.

"By the mid-60s it became apparent that most minor league franchises could not pay for themselves and the simple reason behind that was the fact that people in those cities could watch the National Hockey League for free on the TV sets instead of paying to see the American Hockey League or another league."

Free agency, television and the 1967 Expansion were the first steps, and the WHA was the last. Pollock quickly moved to cut away the excess in the organization. The pride of Frank Selke, the extensive system of professional feeder clubs, was outdated and no longer profitable. Sam the businessman had spoken.

It was a move that Frank Selke probably would have made himself. If there was a major difference between Selke and Pollock it was that Selke was a front-line producer, a farmer-businessman, while Pollock was the quintessential entrepreneur or middleman. Frank thought in terms of seeding, weeding and feeding (no rhyme intended) and taking the produce to market. Sam thought in terms of the deals that could be swung in the marketplace.

Each man was a visionary in his own era. Such leadership is at the heart of the Canadiens' tradition of success.

9

The Surprising Sixties

Blessed are those that nought expect,
For they shall not be disappointed.

This quotation from John Walcot, Lord Mayor of London in the fifteenth century, may best summarize the credit and the curse of the Montreal Canadiens' Team of the Sixties.

"I really don't understand why everybody is so anxious to compare the Montreal Canadiens of the 1950s with the team of the late '70s. There was a team in the middle that might have been as good."

That is the opinion of Sam Pollock, general manager of the Montreal Canadiens from 1964 to 1978, the architect of two of the three Canadiens' powerhouses.

With respect to Lord Mayor Walcot, the credit to which we refer is for winning five Stanley Cups. Here we add our own asterisk: the Stanley Cups won by the 1960s team came in 1965, '66, '68, '69 and 1971. The championship won at Toronto, April 14, 1960 was won in the 1960s if you use the calendar as your only rule; the same qualification applies to the cup won in Chicago, May 18, 1971. Had it not been for unbelievable goaltending by Johnny Bower and the late Terry Sawchuk in the 1967 playoffs, the 1960s Canadiens would have duplicated the feat of five straight.

The 1960 Cup, the fifth in a row, most obviously belonged to the 1950s edition of the Canadiens. The 1971 championship was a glorious close to a chapter of the club's history that is unjustifiably ignored. As for the 1973 Cup, the best that can be said is that it was won by a team in full transition, two years after the team of the 1960s retired gracefully and two years before the team of the '70s began toying with any and all comers.

To help you understand our point of view, and explain why this chapter begins with a quotation from a Mayor of London who lived five-and-a-half centuries before the 1960s Canadiens skated at the Forum, it is necessary to return to the 1950s.

There was no real reason to believe that the Montreal Canadiens that won five straight Stanley Cups would stop there, as the Age of Camelot on the Potomac dawned. Up front, Jean Beliveau, Bernie Geoffrion and Dickie Moore were twenty-nine years old and other stalwarts like Henri Richard, Ralph Backstrom, Billy Hicke, Phil Goyette and Don Marshall were even younger.

On the blueline, Doug Harvey, Tom Johnson, Jean-Guy Talbot and Bob Turner anchored a stingy defence. They were, respectively, thirty-six, thirty-two, twenty-eight and twenty-six. Goalies Jacques Plante and Charlie Hodge were thirty-one and twenty-seven. As well, very capable rookies like the Tremblays, Gilles and Jean-Claude, and Bobby Rousseau, were being worked into the line-up slowly. The Canadiens also had legions of good young players scattered throughout North America, awaiting the call to the Forum.

Maurice Richard hung up his skates one day during September training camp (after scoring four goals in a morning scrimmage) but the team that had ravaged the league during the previous decade was basically intact. The Canadiens proved it by finishing first in the regular season with 92 points, the same total as the year before, and would better that mark with 98 the following season. In all respects, the team of the Fifties was still alive and thriving.

The derailment, as would be the case in the early 1980s, came in the playoffs.

"We still had a very competitive team," Frank Selke recalled, "and we made few changes in those two years because we had few to make. You do not go about disassembling a first-place team because of a playoff setback. The team was sound in 1960-61 and we had every right to expect a good result in the playoffs."

How sound were the Canadiens? Jean Beliveau and Bernie Geoffrion finished first and second in the scoring race, with Boom Boom scoring 50 goals, only the second time ever that feat had been accomplished. Dickie Moore and Henri Richard joined their two teammates in the top ten in scoring. Beliveau, Geoffrion and Harvey were on the first all-star team, Moore and the Pocket on the second.

In the playoffs they ran into a Chicago Black Hawks team that had been under construction for almost a decade. Jim Norris and Arthur Wirtz had spent a lot of money in the late 1950s to give Chicago a winner and they had received some significant help. The National Hockey League was well aware that a franchise in Chicago was a necessity, and they knew that the Black Hawks were being held back because they lacked the most important thing of all: the ability to play as a team.

After some success in the 1930s, the Black Hawks headed for the league's nether regions and took up permanent residence there. Between Stanley Cups (1938 and 1961) the Black Hawks finished last ten times and never higher than third. Emile Francis, a goalie with the 1950-51 team, remembers that quality players did not seem to last a long time in Chicago.

"We had a rookie left winger named Bert Olmstead with us that year and the word got out that the Canadiens wanted him. Before you knew it, Montreal, Detroit and the Black Hawks made a three-way deal and he was on his way to the Forum. It wasn't easy playing for Chicago back then; it was the place where teams unloaded excess baggage."

Bringing back the Black Hawks to respectability became an NHL reclamation project, not unlike the Marshall Plan that resurrected Europe in the post-War years. Players like Eddie Litzenberger, Ab McDonald, Dollard St. Laurent, Reggie Fleming, Murray Balfour and Bob Turner came over from Montreal and joined Toronto castoffs like Tod Sloan, Eric Nesterenko and Jim Thomson, former Red Wings Al Arbour and Ted Lindsay and longtime New York Rangers defensive stalwart Jack Evans. The latter four and Montreal's St. Laurent were despatched to Chicago by their respective teams as punishment for their abortive efforts to establish a players' association in 1957. When the 1960-61 season rolled around, however, they were no longer complaining.

There they joined the first crop of "original" Black Hawks, raised in the Chicago farm system, most of them in St. Catharines, Ontario: Bobby Hull, Pierre Pilote, Stan Mikita, Kenny Wharram and Chico Maki. Goalie Glenn Hall was acquired in a trade with Detroit and centreman Red Hay came out of college ranks.

That was the team that bumped off the Montreal Canadiens in successive semi-finals in 1961 and '62, winning the Stanley Cup the first year in a six-game series with Detroit then losing it to Toronto in the same number of games the following season.

The Canadiens were still a strong club, finishing in first with 98 points in 1962, 13 better than second-place Toronto who were 10 points in front of third-place Chicago.

"We handled Toronto all year but a combination of injuries and a very physical Chicago club did us in both years," Frank Selke recalled.

The first moves at disbanding the team of the 1950s came in the 1961 off-season when Doug Harvey was dealt to the New York Rangers, even though he had won a spot on the first all-star team and the Norris Trophy as the league's best defenceman. He felt it was his punishment for union activity of the same kind that had resulted in so many one-way tickets being issued to Chicago four years earlier.

"Of course it was that. If I hadn't won the Norris Trophy from '57 through '60 and if we hadn't been winning all of those championships, I would have been long gone. But Selke wasn't stupid; he knew if he traded me in 1957, they would have lynched him at the corner of Atwater and St. Catherine."

Harvey, Turner and St. Laurent were replaced by J.C. Tremblay, Jean Gauthier and Lou Fontinato, all capable defencemen. A year later, Jacques Plante was traded and Bernie Geoffrion, often injured, retired in 1964.

If the Montreal Canadiens had a major weakness in the early 1960s, it was size. Too many times, it seemed, bigger clubs were battering the small Canadiens forwards along the boards and the playoffs became a grind. Frank Selke, and later Sam Pollock, set about remedying that problem in a hurry.

In 1963 the airlift began. Three huge defencemen (especially for that time) joined the team: Jacques Laperriere, Terry Harper and Ted Harris. Bryan Watson, a fourth defenceman who occasionally played forward, also signed on. The Montreal Canadiens would be pushed around no more. Just to make sure, Frank Selke reached into the American Hockey League for a player everyone said would garner instant respect for his teammates.

Gilles Tremblay remembers the new policeman's arrival.

"He showed up in training camp with a reputation of a good hockey player and one who hadn't lost a fight in the AHL. A lot of teams wanted him and it wasn't hard to see why. In our first game in Boston, he got into a fight with Ted Green right off the opening faceoff, won the fight, and all of a sudden we had a lot more room to skate again."

John Ferguson had a mission. He was going to be the meanest son-of-a-bitch in the NHL and he would waste little time in delivering that message, in person, to the benches of the other five teams. Unlike many other players, he had chosen the Canadiens, and not vice versa.

"I was in the AHL with Cleveland and I made the all-star team in 1962. The New York Rangers had seriously scouted me and I had the chance to go to either the Boston Bruins or the Rangers but I had always been a

Canadiens fan. I told Jackie Gordon that I preferred to go to Montreal and if I didn't make it there, I could always make it in the other two cities."

As it was, Ferguson ended up in Montreal and his fierce, fearsome grinding allowed the Canadiens to become the Flying Frenchmen again.

One thing that opponents of fighting in the NHL never seem to understand, as is well evidenced by a 1985 campaign against hockey violence and so-called goons in a major U.S. sports publication, is that it has been historically accepted as an integral part of the game. There is no question that there is little room for brawling, which is tedious, time-consuming and diminishes the game. Former league president Clarence Campbell described the place of fighting accurately, when interviewed on the topic a decade ago.

"They'll never take it out of the game because it is an outlet, a safety valve, that allows players to get some built-up tension out of the way and to continue on about their business. If you tried to stop it, animosities would grow and linger and they would eventually lead to some very ugly stick incidents. I am convinced of that."

A large majority of players agrees with that statement. Several European players, Mats Naslund of the Canadiens among them, smile quietly when they are questioned about the big bad NHL with all of its Rambos ready to let gloves fly at a cross-eyed glance or any other such perceived slight.

"Do you really think that there is no dirty work back home? The Russians are the best in the world with their sticks and skates and a kick in the back of the leg is more dangerous than a punch on the nose. The strangest thing is that more fuss is made about fighting here; back home it is not much of a topic, maybe because the fans don't really notice the stickwork."

Fighting has its historical place in the dynamics of the hockey game. Few modern hockey fans are aware of the sport's beginnings. Most expect perhaps that the game just happened on some icy lake or river a century or so ago and evolved from there. Nothing could be further from the truth. Hockey began as a rough game and always has been.

A variety of stick and ball games were played on ice in northern England, Scotland, the Netherlands and North America in the nineteenth century. It is believed that the original version of ice hockey combined several of the European games, and was played for the first time in Canada, sometime in the early nineteenth century. The official history of the game is that variations of bandy (Russian) and shinty (later corrupted to shinny) were played by British soldiers in Halifax and Kingston around 1850 and hockey developed at the Lake Ontario garrison in the same period.

Says *The Canadian Encyclopedia*:

> In 1879 the first organized team, the McGill University Hockey Club, was formed, and with the advent of a basic set of rules the sport quickly spread across Canada . . .
>
> Early hockey was played in rudimentary conditions, mostly outdoors on patches of natural ice, with snowbanks for boards and wooden posts for goals. There were 9 players per side on the ice, and the puck could not be passed forward. The on-side rule and primitive face-off ("bully") were adapted from rugby. With speed and rough play the game had immediate attraction, and strong local rivalries developed.

Most of the sport's earliest stars were rugby players who were looking to stay in shape during the traditionally lazy winter months. Thus, the earliest version of ice hockey developed as rugby on ice. Contrary to popular belief, the rugby influence was not weaned early from the sport. The twenty-minute period surfaced in 1910 and the forward pass rule was softened in 1918 (the year the NHL was formed) to allow it in the neutral zone— between bluelines.

It was not until the 1930-31 season, the NHL's thirteenth, that the forward pass was allowed all over the ice. Players like Howie Morenz, Aurele Joliat, the Cleghorns, Frank Nighbor and the like played a game much closer to rugby than to modern hockey. Morenz was especially valuable because his speed allowed him to elude defencemen and either shoot directly on goal or leave drop passes or laterals for his wingers. He and other speedy forwards were not averse to "crashing" the opposition's defensive line, much like rugby ball carriers do, hoping to create an opening.

Defencemen, on the other hand, were free to practically tackle any fast forward aiming to advance the puck, also in the rugby manner, and most contact took place in the centre of the ice surface and not along the boards, as is the case today. All of that violent action in open ice, with its sticks, elbows, knees and skates, led to major league stickwork that would shock today's staid burghers, and some serious brawling that would occasionally spread into the spectator stands.

Accordingly, when John Ferguson, Ted Harris, Terry Harper, Jacques Laperriere and Bryan Watson showed up in 1963, everyone knew why they were there.

"We knew that we would have trouble winning until we could handle the rough going," said Gilles Tremblay.

"It was necessary to get players like these to let us play our game. On a hockey team with 18 to 20 players, there are role players. Guys like Yvan Cournoyer, Bobby Rousseau and myself were there for our speed on wing and ability to get scoring chances. Jean Beliveau, Henri Richard and Ralph Backstrom were there for their ability to set up scoring opportunities and Ted Harris, Jacques Laperriere and Terry Harper kept our defensive zone under control. Fergy, Claude Larose and players like that gave all of the rest of us room to manoeuvre, to do our jobs, while they kept the other team's heads up. No Stanley Cup winning team I can think of has ever done it without the tough players who keep the opposition honest."

Another aspect of the team dynamic that the novice might find curious is the place held by the so-called "team policeman". One would assume from the hue and cry in the stands that this player is a marginal one, forever banished to the fringes of the group, never to be discussed in polite company and never really accepted by his more honest teammates.

That is patently false. The player who fights for his teammates, or is at least willing to drop his gloves so that less pugilistic players are free to do what they do best, is as essential to a team as any other player. He is accepted as such, a full contributor.

"We all have our jobs on a hockey team," said Yvan Cournoyer. "And we respect a player who does his job because he is bringing something special to the team. John was a rough and hard hockey player because the Montreal Canadiens needed a player like that. Without him, and guys like Terry Harper and Ted Harris on defence, we would not have been as good as we became."

His teammates respected Ferguson and they let him know it.

"It was really important to me that the guys felt that way. One year the Canadiens veterans voted me the most valuable player and that was the year that Cournoyer led the team in scoring. What impressed me was the fact that in the Canadiens scheme of things you could be a leader not only as a goal scorer but also as an aggressor."

John Ferguson assumed a leadership role, but he was a special case. Ferguson lasted all of 12 seconds in his first game before he became embroiled in that first ice fight with Ted Green. What most denigrators of his style of hockey might not realize is that Ferguson also scored twice in that game, a 4-4 tie.

"Fergy disrupted the other team, all over the ice," said Jean Beliveau. "When he was in the other team's zone, the goalie had to keep an eye on him at all times and that helped the rest of us who were making plays and taking shots. But he was just as valuable off the ice. John hated to lose and players on his team were afraid of him a bit. With a guy like him on your team, you don't want to fool around. He doesn't have to say anything; all he has to do is look at you, like the Rocket used to. But he was the nicest man to his teammates."

Ferguson believed in more positive reinforcement in the room.

"In the dressing room, I assumed that it was my responsibility to get things going and to move on issues to help all the guys give their best. If someone was lethargic, I had a way to make them deal with the situation by feeling good about themselves and I told them they could always count on me."

His presence counted, and when the brash young Boston Bruins strutted into the Forum in April of 1968 for the first game of their Stanley Cup semi-final, it was Ferguson who took the situation in hand.

All pre-playoff talk had centred on intimidation; the only question was which team would wear out the other first. Halfway through the first period, Green and Ferguson came together. Ferguson got position on his adversary, pulled his jersey over his head, and whaled away at the Boston defenceman. He came away a clear-cut winner and Montreal blitzed the Bruins in four straight.

"When you get right down to it, I made it my business to be an absolutely miserable son-of-a-bitch on the ice all of the time. But in the room, we tried other methods. We were very close and it was a team composed of comedians who always knew how to deal with pressure, guys like Larose, Laperriere and Harper. Those guys never stopped and kept all of us loose."

Those who watched him on the ice, or saw him adamantly refuse to socialize with players from other teams even in the off-season, would be surprised to discover that Ferguson was one of the ringleaders when it came to Canadiens' high jinks and pranks. When the popular Bryan 'Bugsy' Watson was traded to the Chicago Black Hawks in 1965, he telephoned the Canadiens' dressing room about two weeks after his departure and asked the equipment manager to forward his favourite pair of skates. He received them about ten days later, painted bright pink. The two teams laughed about that one for weeks.

How important were Ferguson's leadership qualities? When Beliveau and Ferguson announced they were retiring in 1971, Sam Pollock called Ferguson and offered him the team captaincy if he would reconsider and play another season.

"I decided to stay retired but that was a very important

gesture by Sam," Ferguson said. "That told me that my contribution to the Montreal Canadiens had been noticed and appreciated."

If the Montreal Canadiens were a much tougher team in the 1960s, they were a little less gifted offensively than previous (or subsequent, for that matter) editions. The big scorers were in Boston, Detroit and Chicago. In 1965, the Canadiens won their first (true) Stanley Cup of the decade. The team's top scorer that year was Claude Provost, whose main claim to fame usually was his ability to stop Bobby Hull from scoring. Provost was sixth in the NHL scoring race and Ralph Backstrom was tied for ninth. Beliveau and Richard finished further down the list in a year when injuries struck hard.

In the four years that the 1960s Montreal Canadiens won the Stanley Cup, no Montreal player finished higher than third in scoring (Bobby Rousseau in 1966).

"That kind of statistic proves something that we players knew very well—the value of Toe Blake to the Montreal Canadiens," said Beliveau. "In the 1960s we had a very good team but we were not head and shoulders above the rest of the league as we had been in the 1950s. The difference was that we had the very best coach in hockey and a man who could get the best out of his players at all times."

The praise for Blake is unanimous.

"To me Toe was the greatest," said John Ferguson, currently the general manager of the Winnipeg Jets. "He is like my father. I look up to him and I think that he is the greatest coach of all time. Players performed for Toe. He was a great taskmaster and demanded and earned respect. But, most importantly, it was a two-way street. If you earned it, you got his respect too and too few coaches know how to do that."

During the 1985-86 playoffs, Ferguson visited the Forum for the seventh game in the Adams Division final against Hartford.

"The first guy I searched out was Toe. Since I had recently gone behind the bench again, I wanted to make sure that I hadn't gone rusty, so we talked."

Tom Johnson, a member of the team of the 1950s and

current assistant GM with Boston Bruins, tells a story that shows his feelings for his former coach.

"About three or four years ago Gerry Cheevers was our coach and he came to me during the summer with a voucher for me to sign. I asked what it was and he told me it was for several hundred dollars so he could go to a special hockey coaching clinic run by Gary Green (former Washington Capitals' coach) in the Laurentians."

Johnson looked up at his coach and said, "I've got a better idea." He reached into his pocket and pulled out a twenty dollar bill.

"Take this and go to Toe Blake's Tavern in Montreal. You'll learn more about coaching there in an hour than in four days in the Laurentians."

The punch line?

"I wasn't kidding," said Johnson.

Terry Harper saw Blake's biggest contribution as his ability to meld different personalities into a distinct unit.

"There were so many types of personalities that made the Canadiens so successful. All the individual personalities of players were allowed to surface but they surfaced as a group, and Toe made a team of it. He didn't try to change everybody or make anybody the ideal Canadien. He tried to have everyone be what they were. He was above anybody else I ever played for or ever met. He was more interested in the mental aspect of a player."

Blake was strong in game preparation and even stronger during the game.

"Toe knew how to work the rest in between periods," said Harper. "Sometimes he would come in and say absolutely nothing, and other times he would give us hell straight through until it was time to go back on the ice. And yet other times he would come in and say something really hilarious and have us all laughing like crazy. The point is, he knew when to do any of the three. He could tell when we were too tight and needed to relax a bit, or when we were complacent and [he] needed to jump on us. He had a tremendous feel for where the team was.

"The best part was that he brought the whole team along, not just one or two fellows . . . the whole team. He believed in the players and they, in turn, believed in him."

Blake's coaching, the inspiration of veteran leaders like Beliveau and Richard, the new toughness in the persons of Ferguson, Harris, Harper and Larose, staunch goaltending by Gump Worsley, Charlie Hodge and, later, Rogatien Vachon, characterized the team of the 1960s. If we count from 1963-64, by which time the transition from the 1950s edition had ended, the Canadiens won the Prince of Wales Trophy for finishing first four times and won the Stanley Cup five times in eight years.

But for some reason or other, they will always be the team that Montreal forgot.

An educated guess would be that Montreal fans missed the élan of the 1950s. For years the Forum crowd has been likened to that attending world figure skating championships. The fans in Montreal award points for both technical and artistic merit.

In Montreal, not only did you have to win, you had to win with style and panache. The team of the '60s did not fit that bill, even though it won consistently. In the early half of the decade, the flash in the NHL was provided by Chicago where Bobby Hull and Stan Mikita plied their trade. And toward the end of the decade, Bobby Orr, Phil Esposito, and friends captured the imagination of offence-minded hockey fans everywhere. The Canadiens were terrific defensively and competent up front, but despite a few exceptions, Yvan Cournoyer especially, they generally won in a workmanlike manner.

Players like Terry Harper and Jacques Laperriere, both tall and lanky, seemed to blanket the Canadiens' defensive zone, throwing arms, elbows, sticks and legs in the way of opposing forwards and pucks. As a result, Montreal won three Vezina trophies in that period.

Few Canadiens made the first all-star team in those days. From 1963 through 1971, Montreal had 5 First Team and 13 Second Team nominations. Chicago was 20 and 5, Toronto 3 and 8, New York 4 and 7, Detroit 6 and 7 and Boston 9 and 5 during the same period.

No player epitomized the Montreal Canadiens' work

ethic and sense of personal sacrifice more than Harper. Conversely, no player got less respect from the Forum fans, who have been overrated as hockey connoisseurs at certain times.

Harper, a Regina native, was twelve years old when he was severely burned in an accident. For a while it was uncertain that he would ever walk again, but with a quiet sense of self-confidence combined with hard work, Terry built himself up and became a stalwart defender for his hometown Regina Pats.

He arrived in Montreal late in the 1962-63 season and went on to play ten seasons for the Canadiens. A 6' 2", 195-pound defenceman, he was the antithesis of everything the Montreal fans had come to expect from the flashier side of the sport. Harper once scored as many as four goals in one season and even won a fight, a penalty box affair with Bob Pulford very early in his career. However, J.C. Tremblay or John Ferguson he wasn't when it came to offensive prowess or intimidation.

Derek Sanderson perhaps said it best in his autobiography, *I've Got To Be Me*: "Harper can't fight worth a damn but he's got a lot of guts and he keeps coming back, although he usually gets the hell beat out of him." Another thing Sanderson could have said, but didn't, was that his Bruins could never beat the Canadiens when it counted because of players like Harper.

During the 1960s, when he was at his peak, Bobby Hull was asked about the defencemen who were toughest on him, at a time when Hull was shredding defences every night.

"Terry Harper," he said, "plays me as well or better than any defenceman in the league. I can never seem to get around him."

One thing the so-called knowledgeable fans overlooked in their merciless treatment of Harper was his skating ability. He was gawky, all angles, elbows and knees. But the forwards on his team who went against him in practice knew one thing; you couldn't get around him. Skating backwards, he put his flashier defensive mates to shame. Add to that ability a reach that could flick a puck off an attacker's blade from a seemingly impossible long distance, and it is little wonder that Frank Selke and Sam Pollock ignored the braying of the red-seat cognoscenti for a decade.

Harper's abilities also led to one of the more dramatic moments in Stanley Cup history, especially at the Forum. It came on Sunday, May 9, 1971, the third game of the final series against Chicago. Montreal had lost the first two contests in Chicago, 2-1 and 5-3, despite the heroics of Ken Dryden, and were locked in a tight duel with the Black Hawks who knew they could wrap up the championship if they could steal a win at the Forum.

Harper had been the goat of an earlier Chicago score and was hearing the boos from a surly segment of the crowd whenever he went near the puck. Midway through the second period, he picked up the puck behind his net and skated up the left side.

"Boooooooooooooo!" came cascading down from the rafters.

Harper eluded a Chicago checker at the Canadiens' blueline and swung in toward centre ice.

"Boooooooooooooo!"

He cut back towards the left boards, evading another check, and moved towards the Black Hawks' blueline as his teammates all braked to avoid going offside.

"Boooooooooooooo!" There wasn't a fan left sitting.

Just inside the blueline, Harper slid off yet another bodycheck and carried the puck behind the Chicago net. As he skated directly behind the cage, two Black Hawks smashed into him simultaneously. Falling, he still had enough leverage to pass the puck out in front of the net where John Ferguson was all alone in front of Tony Esposito. Ferguson made no mistake and the Canadiens were on their way to a 4-2 win.

A teammate, who prefers to remain anonymous for obvious reasons, summed it up best: "That was the best 'Fuck You' play I've ever seen in hockey. It was all some of the players could do not to give the crowd the finger."

Harper disentangled himself from the two Chicago players and rose to the rare, for him, sound of a standing ovation as all of his teammates on the ice converged on him, rather than Ferguson the scorer. In the stands, fans were cheering wildly, if not looking out of the corners of their eyes in semi-accusation at all of their *confrères* who had had the temerity to boo such a wonderful hockey player.

Harper, Ferguson, Laperriere, Harris, Provost, Larose —they were Montreal's version of Boston's Lunch Pail Athletic Club—eminently forgettable but for one thing.

Nobody told them how to lose.

They won with improbable plays by Terry Harper and the battling of John Ferguson that could take the starch out of a cocky team like the 1968 Boston Bruins. They won with the finesse of Jean-Claude Tremblay who, unlike his defensive partners, did not like the heavy going but could make a puck dance.

They won when they shouldn't have, against Boston in 1969 and again in 1971. They won with veterans like Richard, Beliveau and Backstrom and kids like Mickey Redmond, Serge Savard, Guy Lapointe and Phil Roberto. They won with raw rookies like Rogatien Vachon and Ken Dryden tending goal. The only silverware they collected was the Stanley Cup.

Individual awards, it seems, were for other teams. In terms of league awards, Claude Provost won the Bill Masterton Trophy (1968), Jean Beliveau, Serge Savard and Ken Dryden won the Conn Smythe Trophy, Jacques Laperriere won the Norris Trophy (1966) as top defence-man in the league, Laperriere (1964) won the Calder Trophy as top rookie and Beliveau the Hart Trophy as league MVP.

Including the aforementioned three Vezina trophies, that made ten individual awards between 1964 and 1971. No Canadiens player won the Art Ross in the same period because no Montreal player won the scoring championship. However, nothing can be more patently ludicrous than the fact that the league's least penalized and highest scoring team, historically, has not won the Lady Byng Trophy since Toe Blake turned the trick in 1946. It is quite obvious that players such as Henri Richard, Jean Beliveau and Guy Lafleur were penalized for playing with a team that regularly won the Stanley Cup.

More ludicrous is the fact that the Canadiens are even penalized for their success in post-season play. The Conn Smythe Trophy, for most valuable player in the playoffs, has gone to a player on the losing team only three times since its inception in 1965. In each case the winning team was the Montreal Canadiens. The three years were 1966 (Roger Crozier, Detroit), 1968 (Glenn Hall, St. Louis), and 1976 (Reggie Leach, Philadelphia). Montreal won those final series 4-2, 4-0, 4-0 or an aggregate 12-2, yet the so-called experts could find no Montreal player deserving of the award.

To return to John Walcot, Lord Mayor of London in 1402, the Canadiens of the 1960s may have raised few expectations as individuals. As a team, however, they did not disappoint.

10

Guy Lafleur
The Lion in Flight

It is a typical early spring day in the working-class Montreal suburb of Verdun—grey, blustery and chilly enough to raise serious doubts about the impending arrival of warm weather. The only indication that winter's grip has been broken has nothing to do with temperature: it is 7 p.m. on this dreary Thursday in April, 1971, and it is still daylight. Panchromatic daylight perhaps, but daylight nonetheless, and the celebration of the relaxing of winter's grip is evident. Everywhere in the streets of Verdun, cars and buses must inch daintily around the hundreds of ball hockey games that infest the streets with ruddy-faced kids between the ages of five and fifteen. It may be only a windy 40 degrees Fahrenheit, but most of the players are in the uniform of the day: running shoes, battered jeans, hockey shirts. Their equipment runs the gamut from gleaming new fibreglass-wrapped hockey sticks to those on which the blade has been worn to a mere inch-wide sliver. Everywhere, soggy tennis balls are whizzing at the goal. Everywhere, too, bunches of kids do something the professionals could never master —they play with 100 percent effort for hours on end, and keep a simultaneous play-by-play going in the best traditions of René Lecavalier and Danny Gallivan. "He shoots, he scores!" warbles a red-haired ten year old in a battered Black Hawks sweater, as he picks the top corner. The goalie's reply is muffled, but you don't have to be near to know what he has just said. It is a truism of the streets that the first kids on the block to swear fluently are the goalies.

Shortly after 7 p.m., almost miraculously, the streets clear. On most nights, the games would have at least another thirty minutes to go, but not tonight. Moments later, troops of future stars, wearing ski jackets (a concession to Mom) and clutching a valuable dollar in their hands, emerge from the three-storey row houses and head for Church and LaSalle. There stands the Verdun Auditorium, a brown brick barn where the Verdun Maple Leafs of the Quebec junior league play. Tonight the Maple Leafs will face the storied Quebec Remparts in a playoff encounter. Tonight the local heroes will face off against some very well-known eighteen and nineteen year olds with names like Jacques Richard, André Savard and Guy Lafleur. The single greenback will take care of the 75 cents admission and a soft drink or bag of chips between periods.

The Montreal Canadiens and their wonderful new goaltender, a rangy scholastic type, have the night off in their playoff series with the powerful Boston Bruins. This is the only game in town.

Inside, a curiously mixed crowd of more than 5,000 people has packed the Auditorium to the rafters. The Maple Leaf regulars, Verdun residents and the kids are there and on this night they have been joined by hundreds of more well-heeled Montreal sports fans. National Hockey League scouts are everywhere in the joint and the noise and heat are almost unbearable. The visiting Remparts in their dark red and black are the first team to emerge and skate around leisurely, with the easy grace and confidence possessed by only the very best teams. The message seems to be: "We'll beat you here, we'll beat you anywhere you want to play."

In the middle of a group of four skaters lazily circling the defensive zone in the south end of the building,

Number 4 chats easily and moves effortlessly. Wearing the dark red uniform with the crenellated "R" on the crest, a tiny black helmet perched high on his head and long sweeping sideburns, Lafleur looks more like a bell-hop than a hockey player. Yet this is the player who has filled the Auditorium, an unparalleled scoring machine with 103 goals last year and an incredible 130 goals, 79 assists for 209 points this season. These feats are unheard of even in the frenetic world of junior hockey. His 135 minutes in penalties attest to the less-than-legal attempts of some teams in the Quebec Major Junior A Hockey League to stop him at all costs.

"Il a compté cent buts deux fois? Pas possible!" ("He scored 100 goals twice? Not possible!") Every eye in the joint is on him.

The microscopic examination ends when a blast of sound introduces the Maple Leafs and they skate out in their home whites with blue trim. All night long we will hear "Hey, Hey, Hey, Goodbye". Unlike the 1980s, when the derisive "Goodbye" will dismiss losing teams in the late stages of hockey games, here the accent is on the "Hey, Hey, Hey" and the hit parade favourite blares away *ad nauseam* at every stop in play and during each intermission.

Amid the fanfare, the game gets underway and, again, all eyes focus on the skinny six-footer in red. He patrols his wing easily, almost perfunctorily, and ten minutes into the period a man sitting to our right turns to his neighbour and says: "This is the great player that Sam Pollock is going to draft number one? You gotta be kidding!"

There is a wonderful Québécois expression that imbues high skepticism with an air of juridical finality. *"Il y a rien là!"* ("There's nothing there!")

His companion, a seasoned hockey observer, remains impassive. "What's the problem?"

"He's out for an afternoon skate. He hasn't done a damn thing and he certainly doesn't look interested. He scored all of those goals because this league thinks defence is a dirty word!"

The cooler head prevails. "Not moving, eh? Like Frank Mahovlich doesn't move. Who's checking him?"

"Normand Cournoyer." The *frère de l'autre* as they say locally. The Canadiens' Yvan is known as the Roadrunner; his kid brother with Verdun is a carbon copy and very quick on his skates.

"Watch Cournoyer and tell me if Lafleur is goofing off," he adds.

Two shifts later, the point has been made. Lafleur may not appear to be moving, but Cournoyer, who must check him, is constantly at top speed, his short but powerful legs churning like pistons. With all that he can barely keep up. When you look closely you notice that Lafleur has something Bobby Orr has, the ability to accelerate so quickly and effortlessly, and to move to either side at top speed without losing a step, that he forces the opposition to back off. No matter how good they are on their skates, most professionals are just like the kids who play shinny on a pond; they favour one leg and one side, and when they move to their weak side, they usually are doing it at a slower speed. Orr, Lafleur and few others can go both ways at top speed. As a result, for them the rink is much bigger.

Late in the first period, Lafleur casually picks up a loose puck along the right wing boards near the centre redline and skates into Verdun territory. A defenceman is backpedalling furiously to cut off the angle; Cournoyer got caught on a line change and is motoring hard to catch up. Five feet inside the blueline he takes a short wind-up and shoots on goal. The puck has hit the twine and rebounded six feet in front of the crease before the startled goalie can even react.

It takes even longer for the crowd to react; they seem stunned by the suddenness of it all. Then there is a collective "oh", a quick exhalation, and everyone seems to be talking at once. Nobody is really cheering or booing— 5,000 hockey fans seem to be analyzing the goal.

"Not bad, eh?" smiles the cooler head. "That one would have beaten most pros I've seen."

When the emotional contest is over, an inexorable 5-4 win for the Remparts, Lafleur has scored three times

Toe Blake, David Molson and Sam Pollock celebrate a Rite of Spring in Montreal; another Stanley Cup parade.

J. McKENNA.   C. HART.   P LÉPINE.   G. RIVERS.   A. LEDUC.   W. LAROCHELLE.   A. MONDOU.   N. WASNIE.   A. JOL

1930-31 Montreal Canadiens Team Picture: Aurele Joliat appears ninth from the left, Howie Morenz appears tw to the right of him and Owner Leo Dandurand appears at the far right of the photograph.

Coach Dick Irvin expresses his feelings and a beaming Frank Selke looks on as Jean Beliveau signs his first National Hockey League contract in October, 1953, after two years of wooing by the Canadiens. How did Selke pull it off? "It's simple. I just opened the Forum vault and said 'help yourself, Jean'."

Stalwarts of the Sixties: John Ferguson (top), Yvan Cournoyer, goalie Charlie Hodge and Claude Provost (after a 1964 playoff victory) didn't get an advertising contract for this picture. But they won the game. . . .

RTH.   H. MORENZ.   J. GAGNON.   M. BURKE.   S. MANTHA.   G. MANTHA.   A. LESIEUR.   E. DUFOUR.   L. DANDURAND.

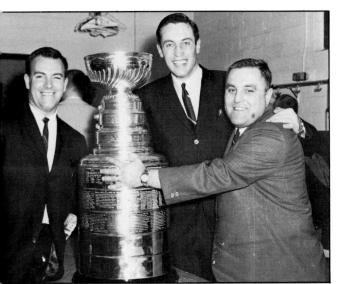

Scotty Bowman, then coach of the St. Louis Blues, captain Jean Beliveau, and Montreal coach Claude Ruel pose after Montreal won the 1969 Stanley Cup in St. Louis. It was Montreal's sixteenth. Three years later, Bowman was head coach of the Canadiens.

The Forum, circa 1966. The hockey rine was looking seedy before a major renovation was undertaken in 1968.

Maurice Richard scores on Sugar Jim Henry in the 1953 playoffs. The Canadiens won the Stanley Cup that year.

Jean Beliveau slides the puck past Gilles Gilbert of Minnesota as Frank Mahovlich looks on. The date: February 11, 1971. The time: 6:42 of the second period. The occasion: Beliveau's third goal in a 5-3 win and the five hundredth of his illustrious career.

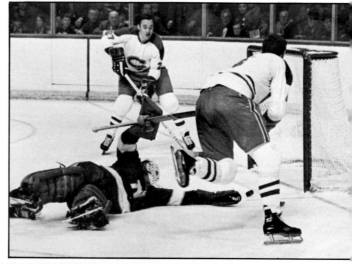

Guy Lafleur score a playoff goal against Philadelphia in 1976.

The generations meet: Jean Beliveau, Guy Lafleur, and Maurice Richard.

DENIS BRODEUR

Ken Dryden. Stops like this one put the lawyer/goaltender in the N.H.L. Hall of Fame before he was 35.

Lise Lafleur, son Martin, and "stepmother" Mrs. Eva Baribeau look on as Guy Lafleur acknowledges the cheers of the Forum Faithful, February 16, 1985, during his official retirement night.

Mats Naslund, 5, always knew he would be a Montreal Canadien. This photo was taken in March, 1967, or about 20 years and 2 months before the Little Viking celebrated his first Stanley Cup with the real Canadiens.

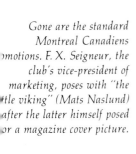

Gone are the standard Montreal Canadiens promotions. F. X. Seigneur, the club's vice-president of marketing, poses with "the little viking" (Mats Naslund) after the latter himself posed for a magazine cover picture.

BOB FISHER

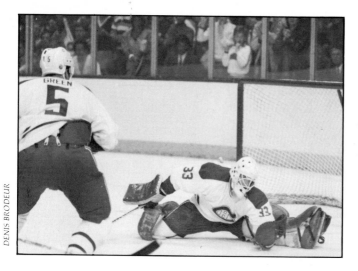

Patrick Roy extends himself in playoff action as Rick Green comes to the rescue. Roy, a rookie, was awarded the Conn Smythe Trophy as top performer of the 1986 Stanley Cup playoffs.

Claude Lemieux eliminates the Hartford Whalers with a backhand high over Mike Liut's left shoulder at 5:55 of overtime, Game Seven. Lemieux scored four game winners in the 1985 playoffs, two in overtime.

Beach party at 30,000 feet. Claude Lemieux, Gaston Gingras and Serge Boisvert (with a rose behind his ear) celebrate the Stanley Cup Championship high above Canada on the flight home.

with almost surgical precision. Scouts from 13 of the 14 NHL teams leave the rink shaking their heads. The members of the Montreal brain trust can be seen smiling as they shrug into their overcoats and head for the exits in animated discussion.

The Verdun kids, their heartbreak behind them, return to their ball hockey the next day. And on a breakaway, more than one announces: "Here's Guy Lafleur going in on goal . . ." before the top corner is picked. They will be joined by kids from coast-to-coast in the coming years.

*   *   *

Guy Damien Lafleur, nineteen, of Thurso, Quebec, is not much older than many of the kids who will grow to idolize him during the next decade. But the age difference is deceptive. In many ways, Lafleur has been a professional hockey player since he was fourteen and that brings with it a certain maturity that goes far beyond his years. In other ways it produces a curious blend of sophistication and naïveté, as if some lessons were left out.

"When it came time to leave home for the first time, I don't know if I was ready," Lafleur smiles, remembering what it was like to be fourteen and preparing to leave the universe that was Thurso, a town in western Quebec closer to Ottawa than Montreal. Until then, the story is the familiar one: smalltown boy from rural Quebec grows up as an altar boy and terrific athlete and gets into all sorts of mischief whenever he can. A sort of francophone Huck Finn.

"There was nothing very special about being a kid," Lafleur recalls. "Like all the kids my age, I hung around with the gang from the neighbourhood and my cousins. Maybe I was a little wilder than some because I was the only boy in a family with four sisters, so I had all the trouble I could handle. My dad came from a large family, seven children, and most Sundays all of us would end up at my grandmother's for dinner. We were almost fifty people. The parents would be inside talking and a lot of us kids would be outside playing sports, cowboys, cops and robbers, you name it. And we could get into our share of trouble, hunting small birds and animals or even each other with our slingshots, and later BB guns."

Guy's biggest scare came when he threw a rock that broke the windshield of a police cruiser passing by. "The policeman was a friend of my dad and I was so scared I ran home and hid behind the fridge," he said.

Hockey started with his first pair of skates at age five. Rejean Lafleur, a welder by trade, built a rink behind the house every winter and welded some pipes into the framework of goals. Potato sacking replaced netting but the twenty or so kids who would play pick-up hockey every day until well beyond last light didn't care. "Nobody had specific positions but one thing was true ... I never once played goalie—you had to be crazy to do that."

Guy Lafleur was one of the crowd and quite unaware of his worth as a hockey player because the pick-up games featured boys of all ages. "All I know is that by the time I was seven or so, I was taking hockey more seriously than some of my friends. I was so bad that I used to sleep in my equipment so I could be ready to play the next morning. Quite often my dad would find me in bed fast asleep with everything on except my helmet and he'd undress me without waking me up.

"On weekdays, we'd start playing at seven in the morning and then we'd play the other classes at lunchtime. After school, we'd play against other teams in the area. It was hockey, hockey, hockey and we loved it."

As Guy got older, he spent more and more time practising with the teaching brothers at l'Ecole Ste. Famille. "I'll never forget my math teacher. He used to tell us that Paul Anka [from nearby Ottawa] had made a lot of sacrifices to make the big time and that if we wanted to be athletes, we would have to make the sacrifices, even at our young ages."

Those words struck home with Lafleur and he went into "serious training" when he was nine. That consisted of slopping out the pigsties at a friend's farm, and helping at milking time with thirty-five dairy cows. Perpetually jammed in high gear, Lafleur also made first contact with his passion for motor vehicles there. "I was nuts about driving their truck and tractor." To build up his legs and stamina, he also started running cross-country after finishing his work, quite often for ten miles or so. "A lot of the kids at school thought I was crazy."

All of Lafleur's ice time was spent outdoors, until school carnival, when he and his teammates played in the local arena for the first time. Afterwards, they couldn't keep him out of arenas. The Singer sewing machine company, Thurso's major employer, had built the indoor facility and later sold it to the town for a nominal one dollar. It was a ramshackle affair. "The boards were pretty far apart in some places and you could see sunlight right through them." But it was hockey heaven to the rising young star and very early each morning, he would sneak into the arena through a hole in the boards and skate leisurely by himself.

All of his ice time and off-ice training began to pay off. "I was nine when I began to break out in hockey," he recalls. "Our team went to the peewee tournament in Quebec City three times, in 1962, '63 and '64, and I won the scoring championship the first year. I'll never forget because Red Storey gave me the trophy. I had my name in the local paper a couple of times, too."

The young player's fame spread further than that. Paul Dumont, one of the top amateur hockey people in Quebec City was so impressed by Lafleur's play at the Quebec tournament that he phoned Rejean Lafleur and asked if his son could move to the provincial capital to play midget or Junior B hockey. Guy was twelve, going on thirteen that summer.

"My dad came up to me and asked me if I wanted to go and I said yes. I kept bothering my dad to go, even if I was twelve, but I didn't know what I was getting into at that age. He thought about it for a long time and then said no. I was too young. A year later, Mr. Dumont called again. This time my dad said okay."

As was the case with many young athletes approaching puberty in rural Quebec, another road beckoned. Guy had been an altar boy for about five years and "it must have seemed that I liked it a lot because the priests decided I should become one of them. The old priest came over to my house and wanted to be sure that my decision to play hockey was the right decision. Did going away to play hockey mean that I had decided against the priesthood?" With all of these weighty matters roiling around inside him, a very young, green kid took the fated bus ride to Quebec City to play for the Canadian Tire and Repair Junior B team.

"It was tough for a fourteen year old kid. I cried, every night it seemed, and several times I called my dad and said I wanted to come home. But my dad wasn't having any of it. He told me: 'You cried for a year to go there, you are going to stick it out. You're not coming back.' Now that I have two sons, I think of how it must have really hurt him to say those things; after all, I was his only son and no father wants to tell his son he can't come home. But he was strong for me."

Strong and supportive. Rejean Lafleur often would drive to Quebec twice a week—a notoriously treacherous drive—to watch Guy play, and hop right back in the car to drive more than two hundred miles straight home to make it just in time for work the next morning.

Guy's eldest son, Martin, is ten. Could he picture him in similar circumstances, leaving home to play hockey more than two hundred miles away, just four years from now? Could he adapt to the role of the anxious father?

"Not in a million years," Lafleur replies nervously.

"I really don't know how my father had the strength to let me go. As a father now, I know it would be more difficult on me than my son. Besides, the situation is quite different these days. Not too many fourteen year olds go away to play hockey any more. They usually find a place near home. Yet, if he had the talent and the desire to make it, I would have a hard time stopping him. But if he doesn't have the talent, I would have to tell him. I would never want my son to become a junior hockey bum, giving away five or six years of his life to hockey when there is no real future in it for him."

In his second year in Quebec City, Guy had made a few friends in school and on the hockey team and life away from home became more enjoyable. By his third year, all of his friends were in Quebec City and Thurso was somewhere he went after the hockey season ended. "By then I was fine. I didn't want to go back home."

The team policy of billeting out-of-town players with families also helped Guy to adjust. When Jean Beliveau had moved to Quebec from Victoriaville, he stayed with the three McKenna sisters. Guy stayed with the Baribeau family at 238 Boulevard Benoit XV in Limoilou, a stone's throw from the Colisée. For six years, Mrs. Eva Baribeau was his surrogate mother. When Lafleur officially retired, February 16, 1985, at the Forum, Mrs. Baribeau was part of the Lafleur family group at centre ice.

"Mrs. Baribeau is a wonderful lady and she became a second mother to me," he recalls. "This stable home life was important to me because it meant that I belonged, I was not a complete stranger in Quebec. But even with that, it wasn't easy. School was hard because we travelled a lot; I missed a lot of school because I was on the road." Lafleur was enrolled in Jean Brebeuf high school but each year, when hockey was over, would return to Thurso and finish the school year at Ecole Secondaire St. Michel in nearby Buckingham, Quebec.

Lafleur lived the standard junior hockey player's life in those days. Education was of secondary importance and some junior hockey operators, while paying lip service to the benefits of good schooling for their players, found that schooling disrupted the team and subtly encouraged players to quit.

All of that changed within a year or two of Lafleur's graduation from junior hockey. The right winger found himself surrounded by college-trained hockey players like Rod Langway, Brian Engblom, Craig Ludwig, Ken Dryden and Chris Nilan on the Montreal Canadiens.

"I can't say I'm all that disappointed that I didn't get a better education because it wasn't available back then. Had it been available, I don't know what I would have done; I probably would have gone the same route as I did. However, if I was about sixteen or seventeen today and getting serious about a hockey career, I would probably go the other way. I know I would strongly advise young guys today to do anything they can to get scholarships or find a way to marry the two, because education is very important. The numbers game is against you when you are moving up through hockey; only a very small group of players ever make it. If you can do both, you won't have lost X number of years and have to start all over again at twenty-one or twenty-two."

Lafleur played ten games of Junior A his first year with the Quebec Aces and scored two goals and seven assists. "Mr. Dumont did not want me to move up too quickly; I was much younger than the other guys and I weighed only 133 pounds at the time." Lafleur moved up the following year and would play three years for the Aces and another two for the Remparts following a name change for the team.

At sixteen, he was labelled "can't miss" by the NHL scouts. Three years later (players weren't drafted until they were twenty in those days) the tag had changed to "franchise player". Guy Lafleur was going to be something very special in professional ice hockey.

Canadiens' scouts were particularly interested in the player who wore Number 4 with the Remparts, in honour of his idol, Jean Beliveau. At the time, a banner crop of French Canadian talent was emerging. Players like Rejean Houle, Mark Tardif and Gilbert Perreault with the Junior Canadiens and Marcel Dionne of the St. Catharines Black Hawks of the OHA league were regularly making headlines. In 1969-70, Drummondville's Dionne scored 55 goals and added 77 assists for 132 points—league records in all three categories—in a 54-game season. Victoriaville's Perreault was just behind with 51-70-121 in a league which was recognized as Canada's best at the time. Lafleur's totals that season were an astounding 103-67-170 in 56 games (and 25-18-43 in 15 playoff games!). Many hockey observers discounted that performance, however, claiming that the QMJHL was weak in comparison with the OHA. That argument would retain some validity for only one more season, and then Lafleur would shatter it once and for all.

The question was: where would Montreal go? Would the Canadiens go after Perreault, an extremely popular player, superb playmaker and hard worker? Would they opt for Dionne, offensive machine with terrific puck sense? Or would it be the "quiet machine" Lafleur in the Quebec league?

"In a sense, the decision was out of our hands the moment the National Hockey League decided to expand by two more teams," Sam Pollock says. "Perreault was born in 1950, a year before the other two, so he was going to go in the 1970 draft. The first two positions in the draft would be decided by a coin toss between the two new teams, Buffalo Sabres and Vancouver Canucks, and the best two players in the country, Gilbert Perreault and Dale Tallon with the Toronto Marlboros, were going to go 1-2. There was no question of trying to make a deal with Punch Imlach for the number one spot after he won the toss."

Punch knew his hockey players, especially since he had coached Jean Beliveau in Quebec in the early 1950s. Imlach was one of the few English Canadian hockey men who was comfortable with Quebec and Quebec-born hockey players. He built himself some powerhouses with the Maple Leafs and would have liked to take advantage of his contacts in the French-speaking province but was stymied by his boss, Stafford Smythe. "French Canadians do not represent Toronto or the Maple Leafs," Imlach was told virtually every time he broached the subject.

Now, however, Imlach was his own boss and he knew which of the two, Perreault and Tallon, would pan out. He chose Perreault and the quiet, unassuming superstar was Mr. Buffalo Sabre for his entire career. Tallon, a superb junior hockey player and junior golfer, was an above-average player with Vancouver, Chicago and Pittsburgh but never attained superstar status.

Montreal was shut out of the Perreault derby by expansion, but Trader Sam's machinations were still in evidence: the Canadiens drafted fifth and sixth and managed to secure goalie Ray Martiniuk from the Flin Flon Bombers and speedy winger Chuck Lefley from the

Canadian National Team in a draft that included such notables as Reg Leach, Darryl Sittler, Dan Maloney, Dan Bouchard and a centre with Ottawa 67s named Bill Clement, from Guy Lafleur's hometown of Thurso. Evidence that Sam Pollock is not infallible comes from the fact that Sittler was drafted number 8 that year.

"That draft made us redouble our efforts to secure Lafleur the following year," Pollock says. "1970 was a very good draft and 1971 looked like it might even be better. Lafleur and Dionne had a lot of company that year—the Junior Canadiens had Perreault's winger Richard Martin, centre Bobby Lalonde and defenceman Jocelyn Guevremont; there were players like Ron Jones, Chuck Arnason, Steve Vickers, Terry O'Reilly, Craig Ramsay, Larry Robinson and Rick Kehoe."

Lafleur's output that year was even more outstanding than in 1970; 130 goals, 79 assists, 209 points in 62 regular-season contests and 22-21-43 in 14 playoffs. In 76 games overall, Lafleur scored 152 goals, precisely two a game, and added exactly 100 assists. Dionne was no slouch either, with 62-81-143 in only 46 OHA season games, also more than 3 points a game.

The "good player, bad league" stigma was erased that spring when the Quebec Remparts met the St. Catharines Black Hawks in the final for the Memorial Cup. Quebec upset the Black Hawks in a riot-marred series and all doubts about the quality of the QMJHL were removed.

This is not to say that the Canadiens were unsure of their choice. "We had known for two years that we wanted Lafleur," Pollock says. "Had we not been able to get him, however, Dionne would have been a nice consolation."

On June 10, 1971, league president Clarence Campbell announced that the NHL draft was now in session and that the first pick was Montreal's. The room disintegrated when Trader Sam acknowledged that it was Montreal's pick then called time out. Three minutes later, with time in again and the room abuzz, Guy Damien Lafleur, nineteen years, nine months and twenty days old, became a Montreal Canadien. Marcel Dionne, who would be doomed to practise his sport in quasi-obscurity for most of his career in faraway California, was selected by the Detroit Red Wings moments later. About an hour later, a tall, gangling redhead named Larry Robinson joined Lafleur on his new team. Lafleur would go to Montreal right away and Robinson would join him two years later. More than any other players, these two would epitomize the Canadiens during the 1970s.

Years later, after having been selected by fans to the all-time Montreal Canadiens team (on defence with Doug Harvey), Robinson smiles and is thankful that he did not have the double pressure of being a Quebec-born hockey player and the number one NHL draft pick. "I was picked twentieth that year, in fact, fourth pick by the Canadiens (Chuck Arnason and Murray Wilson followed Lafleur) and there never was any question of being a member of the big team that fall. I went to training camp just hoping to play well and find a place in the organization."

The farm boy from Winchester, Ontario did just that, finding a place on the Nova Scotia Voyageurs where his crunching bodychecks raised eyebrows all over the league. He would play another half-season before being called up, and sticking with the parent club.

"Guy, on the other hand, was practically handed Jean Beliveau's sweater and told he was the replacement for the most popular Montreal Canadien ever. That kind of pressure would have destroyed a lot of players in any NHL city, let alone Montreal. It would have scared a couple of years growth out of me."

The shy blond with the immense sideburns who showed up at his first professional training camp that September agrees with Robinson. "I was very frightened and the stuff they were writing in the papers didn't help. They had me as some kind of saviour coming to a team that had just won the Stanley Cup and had players like Henri Richard, Yvan Cournoyer, Jean-Claude Tremblay and the Mahovlich brothers." Lafleur's first decision was a wise one; he turned down the offer of Beliveau's Number 4 sweater, opting instead for the Number 10 that Frank Mahovlich had worn for two road games after having been traded to Montreal from Detroit the previous year. "That kind of instant pressure I could do without," Lafleur says.

The quiet hockey player celebrated his twentieth birthday at the Canadiens' training camp, a first draft choice, secure in the knowledge that he would spend the coming year with the Montreal Canadiens. Some fifteen years later, retired from the game and President of the Longueuil Chevaliers of the Quebec Major Junior A Hockey League, he would say that he could not imagine how eighteen year olds could endure such pressure at an even younger age.

When Lafleur was drafted, the Entry Draft selected the best twenty year old players available. Considerable pressure was placed on the NHL by the WHA in the mid-'70s when that league, desperate for quality players, began drafting underage players at age eighteen. These included Wayne Gretzky, originally signed by the Indianapolis Racers and then transferred to the Edmonton Oilers when Nelson Skalbania's financial schemes began to collapse. The biggest dent was made by the Birmingham Bulls, who stocked their team with young players for the 1977-78 and 1978-79 seasons. The Baby Bulls included such current NHL stars as Toronto's Rick Vaive, Edmonton's Mark Napier, Washington's Rod Langway, Montreal's Gaston Gingras, St. Louis's Rob Ramage and Minnesota's Craig Hartsburg.

In 1980, the NHL began drafting eighteen year olds (they had selected occasional underage players in the past such as Bobby Orr in 1968 and Mario Tremblay in 1974). There have been complaints that this advanced age has especially harmed junior hockey in Canada.

"The eighteen year old draft by the NHL teams is a veritable disaster," says Lafleur. "This has hurt the entire system of hockey, but the worst affected are the young players who are drafted. When I was twenty years old, I got pretty homesick that first year in professional hockey. It has to be worse for a lot of these players, they haven't matured yet." The young players are hurt in several ways, he adds.

"A lot of these guys are drafted, go to the NHL team's training camp, and then are sent back to junior for a year or two to mature. But it is almost impossible for these guys to come back down to earth. They come back to their junior team, where guys might make $100 a week, with contracts for $75,000 or $100,000 in their pockets. They lose all motivation and quite often their progress stops dead. And there isn't a junior hockey coach who knows more than this kid's agent. Junior hockey and the team become a pastime for these guys; they are just marking time until they go up to the NHL."

Lafleur has lived the uncertainty of the NHL rookie season. In his case it was doubly hard, because he was the heir apparent to Jean Beliveau, the most beloved hockey player in Quebec, and was going to play in the Forum Fish Bowl.

One Saturday night in February, 1972, many in attendance at the International Peewee Tournament in Quebec City, where he had starred just a decade before, were surprised to see Lafleur in the press room. Nattily attired in a dark blue velvet sports jacket, grey slacks and tie, the rising young hockey star chatted easily with friends like *Le Soleil* columnist Roland Sabourin and other journalists. He paused only to sign autographs for the young hockey players who gathered up their courage to invade the press room.

Earlier that day, the Canadiens had played the Chicago Black Hawks in a rare afternoon game.

"Guy's here all the time," Sabourin said quietly, telling the Quebec media's big secret. Montreal writers who might be seeking the rookie's time and attention for interviews and feature stories would have a hard time finding him at his Longueuil apartment; whenever Montreal was home, Guy went home, to Quebec City, making the 300-mile round-trip at every available opportunity.

"I had been in Quebec City for six years and I would head up there regularly because I knew Quebec and I didn't know Montreal," he recalls.

"When I got to Montreal, just about all the players were married. I think the only bachelor was Pierre Bouchard, for all the obvious reasons," he laughs. "He still is single today and hasn't changed." Lafleur turns serious again and the pain of that first year returns.

"I had all of my friends in Quebec and I would head back there constantly. I really missed it. In Montreal I was lost. Even though Quebec was a pretty big place, it just was not Montreal." All of those sports and entertainment editors with the big Montreal dailies who sought "Rookie captures the Big City" features, with Lafleur flashing his sideburns and flowered shirts to the beautiful ladies in Crescent Street or Rue Saint-Denis discos would be disappointed. Lafleur was not averse to doing the town; it just wasn't the same town that the locals thought.

When there wasn't enough time to get away to Quebec, Lafleur would prowl his Longueuil apartment like a caged lion. Yet this was not a case of a terribly introverted young man hiding out. Rather, Lafleur was the type of person who preferred to scout the terrain first, then make a sortie. After years of headlines and adulation in Quebec, Lafleur had a cocky ingenuousness that was attractive to many. He wanted to be in control of situations, not vice versa.

The Huck Finn of Thurso would surface in the weirdest ways. A combination of his self-imposed incarceration in his apartment and his natural insouciance resulted in a strange introduction to the future Mrs. Lafleur.

Lafleur, perhaps a bit desperate for company, befriended the janitor in his apartment building and the two would often share short conversations. "Why doesn't a good-looking guy like you go out more often?" the janitor ventured, asking the most obvious question in Lafleur's world. "Montreal has some of the best-looking women in the world; downtown is crawling with them." A touch embarrassed at the turn in the badinage, Lafleur made some quick excuses about being on the road with the team a lot and not having the time to meet a lot of women.

"Have I got the answer for you!" replied the janitor. "There's a gorgeous stewardess on the eleventh floor you should meet. She's even from Quebec City." Pushed and prodded, Lafleur found himself in the girl's apartment where she was discovered on her hands and knees, scrubbing her kitchen floor.

After the basic introductions were dispensed with, he endeared himself to her forever by blurting tactlessly: "If you want to go out with me, you'll have to lose about fifty pounds."

Lise Barre was equal to the challenge: "Get out!"

On to Chapter Two of the Hockey Star and the Stewardess. Lafleur's janitor buddy had given him a master key so that he could use the sauna at all hours. One morning at about three a.m. and about three months later, Lafleur returned to her eleventh-floor apartment and let himself in. The coast was clear, she was away on flight duty, the janitor had said.

"I don't know what I had in mind," Lafleur recalls. "Maybe I thought I could find out what she was like by looking around her place. I had not seen her up close since she kicked me out and it seemed like she *was* losing weight." The amateur anthropologist prowled the apartment, checking out the furniture, the record collection and the stereo. He found a bottle of cognac by the sofa, poured himself a drink, turned on the stereo and sat back. He was on his second drink when the lessee walked in at about four a.m.

Mr. Smooth proved how quickly he could react; after all, this is a man whose lightning reflexes would terrorize the opposition for a decade.

"What are you doing back a day early?" he demanded to know.

The future Mrs. Lafleur had seen all the Rock Hudson-Doris Day pictures too.

"Get out," she said, in a touching replay of their previous farewell of three months past. "Or I'll call the police," she added, grateful for the extra line of dialogue. And then to avoid more early morning surprises, she moved out and returned home to Quebec City, breaking her lease and telling management that their building was not big enough to share with that hockey player who lived on the first floor.

"Who does he think he is? Maurice Richard?"

Lafleur used his connections to discover her address in Quebec. He drove there and contritely mumbled something about love at first sight and his overall weirdness. When he returned to Montreal, the girl he would marry a year later was in the car with him.

On the ice, life was just as eventful. Lafleur was not as shy but still was being worked gently into a team that, while rebuilding, had all the elements necessary to re-emerge as champions. That year, the Canadiens finished third in the East Division standings with 108 points, behind Boston's 119 and New York Rangers' 109, a repeat of the previous regular season. The Bruins' Phil Esposito and Bobby Orr finished 1-2 in the scoring race ahead of the Rangers' GAG (goal-a-game) line of Jean Ratelle, Rod Gilbert and Vic Hadfield. The Canadiens were ably represented in the top ten scorers by Frank Mahovlich, Yvan Cournoyer and Jacques Lemaire.

While Lafleur would not have to wait two full years before cracking the regular line-up as had Cournoyer in the mid-60s, he spent most of the season on the third and fourth lines, ending 1971-72 with 29 goals and 35 assists for 64 points, respectable totals. But that was 13 points behind Marcel Dionne of the Red Wings 28-49-77 and 10 points behind Sabres' rookie Rick Martin, with 44-30-74, and some grumblings were being heard in the reds.

Lafleur did not win the Calder Trophy as best rookie for 1971-72, but neither did Dionne or Martin. Canadiens fans were mollified when it was announced that Ken Dryden was the top newcomer, and especially gratified considering the fact that it was the rangy goaltender's second major award, following the Conn Smythe trophy he had won as best player of the previous year's Stanley Cup playoffs. They were not so happy when the New York Rangers bumped off the Canadiens in the playoffs, before losing to the Bruins in the final.

Montreal recaptured first place in the East Division the

next year, finishing 13 points ahead of Boston on the strength of 52 wins, 10 losses and 16 ties and went on to win the Stanley Cup by beating Chicago in the final. Despite the championship, more grumblings were heard about the number 1 draft as Lafleur's production dropped marginally to 28 goals, 27 assists for 55 points in 69 games. The right winger added 3 goals and 5 assists in 17 playoff games but the natives were restless . . . Dionne had turned in 40 goals and 50 assists and Martin scored another 44 goals.

A year later it was even worse. Rick Martin reached the 50-goal plateau, finishing sixth in the league scoring race with 52 goals and 34 assists for 86 points. Dionne was just behind with 78 points and young stars like Bobby Clarke and Darryl Sittler were emerging in Philadelphia and Toronto. For the first time in four years, the Canadiens had no players in the top ten scorers and were eliminated by the New York Rangers in the playoffs. Lafleur slipped to 21 goals and 35 assists for 56 points, a full 30 points behind Martin, a statistic thrown up time and time again by the cognoscenti on the hotlines. Worse than that, all he could produce in the six-game quarterfinal loss to the Rangers was a single, measly assist.

The consensus was the Canadiens had blown it. Sam Pollock was fallible. Imagine what a pure shooter like Martin would have done in his hometown, they speculated, conveniently forgetting that Martin was doing so well because his centre from the Junior Canadiens days, Gilbert Perreault, was playing with him. Would it not be great to have such a playmaker as Dionne on the Canadiens, they wondered aloud, forgetting, too, how easy it was to concentrate on individual stats when a team was going nowhere.

If anything positive could be said about the playoff loss to the Rangers, it was that another rookie, Steve Shutt, who had scored all of 15 goals and 20 assists in 70 regular-season games, had come alive during the playoffs with 5 goals and 3 assists in 6 games.

Claude Ruel, who had briefly coached the Canadiens

after Toe Blake's retirement, and would do so again after Bernie Geoffrion's resignation, was the man who worked with the young players.

"We selected Guy Lafleur number one because he was the best player available in the draft in 1971," he says. "We knew that Dionne was a very good hockey player; and certainly so was Martin—we did not have to go very far to see that, he played in our own building. But Lafleur was the best of the three and the only question was when he would begin to show it in the NHL. It was a question of confidence, for sure; somebody with his speed and shot, who scored all of those goals in junior, does not suddenly lose that ability. Especially not when he's twenty-two or twenty-three years old. It was a matter of time and when he would start putting them in."

Another factor that hampered Lafleur's development was that he played out of position for long periods of time during those first three seasons. The Canadiens had a rich harvest of wingers—Yvan Cournoyer, Claude Larose, Reggie Houle (although he was a left-hand shot), Phil Roberto, Chuck Arnason and Jim Roberts on the right side and Marc Tardif, Frank Mahovlich, Chuck Lefley, Houle, and three rookies—Murray Wilson, Steve Shutt and Yvon Lambert on the left.

With the retirement of Jean Beliveau and the trade of Ralph Backstrom to Los Angeles to set up the Lafleur draft, the Montreal team considered itself shorthanded at centre. "Considered itself" is the operative phrase; Jacques Lemaire and Pete Mahovlich would settle into those positions and carry the team through the rest of the decade. However, when Lafleur joined the Canadiens, the team noted his skating ability, size and speed, and pencilled him into the line-up as a centre.

"A lot of people look at Guy Lafleur's first three years and forget that," Ruel says. "He was playing out of position, and not complaining. Centre demands a lot more than the wing and it is quite a change for a player coming off the wing. Going from centre to wing is much easier. One good thing that came out of it was the fact that Guy really improved his passing game during those three years and that would really help him during his big scoring years later on. He was a great scorer, that was obvious to everyone. But he was also the best passing winger in the league when he was at the top." Not too many wingers have ever chalked up 80 assists in a season, as Lafleur did in 1976-77.

After three years of unfair comparisons with players who had been able to step into the lineups of their new teams and play thirty minutes or more a game without pressure, was the Flower ready to bloom?

That question was answered in Lafleur's fourth season. Several events conspired to help Lafleur break out. The WHA had lured away Rejean Houle and Marc Tardif the previous season and Frank Mahovlich left to join the Toronto Toros after the 1973-74 season ended. Veteran defenceman Jacques Laperriere retired, Chuck Lefley was traded and suddenly the Canadiens included names like Van Boxmeer, Risebrough, Tremblay and Chartraw. Lafleur was a veteran and, in the tradition of the Canadiens, was expected to lead rather than follow.

In training camp that fall, off came the helmet and *le Démon Blond* was born. Lafleur was teamed with veteran Pete Mahovlich and Shutt, the chubby Toronto sniper who had shown a very nice touch around the net in the previous playoff round, and all three took off.

Maurice Richard and Bernie Geoffrion had been the first two National Hockey League players to score 50 goals in a season. That they were francophones and Canadiens was a source of immense pride for Montreal fans.

Since then, it seemed, 50-goal scorers belonged to everyone else. Montreal might win Stanley Cups but other teams had the glamour boys who filled the nets, players like Bobby Hull, Phil Esposito and Johnny Bucyk. That rankled in a city where the fans award points for artistic and technical merit. At the Forum, the home team not only had to win, it had to win with style.

When players with names like Vic Hadfield (a journeyman to Montreal fans) and Mickey Redmond—a player traded away by the Canadiens to obtain Frank Mahovlich —began to reach the sacred plateau, Montreal fans could not hide their frustration. Before Boom Boom beat Toronto's Cesare Maniago on the last weekend in the season in 1960-61, Jean Beliveau had flirted with immortality with 47 and 45 goals in 1955-56 and 1958-59. Yvan Cournoyer titillated them in 1968-69 with 43, and came even closer in 1972-73 with 47, while his linemate Jacques Lemaire chipped in 44 the same year. Frank Mahovlich, who would get as close to the magic mark as 48 goals with Toronto Maple Leafs and 49 with Detroit Red Wings, would net 43 in 1971-72.

But that was as close as it got. The Flying Frenchmen were not reaching the heights of goal scoring. Even worse, the last time a Canadien had won the league scoring title was way back in Geoffrion's 50-goal season, 1960-61, when he and Beliveau finished 1-2 with 95 and 90 points respectively. Since then, the scoring title was a consolation prize for the perennial also-rans, the Chicago Black Hawks (Bobby Hull twice, Stan Mikita four times) and the Boston Bruins (Phil Esposito five times, Bobby Orr twice) with Gordie Howe capturing the other title in that fourteen-year period.

That all changed on March 29, 1975. Denis Herron wore the blue, red and gold of the Kansas City Scouts and his white fibreglass goalie's mask was painted with warstripes. A ferocious countenance perhaps, but not enough to deter Guy Damien Lafleur. Despite missing ten games because of a fractured thumb, broken by a vicious slash in a game against the fledgling Washington Capitals, Lafleur went into Montreal's 76th game with 49 goals. Early in the game he teamed up with Mahovlich to score Number 50 and the Forum went crazy.

Poor Denis Herron would become Lafleur's personal property after that, giving up the Flower's 50th goal in 1977, again with the Scouts, and also in 1979, after moving to Pittsburgh Penguins. Shortly thereafter, the Chambly, Quebec native caught a break; he was traded to Montreal, where he could watch as Richard Sevigny gave up the 50th goals of the season to St. Louis's Wayne

Babych and Quebec's Jacques Richard. Upon leaving Montreal for Pittsburgh in 1982, Herron's semi-centennial bad luck would return and he would be the victim of Michel Goulet's and Tim Kerr's 50th goals in 1984 and Wayne Gretzky's in 1985.

The renewed Lafleur, playing ten fewer games than the rest of the competition, finished fourth in the NHL scoring list in 1974-75, with 53 goals and 66 assists for 119 points, behind Bobby Orr, Phil Esposito and Marcel Dionne. Mahovlich was fifth, two points behind Lafleur, and Montreal finished the season in a three-way tie with Philadelphia and Buffalo for overall first place with 113 points. More importantly in the eyes of Montreal fans, Lafleur was 24 points ahead of Martin. The latter would get some measure of revenge when the Buffalo Sabres edged out the Canadiens in the playoffs that year.

That would be the last playoff disappointment of the decade. For the next three years, Lafleur owned the league and Montreal was on the way to four straight Stanley Cups. The young man who had imposed a rigid self-exile to his Longueuil apartment just three years before would begin to fully understand what life in the Forum Fish Bowl was really all about.

In the first years of their marriage, the Lafleurs set up housekeeping in Vercheres, a francophone community on the South Shore of the St. Lawrence across from Montreal. It was a nice neighbourhood, but "too nice", recalls Lafleur. "There were too many 'fans' in the area and we were looking for peace and quiet." One thing they weren't looking for was danger, for themselves or baby Martin, born in 1975.

During the quarterfinals of the 1976 playoffs, knowledgeable observers noted that Lafleur was skittish and seemed even more frenetic than usual on the ice, passing when he should shoot, shooting when he should pass. Management knew what was behind the erratic behaviour but was not talking. Halfway through the playoffs, the Flower seemed to blossom anew and Montreal ended the two-year reign of the defending champion Flyers in four straight to win the Cup, Lafleur wrapping up the post-season tournament with 7 goals and 10 assists in 13 games, including the winning goal in the 5-3 clincher over the Broad Street Bullies on May 16.

Ten days later, the real story surfaced. Montreal police, investigating a spectacular $2.8 million Brink's robbery that had taken place in March, received a tip from an informant that Lafleur would be kidnapped and held for a very large ransom during the playoffs. This was reported to Sam Pollock, and the managing director immediately hired private security guards to accompany his star everywhere he went, at home and on the road. At home, Lafleur was under close police surveillance for three weeks until the same informant contacted the Brink's investigators.

"It's okay, the heat's off," he told the police. "The guys who were going to pull this off were picked up on something else and they won't be going anywhere for a long time."

Jean Beliveau handled the affair for the club and was in constant contact with the police. "I had to devote almost all of my time to the affair. Guy's home was under constant surveillance and he was always under guard." Beliveau knew what it was like to be a target. He hadn't forgotten the night that burglars had cleaned out his Longueuil home while he was playing a televised game at the Forum.

What really hurt Lafleur was that his erratic performances in the first two series against Chicago Black Hawks and New York Islanders had led to a lot of booing from the home fans.

Lise Lafleur was quick to rise to the defence of her husband. "If they only knew what he was going through, they would have been less unjust toward him. It is unbelievable how these events tortured him; he lost about a dozen pounds in three weeks." For the Lafleurs, the ordeal lasted the full three weeks. During the first, Mrs. Lafleur and her infant son moved into the Bonaventure Hotel, where the team was staying during the playoffs. A week later, she returned to her parents' home in Quebec City.

Such is the size of the Canadiens' entourage that few of his teammates suspected that anything untoward was happening, even with extra private security guards around the team.

"It was quite common for the team to hire people to ensure that we had a quiet time during the playoffs," says Pete Mahovlich. "Most of us just assumed that these guys were there for the whole team. Guy never mentioned a thing to us at all about the kidnapping threat."

That was virtually the only secret in the superstar's life in the late 1970s.

The young man who spent much of his first season escaping down Highway 40 to Quebec City at every opportunity became Montreal's latest matinee idol. Lafleur's sharp-chiselled features adorned the covers of sports, gossip, fashion and news weeklies and monthlies as he moved into the fast lane lifestyle of the national superstar. He flew to exotic Monaco to film commercials for General Motors' Monte Carlo sedans ... but drove a Ferrari in real life. The young man who had once sequestered himself in his Longueuil apartment now owned Crescent Street and had a regular table at trendy places like Thursday's and the Auberge Saint-Tropez— pronounced the "Sane-Tro" by Montreal's In Crowd. Lafleur's new business agent, Jerry Petrie, entertained offers from all sectors, accepting some, turning down many, many more.

Lafleur may not have been more popular than Maurice Richard or Jean Beliveau in their day, and like them he had to share the glory of the Canadiens with a raft of superstars like Shutt, Dryden, Lemaire and the Big Three. But his timing was the best. This was the television age, the era of McLuhan's Global Village, and more people were able to witness, and appreciate, his wizardry on the ice. Just as important, French Quebec was exploding politically, socially and economically, with a proud new Parti Québécois government in office in Quebec City. People such as racing's Gilles Villeneuve, singers Robert Charlebois and Diane Dufresne, financier Paul Desmarais and Lafleur himself were symbols of the new vibrancy. A new pantheon of native idols had emerged, to be worshipped avidly by most Québécois.

Style took on a new importance as Quebec looked at itself in the collective mirror with new eyes, and liked what it saw. Guy Lafleur was part of Quebec's emerging élan. He had moved to centre stage when he shucked his helmet and began scoring goals with panache, his blond hair trailing behind him like the tail of Halley's Comet.

Others were filling the net in the NHL: Phil Esposito, Rick Martin, Reggie Leach, Jean Pronovost, Danny Grant, Marcel Dionne and Pierre Larouche. Only Larouche could match Lafleur for style and he laboured in near anonymity in Pittsburgh. As far as Montreal was concerned, the others were plodders, possessors of big shots, cannons which simply blasted the rubber into the net. Lafleur was *un artiste*, a magician who could lift 18,000 people from their seats with his end-to-end rushes. At home, Lafleur's linemate Steve Shutt increased his scoring in increments of 15, with consecutive years of 15, 30, 45 and 60 goals, but was never considered a threat to Lafleur's deity. A very smart man who often hid his intellect behind a ready smile and constant kidding, Shutt took the pressure off the fans by describing himself as a "garbageman"—someone who "just hangs around and picks up the leftovers of Lafleur, Lemaire or Mahovlich."

Conversely, while the Québécois love-in was in full swing, Lafleur quietly moved to an English West Island suburb called Baie d'Urfe. He would not discuss politics in public but quietly let the PQ and others know that he was not enamoured of their policies. He was once (a rare occasion) quoted on the subject in an English Canadian magazine:

> I try to understand the Parti Québécois, but so far it's not very good. I live in an English suburb of Montreal, I want my son to go to English school. I want him to learn English. I had to, to play hockey in Montreal. Some of my best friends are English. On the team we get about half and half. It's a family, we work together and for each other. I'm not taking a public political question, but I've got my own idea

about the way it goes. And I would say that I am an anti-separatist.

That comment helps to explain why, when Lafleur became involved in a noisy contract squabble in 1982, Premier René Levesque, who made notably less money, was quick to criticize the superstar. The fact that the PQ honeymoon was over and that one of Lafleur's reasons for his threatened holdout was Quebec's onerous tax system, (attributed by many to PQ financial ineptitude) seemed secondary.

By then, Guy Lafleur could practically do or say anything at all with impunity in Montreal. The French Canadian Huck Finn had emerged and was thriving in the fantasyland of the Montreal Canadiens. All the glitzy new magazines that had sprung up clamoured excitedly for his every word. "What does Mr. Lafleur think about this spring's fashion statement? Which car does Mr. Lafleur drive? Is it difficult to live the life of a highly paid athlete in the 1970s? Is all well in the Lafleur household?"

Guy loved the lifestyle and was not afraid to say so, with a characteristic combination of sophisticated naïveté and disarming honesty. "Hockey is number one in my life," he proclaimed. "I must be truthful and say that it even comes ahead of wife and family," he added, in a tone which implied: "I worked all those years as a kid and teenager to become a hockey player, not a husband and father. The other two were incidental." At home, Lise Lafleur, a remarkably strong young woman, turned the other cheek. She would occasionally put her foot down, like the time Lafleur and son Martin posed for a magazine cover photo. Guy was reminded, none too gently, that, in the real world, the family had gone through hell for three weeks during the 1976 kidnap scare. "I don't want the crazies knowing what Martin looks like," she said. There were no more cover shots.

Guy spent a lot of time with his teammates on Crescent Street. Steve Shutt fondly reminisces, "We played hard and we partied hard." Lise Lafleur stayed home.

Guy explained his philosophy to *Weekend Magazine* in 1978:

> She knew what the situation was before she married me, and understood. It's tough for me and tough for her to accept. Lise is not really a hockey fan, but she is, I think, my biggest supporter. I want her to be happy. We both pursue separate activities by mutual agreement. If I'm home one night a week and that's the night she usually goes out, that's fine. At heart I am a family man, but when I'm home I can't sit still. So after I wash the car and play with Martin, I drive Lise crazy sometimes.
>
> Sometimes, I think she is glad to be rid of me. We are discussing more children, but I don't want them right now. I don't want to father them and then hit the road; that's not right.

Lafleur gave that interview many times, seemingly oblivious to the divorce rumours. Quebec truly had changed; had Beliveau or Richard before him ever uttered such statements, both would have been roundly denounced from every pulpit in the land.

In 1982, his on-ice fortunes waning, Guy Lafleur had a conversation with a man he admired and respected, Roger Barre, his father-in-law. Roger Barre was dying.

"Guy, you are getting older and the hockey days are getting shorter," he told the thirty-one year old superstar. "You owe it to yourself, Lise and Martin to settle down for a while."

There was a reason for the conversation. One March night a year before, Lafleur had eaten dinner at Thursday's with teammate Robert Picard. Guy was mentally tired, in the middle of an ongoing battle with the tax man and at a rocky time in his marriage. There was wine with dinner and a couple of liqueurs afterwards, then the two players moved on to a nearby disco for a nightcap. At two a.m., Lafleur hopped into his Cadillac (the club had asked him to part with his Ferrari) for the drive home to Baie d'Urfe, about twenty-five miles up Highway 20. Picard suggested that Lafleur not drive. "I'm okay," Lafleur retorted.

Columnist Ted Blackman of *The Gazette* had written:

> Lafleur had been known as a chain smoker, but not much of a capacity drinker. It's an industry gag that *La Presse* always gets its annual scoop ("Lafleur Blasts Coach, Teammates, Mom, Apple Pie") during a long team flight from Los Angeles, when he's had the time for a third cocktail and pours out his frustrations.

About twenty minutes after Lafleur left Crescent Street, the Cadillac swerved off the highway, sideswiping a light standard and ripping out about twenty yards of Frost fence. A fence post came through the windshield, gouging the star's right ear. He missed decapitation by millimetres. The accident occurred because Lafleur had fallen asleep at the wheel. Ironically, dozing off may also have saved his life.

All of this was part of the emotional baggage Lafleur carried into the meeting with his father-in-law. Mr. Barre also had some sensible financial advice. "He told me this would be the best time for me to get a better contract." Lafleur still had four years remaining on his current deal, which called for $375,000 a year. He went to Larry Robinson, who already was renegotiating his contract, and suggested the two combine forces. They did, and both got their raises. However, they scored few points with fans (or the Quebec premier) with their public complaints about the Quebec and Canadian tax situations. Lafleur's remark that it would be better to play for an American team was particularly tactless.

Veneration of the superstar was still high in 1982, but his popularity had begun to wane. The celebrated outbursts that grew out of his on-ice frustration disillusioned some fans. The first such explosion had come four years before, in 1978, when Lafleur suddenly demanded a renegotiated contract.

The 1978 contract hassle was a precursor to other public disagreements Lafleur was to have with management. The fact that management no longer included Sam Pollock, who had left the club in September, after the Molson sale, is significant.

Most hockey fans and the Forum's second floor were equally at sea when a French newspaper reported out of the blue that Lafleur had been distressed to discover in a Toronto newspaper that, while he was earning only $180,000 a year, Canadiens' goalie Ken Dryden was reportedly pulling down somewhere between $325,000 and $350,000.

The fabled Forum press corps swooped down on this story like angry paratroopers and Jerry Petrie was called to a hurriedly scheduled meeting with the club's new managing director, Irving Grundman. The latter had to act fast to head off trouble, because he still was defending himself for having lost the popular Pierre Bouchard in the league's waiver draft a month before.

Three facts were significant in the Lafleur situation. He was far off base with his claims about the salaries earned by Dryden and other Canadiens veterans. As well, the media reported that Lafleur had delivered an ultimatum to the team, threatening to sit out upcoming games if nothing was done about his salary demands. (As a result, the crowd of reporters outside the Canadiens' dressing room at Maple Leaf Gardens for the October 25 game almost outnumbered the fans in the paying seats.) This was later denied by both Grundman and Petrie. Finally, Lafleur eventually won the showdown and was given a renegotiated contract by Grundman, something insiders say would never have happened during Sam Pollock's tenure.

Lafleur played in that lacklustre 4-4 tie and tried to back away graciously from what had become an incendiary situation. Just before the game began, Petrie read a prepared statement, purportedly prepared by Lafleur, to the press: "Certain remarks have been made to certain members of the press which are regrettable, and as a result the matter has been blown slightly out of proportion. I just want to devote my full time and energy to playing hockey for the Canadiens and helping our team win another Stanley Cup."

He did just that, scoring 52 goals and adding 77 assists for 129 points to finish third in the league scoring race behind Bryan Trottier and Marcel Dionne. He added another 10 goals and 13 assists in 16 playoff games as the Canadiens won their fourth straight Stanley Cup. But something had changed. It was impossible to define, but somehow the Lafleur holdout had struck a nerve with the Canadiens; after all, Richard and Beliveau never had threatened to sit out during their careers. Something was irretrievably lost, but it was difficult to say exactly what. Before Lafleur would retire, there would be other interviews, some on salary matters, others on the weaknesses of management. There were also whispers about complaints by Lafleur of the linemates he had been saddled with, hints that Steve Shutt had slowed down, that newcomer Keith Acton wasn't getting him the puck enough.

There were other factors contributing to the change. Guy Lafleur was about to get more competition on the ice for the unofficial title of most spectacular player in the NHL.

The 1979-80 season was special. The Nordiques had joined the league, along with the Winnipeg Jets, Hartford Whalers and Edmonton Oilers with their young new scoring sensation, Wayne Gretzky. Over the past several seasons, Montreal had become very aware of the rising power of the New York Islanders and their emerging stars like Bryan Trottier, Mike Bossy, Denis Potvin and Clark Gillies. In 1978-79, the Islanders had edged out the Canadiens, 116 to 115 points, for the overall league championship, only to be ambushed by their cross-town rival, the Rangers, in the playoffs.

In 1979-80, Lafleur again would attain the 50-goal mark, scoring exactly that many and adding 75 assists for 125 points, but some of the magic was disappearing. Gretzky tied Dionne for the league leadership in points with 137 and Bossy scored 51 goals for the Islanders. The latter was a Montreal native who had escaped the Canadiens' talent net, despite a pro-Bossy clamour in the Montreal newspapers—proof that the club shared the opinion that scoring feats in Quebec junior hockey were overvalued. As a result, Bossy was Bill Torrey's first draft pick in 1977, but the fifteenth overall, after such players as Dale McCourt, Barry Beck, Robert Picard, Jere Gillis and Lucien Deblois. Selecting tenth, Montreal picked Mark Napier, who had scored 60 goals for Birmingham of the WHA the previous season, after 156 goals in three excellent years with the Toronto Marlboros of the OHA.

Bossy, meanwhile, had scored 308 goals in four seasons of junior with Laval Nationals and was considered a pure shooter. However, there was a *caveat emptor* as to his ability to play defence.

"Get me the scorer," Al Arbour told Torrey. "We'll teach him to play defence."

Bossy was an immediate hit in the NHL, winning the Calder Trophy as Rookie of the Year, setting a rookie scoring mark of 53 goals and earning a spot on the league's second all-star team behind Lafleur. That same year, Lafleur scored 60 goals, but it was the only time that he ever outscored Bossy.

Every year thereafter, Bossy scored more goals than Lafleur and whispers were heard even in Montreal as to who the real best right winger in the NHL might be. Lafleur was the first player to have six consecutive 50-goal seasons before that string was broken in 1980-81. Bossy has never had a sub-50-goal season to date in his nine-year career.

Montreal was still a powerhouse in 1979-80, finishing third overall with 107 points, behind Philadelphia's 116 and Buffalo's 110. Yet that result was somewhat inflated, since the Habs played in the notoriously weak Norris Division with Los Angeles Kings, Pittsburgh Penguins, Hartford Whalers and Detroit Red Wings, while Buffalo was in the tough Adams with Boston, Minnesota, Toronto and Quebec. The Flyers fought it out with the Islanders, Rangers, Atlanta Flames and Washington.

That spring, Montreal entered the best-of-five quarterfinal against the Whalers with a good shot at their fifth straight Stanley Cup, a challenge to the powerhouse history of the late '50s. The Habs swept the Whalers 3-0, but late in the third period of the third game, a journeyman player named Pat Boutette kneed Lafleur as he was skating past.

Lafleur was out for the rest of the playoffs, joining fellow 50-goal scorer Pierre Larouche on the sidelines. With 100 goals out of the line-up, the Canadiens went down in seven games to the rising Minnesota North Stars, something which never would have happened with Lafleur and Larouche playing, and the dream for five straight ended. Later that spring, the Islanders launched their four-year conquest of the Stanley Cup.

Contrary to the popular mythology of the mid-1980s, the Montreal Canadiens did not roll over and die in the ensuing years. The team maintained its position in the upper echelons of the NHL, especially during regular-season play, with first-place finishes in 1980-81 in the Norris Division and 1981-82 in the revamped Adams Division, before slipping to second place behind Boston in 1982-83. Popular mythology, created daily in the local media, painted the so-called "Grundman years" as a total failure, a damning canvas of Forum futility. That, of course, is not true.

However, two factors combined to attach a label of ineptitude to the once-proud franchise. The first was Montreal's poor playoff record; they were embarrassed 3-0 by the upstart Edmonton Oilers in 1980-81, and then lost a heartbreaking series to the dreaded Nordiques in overtime in the fifth game of 1981-82 divisional semi-final. The following year, the Sabres blew out Montreal in three straight, once again in the opening series.

The second, and most important, factor was that Guy Lafleur had plunged into a precipitous decline and was not producing as he once had. An injury in 1980-81 caused him to miss 29 games and *le Démon Blond* scored 27 goals and 43 assists for a mere 70 points. He would remain stuck at the 27-goal level for the next two years, breaking loose with only 30 goals in 1983-84. What frustrated Lafleur, and Montreal fans, during this period was that just about every scorer worth his shot was popping in 50; people like Rick Kehoe, Dennis Maruk, Dino Ciccarelli and Al Secord. Bossy was still Bossy, averaging 60 goals a season and 20 in the playoffs while Gretzky was sublime, scoring 55-92-71-74 to Lafleur's 27-27-27-30.

Whether or not Lafleur himself made conscious comparisons with Gretzky we will never know. The two played together for Team Canada in 1981 and got along well, with Edmonton fans chanting "Guy! Guy! Guy!" whenever Lafleur carried the puck. Unfortunately, Team Canada was humbled by the Soviet Union in that competition.

Worse still, the two played against each other in the 1980-81 quarterfinal and Gretzky owned the ice in their first head-to-head confrontation. It really stung when Canadiens' goalie Richard Sevigny showed that even if the Flower didn't, his teammates did make such individual comparisons, vowing on the eve of the first game that "Guy will put him [Gretzky] in his pocket before the series is over." All Lafleur had to show for the series was a single assist and one minor penalty. His nemesis ended the playoffs with 7 goals and 14 assists for 21 points.

Nobody could foretell that Lafleur would score only two more Stanley Cup playoff goals in his career, both in the 1981-82 series loss to the Nordiques. The last came April 10, 1982, a power play goal at 19:34 of the third period that allowed Montreal to escape the ignominy of a shutout.

A year later, after the Canadiens' worst season in living memory—35 wins, 40 losses and 5 ties in 80 games—the team would rise up and smite the Bruins and Nordiques in the playoffs and take a 2-0 lead on the defending champion Islanders before succumbing in six games. Lafleur's contribution in the 12 games would be three assists. His 30 goals and 40 assists in the regular season would be deceiving, too. Most of those were scored in the first half of the season.

In late February, with Montreal's record at 28-30-5, Bob Berry was fired as coach and replaced by Lafleur's former linemate, Jacques Lemaire. In the remaining 17 regular-season games and 12 playoff games, Lafleur would only score twice, ending the 1983-84 season and playoffs mired in the 26-game scoring slump.

In the 1984 off-season, as he had the year before, Lafleur worked hard to keep in shape and reported to training camp in top condition. But the magic was irretrievably gone. In 19 games, he scored just two goals, one each against Buffalo and Philadelphia, and both in October. Added to that were three assists, the last on a Mark Hunter goal on November 1 in a 6-5 win over the Islanders. The Flower spent long stretches of games rivetted to the team bench, kept there by Lemaire, a stickler for defence. Yet, Lafleur's skating and defensive play were better than they had been in several years.

He was skating well, as even the opposition would admit. Craig Ramsay, Larry Playfair and several other Sabres discussed Lafleur's last season on the afternoon of the Flower's public retirement ceremony.

"The strange thing was that he was skating much better this year than the last two seasons," said Ramsay, who would win the Frank Selke trophy as top defensive forward in the NHL that season. "He wasn't putting it in the net like he had before, but I always had the impression than when he got a couple, he would return to normal. Before every game, our coach would say something like: 'Let some other team wake him up, don't let Lafleur kill us.'"

Playfair agreed: "Say what you want in the press box; when you're down here on the ice, you see a different Lafleur and this guy can still play hockey."

On Saturday, November 24, Montreal beat the Detroit Red Wings 6-4 in a lacklustre game at the Forum. The win gave the surging Canadiens a 13-4-2 record and the club was playing superbly under Lemaire's defensively oriented system. So far in the young season, they had defeated the challengers in their division: Buffalo, Boston, and Quebec (twice). The Canadiens had also logged wins over the cream of the rest of the NHL—New York Islanders, Philadelphia Flyers, Edmonton Oilers and Chicago Black Hawks. Strangely enough, three of their four losses had come at the hands of the league's have-nots— Detroit, Toronto Maple Leafs and Pittsburgh Penguins.

When the team skated off the ice after the game, few

fans suspected that Guy Lafleur had played his 961st, and last, hockey game with the Montreal Canadiens.

Even though Guy Lafleur had not been scoring, his teammates and the fans were still rooting for him. But he was an open, festering wound that club management strove to cauterize. Shift after frustrating shift, Lafleur skated through his slump, seemingly a shell of the player who had terrorized a generation of NHL teams. As the Sabres said, his skating was still there, but every time he touched the puck it seemed he would instinctively make the wrong move. Each time he skated to the bench at the end of a shift, a collective sigh would float down from the seats. Everyone ached to see the Lion in pain, unable to shake it off. Forum games became group empathy sessions.

As well, although club management would not admit it, Lafleur posed too much of a challenge to the authority of Lemaire. A still-young thirty-three, Lafleur should have had several good years ahead of him. After all, his predecessors, Richard and Beliveau, had played to the ages of thirty-nine and forty-one respectively. They, too, had endured late-career slumps, only to finish strongly. Most importantly, both had finished their careers on Stanley Cup winners.

However, neither had railed against the team or management during their careers. The club feared another Lafleur outburst; they felt it would be devastating to a young, new team in full reconstruction. Ever since Henri Richard's celebrated criticism of Al MacNeil during the 1971 playoffs, management was hypersensitive to the slightest rumblings of a veteran.

The Friday before the Detroit game, and the day after a 3-2 home win over Chicago in which Lafleur hardly saw any action, the player held a long meeting with Lemaire. They discussed his contribution to the team.

"Before I retired, I was skating very well but they weren't letting me play," Guy says. "I was getting eight or nine minutes a game on the ice and that wasn't enough—I couldn't build up my confidence that way. And they knew that I was losing my confidence. There was a psychological war going on." Lafleur asked Savard several times for a trade but the general manager refused. "We can't trade you; you're part of the building," Savard told him.

"Then Serge would say to me: 'Go talk to Jacques,' which was his way of washing his hands of the affair. I spoke with Jacques but he had his own style. I respected that. On the Friday before I retired, I sat down with him and said, 'Listen, Jacques, we played together and had a lot of success and I was getting about 25 minutes a game. If you think at my age I'm not capable, say so, but I know I can still play if you give me the chance to prove myself.' There didn't seem to be a problem. We were scheduled against Detroit the next night and he said I was going to play on a regular line, I was going to play on the power plays and I might play on another line or kill penalties. I wanted to play 17 or 18 minutes, not 25 or 30—so I could get my confidence back."

Lafleur returned home and told his wife about the meeting. "She didn't believe a word of it; she said I was deluding myself if I thought Lemaire was going to do that for me. I told her I thought things would be fine."

On Saturday morning, Lafleur showed up for the team skate and was in high spirits. He was so keyed up, he returned to the rink at three p.m., surprising club president Ronald Corey who was in the team's exercise room.

"What are you doing here?" he asked Lafleur.

"I'm getting ready," Lafleur replied. "I spoke with Lemaire and I'm going to get some ice time tonight."

"Perfect," said Corey. "I hope things will go well and you pop a couple."

Lafleur was on the ice once in the first period, and twice in the second.

"After the second period, I asked Mr. Charest [the Forum policeman stationed just outside the team dressing room] to get Serge Savard, it was urgent. Savard didn't come downstairs because he knew. When he came down after the game, I said to him: 'It's over. You got what you wanted. It's over.'"

Just two weeks before Lafleur retired, Steve Shutt had been traded to Los Angeles Kings.

"It was all part of the plan. Mr. Corey had come in with a five-year plan to rebuild the Canadiens and I always thought that this attitude made a lot of sense. And when Serge became general manager in 1983, I thought they had picked somebody who would know what to do. But a little while after he took over, I found out from somebody with impeccable contacts—he had the scoop, as they say—that Savard had said he would get rid of all the players who had played with him and Lemaire over a period of three years. I didn't believe it at first but this person told me this was the mandate.

"When Steve left, I knew I was next."

A little under three months later, with the crowd chanting "Guy! Guy! Guy!" for five full minutes before he appeared, Lafleur skated onto the Forum ice for the last time. The Canadiens wore their home whites, the Sabres their distinctive blue-and-gold. Guy was in road red, the uniform of fable.

Standing at centre ice, awaiting him, were Guy's parents, Rejean and Pierrette, Madame Baribeau, his second mother from Quebec City, Lise Lafleur, and son Martin. For the first time in her life, it seemed, Mrs. Lafleur got a real look at her husband's world. She stood in her chic blue dress, a gold corsage above her right breast, and appeared overwhelmed by the ovation, looking on uncomprehendingly as Guy Lafleur drank from the heady wine of the fans' cheers for a last time. It was as if the fans were saying: "Guy's fantasy land is as much a real world as any other. This ovation is real. His special career and what it meant to all of us is real."

There were more than 18,000 paying customers, 200 journalists and media technicians and some 40 professional hockey players in the building and all unabashedly took part in a standing ovation that lasted a shade under five minutes. There were few dry eyes in the house, Lise Lafleur's included. In front of her, Martin bravely bit his lower lip throughout the special ceremonies.

Buffalo Sabres' assistant coach Roger Crozier stood on

the visitors' bench, clapping steadily, and forcing some of his players off the bench and onto the ice. There they clustered with a phalanx of photographers. "Guy! Guy! Guy!" cascaded down from the rafters. The Sabres and Canadiens banged their sticks on the ice and the boards in the kind of tribute accorded only to Morenz, Richard and Beliveau in this building.

Guy skated over to his former teammates, going down the bench shaking hands, stopping here for a word with Mario Tremblay, there for a joke with Larry Robinson. Then, to tumultuous cheering, he skated to the Sabres' bench and repeated the process. Tough hockey players like Larry Playfair and Mike Foligno were beaming ear-to-ear, past animosities and ice battles forgotten. They would admit later to being thrilled. With electronic flashes bouncing lightning bolts off the protective glass over the boards just behind them, Lafleur stopped and shared a quiet moment with Gilbert Perreault. A couple of Sabres players were on the other side of the mob of photographers and Lafleur couldn't see them; thinking he had pressed the flesh with the whole team, he shook hands with Foligno and returned to centre ice after a parting word to Perreault. You could see the disappointment on Paul Cyr's face all the way up in the press box.

As the great Bobby Clark once said: "There are players in this league that make fans of the rest of us. Lafleur was like that. He was the kind of player you not only played against, but you watched when he was on the ice."

After the emotional press conference on November 26, 1984, during which a distraught Lafleur announced his retirement, the Canadiens' management apparatus went into high gear. Guy was quietly enrolled in business courses and became a member of the second floor team.

For a while, it seemed to work. The shaken warrior who announced his retirement in late November was gone when Lafleur stepped to the microphone at an Ad and Sales Executives Club luncheon in early February, a week before his on-ice good-bye.

Tanned from a southern holiday, he was relaxed and

his pinstripes fit. The three hundred businessmen in the room cheered "Guy! Guy! Guy" as Lafleur made his way to the podium.

"The difference between my new life and my life three months ago is that I didn't have to carry a piece of paper on the ice with me," he joked, referring to his speaking notes. "I am no longer a hockey player. I am embarking on a new career and I intend to work as hard at it as I did hockey. For those of you who keep mentioning rumours of me returning for the playoffs, I must say that I won't be back this season." He paused. "I won't be back for-ever."

He made a passing reference to his past differences with management. "Now I can understand how they think upstairs. Now they're on my level ... the second floor."

Forever is a very long time, especially if you are a thirty-three year old man who has been in the limelight for two decades. In Lafleur's case, forever on the second floor was less than a year. In mid-September, the *Journal de Montréal* reported that Lafleur was locked in yet another salary conflict, this time over his future salary as a public relations representative with Montreal. With still one year to run on his $400,000-plus playing salary, Lafleur was offered a very generous $75,000 a year, with a liberal expense account and ten percent increases each year, to start in 1987.

The Flower's response was predictable. He suggested that a move to Quebec City might result in him working in the automobile industry and doing some public relations for the Nordiques.

This time, however, the second floor was firm. "I am saddened by Guy's decision to resign," said Corey. "In view of what he said publicly about a private matter, I had no alternative but to accept it, effective immediately."

"I was told I was resigning," says Lafleur. A few days later, Lafleur speculated on a possible return to a playing career, and got Serge Savard's permission to speak with other teams in the league. There were talks with the

New York Rangers, Pittsburgh Penguins and Los Angeles Kings, but all eventually fell through.

"Rogatien Vachon [Kings' GM] is Serge's biggest chum so there was little real chance there. The Rangers were in the process of dropping all of their veterans, like Mike Rogers and Pierre Larouche, so little happened there, too. Pittsburgh was a real possibility because Eddie Johnson liked the idea of teaming me up with Mario Lemieux but he had to clear it with Eddie deBartolo, the owner."

Lafleur gave all teams a deadline of 5 p.m. EDT on Friday, October 11, to come to some agreement, but Pittsburgh could not meet it. Later that day, he announced that he would not return to action. If there was a measure of revenge it came when the Canadiens included him among the eighteen players protected by the club in the waiver draft earlier that week.

Serge Savard did not see it that way: "We protected Guy so that he would retain his choice of team if he decided to return to action. If he had been unprotected, he might not want to go to the team that claimed him and after all he meant to Montreal for so long, it would be unfair to leave him in that situation."

What if Lafleur wanted to return to Montreal?

"Not a chance," Savard said.

* * *

It is a cold blustery Boxing Day, 1985, in Paris, France, not unlike that cool April day in Verdun a lifetime ago. No children play ball hockey in the streets, yet a lot of young boys find their way to the squat concrete-and-steel building that is the Palais Omnisport Paris-Bercy, an impressive indoor facility that today will be home to the first two games in an international ice hockey tournament. Guy Lafleur, who has not suited up for a professional hockey game during this calendar year, sits quietly in the dressing room of the Français Volants, the Parisian team in France's First Division. The Français Volants, who wear the real *bleu-blanc-rouge* and who literally are the Flying Frenchmen, will face off shortly against Riga Dynamo of the Soviet Union's Elite League.

For once, Lafleur's salary is no point of contention: "They're paying me $1,000 and have chipped in three airline tickets and my room at the Intercontinental," he smiles. Professional hockey players wear longjohns under their uniforms and elaborate padding. The rest of the Français Volants, who include several former pros such as Patrick Daley, who was a linemate of Mike Bossy at Laval, and Ottawa's Larry Skinner, a former Colorado Rockie, are no different. Lafleur, on the other hand, looks like a small boy about to play shinny on a backyard rink; his underpinnings are the most basic, a T-shirt, blue jockey shorts and well-worn streamlined shoulder pads to which his elbow pads have been attached.

He skates out onto the POPB ice with his new teammates to do battle with the Russians. Three hours later, he rolls his eyes and answers questions from French journalists who hang on every word. "What's it like to lose 16-1?" is the first. "No fun at all," he retorts, with a little smile. "But these guys would have given a lot of NHL teams trouble. I am not here as the team's saviour; I'm here to help sell hockey."

Lafleur, and his linemates Daley and Christian Pouget, a speedy centre who plays for the Trois-Rivières Draveurs in the Quebec Major Junior Hockey League, are the only ones who can hold the fort against Riga and emerge from the game a minus-1, victims of Riga's fourteenth goal.

In some ways, the POPB was the Montreal Forum all over again. Many expatriate Quebecers and Canadians (and some make sure that you note the difference) are in almost obligatory attendance. Here and there, a cherished Canadiens sweater makes an appearance.

Most have been stationed here with the Maison de Québec or the Canadian embassy for several years and have not lived through the frustrations of Lafleur's later years. They "ooh" and "ah" at every move and groan with every close call. The Soviets run up the score, 11-1, 12-1, 13-1 ... but the crowd remains. A late goal by *le Démon Blond* will make it all worthwhile. It never comes. Lafleur has laced on skates perhaps ten times in the past four months and is puffing at the end of his shortened shifts. More importantly, the Soviets double-team him for three periods. Every time he steps on the ice, a left winger and a defenceman are on him constantly.

On Saturday, the Français Volants will play in the consolation final against a team that promoter Thierry Lecarriere has euphemistically called *la Sélection de Montréal*. In truth, they are the last-place Granby Bisons of the QMJHL, bolstered by one centre and lanky Laval Titans' goalie Mario Brunetta, a Quebec Nordiques draftee.

Naturally, they all are in awe of Lafleur, and before the game make a pilgrimage to the Parisian dressing room for the mandatory autographs and signed sticks. During the game, however, the Bisons are all business and, while they show healthy respect for the Flower, they bang and bump the Français Volants at every turn. The only player who seems intent on bumping Lafleur is young Stephane Roy, as they say in Quebec, *le frère de l'autre*, whose older brother Patrick will tend goal for the Montreal Canadiens against the New Jersey Devils that very night.

More than 7,000 people, the second largest hockey crowd ever to gather in Paris, watch in hopeful anticipation as the two teams bump and grind, eschewing the European style for a more North American game. Yet there are constant reminders that this is Paris. The house P.A. announcer, a cross between Bill Murray and René Lecavalier, keeps up an incessant spiel during the game. "What a bodycheck, ladies and gentlemen! How about a large hand for our Paris Volants?" Beside him at rink level is the stadium organist, pumping away furiously at every stop in play. The 17,000-seat facility, opened in February, 1984, has an oversize European ice surface, unobstructed sightlines throughout and padded seats that prove unnerving: wayward pucks disappear into the ether when they clear the glass, the house lights are off during play so you can't see them and the padded seats swallow them without the slightest sound.

The bump and grind goes on until Granby defenceman Mario Barbe is assessed a penalty at 4:57. A minute later, the Français Volants score and the crowd cheers happily. Moments earlier, Lafleur rang a point shot off a goalpost.

In the second period, the teams exchange goals and, with 20 minutes to play, the home team leads 2-1. As the French fans line up for their hot dogs (French sausage and Dijon mustard on a baguette) in the POPB corridors, the talk is all Lafleur. "Will he ever score?" The crowd seems resigned to the fact that the magic is gone, and the expatriate Quebecers and Canadians are taking it the worst.

The third period begins on a dismal note for the home side as Granby scores on a power play at the 13-second mark and presses to go ahead. Lafleur leads several rushes, taking good hard slapshots from just inside the blueline. Mario Brunetta is 6-feet, 2-inches tall and a standup goalie. He glides out to cut down the angle, smothers the shot in his pads and kicks the rebound into the corner.

The fans are in a state when shortly after the six-minute mark, Lafleur repeats the manoeuvre, hesitates, and then shoots. Brunetta handles the puck easily, but Lafleur's hesitation had a purpose. His centreman Pouget is bearing down on the goalie through the slot and Daley, who has not forgotten the North American hitting game, draws a bead on a defenceman who scrambles after a rebound kicked too quickly. Daley swoops behind the net from the right wing, with Lafleur trailing, and crunches the defenceman. His momentum carries both away from the puck, which lies a little behind and to Brunetta's right. Lafleur sails in, scoops it up and, moving laterally in one fluid motion, puts it into the far corner behind a startled goaltender as he completes his semi-circle. Both the Rocket and Gros Bill scored their last goals on plays started behind the net.

Daley and Pouget, their sticks raised high, race for the Flower. It takes even longer for the crowd to react; they seem stunned by the suddenness of it all. Then there is a collective "oh", a quick exhalation, then everyone seems to be cheering and talking at once.

11

The Seventies

In Philadelphia, on a warm September Sunday in 1975, the 21st it was, their minds were on The Bull, Lefty, Mike "The Hammer" Schmidt and the Philly juggernaut that was thick in the fight for the National League's East Division crown. As well, a young coach from the West Coast named Dick Vermeil was proving that fanatical dedication to the work ethic would soon forge championship contenders of his National Football League Eagles, and the improving 76ers were readying for another National Basketball Association season.

In the Spectrum, across the street from Veteran's Stadium, the Stanley Cup champion Philadelphia Flyers, a.k.a. the Broad Street Bullies, were warming up for a season of mayhem on the ice and a run at a third straight championship. Tonight's exhibition game would be the return engagement of a weekend home-and-home series with the Montreal Canadiens, a powerhouse-in-the-making which just might be ready to challenge their supremacy.

Accordingly, the Flyers had bumped and battered the Habs during a 5-4 win at the Forum in the Saturday night encounter. There were 21 penalties handed out, including majors to Dave "The Hammer" Schultz and Montreal's feisty sophomore Doug Risebrough. Schultz added insult to injury when he scored the winning goal, tipping in an Ed Van Impe shot with less than three minutes remaining.

Exhibition game notwithstanding, a message had been delivered: "The Cup is ours; if you want it, you'll have to take it away from us. Love, The Philadelphia Flyers, R. E. Clarke, captain."

Risebrough became embroiled with Schultz after the Philadelphia winger had abused newly appointed team captain Yvan Cournoyer (Henri Richard had retired in the off-season) with a crosscheck that reinforced the message on a more personal note. Guy Lapointe read it loud and clear . . . the heavyweight rearguard came to his captain's rescue with some of the nastiest threats against The Hammer's personal wellbeing one might ever hear, from a distance of twenty feet or so and over the heads of two linesmen and referee Bryan Lewis.

After the game, William Scott Bowman congratulated his young centreman for his temerity and his good sense —Risebrough had tackled Schultz from behind, secured a solid headlock and hung on for dear life—and then began making clucking noises at some of the larger physical specimens filling the Canadiens' home whites.

What follows is a re-creation of Scotty's lecture: "Young Douglas weighs only 177 pounds soaking wet and the trainer suspects he has batteries in his pockets when he climbs on the scales," he said, his voice deceptively soft.

"There are others in this room who, in the interests of team unity, will remain nameless, but who tend to be a lot larger than six feet tall and 200 pounds in weight— without batteries in their pockets. Again, to protect the innocent, I must point out to these same anonymous types that the gentlemen from Philadelphia love it when someone like Mr. Schultz crosschecks our captain into the ice and our people waggle warning fingers at said honoured opponent. I wish to leave you with this question to ponder as we fly south to the wonderful state of Pennsylvania. What do you think the Flyers would have done if one of our players, heaven forbid, dared to reserve such treatment for their captain, a certain Robert Earle Clarke?"

That evening at the Spectrum, the Canadiens team that skated out in road reds for the warmup was noticeably larger than the team that had worn the home whites the night before. In the lineup were healthy young red-meat-eaters with names like Sean Bryan Shanahan (6'3", 205 lbs.) Glenn Michael Goldup (6', 187 lbs.) Pierre "Butch Jr." Bouchard (6'2", 202 lbs.) and Rick Raymond Chartraw (6'2", 210 lbs).

Late in the third period, Montreal led 6-2 when young Mr. Risebrough pondered the question posed by his coach at the end of the previous evening's meeting. As he and Mr. Clarke skated back to their respective benches, they began exchanging pleasantries. Not content with simple expression of intent, they dropped their gloves and had at each other. As the two young men tussled, the answer to Mr. Bowman's question was delivered in the person of Schultz vaulting the boards and racing into the melée. He was joined by all of his teammates and Risebrough was joined by all of his.

In the words of Stephen John Shutt, a much better goal scorer than historian: "We kicked the living daylights out of them."

Schultz, who would end the evening with trios of penalties (three each of minors, majors and misconducts), was intercepted by Chartraw and the two replayed a first-period set-to, Chartraw 2, Schultz 0. Mr. Jack McIlhargey was thoroughly drubbed by Mr. Bouchard and left to sputter: "I'll get you for that next game!" Never at a loss for words in Canada's two official languages, Bouchard opined as to the low probability of such an encounter. "I'm not worried, you'll be in the minors by then."

Mr. Gary Dornhoefer, a.k.a. High Cheeks for his habit of obscuring the vision of opposing goaltenders in the crease—in all senses of this word—was being throttled by a large Canadien in front of the Montreal bench. "For Pete's sake, Scotty," he implored, "call him off. I can't breathe!" Meanwhile, the aforementioned McIlhargey had separated himself from Bouchard, with the help of overtaxed linesmen, and encountered Mr. Goldup. Alas, it was not be McIlhargey's night. Even notorious non-combatants were involved, including Jim Roberts and Bill Barber, Guy Lafleur and Mel Bridgman (Guy, of course, discovered he was a lover and not a fighter), Mario Tremblay and the same Mr. Bridgman (who, in turn, discovered to his chagrin that young Mario was a lover . . . of fighting) and all the way back to the original twosome, Messrs. Clarke and Risebrough.

The referee for the encounter, Mr. Bruce Hood, assessed some 322 minutes in penalties for the entire contest, 250 of which were the result of the bench-clearing festivities. Five of those went to Andre "Moose" Dupont, the former Jr. Canadien who thumped William Scott Bowman during the melée. "I figured this was Scotty's idea all along," he fumed after the "pretend game" was over.

Mr. Shutt, the amateur historian, reflected on that innocuous encounter a decade later: "We won the Stanley Cup that night. It just wasn't official until next May. If you are going to beat the Stanley Cup champions, you have to beat them at their style because they dictate the game. Philadelphia was a tough team so we had to prove that we were tougher, to break them mentally. And even if we didn't win all of the fights, which we did anyhow, they knew that fighting us was not going to help them.

"Sitting in the dressing room after the game, a lot of guys were smiling. We knew we had them. Better still, they knew it, too. And once you beat them at their style, you could impose your style on them and we knew they could never skate with us."

Scotty Bowman, also assessing the impact of that exhibition game played ten years earlier, agreed.

"The Broad Street Bullies played their style of game and used it effectively. I would never think of criticizing their team make-up or the job Fred Shero did, because as a coach, you go with what you have. And although Dave Schultz and I have had our disagreements over the years, I could not criticize his style of play. You had to give him credit . . . he played nine years in this league and came out of it with two Stanley Cup rings. He did what he had to do.

"We just had to find a way of countering what the Flyers had going for them." Eight months later, spotting Rick Chartraw and Pierre Bouchard as forwards, the Canadiens swept the Flyers four straight in a relatively tame series. Sam Pollock's team of the '70s had arrived and was on its way to four straight championships and a raft of league records.

If ever Sam Pollock's draft movement bore fruit, it was with the team he assembled in the 1970s. The 1968 and 1969 drafts ended an era, with the disappearance of territorial protection. However, that did not prevent Sam Pollock from assembling an impressive cast of home-brews.

The 1975-76 team comprised the following players:

Goal: Michel Larocque, Ken Dryden.

Defence: John Van Boxmeer, Guy Lapointe, Serge Savard, Larry Robinson, Don Awrey, Pierre Bouchard, Rick Chartraw.

Forwards: Jim Roberts, Doug Risebrough, Guy Lafleur, Yvon Lambert, Yvan Cournoyer, Mario Tremblay, Glenn Goldup, Ron Andruff, Murray Wilson, Pete Mahovlich, Doug Jarvis, Steve Shutt, Bob Gainey, Jacques Lemaire, Sean Shanahan.

All but Dryden, Awrey, Lambert, Mahovlich and Jarvis were obtained in the draft or, in the case of some of the veterans, came up through the ranks of team-sponsored junior franchises. Dryden was originally drafted by Boston, Awrey was obtained in a trade from St. Louis, Lambert was originally a Detroit draft pick, Mahovlich was obtained in a trade from Detroit and Jarvis from Toronto.

In the four-year Cup sweep, players would come and go. Additions who would wear at least one Stanley Cup ring included Bill Nyrop, Brian Engblom, Rejean Houle (back from the WHA), Pierre Mondou, Gilles Lupien, Pierre Larouche, Pat Hughes, Rod Langway, Cam Connor and Mark Napier. Nyrop was drafted in 1972, Connor and Lupien in 1974, Mondou, Engblom and Hughes in 1975, Napier and Langway in 1977. Only Larouche came in a trade.

In all, that meant that sixteen players who had been draft choices would play for at least one Stanley Cup winning team in the four-straight streak from 1975 through 1979. It also meant that the Canadiens did something few teams have ever accomplished—they managed to rebuild and rejuvenate while they were winning championships.

The 1970s Canadiens started a year late. Very few Canadiens fans expected the team to win the 1970-71 Stanley Cup and they were properly thankful for the championship. They were not too happy, however, with the spate of defections after the season. Gone through retirement were Jean Beliveau and John Ferguson, the latter to attend to his burgeoning business interests. Ralph Backstrom had been traded to secure the Lafleur draft and Rogatien Vachon followed him west in 1972. A year later, more changes were made with the departure to the World Hockey Association of Houle, Tardif and J.C. Tremblay, and the trades of Terry Harper and Chuck Lefley.

The team which had won in May, 1971 was the 1960s edition of the Canadiens. By 1975-76, the Stanley Cup winning team of '70-'71 was a faint memory as only Lapointe, Cournoyer, Savard, Peter Mahovlich, Lemaire, Bouchard and Dryden remained, and of those players only Cournoyer, Savard and Lemaire were real '60s vintage—the rest were transition era and soon-to-be '70s bedrock. Despite such a talent drain in a short four-year period, Montreal managed an interim Stanley Cup in 1972-73.

You did not have to travel far in 1970 to know how good the 1970s Canadiens were going to be. Playing for the Montreal Voyageurs of the American Hockey League at one time or another that season were Peter Mahovlich, Bouchard, Dryden, Lapointe, Dennis Hextall, Jude Drouin, Guy Charron, Chuck Lefley, Bob Murdoch, Phil Roberto, Reynald Comeau and Bobby Sheehan. They made a shambles of the AHL and some knowledgeable hockey people, noting the weakness of several franchises in the Western Division, felt that if the Voyageurs played in that NHL division, they would have made the playoffs.

A year later, the Voyageurs franchise would move to Halifax and continue its domination of the AHL, becoming a first professional home to future Canadiens named Gainey, Tremblay, Risebrough, Chartraw, Lambert, Guy Carbonneau and Keith Acton.

As mentioned earlier, the Canadiens of the 1960s carried over into the spring of 1971 and the surprise victory over the Bruins that paved the way for Stanley Cup Number 17. The Shot Heard Round the Dressing Room —Henri Richard's blast at interim coach Al MacNeil after the latter benched him in Chicago in the fifth game of the series—was to have long-term repercussions that would shape the team for the rest of the decade. Henri picked up his pride, scored the tying and winning goals in a 3-2 win over the Black Hawks and embraced MacNeil at centre ice.

Yet his tirade could not be undone. Someone had to go. Would it be the French Canadian team captain, bearer of that proud name Richard, which meant so much to the Canadiens? A fierce competitor who never gave quarter nor asked for the same from opponents much larger than he, Henri was a fixture in Montreal.

It was MacNeil who left, and of his own volition. The Richard criticism had resulted in death threats against the soft-spoken coach and his young family.

"There were many things involved in me finding myself as head coach of the Canadiens," said MacNeil. "I had known Sam Pollock for many years, well before he became GM of the Canadiens. I was captain of his club in Hull-Ottawa and he asked me to stay there and coach the team. I said no because I wanted a shot at playing in the National Hockey League."

MacNeil started out with Montreal and spent eight years in the NHL, most of them with the Chicago Black Hawks. When he retired, Pollock came calling and offered him a choice of two Canadiens farm teams, Cleveland and Houston. MacNeil opted for Houston and coached some impressive young talent, including such future stars as Guy Lapointe, Jude Drouin and Tony Esposito. A year later he ended up in Montreal coaching the AHL Voyageurs.

Pollock did not have to go far to find a coach for the Montreal Canadiens when Claude Ruel decided the pressure was too much for him in December, 1970.

"I took over and looked forward to a good long run behind the Montreal bench," said MacNeil. "I felt I was a career coach and I got along with a lot of the younger players like Tardif, Houle and Lapointe. But I ran into problems with some veterans. The team was pretty established and they balked at some of the things I wanted to do."

It was an up-and-down year for Montreal, thanks to mediocre goaltending, but Ken Dryden was called up and was brilliant in a seven-game defeat of Boston and a six-game triumph over Minnesota. MacNeil found himself coaching the Canadiens in the Stanley Cup final.

"I was playing the kids a lot and after game five Henri, who had been sitting on the bench a lot, blasted me. He said I was a bad coach. Then the Forum started getting phone calls with bomb threats. Remember, this was just after the Kidnap Crisis and the *War Measures Act* and French-English relations were not so good."

When MacNeil coached the next two games, a special bodyguard stood behind him at the Forum and in Chicago, and others were posted at home with Mrs. MacNeil and the couple's young daughter.

The MacNeil family took a Florida vacation after the Stanley Cup was clinched and when the Maritimer returned to Montreal, he told Pollock he no longer wished to coach the Canadiens.

Fifteen years later, Henri still regrets that the incident had French-English overtones. "This was a player-coach situation, nothing more. I meant what I said when I said it, and regretted it two minutes after because of the way it came out. Al and I made friends when it was over but his wife wouldn't speak to me after that and to tell you the truth, I don't blame her."

The soothing balm of another Stanley Cup notwithstanding, it was much easier to quietly promote the English-speaking interim coach to General-Manager of the new Nova Scotia Voyageurs and seek a replacement behind the bench. Sam Pollock was criticized in some quarters for not backing his coach, but the decision was MacNeil's. Pollock agreed with his former coach because he was a skillful player of the percentages. There was no percentage whatsoever in management coming down on a consummate professional like Richard, the man who had won the Cup for the Canadiens and whose ferocious competitive drive was an asset 99.9 percent of the time.

As well, finding a coach was not likely to prove difficult. One of Sam's protégés, Scotty Bowman, had accomplished miracles with trades and veterans on their last legs and had carried the St. Louis Blues to the NHL final three years running. However, the Blues' owners, the Solomon brothers, were upset because Scotty would not let them play with their new toy, and life was becoming tense in the Missouri metropolis.

Sam and Scotty went back a long way with the Montreal organization. Bowman, a Verdun boy from the neighbourhood which had spawned Donnie Marshall and Buddy O'Connor, played for the Junior Canadiens until a head injury in 1951-52 ended his playing career. In the third period of a game, Bowman got a breakaway and was chopped down by a vicious two-hander to the head wielded by Jean-Guy Talbot.

"That was it for me. I never was the same player afterward. I just didn't have the confidence. I had a lot of headaches and blurred vision and things like that in the off-season and the club recommended that I quit as an active player."

The club paid Bowman's tuition for business courses at Sir George Williams College and he began coaching for them at midget level. Two years later he was coaching in the Canadiens system and in 1957, became Pollock's assistant with the Hull-Ottawa Junior Canadiens, who would win a Memorial Cup.

The rich benefits of Canadiens' tradition were quite evident when Bowman went to St. Louis in 1967 and wrote his own ticket.

"Frank Selke and Sam Pollock had put together the biggest system out there and coaches and general-managers in the Canadiens' system were coveted by the new teams. After all, we knew where all the good players were and the new guys wanted that knowledge."

Bowman made immediate good use of his Canadiens' contacts and stocked his team with former Montreal players and farmhands. It paid off right away and the Blues were the toast of St. Louis. In the West Division final, spurred by such stalwarts as Dickie Moore, Noel Picard and Bill McCreary, the Blues led the Philadelphia Flyers 1-0 and three games to two, late in the sixth game. The Flyers scored a lucky goal to tie it and won it with an even flukier score in overtime. The Blues were down and the Flyers looked to win game seven on momentum alone.

During the playoffs, Bowman had been keeping close tabs on the Blues' farm team in Kansas City, player-managed by one Doug Harvey.

"I really thought Doug would be able to help us but league rules stipulated I couldn't bring him up until their playoffs were over. After our sixth game, he called me and said his team had been eliminated. I told him: 'Come on up, we need you!'" Harvey was the first star in the Blues 3-1 series clinchers.

Montreal defeated St. Louis 4-0 in the Stanley Cup final that May, but that statement does no justice to the task accomplished by Bowman. The scores were 3-2, 1-0, 4-3 and 3-2, as a patchwork quilt of over-the-hill veterans and the rawest of raw rookies fought the Canadiens tooth and nail. A year later, the teams met again in another 4-0 whitewash and again the scores were respectable. In 1969-70, the Blues appeared in their third straight final, against the Bruins this time, succumbing in four games once more.

Sam Pollock watched and waited as his former assistant wrung superb results from the Blues. When the Richard-MacNeil affair became front page news, Pollock was determined to hire Bowman.

That decision proved as important as the acquisition of any player who played for the Canadiens during the rest of the decade. Bowman led the transition Canadiens to a respectable third-place finish in the East Division in 1971-72, one point behind New York Rangers and 11 behind Boston.

A few off-season player moves later, the Canadiens led their division in 1972-73 and captured the Stanley Cup. It was to be Bowman's first of five in eight years of coaching in Montreal, a winning percentage which would challenge the numbers turned in by the immortal Toe Blake in the 1950s and 60s.

However, there was a world of difference in their coaching styles. Peter Mahovlich smiles as he recalls the man who coached him to three of his four Cups with Montreal.

"First off, you have to start with the premise that Scotty is a liar. He would say and do anything to you so that the team would win. Some people would say we won despite Scotty, or even in spite of Scotty, but that isn't true either. He was an excellent coach, especially in game situations. He was terrible when it came to personal relationships . . . he didn't have any."

Players like Shutt, Henri Richard and Lafleur recall one of Bowman's quirks. Says Shutt:

"The strangest thing with Scotty would be that the farther ahead we were in a game, the more agitated he'd become. If we were playing a tight 2-1 game, he kept quiet and didn't say anything. But if we were up four or five goals, he'd go crazy . . . he'd be screaming at us to stay on them, not to goof off and let the other team into the game."

What do players talk about in those mini-huddles before a face-off? The ensuing tableau is fictional, but not too far from the truth.

(Montreal is leading 8-3 over some expansion team and has a powerplay late in the game.)

GUY LAFLEUR (looking over at the Canadiens' bench where an agitated Bowman is pacing nervously, chomping ice cubes like a Cuisinart) Come on, Shuttie, let's pop a couple more.

STEVE SHUTT: Jeez, I dunno. It would be really rubbing it in. The game's almost over.

LAFLEUR: I wanna see if we can give 'im a heart attack.

SHUTT: There isn't a guy on the bench who'll give him mouth-to-mouth.

LAFLEUR: I know. I wanna see which guys jump on the St. John's Ambulance crew to stop them.

SHUTT: You're on!

Toe Blake's style was to talk to players individually and privately, even though he was not beyond chewing out the entire dressing room when he felt it was warranted. Bowman chose to castigate his miscreants in front of their teammates, and even players who did not get along took exception.

Henri Richard became involved in a celebrated slapping incident with Serge Savard in Vancouver in November, 1972. The team had just skated to the dressing room after a 9-1 humiliation of the Canucks when Jacques Laperriere, seething over something written the day before, yelled: "Let's keep the goddamn newspaper guys out of the room!" The team, from the highest levels of management down, was in one of its periodic kill the messenger moods.

Some players were steaming about a humorous road trip story that had appeared in a Montreal newspaper and which had been read over the telephone to them but that none had read personally. Others were under instructions to act angry. Management wanted to put the media on notice.

"That's a good idea," Savard chimed in. A superb defenceman who had overcome broken legs in consecutive seasons to win the Conn Smythe Trophy in the 1969 Stanley Cup series, he had become a leader of a vocal faction of Young Turks that had been feuding with the press since the Canada-Soviet Union series two months earlier.

Richard, in his second season as team captain and very much Old School, intervened.

"Cut the crap. They have their job to do just like anyone else."

After a heated exchange, Savard challenged the team captain.

"If you like them so much, why don't you sleep with them?"

Many teammates and opponents will tell you that of the famous brothers, it was Henri and not Maurice who had the shorter fuse. Livid, the 5′7″ captain strode over to the 6′2″ defenceman and slapped him hard across the face ("I opened my fist at the last second") with a crack that could be heard outside the room. Players jumped in to separate the two and it was agreed that what had happened would "stay in the dressing room." It didn't, because several players were quite shaken by the incident. Richard and Savard hardly spoke for a long time afterward.

A year later, Savard missed a practice and Scotty Bowman railed about it during a team practice, upsetting Richard.

"It was near the end of the practice and we were all down at one goal, leaning on our sticks, when Scotty began calling Savard all sorts of names and talking about a guy he was hanging out with. Scotty said things like the guy was just divorced and him and Serge were in all the bars and hockey players shouldn't be so dumb as to be in such situations because they hurt the team," says Richard.

The diminutive team captain interjected.

"Scotty, if you have something to tell Serge, tell Serge. He isn't here now." The coach got the hint.

"Scotty played favourites, no doubt about it, and he loved playing one guy against another," adds Mahovlich, who was immersed in a classic feud with Bowman in 1977 when he was traded to Pittsburgh. Bowman was not often happy with his big centre and said so to the press. Peter had his own friends with the media and matched Bowman headline for headline before Pollock did everyone a favour and arranged a deal with Pittsburgh.

"The important thing is, Scotty's way worked. His teams might have hated him, but he got them to play to their capabilities and not too many coaches can say that. Agree or disagree, love him or hate him, he won and that's all people remember now."

That comment is heartily endorsed by Al Strachan, hockey writer for Toronto's *Globe and Mail*, who then was covering the Canadiens for the *Gazette*.

"The players hated Scotty 364 days a year. On the other day, they cashed their Stanley Cup cheques. Scotty played the media like a fine violinist and that upset his players to no end. But his attitude was win at all costs and the players trusted him behind the bench. He was a bit of a loner but he would often take the writers out to dinner and answer any and all questions we had."

Strachan remembered an incident that was classic Bowman.

"The team flew into Minnesota and was on a pretty good streak when Scotty called in the press and announced that he was benching Steve Shutt that night. This was the year Shutt ended up with 60 goals so he was really pissed off. Shutt told Lafleur, who wasn't too happy to be losing his left winger, and the veterans' committee called a meeting. They then took the grievance to Bowman who let them talk him into reinstating Shutt, who played that night as the Canadiens bombed the North Stars."

It worked. Bowman refused to let his team get complacent. He was always a step ahead of his players and they knew it.

Internal conflicts notwithstanding, the Canadiens team that emerged in the 1975-76 season was formidable. Shutt and Lafleur, who had played alongside Henri Richard two seasons before, now were paired with Mahovlich on the "doughnut line", a term coined by Pierre Bouchard ("a hole in the centre").

Veterans Jacques Lemaire and Yvan Cournoyer were an entry and played with left wingers like the smooth-skating Murray Wilson on a second line. The checking line was the best in the business, centred by Doug Jarvis, a rookie from the Peterborough Petes School of Higher Defence, and one of the best face-off men in the league. He was teamed with veteran Jim Roberts and the incomparable Bob Gainey, a player who was to defence what Lafleur was to offence.

The fourth line comprised "Piton's Raiders"—Doug Risebrough, Mario Tremblay and Yvon Lambert—three young players who hit anything that moved, scored important goals and wreaked havoc in the opposition's zone. "Piton" was Claude Ruel's nickname—he often remained late after practice working with the rookies.

"And then if you could take care of that group of forwards," says former Bruins coach Don Cherry, "you came up against the Big Three at the blueline and Dryden in net. The 75-76 and 76-77 Canadiens teams may have been the best ever in the NHL. They were certainly better than the 1980s Oilers because of the defence."

Boston had Bobby Orr. The Flyers had a staunch defensive corps of Tom Bladon, Ed Van Impe, the Watson brothers and Moose Dupont. But Montreal had Serge Savard, Guy Lapointe and Larry Robinson. All three could skate, shoot and hit with authority. Any of the three had the ability to break a game wide open with a pass, a rush or a bodycheck. Savard and Robinson were two of the best at "head-manning the puck"—spotting a streaking winger at centre ice and hitting him in full stride on the blade of the stick with a long pass.

Lapointe was a good passer as well, but his strengths were skilled skating, joining forwards on rushes, and playing the point on a power play. His prowess at the blueline, especially his devastating slapshot which he kept low and on net, was second only to Orr's and just ahead of another superb defenceman in New York named Brad Park.

Teamed with the Big Three were two quality defensive defencemen—Bill Nyrop and Brian Engblom—and an all-purpose backup, Pierre Bouchard, who played an important role in heavy traffic.

Ken Dryden is uncomfortable with long-winded or romanticized descriptions of his talent. Suffice it to say, therefore, that he is one of the very few members of the NHL Hall of Fame selected before his thirty-fifth birthday. In a little more than seven years with the Canadiens, he had a 2.24 lifetime goals-against average and 46 shutouts.

In post-season play, he played every minute of every game in leading Montreal to six Stanley Cups, or a Stanley Cup winning percentage of .750, highest ever in the NHL for a player who played five seasons or more. There are many who feel that Montreal would have won one of the Flyers' championships had Dryden not elected to sit out the 1973-74 season in a salary dispute. He is also the only player ever in NHL history to win a major NHL award a year before winning the Calder Trophy as top rookie. (He won the Conn Smythe Trophy for best performer in the 1970-71 playoffs, and won the Calder in 1971-72.)

This team would provide Montreal fans with the Firewagon Hockey to which they had become accustomed. In 1975-76, the Canadiens finished the regular season with 58 wins, 11 losses and 11 ties for 127 points, breaking the record of 57 wins and 124 points set by the Boston Bruins in 1970-71. If it was possible, the 1976-77 version was even better, setting records which still stand for most wins—60, fewest losses— 8 (80-game schedule) and most points—132. A year later, the Habs "slipped" to 59-10-11 for 129 points.

In these days of the one-way Edmonton Oilers and the Disappearing Veteran, in which thirty year old veterans with big contracts who have learned a few things about defence mysteriously lose a step so that cheaper non-defensive nineteen year olds can take their place, the scoring feats of the Canadiens might not be considered prodigious. Boston Bruins scored an incredible 399 goals in the 1970-71 regular season and that total was not surpassed until 1981-82, when the Edmonton Oilers net-ted 417 goals, and then added 424, 446 and 401 in the next three seasons.

However, Edmonton would allow 295, 315, 314 and 298 goals against. That meant that the Oilers finished those seasons with plus-minus figures of +122, +109, +132 and +103, about 1.25 to 1.5 goals a game more than their opponents.

Montreal was a better-balanced and much more devastating team. The 1970s Canadiens established league records in points, wins and losses, because while goals poured in at one end, they stayed out at the other. From 1974-75 through 1978-79, Montreal's plus-minus figures were 374-225 (+149), 337-174 (+163), 387-171 (+216!), 359-183 (+176) and 337-204 (+133). In that five-year stretch, Montreal outscored the opposition by 837 goals in 400 regular-season games, or 2.09 goals a game. In 1976-77, the per game differential was a phenomenal 2.76 goals a game! That team never could have been defeated 11-0 by Hartford Whalers or 11-9 by Toronto Maple Leafs, off-night or not, as were the Oilers.

1971 was a pivotal year in yet another way for the fortunes of the Canadiens. On December 31 of that year, scant hours before new capital gains tax provisions were to take effect, the Molson family sold the Canadian Arena Company (the Montreal Canadiens and the Forum) to a consortium of Edward and Peter Bronfman, the Bank of Nova Scotia and John Bassett's Baton Broadcasting of Toronto for about 15 million dollars. The new group was called *Placement Rondelle* (literally, "Puck Investment"). In 1958, Peter, David and William Molson had purchased the team for 5 million dollars from cousins Hartland and Tom, who in turn had bought the Canadian Arena Company in 1957 from Senator Raymond.

The Molsons had proven beneficial for the Montreal Canadiens. They allowed Frank Selke and Sam Pollock all the room necessary to manage the dynasty and underwrote the $9.5 million renovations that took place in 1968 which made the Forum one of the best rinks anywhere to watch a hockey game.

Jacques Courtois, a well-known Tory lawyer from

Montreal, was appointed president, while Bassett and the brothers Bronfman were named to the new board of directors. Along with the Bronfmans came financial adviser Irving Grundman, who would become involved in the business side of the Canadian Arena Company operations. All the other vice-presidents, Pollock, Toe Blake and Jean Beliveau, remained in their posts and little changed over the next seven years.

In 1978, the team was sold yet again. This sale had repercussions in the front office that eventually reached ice level.

Oddly enough, the deal began on a baseball field—the most uncomfortable, god-awful baseball field ever to plague the major leagues in a modern era—Exhibition Stadium in Toronto. In 1976, John Labatt Ltd. of London, Ontario became the majority owner of the expansion Toronto Blue Jays and watched in amazement as the baseball team tie-in boosted the company's share of the lucrative Ontario beer market by two percentage points, a major gain in the cutthroat beer wars.

Labatt's marketers immediately twigged to the sports connection and looked around for other vehicles. A purchase of the Canadiens, it was decided, would be a two-edged sword. Not only would Labatt become associated with the best club team in the sport, it could excise Molson beer from the high-profile Canadiens' TV broadcasts.

Strolling happily along a sunny Montreal sidewalk with a company lawyer, in search of a cab after leaving the press conference at the rue Notre-Dame headquarters of Molson's brewery where the sale of the hockey team just had been announced, Peter Bronfman answered the journalist's question with canary feathers in his mouth: "It was a seller's market."

Very aware of the Labatt interest, and very anxious to maintain a television partnership of more than a quarter century's standing, Molson Breweries of Canada Ltd. had just paid 20 million dollars for the Montreal Canadiens. However, the building and the team were separated this time which would explain Peter Bronfman's good humour. The separation was worth a 30 million dollar long-term lease, which is still in effect today.

The sale reached into the Canadiens "upstairs dressing room" in the departure of Sam Pollock. During the seven-year ownership of the club by Peter and Edward Bronfman's Edper Investments, Pollock had acquired an equity interest in the company. When the sale took place, he was deeply involved in the Edper scheme of things and reluctant to divest.

"I had been involved in hockey and the Montreal Canadiens ever since I had left high school. It was time to go. I never for a moment doubted that I would miss it, but I had a unique opportunity with Edper and I wanted to take advantage of it."

The Pollock departure had immediate repercussions. Scotty Bowman fully expected to be named general manager in his place, but when the 1978-79 season got under way, Irving Grundman had inherited the new title of Managing Director.

Grundman had joined the Canadiens with Edper in January, 1972, and had taken an advanced course in Sam Pollock 101. The two worked side-by-side for six years, eating lunch together almost every day and discussing the intricacies of the business and hockey aspects of the Montreal Canadiens. Whether or not it ever came to annointing a successor, the coach was to eventually find himself on the outside looking in.

"Scotty and I always had gotten along and we didn't have what you might call a personality problem. But when we talked that summer, he laid it on the line. 'I won't work for you', he told me. I told him that was too bad because I thought he was the best hockey coach available, I still think he is, and I would like him around."

Grundman tried to persuade Bowman to stay with the team: "Scotty, I don't see myself doing this job more than two, three years at the outside. I wouldn't have any problems nominating you for it when I step down. All you have to do is wait a little."

Bowman couldn't wait, but remained behind the bench

for the next season and the team's fourth-straight Stanley Cup. While he did not sulk in public, he was abnormally quiet with the team.

"It wasn't vintage Scotty," says Steve Shutt. "It was a strange year. We did all right in the standings even though we weren't steamrolling teams like we had in the past. We still would win the big games against most teams, although the Islanders played us very tough. And all through this Scotty was really calm. Like he was somewhere else."

Irving Grundman received a hot-and-cold reception as new head man for the Canadiens. The hot came when he showed his straight-A marks in Pollock 101 when three WHA grads, Mark Napier, Cam Connor and Rod Langway, joined the team. The three were officially signed to contracts and attended camp, but Grundman kept saying that some technicalities had to be worked out and that their contracts could not be registered with the league office. Until they were registered, their status was that of unsigned draft choices and Montreal had three fewer players to protect in the new league waiver draft on Thanksgiving Day.

The cold came when the Canadiens allowed the very popular Pierre Bouchard to be drafted by the Washington Capitals in that same waiver draft. The way the clubs had worked it was that Washington would claim Bouchard, place the defenceman on their protected list, and trade him back to Montreal after the draft—a standard Pollock-Macchiavelli scenario. However, the league ruled that this process contradicted the waiver draft rules and that Bouchard would have to stay with Washington.

"I went to lawyers and I showed the rule to Sam and everybody agreed that our trade agreement should have been okay the way the rule was worded," Grundman said many years later. "John Ziegler chose to rule against us."

As it turned out, Ziegler was worried about a player strike. Player union head Allan Eagleson had threatened a strike when all parties came to the conclusion that free agency in the NHL was a paper tiger. The waiver draft gave a semblance of mobility to the players.

The incident was an embarrassment for Grundman and the club which had been the class act of the league for so long. Even within the front office all sorts of rumours flew. One story claimed that Scotty Bowman was the real Macchiavelli in the affair. That version said Bowman had sat on the committee that drafted the wording of the waiver re-trade rule and had told Grundman it was all right to make the deal with Washington, knowing, of course, that it wasn't, only to go whistling loudly and innocently by the distraught general manager's office after the situation backfired. Both Bowman and Grundman deny the story. Since coaches rarely get involved on league rule committees, their denials are credible.

Sam was gone, the fans lamented. Would the winning teams follow him into retirement?

One winning team stuck around. On May 21, 1979, at approximately 10:45 p.m., team captain Serge Savard skated around the Forum ice with the 22nd Stanley Cup in the club's history. A few moments later, Bob Gainey was hoisted on his teammates' shoulders when it was announced that he had won the Conn Smythe Trophy as best individual performer in the playoffs. The Canadiens defeated the New York Rangers 4-1 in the final game, holding the Broadway Blueshirts to three shots in the second and four shots in the third period. Gainey was a huge part of the Grand Suffocation.

Sam Pollock and Frank Selke might be on the sidelines, and maybe Scotty Bowman's victorious smile was a wee bit thin-lipped, but this team on the ice was only the second-ever to win four straight Cups. In a few months they would embark on a quest for their fifth.

Bob Gainey was 25, Guy Lafleur, 27, Steve Shutt, 26, Larry Robinson, 27 and Pierre Larouche, 23. They had been joined by some terrific young players like Mark Napier, Rod Langway, Brian Engblom and Cam Connor in the last year. The transition to the team of the '80s should be smooth and uneventful. The drive for five should be quite interesting. And the spirit of Sam still lived!

The Canadiens and the rest of the NHL teams would return to the Forum in three weeks, June 11, for the NHL Entry Draft. This year, Montreal would not enjoy the greatest position, their first pick being Number 27 overall, a young defenceman named Gaston Gingras. Still, a diminutive Swede named Naslund would be found as the 37th pick overall, a high-scoring Chicoutimi centre named Guy Carbonneau would be 44th and goalie Rick Wamsley of Brantford Alexanders would be number 58.

Better still, Montreal had the number 1 pick all locked up for the following year, and every scout in the league was predicting a bumper crop in '80.

12

La Guerre

In May, 1979, the Montreal Canadiens won their 22nd Stanley Cup and the province of Quebec was their oyster. Four and a half months later, they were involved in a dire struggle with a new challenger, the Quebec Nordiques.

Things would never be the same again for the Canadiens.

*　　*　　*　　*　　*　　*

Images of la Guerre . . . Part 1

The Quebec Nordiques and the Calgary Flames have finished their pre-game skate and are back in their dressing rooms, and the attention of the full house at the Colisée on this chilly November evening in 1985 turns to a weird device suspended about twenty feet above the ice, right beside the scoreboard.

The four-sided black-and-silver contraption hovers over the rink like a shroud. *"Qu'est ce que c'est?"* ("What is it?") The question travels around the Colisée like the ubiquitous Wave.

Moments before the teams are to come onto the ice for the start of their National Hockey League contest, the house lights dim, then are extinguished. A single spot illuminates a portable lectern at centre ice, where the house announcer begins his spiel. "Tonight the Nordi-

277

ques would like to honour one of our own . . ." He introduces André-Philippe Gagnon, a remarkable Québécois
performer who has recently wowed audiences in Paris
and Burbank, Ca., with his imitations of Joe Cocker and
the entire "We are the World" aggregation, with the
accent on Kenny Rogers, Willie Nelson, Bruce Springs-
teen and Bob Dylan.

Then while the mostly unilingual (French) audience
holds its collective breath, the mysterious black-and-silver device is transformed into a rear-projection screen
and the silence in the arena is broken by the ever-familiar
"He-e-e-e-r-r-r-e-e's Johnnnnnnnnnnnny!" A video of
Gagnon's recent seven-minute appearance on the Johnny
Carson show is played back to a standing ovation.

Gagnon is the hottest ticket in French Canadian entertainment after his triumph on the Carson show—he sells
out two weeks of performances at Montreal's Place des
Arts in two days—and is *un petit gars de chez nous*, hailing
from just outside Quebec in Loretteville.

The video extinguished, he is introduced to a standing
ovation and escorted on the ice by Mr. Everywhere, team
president Marcel Aubut. Gagnon receives a complete
Nordiques outfit, sweater, pants, socks, pads. He has the
crowd in stitches with his imitations of Aubut, coach
Michel "Tigre" Bergeron and Peter Stastny.

As everyone knows in these parts, everything is fair in
l'amour et la guerre and the Nordiques have scored an office win over their arch (in all senses of the word) rival
Montreal Canadiens. Johnny, Ed and Doc are the latest
fleur-de-lys conscripts in their perpetual struggle against
the *bleu-blanc-rouge*.

This game transcends a mere sixty minutes of body
contact on a 200 by 85 foot ice sheet. Any popular Que-
becer can expect to take part at any time.

After the 1984 winter and summer Olympic Games,
both the Nordiques and Canadiens almost drew and
quartered Québécois gold medalists Gaetan Boucher
(speedskating) and Sylvie Bernier (diving) in their frenzy
to "honour" them first. The internecine struggle between the two franchises reaches into every nook and

cranny of North America's French collectivity. Picture Kojak in a Nordiques or Canadiens sweater saying "Who loves ya, baby!" with a Québécois accent.

The on-ice activities of two of the NHL's most talented and colourful teams often pale in comparison with the marketing war being waged on all fronts.

*   *   *   *   *   *

Images of la Guerre . . . Part 2

Defenceman Brad Maxwell sprawls exhaustedly in the visitors' dressing room of the Forum, the most famous hockey rink in the world. His shoulder pads and blue-and-white sweater lie in a crumpled heap at his feet. He is still wearing one elbow pad and has only loosened his skate laces. He is surrounded by a solid phalanx of hockey beat reporters, print and electronic. There is an angry red welt across his right arm, in the very spot where the shoulder pad ends and the elbow pad begins.

Quebec and Montreal have tied 4-4 in this New Year's Eve 1984 matchup, the teams' second game in four days.

"These guys really hate each other," he says in a dull monotone, equal parts amazement and fatigue. Nothing has prepared him for *la Guerre*; after all, he had only eight years and 450 NHL games under his belt before he was traded to the Nordiques by Minnesota North Stars two weeks earlier.

"Minnesota and Chicago, and Minnesota and St. Louis always have been good rivalries but nothing like this. In four days, we have just played *two* seventh games of the Stanley Cup final."

In the 1984-85 season, the Canadiens and Nordiques met for an incredible 17 games, 2 exhibition, 8 regular season and 7 in their seesaw Adams Division final, won in overtime by Peter Stastny. With the exception of the first game of the playoffs in which both teams came up flat two days after thrilling last-minute wins over Adams Division rivals Boston Bruins and Buffalo Sabres, all games were emotional rollercoasters, fraught with intensity rarely seen since the old six-team NHL.

"There is no such thing as an exhibition game between Montreal and Quebec," Stastny says with a grim smile. That is because the Montreal Canadiens and the Quebec Nordiques conduct their war on many planes, from the ice to the front office, from Abitibi to the Gaspé, in public relations, advertising, marketing, the newspapers, on radio and television, in the NHL boardroom and in courtrooms.

Who would have figured it as recently as seven years ago?

In 1976, with the upstart World Hockey Association failing on most fronts, a thirty year old Quebec City lawyer named Marcel Aubut was appointed president of the Nordiques and given a single mandate. "Get the Nordiques into the NHL," he was told. Otherwise there will be no Nordiques, was the unspoken corollary.

A tall order in most situations, it was virtually impossible in the world of Quebec hockey. After all, Aubut had everything going against him; *la Métropole*, as Montreal is known even in Quebec City, was 142 miles upriver. The Canadiens were in the midst of a four-year Stanley Cup reign. Sam Pollock, acknowledged as the model for the current generation of NHL hockey executives, was in charge of the Canadiens.

Pollock, although he will modestly deny it, was the most influential man in NHL boardrooms. As a hockey fan, he respected Quebec's aspirations for admission to the NHL. As a businessman, he considered Quebec City as little more than a daycare centre for rising stars like Jean Beliveau and Guy Lafleur. Quebec City was Montreal turf and it was inconceivable that it be surrendered to a rival team.

Nobody could reckon with the chutzpah of Aubut, a cross between Rimbaud and Rambo. While the three-piece pinstriped suit is his uniform, it would not be too difficult to picture him in jungle fatigues, carrying an AK-47 with bandoliers of ammo crisscrossing his chest. The only way to describe Aubut's eventual impact is to say that he methodically blew away all opposition.

"Marcel is nothing like most people from Quebec City," says veteran *Le Soleil* columnist Claude Larochelle. "This is very much a closed town, a civil service town, and we don't seem to develop the go-getter type of person." Some outsiders might go further in their descriptions of attitudes of North America's most picturesque and only walled city, perched high on bluffs above the St. Lawrence River.

"It's not closed, it's cloistered," says one French-speaking journalist from Montreal, who begs anonymity. "There's an old joke that goes like this: 'What do you call a seventy-five year old man who was born in Sherbrooke, moved to Quebec City when he was a baby and has lived there all his life? Answer: The Sherbrooker.'"

The difference between Quebec City (half a million people, almost totally French-speaking) and Montreal (just under three million, a cosmopolitan mix with hundreds of thousands of Jews, Greeks, Italians, Portuguese and yes, *les anglais*) are a lot more profound than just size and language spoken in the street.

Historically, the two cities have banged heads for nigh on four hundred years, going back to the time when Samuel de Champlain and the *coureurs de bois* started blazing trails in the northern woods on both sides of the St. Lawrence. The fur trade opened the way for farming, which in turn led to settlements. Montreal and Quebec began as fur trade depots and grew in importance as hardy Bretons and French soldiers began hacking out farms in the wilderness and raising families.

By 1759, when Wolfe's British troops snuck past sentries in the dead of night at Cape Diamond and routed Montcalm's French army on the Plains of Abraham, the competition between the two cities was well ingrained in the collective psyches of all denizens of New France. It would be only a mild exaggeration to say that Montrealers laughed at Quebecers for being caught asleep at the switch. Fifteen years later the catcalls were reversed when an American Revolutionary army under General Robert Montgomery marched out of New England, up the Richelieu River and captured Montreal, only to be stopped at the walls of Quebec City on New Year's Eve.

That's how far back this rivalry goes.

(Incidentally, both Montcalm and Wolfe died of battlefield wounds that day, a lesson not lost on the current belligerents.)

Both cities took turns moving to the fore in economic, social and political importance until Montreal finally gained the upper hand in the late 19th century. Montreal became the economic engine of the province of Quebec, a vibrant metropolis that was propelled to international prominence by its public relations-conscious mayor, Jean Drapeau. The Main, Peel and St. Catherine, Mount Royal, the Metro, Place Ville-Marie, Central Station ... all were known across Canada and received some recognition outside Canada's borders.

When Quebec abandoned its rural roots after the Second World War, its young men and women went to Montreal to find jobs in factories and plants owned by companies with names like Northern Electric, Canadian National Railways, Steinberg's, Dominion Engineering and Canadair. There a cosmopolitan mix of Jew, Italian, Greek, German, *Canadien français* and English Canadian lived in fragile harmony and learned to work together at building one of Canada's two major metropolises.

Eventually, economic inequity and social unbalance gave birth to *la Révolution tranquille*. In Montreal, young *Canadiens français* students became *québécois*, started the first demonstrations against restaurants like Murray's that provided English-only menus, and sunk the roots of modern Quebec. There, a new nationalism, founded by young revolutionaries and nurtured by an emerging phalanx of artists, songwriters, actors and playwrights, gave rise to a new pride and new sense of accomplishment.

While all the action and innovation was taking place in *la Métropole*, Quebec City was becoming more of a walled city than ever. Home to *l'Assemblée nationale*, the provincial legislature, it seemed caught in a time bubble, perpetually five years behind the rapid changes wrought in Montreal. It gave the impression of a city under siege, its self-satisfied bourgeois citizens standing smugly on the ramparts and staring down curiously at the rabble trying to swim the moat far below. Quebec was a civil service paradise, forever middle class and comfortable. It was also terribly jealous of the excitement in Montreal.

Such a background produced Marcel Aubut. It shouldn't have; his demeanor was more that of a hustler on Montreal's Main than a good *bourgeois* from the genteel *Grande Allée*. While Aubut lives there now, a dues-paid member of Quebec City's elite, he started out as a farmer's son from a tiny hamlet outside Rivière-du-loup. He left the farm at age twelve to go to school at the Quebec Academy but he never forgot his roots. There are three vehicles parked in the Aubut driveway, two luxury cars and a black four-wheel drive Toyota. Guess which one Aubut drives at breakneck speed along Quebec City's precipitous slopes?

Graduating at the top of his class at Université de Laval in suburban Ste. Foy, Aubut made his reputation with the ink barely dry on his law degree.

In a civil action, Aubut found himself staring down a lawyer with a reputation, Jean Lesage, a pillar of Quebec society, who as Quebec's premier from 1960 to 1966 was the acknowledged Father of the Quiet Revolution. Had Aubut been from a proper Quebec City family, he would have known his place—which definitely was not facing a living legend in a Quebec courtroom at age twenty-five.

"I was scared shitless for about two minutes," he admits with characteristic candour. "Then I sat down and went to work. I realized quickly that I was in a no-lose situation: a loss to Jean Lesage for a young lawyer was no disgrace."

Aubut never had a chance to test that hypothesis; he won his case. He also won a new important friend. Lesage did not sulk; instead, he adopted Aubut as his protégé and the young advocate's career surged forward. There are many Quebecers today who feel that one day Aubut will follow in Lesage's footsteps as premier of the province.

"Jean Lesage had a reputation of a winner when he left

politics and he didn't like to lose," Aubut recalls. "But he said he saw something in me that he liked, even though I beat him."

What the late premier saw was straight-ahead drive and frankness, a combination he felt could be useful in many situations. A member of the Board of Directors of the Nordiques, he knew that the team could benefit from somebody like the brash young lawyer he had faced in court.

Aubut joined the club in 1976, the same year that the separatist Parti Québécois government of René Levesque was first elected. Aubut was to represent the Nordiques in the first round of merger negotiations with the National Hockey League. He faced an impossible task—NHL President Clarence Campbell, by no coincidence a Montrealer, had been quoted as saying that it would be "unthinkable that Quebec would be accepted into the league." So Aubut targetted Campbell and worked on him mercilessly. He failed miserably.

Their desperation for a chance to play the Montreal Canadiens on any terms grew to a frenzy in 1977 when the Nordiques won the WHA championship, the Avco Cup, and the Habs captured their second straight Stanley Cup.

Aubut rolled up his sleeves and worked even harder. In 1979, with the WHA teetering on the brink of dissolution, he was 0 for 2.

"We just couldn't get past their conditions for entry into the league," Aubut recalls. "They kept saying that Quebec City was too small and there wasn't enough money in the area to support a team. We said they shouldn't worry, Carling O'Keefe brewery was prepared to spend a lot of money. We also argued that being so close to Montreal would be good for a natural rivalry to build, not bad. They kept saying that our rink (the old Colisée) was substandard and that they would consider us if we built a better one.

"And when we'd go to the City of Quebec for financial support they would tell us to get a franchise first, then they would find money for the rink. It was a vicious circle."

Aubut and two other WHA team representatives, Michael Gobuty of Winnipeg and New England's (Hartford) Howard Baldwin, took to flying into Chicago regularly for strategy sessions that would last long into the night. They split the 17-team NHL in three, and began an intensive lobbying campaign to get enough votes from the NHL Board of Governors.

Aubut kept losing, even though several auspicious events had occurred. First, Clarence Campbell retired and was replaced by a Detroit lawyer named John Ziegler. Then Sam Pollock left the Montreal Canadiens when the Bronfmans, Peter and Edgar, sold the team. The latter event had a catch; the Bronfmans sold to Molson Breweries and the Nordiques were owned by a rival brewery.

The Quebec representative spent months on a private jet canvassing his group—Boston, Detroit, Montreal and Toronto—and turned on the pressure. But he couldn't get over the arena stumbling block and when NHL president Ziegler gave the WHA trio a February, 1979 deadline, even Aubut lost hope.

Yet politics and sports make strange bedfellows in more places than Texas football and the South West Athletic Conference (SWAC). Guy Bertrand, a prominent separatist lawyer who was also player-agent for some Nordiques players (he prompted some nervous giggles for his suggestion in 1976 that a Team Quebec be formed to compete in the first Canada Cup) called Aubut, a well-known federalist. Quebec had not yet held its May, 1980 referendum on separation and the phone call was the equivalent of a Castroite volunteering to work on the Committee to Re-elect Ronald Reagan.

Bertrand offered a meeting with René Levesque and Aubut was sitting in the premier's office a few days later.

At the time, the PQ government could only watch helplessly as scores of multinationals left the province, unwilling to chance separation from the rest of Canada. A wary premier said he could not come up with any money without some sort of guarantee that big business would be onside.

"I told him I would be back with a Carling O'Keefe director and we met again a couple of days later," Aubut smiles.

Striding into the meeting with Aubut was Lesage, who was Levesque's boss in the 1960 Liberal government before Levesque renounced a united Canada, a man still very much respected by Levesque and many of his ministers and backbenchers. An hour later, Aubut and Lesage left the meeting with five million dollars in provincial government money. The federal government, matching Quebec dollar for dollar in a pre-referendum spending competition, chipped in another five million, as did the city.

The NHL could no longer refuse, even though the next vote saw the Molson bloc (several Canadian teams including Montreal) turning thumbs down.

The Canadiens capitulated when large parts of the province suddenly began boycotting Molson's beer in favour of O'Keefe. Aubut smiles smugly when asked about his part in the anti-Molson campaign that "miraculously sprung up", as he put it. "I don't sell beer," he laughs.

When the first puck was dropped to start the 1979-80 NHL season, the Edmonton Oilers, Winnipeg Jets, Hartford Whalers and Quebec Nordiques were proud new members of the club.

In Quebec's case, however, the cost was steep and they were practically secret new members. Part of the price the Nordiques had to pay for admission to the NHL, and to recognize Montreal's original territorial imperative, was a five-year moratorium on sharing TV revenues in Canada. Time passed and Montreal and Quebec (read Molson's and O'Keefe's) began readying plans for the upcoming TV rights negotiations.

Molson's moved first and in 1982 offered to buy Quebec's rights for Hockey Night in Canada. Aubut said they would have a deal, if O'Keefe would be given the opportunity to sponsor some playoff games. Molson said no and made a very, very expensive mistake.

Aubut did not get mad, he got even. He started by

buying the rights to a few NHL games played in the U.S. and selling them to a French pay TV station in Montreal. Molson immediately challenged the move, claiming that it contravened the league's broadcasting agreement.

"There wasn't a word about pay TV in the agreement," says Aubut. "They also specified Canadian games."

Ziegler ruled in Aubut's favour.

Not satisfied with occasional Nordiques away games on pay TV, Aubut then went for the jugular. He had accurately read the currents in the league boardrooms. Many American owners were tired of being treated as parvenus and weak sisters by Montreal and Toronto and Aubut found a receptive audience when he started touring the U.S. with the idea of a new TV agreement in Canada.

He went to the New York Islanders first, convinced that if he could deliver the Stanley Cup champions, other teams would follow. The Islanders agreed and so did the other American owners. A long court fight ensued and Aubut won again. Every Friday night and on occasional Sunday afternoons during the last two hockey seasons, CTV has broadcast an NHL game. The CBC maintains its traditional Hockey Night in Canada telecasts on Saturdays. The cherry on the sundae was the fact that Molson's had to spend 26 million dollars to secure its Saturday night position, only to have Aubut and O'Keefe undermine it by putting together its Friday night package for a mere 10 million dollars.

"I did it team-by-team because I knew the American owners were fed up by the Montreal-Toronto axis," he says. "Each time before they had signed with Molson, they weren't given a choice. This deal gave them a choice, and more power in the league, too. They liked that, and the million dollars or so each team got in the new deal."

Aubut liked the new recognition and power the TV deal gave Quebec in the NHL executive suites. All that remained was to carry over the newfound power onto the ice.

Not everything worked out in the long run, however. By the end of the 1985-86 season, the CTV deal was falling through. The network was not happy with the broadcast schedule for the regular season and the playoffs and threatened to pull the plug.

The Nordiques could not match Montreal when they first joined the NHL. Facing them was a juggernaut with four straight Stanley Cup championships in its trophy case, and names such as Lafleur, Steve Shutt and Lemaire up front and Lapointe, Robinson and Savard on defence.

Eventually, circumstances began to work in Quebec's favour. After winning their fourth Cup that May, a year after Pollock had left and named Irving Grundman as GM, the Canadiens' brass watched in quiet horror as perennial all-stars Dryden and Lemaire retired, the latter to accept a playing-coach position in Europe. Then Bowman, smarting over the Pollock snub, left for Buffalo.

The Nordiques could not ice a team strong enough to compete with Montreal, yet they managed to acquit themselves quite nicely in head-to-head competition, even though Quebec would not make the playoffs that year and the Canadiens would battle Buffalo and New York Islanders for the top three spots in the regular season.

The early NHL Nordiques contented themselves with winning off the ice. The original team that had played in the World Hockey Association in 1974 wore a dark blue uniform with red shoulder stripes. The team that joined the NHL essentially wore a Quebec flag with a Nordiques crest slapped on it. The Nordiques were blatantly marketed as Quebec's team, *l'équipe des Québécois*, and they stocked the line-up with native-born French Quebecers. The Canadiens, their *bleu-blanc-rouge*, and their English front office were snidely referred to as *"l'équipe des anglais"*.

Remembers Steve Shutt: "It was a disgusting piece of crap for them to pull and the kind of problems it caused weren't worth it. First, it really upset the French players on our team because they were not used to being called *les anglais* by people in their own hometowns. We had worked through the nationalism of the late 1970s without any of that stuff working its way into the game and all of a sudden, the sports pages looked like the op-ed pages. If the Nordiques wanted to get us emotional about them, they succeeded. We hated them and the crap they were pulling and a guy like Lafleur who practically grew up in Quebec City was in an impossible situation."

These subtleties were not lost on the voracious press corps in both cities. Dailies commissioned polls to determine the popularity of both teams and published maps of a Quebec divided into "Quebec blue" and "Montreal red". Emotions rose to fever pitch in *tavernes* all across the province, spread to the Forum and the Colisée, and finally onto the ice.

Lafleur, who like Beliveau had played his junior hockey in Quebec City before moving up to Montreal, began hearing boos when he returned to his second home. Games took on a chippy nature. Montreal fans in Quebec and Nordiques fans at the Forum, gently tolerated before, became the targets of verbal and occasional physical abuse.

"I think we went through a period of adolescence," Aubut recalls. "And a lot of things happened that I would rather have not happened." One of those came during what should have been Quebec's proudest moment— their defeat of the Canadiens in the best-of-five opening round in the 1981-82 NHL playoffs. Montreal GM Grundman, Mrs. Grundman and Montreal players' wives were spat upon by Colisée fans. Grundman was subjected to anti-Semitic insults, and the Canadiens demanded extra security from the Nordiques.

That incident overshadowed some brilliant manoeuvering by Aubut within a year of his team's entry into the NHL that would drastically alter his on-ice product. In the late spring of 1980, he launched Operation Europe and stage-managed the defections of brothers Peter and Anton Stastny from Czechoslovakia.

In an operation worthy of spy thrillers, the brothers were spirited away from their Innsbruck hotel in a red

Mercedes and taken at high speed through the Tyrolean Alps to Vienna, where they received visas at the Canadian embassy and then boarded a plane for Canada.

The next season, Peter scored 39 goals and added 70 assists to set a record points total for an NHL rookie. Anton chipped in 85 points on 39 goals and 46 assists and the Nordiques had instant respectability. Ever since the arrival of the Stastnys, the Nordiques have been a competitive team.

"It was like getting two number one draft choices," Aubut cackles, adding that the whole story of the defection would make a great book someday.

"They added stability to our team, and a tremendous amount of discipline and dedication. Our Québécois players tend to get too emotional out there and lose their tempers. Peter, especially, showed our guys how to keep their minds on the game."

That was a tall order for Stastny—now the team captain—who spoke little English and no French when he defected. He occasionally had to work on the coach, too, a banty rooster named Michel Bergeron, who had a reputation for chewing gum at 5000 rpms behind the bench and taunting opposition players in pre-game warmups in Quebec's junior league. Bergeron also was known as a winner, an intense, emotional guy who would torment officials and the opposition.

Bergeron proved to be Aubut's second major coup of 1980. He had found a coach with the same otherworldly drive that he possessed and Quebec began its serious love affair with the Nordiques.

The fiery Bergeron, five-feet, six-inches of scrap and yap who looks like he should be throwing dice in an alley (while Aubut hangs out around the corner holding the money), hides a shrewd hockey mind behind his explosive exterior. He is lovingly called *"le Tigre"* in Quebec and he will do anything to win.

After defeating the first-place Canadiens on a Dale Hunter goal in overtime of the fifth game of the 1981-82 series, the Nordiques polished off the second-place Boston Bruins in the division final before succumbing to the Islanders in the conference final.

A lot of the success for the playoff performance went to Bergeron, who thoroughly outcoached Montreal's Bob Berry and Boston's Gerry Cheevers.

"I have two major priorities in my life," says the youthful Bergeron, "my family and coaching the Nordiques." Those close to him might question that order, remembering his daily round trips of 180 miles when he coached junior hockey at Trois-Rivières. After running his team's practice, Bergeron would hop into his car and drive to Montreal, where he would watch Canadiens' practices run by Bowman. Afterwards he would sit and talk hockey with his guru, assailing him with question after question.

"How else do you learn? Scotty was nice enough to talk to me and help me and I was serious enough about being a hockey coach to go out of my way to learn." In 1985, after Bergeron's Nordiques eliminated Bowman's Sabres in the first round of the playoffs, Bowman said some derogatory things about his former star pupil. "That's hockey," Bergeron laughs.

Bergeron wasn't laughing in November, 1985 when he started suffering from headaches and double vision. After a week in hospital, his condition was diagnosed as post-viral encephalitis and he travelled to Minnesota's famed Mayo Clinic for treatment.

He was still suffering blurred vision when he returned behind the bench in late November. The players, relieved to have him back because the team was 3-8-1 under assistant coach Simon Nolet and 13-2 under Bergeron, were merciless. "I hear the Flames are going to play nine guys tonight because Michel can't tell the difference," said one. "That's nothing, I hear he's going back to the Quebec junior league to coach the Shawinigan Cataractes," retorted another. This is the terrible humour found in winning dressing rooms.

Coincidental with a winning record were several quiet changes. First, all vestiges of nationalistic marketing quietly disappeared, as Aubut and the Nordiques were genuinely embarrassed by the events in their rink during the Canadiens' playoff. Secondly, the team also quietly dropped their "francophone first" policy, opting for the best players they could find to play the roles defined by management. When hometown boy Réal Cloutier, who had scored 283 goals in five years with the WHA Nordiques and another 122 in three-and-a-half NHL seasons, began making impossible salary demands and undermining Bergeron, management was strong enough to trade him to Buffalo for Tony McKegney, André Savard and Jean-Francois Sauvé. The most surprised person in Quebec was Cloutier, who had gambled that the Nordiques were afraid to trade a homebrew superstar.

It was the first of several brilliant deals for Quebec GM Maurice Filion. McKegney and Savard contributed handsomely to the team until an injury ended Savard's career. McKegney was later traded to Minnesota for Maxwell and Brent Ashton. The diminutive "Tattoo" Sauvé anchored the team's power play before going to Europe and Ashton has been a 30-goal-a-year power forward, adding muscle to the Stastny line.

The Nordiques, like the Canadiens' "French Foreign Legion" of eight Americans, two Swedes and a Czech, have a core of players with names like Shaw, Price, Mann, Hunter, Siltanen, Kumpel, Moller, Gillis and Malarchuk.

In the team's early days, there was the "Farrish factor", named after journeyman defenceman Dave Farrish (NY Rangers, Toronto and a variety of stops in the American Hockey League). After a trade from Quebec City, the English Canadian complained that anglophones did not get a fair shake with the team. The report was widely circulated across North America and there was little the Nordiques could do or say to refute the charges. In truth, the universal equation of sports grousing could have been applied to identify the root causes of Farrish's discontent: the vehemence of sour grapes is always inversely proportional to time played.

Today's non-French players scoff at any suggestion of

language favouritism by the club, or of problems of settling into a city that is 95 percent French-speaking.

Dale Hunter of Petrolia, Ontario parades in his long underwear under the stands before a game with the Gretzky Oilers and kibbitzes easily, in English, with two Colisée security guards. He grabs a peaked hat from one and goosesteps a few feet down the corridor to the general mirth of all.

"Anybody who says anything bad about this city is nuts," he states with the trademark pugnacity that has earned him both the respect and enmity of opponents around the league. "This city is tremendous. It is not too big, so you don't fight the rat race, and it's not too small, so you can get all the services you'd find in other places around the league. There is an English community here and they help out with things like babysitting services, schools and helping wives and families getting settled. And the French people are wonderful, too, especially if they recognize you as a Nordique."

"This is the major leagues," says Mark Kumpel of Wakefield, Massachusetts, a member of the 1984 U.S. Olympic team. "No hockey player in his right mind would worry about coming here and not being able to speak English. Could you imagine some guy choosing to stay in the AHL because his team was in the States or English Canada? That's insane."

Quebec City is also popular with hockey beat writers and players for other teams. During the 1984-85 Campbell Conference final playoff, the late Pelle Lindbergh treated several of his Philadelphia teammates to *calèche* (horse and buggy) rides in and out of some of the older town's tiny, cobblestoned streets. He wanted to show North American-raised Flyers what it was like back home in Sweden.

This is not to suggest that there are no French Quebecers playing for the Nordiques. Far from it, with goalies Mario "Goose" Gosselin and Richard Sevigny, Gilbert Delorme, Normand Rochefort, Robert Picard, Alain Côté and Michel Goulet.

Goulet, whose aristocratic bearing evokes the *sieurs* of

New France, is arguably one of the best four left wingers in the game—comfortable in a group which includes Montreal's Mats Naslund, Philadelphia's Brian Propp and Edmonton's Jari Kurri—a tall, smooth-skating sniper who has averaged 56 goals a year for the last three seasons.

Soft-spoken by temperament, he is ice to coach Bergeron's fire and sometimes the combination sets off explosions in the Nordiques camp. Early in 1985-86, when the Nordiques were struggling with only three wins in fourteen games, it was Goulet who was singled out by Bergeron for lackadaisical play.

"I don't accept that kind of criticism," Goulet says. "If we are a team, we are playing badly as a team, not because somebody thinks one or two individuals are letting the team down." Of course, it made headlines.

Goulet, who evokes cheers of "Goo! Goo!" in the Colisée when he sweeps down ice, was a natural target after his celebrated 1985 training camp salary holdout. Three months later, he still was not talking to GM Filion.

Is it harder for a French player to play in Quebec City?

"I can't really say, although it seems that players from Quebec are expected to produce more by the fans. I like it here and I like this kind of pressure. I don't spend too much time worrying about whether or not this market is big enough for me to get off-ice work making commercials, or whether or not I get a lot of attention like I might in the bigger media centres."

Besides, Goulet gets all the media attention he wants during playoff time as the Nordiques and Canadiens wage their little war *en famille*. Suddenly, as the snows recede and warming breezes waft down the rue St. Catherine and the Grande Allée, young men from Timra, Sweden; Bratislava, Czechoslovakia; San Diego, California and Red Deer, Alberta discover the true meaning of a Québécois family feud.

"The strangest thing," says Hunter, "is that we probably respect them (Montreal) more than any team in the league. I don't think we hate them or they hate us (although both teams will admit to loathing Boston) but the circumstances dictate that the series becomes a war."

The animosity came to a head during the sixth game of the Adams Division final, Good Friday, April 20, 1984. Late in the second period of the game in Montreal, Quebec led 2-0 but trailed 3-2 in the series. A series of fights broke out and just when it appeared that order was about to be restored, Quebec's Louis Sleigher sucker-punched Montreal's Jean Hamel, a former Nordique, along the boards.

When the teams emerged for the third period, the Canadiens went after Sleigher, who received a thorough correction from Chris Nilan and another bench-clearing brawl erupted. During the festivities, Peter Stastny had his nose broken by Montreal's fiery Mario Tremblay and entered the team dressing room for repairs.

"Fix it so I can play," he told a club doctor, who advised him that the procedure could be excruciating. "I don't care," Stastny retorted and the doctor did as obliged. Only then did Stastny discover that he had been assessed a game misconduct and could not return. Montreal poured in five straight goals and won the series 4-2.

A year later, his oft-fractured proboscis long repaired, Stastny got a measure of revenge with an overtime goal in the seventh game of the Adams final to eliminate Montreal.

That series, chippy and emotional, was quieter than the preceding one and play in the 1985-86 season showed that the teams have left a lot of the vindictiveness behind.

One reason is that—and one might earn the wrath of dyed-in-the-wool fans for saying it—the Nordiques and the Canadiens have come to resemble each other. Quebec has built a tougher defence and the Canadiens a more prolific offence. Both teams feature a pair of explosive European snipers, Quebec's Stastnys and Montreal's Swedish pair of Naslund and Kjell Dahlin. Both have strong defensive forwards (Quebec's Paul Gillis, Ashton and Alain Côté; Montreal's Bob Gainey, Guy Carbonneau and Mike McPhee). Add to that such top talents as

Montreal's Bobby Smith and Quebec's Goulet, and two exciting young Quebec-born goalies in Gosselin and Patrick Roy, and the family feud could go on for years.

The Nordiques, through other intermediaries, have strengthened their defence with former Canadiens Robert Picard and Gilbert Delorme. Neither will admit it, but their presence in the Quebec dressing room and on the ice tends to cool certain situations.

"You cannot forget that you played with people like Larry Robinson, Craig Ludwig and Gaston Gingras on defence and behind guys like Tremblay, Gainey and Nilan," says Delorme. "These guys were and are my friends, but there are no friends on the ice, just guys in the other uniform."

Picard, acquired in a mid-season trade for Mario Marois, parrots the same cliché. "When you're playing a game, there are no friends—even if you played with them before."

Nevertheless, one cannot help but notice that when Delorme and Picard are in the thick of the action against former teammates, a corner altercation or a slashing incident in front of the net cools off with only a few harsh words spent. The gloves usually stay on.

All bets are off where Dale Hunter is concerned. "You can't help but feel you are always fighting an uphill battle against them," he says. "Everything about playing in Quebec is reflected in Montreal because of what Montreal has always meant to hockey. It upsets us because we don't get a lot of respect, even though we have been fighting those guys even-up for five years. We can't even go on a road trip without passing through Montreal airport."

It has gotten so that the Nordiques are wondering if the stylized "N" on their crest stands for Rodney Dangerfield's "no respect". A classic example of what it means to be a Quebec Nordique came at Christmas, 1985. During the holidays two Soviet teams—Central Red Army and Moscow Dynamo—toured North America and played various NHL teams in a 10-game series. The Aeroflot jet carrying the Red Army, in reality the

Soviet national team, had barely touched down when the Russians had swished by the Los Angeles Kings and Edmonton Oilers in one-sided victories.

Soviet coach Viktor Tikhonov, a veteran of many North American exhibitions, told reporters in post-game interviews in Edmonton that he was "really looking forward to our New Year's Eve match at the Forum against Montreal."

He wasn't kidding. The Red Army dismantled the Habs 6-1 in a one-sided contest. Late in the third period, the knowledgeable Forum crowd admitted defeat and accorded the Soviets a standing ovation. Even the stone-faced Tikhonov allowed himself a gold-toothed smile.

So what does this have to do with lack of respect for the Nordiques? In between shellackings of the Oilers and the Habs, the Soviets "passed through Quebec" en route to Montreal and were thoroughly thrashed, 5-1. The victory ignited Quebec, sending the team on a third seven-game winning streak of the year and into first place in the Adams Division. No one noticed.

"You figure it out," growls Bergeron. "We have the Stastnys, two of the best players in hockey; we have Michel Goulet who scores 50 goals a year, every year; we have a good defence and terrific goaltending and we play well on the road. We are very tough at the Colisée. We beat all of the contenders—Edmonton, Philadelphia, Edmonton, Montreal and Washington. And still they put us down."

He stops dead in mid-diatribe, and smiles broadly. "That's good. It makes my job a lot easier because I don't have to waste a lot of time trying to motivate this team. They do it themselves."

*   *   *   *   *

Images of la Guerre . . . Part 3

The Canadiens and Nordiques have finished their pre-game warmup on this February night in 1986 and the black-and-silver device again hovers about twenty feet above the ice surface. Directly below, a huge red carpet covers the Colisée ice surface from blueline to blueline. Off to the left, at the south end, a shimmering blue and violet tent is formed by young men holding up special flags on poles. The houselights dim ... and are extinguished.

A single spot illuminates a portable lectern.

"Ladies and gentlemen," the tuxedoed P.A. announcer intones, "the Prime Minister of Canada."

The black-and-silver screen flickers to life and The Right Honourable Brian Mulroney, Prime Minister of Canada, tells the Colisée crowd how proud he is to have been appointed Honorary Chairman of the Organizing Committee for the 1987 National Hockey League All-Star games, to be held in Quebec City and to feature the NHL all-stars versus the Soviet Union.

In *tavernes* and *brasseries* all across Quebec, fans impatiently awaiting the appearance of the Canadiens and Nordiques instead are introduced to the Prime Minister, Quebec Premier Robert Bourassa (on video) NHL President Ziegler, Aubut, NHL Players Association head man Allan Eagleson and other sundry political types.

The crowd is getting restless as the ceremonies drag on and desultory boos trickle down from the upper reaches of the Colisée. At TVA studios in Quebec and Montreal, the switchboard is a Christmas tree of blinking lights.

And then, the finale. With a flourish, thirty young dancers in provocative costumes sashay out of the tent and move with more enthusiasm than art through a choreographed piece of modern dance.

The number finished, they stream off the ice and are replaced by two annoyed hockey teams.

Marcel Aubut is smiling from ear to ear. "Le Tigre" Bergeron is snarling. Somewhere in the background, Marcel Filion is trading veteran Wilf Paiement to the New York Rangers.

Life, and *la guerre*, go on.

13

The Interregnum

Montreal, 10:20 p.m., April 27, 1980: A Runyonesque gathering is engrossed in the kaleidoscopic swirl of myriad television images in a store window on this chilly spring evening.

The Granada TV Rental outlet is about 200 yards east of the Forum. There, 18,000 hockey fans are sweating through what the National Hockey League calls Game 7 of Series K. Outside the Granada showroom, watching the five television sets with their multiple images of the seventh game of the semi-final involving Montreal Canadiens and the youthfully tenacious Minnesota North Stars, is our crowd. Official "paid" attendance: nine (we don't count the passersby).

Montreal Urban Community Police patrol car 25-4 is parked directly at the curb, about ten feet from the store window. Inside are four cops, the two regulars assigned to that car and two others from Car 25-31, which is parked across the street. Directly behind them is a Diamond Taxicab, its driver chewing on a cigar. At the corner sits an empty bus from Line 165. The bus driver is standing to the right of the storefront. He feels the cold and zips up his regulation grey sweater.

Two other players in this little vignette are feeling no cold at all. Fresh from a tavern just down St. Catherine Street, one of them lies sprawled against the rear fender of the patrol car. The other, much livelier, keeps up a lurching commentary while the silent ballet blinks before us in green, yellow, red, white and blue.

"Minnesota is gonna win it," he declares over and over again with the conviction of the truly inebriated. "No way they're gonna lose. The Canadiens are tired. Look at 'em, they're dragging their asses."

The driver's window in the patrol car rolls down.

"Shut the hell up or I'll kick yours!" says the cop.

"It's a free country," sniffs the wino, miffed that no one wants to listen to his colour commentary. The door is nudged open an inch and the wino takes the hint.

Back on television, the Habs are pressing. After opening the scoring on a Mark Napier power play goal at 9:12, they suffered the indignity of giving up a short-handed effort just five minutes later. It was pure fluke. Denis Herron went behind his net to clear a puck up the boards and launch another power-play rush, something a goalie does 500 times a year. The puck hit the side of the net and bounced out to checker Tom Younghans who was alone in front of a deserted cage. Late in the second period, defenceman Craig Hartsburg scored with a point blast on a North Stars' advantage and the Canadiens have trailed since.

Montreal is severely strapped in its drive for five. Late in the third game of the best-of-five opening round game against Hartford Whalers, winger Pat Boutette stuck out a knee and caught Guy Lafleur as he skated past. The blatant foul ended Lafleur's playoff series, but the Canadiens went ahead and won the game in overtime. Two NHL greats, Gordie Howe and Bobby Hull, retired after this game. Several years later, some Canadiens fans would say that this was the last game played by the real Flower.

Also sitting out is Pierre Larouche, Lafleur's linemate. The Canadiens scored 328 goals during the regular season. Larouche and Lafleur, with 50 each, accounted for almost one-third of them. Their linemate, Steve Shutt, who scored three goals in a 5-0 shutout of the North Stars earlier in the series, looks lost. In this game, he does not get a shot on goal.

Still, the game is close because the Canadiens have a rockribbed defence led by the Big Three and ably backstopped by the Little Three, Brian Engblom, Gaston Gingras and Rod Langway. Serge Savard and Guy Lapointe are limping on leg and foot injuries, respectively, so the Little Three are in the thick of it.

Early in the third period, two veteran playoff campaigners—Mario Tremblay and Yvon Lambert—do what they do best. They "muck", banging and bouncing bodies against the boards, and the puck comes free. It is directed back to the point where Rod Langway lets it go. It eludes Gilles Meloche and the game is tied 2-2.

Inside 25-4, the cops are slapping each other on the back. The cabbie lays on the horn and the blare substitutes for the silent roar of the Forum fans we can see in standing ovation.

"Enough!" One of the cops has stepped out of the car and is glaring at the cabbie. Station 25 is just around the corner and this foursome wants to escape the notice of their watch commander.

The goal lifts the Canadiens and they start pressing the younger North Stars. We all have seen this happen many times before. The Lion Awakes.

But a strange thing happens. Even though the Canadiens have the better flow, they aren't getting the shots on net. The North Stars regroup at their blueline, stop the thrust and parry dangerously with several 2-on-1 and 3-on-2 breaks. Herron is called on to make several important saves.

The game ebbs and flows silently in front of us. We cannot hear the announcers in French or English, although the cabby has the game on radio, but we all know that each announcer is saying the same thing: overtime beckons.

There is a strange dynamic to a tight playoff hockey game. Play seems to become constipated as the clock winds down. Instead of pressing in the last five minutes of regulation time, and still having some time left to get even again if the opponent scores, the players all act as if overtime is the real goal, even though a mistake made then will have no redemption. They are avoiding defeat rather than striving to win. You can already hear the post-game interviews in the losing dressing room: "Well, we took 'em to overtime and they just got the break."

Players know they get special dispensation if they lose in overtime, and act accordingly.

As a result, there are weird gaps in the action. Instead of pressing to the advantage, players hesitate and drop back and the puck often just lies there with rival players avoiding it like the proverbial plague.

It is this kind of situation that confronts a Canadiens forward with 90 seconds left in regulation.

Instead of turning on the jets and racing a North Star to a loose puck in the neutral zone, he peels off and heads back to his end. Minnesota's Steve Payne pounces on the puck and relays it to centre Bobby Smith who carries it over the Canadiens' blue line. He "shoots-passes" it to streaking winger Al MacAdam who tips it over Herron's leg. Minnesota 3 Montreal 2. Time: 18:43 of the third period. Can the Forum be quieter than the Granada storefront?

"Nuts, Minnesota's gonna win."

The wino is brave again, and maybe a little surprised that his prediction may come to pass. This time the cop can only give him a hard stare and, forgetting the proximity of the station house, slams his hand down on the wheel, hitting the horn in a bleat of defeat.

"The Canadiens are jinxed. Christ, we didn't even have winter," adds the beery philosopher, invoking Montreal's lack of snow in the winter of 1979-80 as the true portent of the impending loss. Inside 25-4, one of the cops can't help but laugh.

Some 77 seconds remain in the dynasty. Can the Canadiens come back yet another time? Behind the Canadiens bench, coach Claude Ruel cannot hide his concern. Scotty Bowman is in Buffalo. Jacques Lemaire has spent the winter in Switzerland. If Ken Dryden is watching the game, it is on television from Toronto. Lafleur and Larouche are absent. Doug Risebrough is dressed but he's injured and he hasn't played a second in this crucial game. Lapointe and Savard are limping.

Play resumes, and with 40 seconds remaining Meloche stones Napier. The camera pans the Canadiens' bench and all players are watching the game intently. The only players with their heads down are those who have just come off the ice, gulping for air. The mental toughness is still there, these guys are not quitting.

Twenty seconds remain and Meloche gets his toe on a shot from the point. And then it is over. There will be no second "five straight".

You can't help but wonder if somewhere in the building, the Class of 1960 is heaving a sigh of relief. Their "five" is safe.

As the green-shirted North Stars mob Meloche and the white-shirted Canadiens console Herron, the bus driver shrugs, walks quickly to number 165 and drives off. The cabbie follows as the rear doors of Car 25-4 open and two officers cross the street to Car 25-31. The driver of 25-4 throws a last look at the two winos, one sleeping quietly on the sidewalk where his partner is trying to wake him, and drives off. Car 25-31 follows. The winos are still there when the Forum funeral procession comes down St. Catherine Street.

The thing about defeating a champion is the surprise that follows. No matter how battered and torn the champion may have been during the contest, the aura of invincibility is all-pervasive, and even the challenger can't believe it when the last siren, bell or gun is sounded.

At 10:44 p.m., with a minute left on the game clock, it was Minnesota that watched the scoreboard with trepidation. The mystique of the Habs worked two ways. It left Minnesota players asking themselves deep inside: "What are they going to do to win it this time?" Across the ice on the other bench, Habs were asking themselves: "I wonder who's going to pot the tying goal?"

At 10:50, both teams, still disbelieving, were in their dressing rooms. Minnesota's tiny cubicle under the reds on the east side of the Forum was inundated by media types: recorders and cameras thrust into the faces of young, exultant faces and all asking the rubberneck's big question: "How does it feel?"

In the home team's museum/dressing room, the same question is repeated, albeit more quietly. None of the players look up. The torch has been passed to them, and dropped. Tonight the pictures of the Hall of Famers which line the upper wall seem to stare down accusingly.

Off in a corner, Doug Jarvis sits quietly, uncomprehendingly. A superb defensive forward and product of the wonderful Peterborough Petes' training ground that has sent so many great players to Montreal and other NHL teams, this is the first time he must face a Stanley Cup loss in his NHL career. He joined the team in 1975-76 and in each year of his four-year career has returned home in the spring as a Stanley Cup champion.

The realization dawns: these guys don't know how to lose. The learning process is a painful and time-consuming one. For the Canadiens, it started a year earlier.

Shortly after the 1978-79 season ended, Al MacNeil announced he was leaving the organization to accept the coaching job with the Atlanta Flames. To some that was minor news. But to those who covered the Canadiens and knew how well MacNeil had done his job preparing young players in Nova Scotia for eight years, it was seen as an important defection. MacNeil made his announcement early because he wanted to be ready for the NHL draft.

His was not the only significant departure from the club that year. Few people close to the team doubted that the Stanley Cup-clinching game in May was Scotty Bowman's last behind the Canadiens' bench. He had brooded for a year over the appointment of Grundman as managing director and the creation of a hockey management board.

Bowman made his move one weekend in early June. He was locked into heavy negotiations with Buffalo Sabres and they were pressing for an answer.

"I was in constant communication with both teams and finally decided that I was going to meet with the

Canadiens' board on Monday. Buffalo started pressing because the draft was just around the corner and they wanted all of this resolved. I called Mr. [Seymour] Knox because he had given me a deadline of midnight Sunday. He was upset because this already was an extension of an earlier deadline."

Bowman did not want to coach any longer. He felt he had earned his promotion into the front office, whether with Montreal or another team, and was determined to obtain the front office position. Many years and many coaches later in Buffalo, he would discover that there was no coach good enough to work for Scotty Bowman, general manager—with the notable exception of Scotty Bowman, coach.

"Buffalo was worried about my decision. They wanted to know a week earlier and that's why I ended up coaching. I said to them: 'I'll come but I'm not going to coach.' That was the bottom line and finally they agreed to this. But I needed more time to meet with the Canadiens and probably, to really make up my mind.

"So I told them: 'Look, you've been fair with me, I'll be fair with you. I'll agree to coach for you for one year if you give me this one-day extension.' I didn't want to start off with them thinking that I was just trying to use them as a way of staying with Montreal."

Bowman decided that Sunday and phoned Knox and, later, Molson's president Morgan McCammon. He still wanted to meet with the Canadiens' board the following day, Bowman told them, but his mind was made up. That Monday Bowman met with Canadiens' president Jacques Courtois, Jean Beliveau and Irving Grundman to tell them of his decision.

"We had a good conversation and parted as friends. It was a good way to leave and I thanked them. There was no animosity."

When the draft meetings opened later that week, Scotty Bowman sat at the Buffalo table and MacNeil was with Cliff Fletcher's Flames.

After the management defections came the player moves. Less than a week after Bowman's announcement, thirty-three year old Jacques Lemaire joined the exodus. Lemaire still had several productive years ahead of him in the NHL; indeed, he had played better as he matured, replacing Peter Mahovlich between Shutt and Lafleur on the club's top scoring line and adding a component it had never possessed, defence. All this from a player of whom it was said in his earlier years: "He could go into a corner with eggs in his pockets and come out with all of them intact."

Lemaire, always a quiet and serious individual, was one hockey player who took his *métier* to heart. He worked hard and taught himself the defensive game in the NHL. He also was good with the younger forwards. His studious approach to the game left little doubt that he could turn to coaching after his playing days were over.

There was only one roadblock. Lemaire was a very shy, intensely private person who hated the Montreal Canadiens' fishbowl. He never begrudged the media people their jobs; he just didn't like the cameras pointed at him.

When the Swiss came calling for a player-coach who could speak French, Lemaire was the right man.

"I feel that at thirty-three, I am very fortunate to have this opportunity," he told a news conference, one of many which would keep the Montreal hockey writers away from their beloved golf courses during this summer of change. "After sitting back and analyzing everything, and considering the alternatives, I have decided to go over there as a playing-coach. I want to continue in hockey after my playing days are over and I think this will give me some experience in coaching and managing."

Lemaire would be taking a salary cut, but it was worth it, he said. He earned 150,000 dollars a year with Montreal in 1978-79 and the contract with Sierre was for 75,000 U.S. dollars a year. However, it was tax-free and the Lemaire family would be provided with a free house and automobile.

Three weeks later, and a scant six weeks after the last Stanley Cup parade, Ken Dryden announced his retirement. He had talked it over several times with Irving

Grundman during the preceding season and the Canadiens had ample warning. Despite his relatively young age, thirty-one, Dryden felt it was time to move on to other things. The hockey writers were reached at their respective golf courses July 8, a month before Dryden's birthday, and summoned to a hastily convened press conference.

"Retiring was a lot easier yesterday than it is today. But it is a decision that I've taken and will have to live with. To have lived in Montreal, to have played at the Forum, to have played before the people of Montreal and to have played with the kind of people I've had the opportunity to play with, makes for a truly remarkable experience."

Another player who had provided Montrealers with many remarkable experiences during his career would be third on the retirement match that summer. Yvan Cournoyer, the Road Runner, had missed much of the last season and the Stanley Cup playoffs after back surgery in January, his second such operation. The thirty-five year old right winger went to training camp that September and was flying, scoring two goals in a 3-3 tie with Philadelphia and another against Chicago.

However, he did not suit up for the two last exhibition games against Toronto and Boston and took his turn before the microphones October 10.

"I tried it and found out I just can't do it," he said. The back was too sore and, although Cournoyer had shown oldtime form, he knew that the wear-and-tear of a full season would be too much. He would hand the captain's "C" officially to Serge Savard. The rangy defenceman had worn it during the Stanley Cup conquest earlier in the spring and now it was his for good. In one summer, Montreal lost three players with twenty-five Cups among them.

"Talk about your house of cards," Grundman reminisced.

"We lost talent at every level that summer and those of us left had to work even harder to maintain our previous level. As much as the losses of the players hurt us, we felt that the nucleus of players who remained was good enough to keep us at the top of the standings. We still had the best defence in the league and we had players like Larouche, Shutt and Lafleur to put it in the net, and Jarvis and Gainey to check the other teams' forwards."

Bunny Larocque finally would get his wish to become number one goalie with the Canadiens, but Montreal needed a dependable back-up who could challenge Larocque for the top spot if necessary. Young forward Pat Hughes, Mark Napier's brother-in-law, was traded to Pittsburgh for Denis Herron, a smart move.

Not so smart a move was the appointment of Bowman's replacement. A variety of people had been considered for the post: Jacques Laperriere, Henri Richard, Dickie Moore, Gilles Tremblay and Claude Ruel. The summer rumour mill was hyperactive in the off-season but none of the guesses came close.

When Red Fisher of *The Montreal Star* scooped the world September 4 with the news that Bernard "Boom Boom" Geoffrion was Scotty Bowman's replacement, the hockey audience was stunned. Glib, funny in a beer commercial sort of way, Boom Boom had been instrumental in launching the Flames franchise in Atlanta. He had shown some talents as a coach, but his strength was public relations, which he was practising for Atlanta when Irving Grundman reached out for him.

"We made a mistake," Grundman admits several years later. "Bernie had coached twice so he had experience and he was a very popular man in this city in his playing days. And although he was famous for his craziness and sense of humour, he was a bright, intelligent man who could communicate. And the thing we needed with a veteran Stanley Cup team was communication."

It never happened.

Geoffrion blitzed into Montreal and immediately took over his press conference, cracking jokes in French and English, the latter a curious combination of French and Georgia Peach accents. His first coaching stint with New York Rangers in 1968-69 had lasted three months into the season before he was sidelined by ulcers. Four years later, he coached the brand new Flames into the Stanley Cup quarterfinals and again quit because of illness.

Montreal's hockey media asked the obvious question: What makes you think you can survive the real heat of coaching the Canadiens?

"I am the new, improved Bernard Geoffrion," he told the masses. "I can handle this. I am serious and I am going to prove it to you."

Both sides agreed to wait and see, especially the veteran journalists who had covered the Canadiens during the 1950s. They had Geoffrion tabbed as right winger on the NHL's all-time Team Strange, with Eddie Shack on left wing and Mike "Shakey" Walton at centre. Boom Boom earned his spot, scoring 393 goals in 16 NHL seasons and engaging in more fun than was legal for fifty people to enjoy.

This was the same Boomer who peered through the hole in his baseball glove in the famed Miller Lite beer commercials in the United States.

Indeed, some scribes remembered, "da Boomer's fun" almost killed him once. The incident occurred in practice. The Toe Blake Canadiens did not waste time on drills and weaves and repetitious "3-on-2s" during their ice training. The best way for the top players in the league to get better was to play against the top players in the league—themselves.

The players were skating hard and having fun in one such scrimmage when Geoffrion went down in a clump. His teammates gathered around and made their usual derogatory comments such as "Hey Boom, the scrimmage ain't on TV" until it was noticed that he was changing colour. Rushed to hospital by ambulance, Geoffrion spent several hours on the operating table as doctors worked hard to minimize the damage caused by a ruptured spleen.

This was the man who would guide the fortunes of a veteran team that had battled Scotty Bowman to a draw over the preceding eight seasons?

It was Boom Boom in the Lions' Den and it ended predictably. Three months and a week after Geoffrion entertained the media wretches at his inaugural press conference, he was in Irving Grundman's office.

Michael Dugas of *The Gazette* was sitting outside Grundman's office when Geoffrion stomped in December 12. He took notes.

"I'm sick and tired of them. They're not acting like professional players. Why should I get sick over a bunch of guys who won't listen to me. Guys are coming in at two or three in the morning [coach, meet Rick Chartraw] laughing and joking around. I'm not going to stick around and let everyone in Montreal blame me for what's happening ... because it's not my fault."

The coach went on to complain about Pierre Larouche strutting through an airport smoking a big cigar on the night of a loss. Captain Serge Savard was too interested in his horses to bother helping Geoffrion. The only player who seemed to care was Larry Robinson, he added.

"I had a dream to coach this team. This dream is a nightmare now. I don't care if you pay me a million dollars a year, I will not stay."

The next day, Claude Ruel began his second stint as head coach of the Montreal Canadiens. The club responded and their opening-game loss in Minnesota in their quarterfinal playoff was their first in 25 games.

There would be no second run of five consecutive championships. But unlike the impression that has been created since, there would be no precipitous plunge from the Olympian heights either.

If those time-bending journalistic historians like to compress Montreal's first forty years to make it seem that the Canadiens have always been the NHL's top franchise, which is not in the least true, the Montreal media, especially the French-language media, still give the impression today that the Irving Grundman years were the club's modern Dark Ages.

The truth is that under Grundman, Montreal finished first in their division three times and won one Stanley Cup. The Canadiens visited no Stygian depths in that era.

In 1979, they were second overall to the New York Islanders, but won the Cup. The Islanders would then win four in a row. However, lost in the shuffle was the fact that over this five-year period, Montreal Canadiens —the supposedly aging giant that stumbled geriatrically from NHL rink to NHL rink—scored 532 points to New York's 531. Other teams in the league, called challengers or up-and-coming at some time during that half-decade, included Philadelphia, Boston and Buffalo. They had 501, 498 and 479 points respectively.

In bottom-line conscious Montreal, however, the Stanley Cup was the only thing. Regular-season results and the fact that the team was perennially competitive meant nothing if the club failed in the playoffs. That the Canadiens were second in goals scored (360) and best in goals against (223) during the 1982 regular season would pale to insignificance after a fluke shot by Dale Hunter trickled behind Rick Wamsley in the first minute of overtime of the fifth and final game of the opening round of the playoffs.

The most unfortunate part of Irving Grundman's two last years as managing director of the Montreal Canadiens revolved about one player.

Montreal's normally demanding media looked at the elimination by Minnesota as pure luck, and with a lot of justification. The Canadiens went into the series without Larouche and Lafleur and with two of the Big Three, Lapointe and Savard, hurting. Doug Risebrough dislocated a shoulder and hardly played.

Going into the draft June 11 at the Forum, the Canadiens knew they were in a position to do themselves a lot of good. They had acquired first pick and the 1980 crop had one word stencilled across it: bumper.

The Central Scouting people, and Montreal's own scouts who had made the trip to Saskatchewan many times, were drooling over a big centreman with Regina Pats who was setting the Western Hockey League on its ear. His name was Douglas Peter Wickenheiser and he had been selected Canadian junior of the year on the basis of a 170-point season (89 goals, 81 assists). If that wasn't enough, he scored 14 more goals and added 26 assists in 18 playoff games.

But Wickenheiser was not alone. The Portland Winter Hawks had a strapping big defenceman named David Babych who was a franchise, the reports said. Not to be outdone by their western cousins, the Montreal Juniors were inspired by a pepperpot centreman from Verdun named Denis Savard. Lower down in the ratings was a huge crop of quality eighteen year olds, many of them defencemen like Larry Murphy, Darren Veitch, Paul Coffey, Rick Lanz, Jérôme Dupont, Normand Rochefort, Moe Mantha, Ric Nattress and Steve Konroyd. Forwards available included Jimmy Fox, Mike Bullard, Brent Sutter, Barry Pederson, Paul Gagné, Steve Patrick, Kevin Lavallee, Mike Moller and John Chabot.

There was a great deal of pressure in the French-language media to draft Savard. An exciting player, he was born with a CH tattooed on his chest and fit the mold of Montreal centres that went back to the Morenz days. He would be terrific with Lafleur and Shutt, they reasoned, and Larouche could form the lynchpin of a strong second scoring line.

But the Canadiens wanted a big centre, something they dearly missed since the Peter Mahovlich trade three years before.

"Although Pierre Larouche was hurt in the playoffs, all indications we had were that he would be all right and he could return between Guy Lafleur and Steve Shutt in the fall," Grundman recalled. "We also knew that Guy was going to be okay from his knee injury. We really studied this thing before the draft was held. All of our people said to go for Wickenheiser."

Montreal picked Wickenheiser, Winnipeg Jets drafted Babych and Chicago selected Savard. That day, Montreal reporters began marking their calendars. The NHL schedule had Chicago coming to the Forum October 11—exactly four months later—for the first Canadiens' home game of the 1980-81 season.

On that night Savard played and starred. The Canadiens, in their infinite wisdom, did not dress their number one pick. When Savard deked Larry Robinson out of his jockstrap and scored, the ovation was very loud. A lot of hockey people still feel that not dressing Wickenheiser for that game hurt the Regina native more than he will ever admit.

As it was, none of the heralded draft choices won the Calder Trophy as best rookie for that season. It was captured by a twenty-five year old veteran rookie named Peter Stastny. However, Savard was not far behind in the voting, thanks to his 28 goals and 47 assists. Babych also had a strong season with 6 goals and 38 assists for 44 points as a rookie rearguard. Montreal's "big centre" finished with 7 goals and 8 assists in 41 games.

The low point of his season came when the Canadiens made a mid-season swing through Alberta. In one of his infrequent outings, Wickenheiser had scored twice and added an assist in a Forum game against the Flames, who had moved to Calgary from Atlanta in the off-season. Yet, he was not dressed for the return game in Calgary, or two nights later for a game against the Oilers. Sitting in the press box was becoming a habit, so Wickenheiser was learning to swallow his disappointment quietly. However, his parents and a large number of friends from Regina drove to the two Alberta games and never got to see him play.

By the midway point of the season, Wickenheiser was a disillusioned nineteen year old.

It would be unfair to intimate that the Canadiens benched Wickenheiser with no reason or for spite. One thing that hurt him was the emergence of a feisty pivot who had spent two years maturing with the Nova Scotia Voyageurs. Keith Acton, a product of Peterborough, had scored 45 goals with the Voyageurs in 1979-80 and was promised a full shot at making the team. He delivered with 15 goals and 24 assists in 61 games.

Wickenheiser's real challenge came from without. As long as he played in Montreal, he would suffer the Savard comparisons and it would get worse as Savard proceeded to set all sorts of records for Black Hawks centremen.

Four years later, and a year after Wickenheiser would be traded to St. Louis Blues, Claude Ruel would admit that "Wickenheiser just wasn't the hockey player we thought he was. He just wasn't good enough and that's the real reason why he was not dressed for that first Chicago game."

Since he was always fiercely protective of the younger players on the Canadiens, Ruel's remark was uncharacteristic. It showed clearly how sensitive a nerve the Wickenheiser draft had become for the entire organization.

Was Wickenheiser a bad choice? Grundman denies it to this day.

"Every scout in the NHL had him listed as number one. Our own scouts had him listed as number one. Central Scouting had him as top pick. We made the right choice according to our own priorities and the information we had at the time. One major factor was temperament. We always tried to assess what kind of person a young player was. Wickenheiser checked out. He was one of the most popular guys in the dressing room here and all of his teammates were cheering for him. He is a class individual and it is unfortunate that it didn't work out for him in Montreal."

The big centre was not in the lineup when Montreal skated out against the Edmonton Oilers' "kiddie korps" in the opening round of the playoffs that spring. The Canadiens were swallowed in three straight and Ruel, a great sergeant, was chewed to bits by Glen Sather's generalship behind the bench.

Also out of the lineup for that series were two long-time veterans. In February, Rick Chartraw was dealt to Los Angeles Kings for a second-round draft choice. A month later, at the stroke of midnight with regard to the trading deadline, Michel Larocque was sent to Toronto for Robert Picard and an eighth-round draft choice.

The Canadiens faced a disturbing summer and this time the storm clouds were clearly evident on the horizon. Guy Lafleur thought Ruel was thoroughly outcoached in the playoffs and said so. Ruel thought Lafleur was thoroughly outplayed, by both Wayne

Gretzky and Lafleur's shadow, Dave Hunter, and said nothing. Others in the entourage hinted at the same problems and it was obvious that a new coach would have to be appointed.

In the summer of '82, Montreal went coach shopping and came up with Bob Berry, a native Montrealer and former Los Angeles Kings star and coach. In three years with Team Surfboard, Berry had managed a very respectable 107 wins, 94 losses and 39 ties. He was known as a strict coach who believed in a system of play. All of these qualities sounded good to the Canadiens' front office.

There would be a few differences in coaching the two teams, Berry acknowledged. "In Los Angeles we had a 500 dollar fine for anyone who showed up with a tan," Berry smiled. The Los Angeles Kings have always been known as the Hollywood Cabana Club by their envious NHL confrères from colder climes. It was always a little too easy to leave practice and head right for the beach.

"I guess we won't need it here. I'm going to give some thought to some new rules but I'm not going to change my coaching philosophy to please anybody. There will be curfews. People will be on time for everything. I don't think this is too much to ask of any professional athlete."

It was quite obvious that Grundman had taken Geoffrion's parting shots to heart, and that the message had been relayed to the incoming coach.

Geoffrion had talked tough and had been openly defied by his players. Claude Ruel, on the other hand, had tried to be more understanding and less demanding of his charges. As a result, they cut him to ribbons in the press. One of the worst culprits was Guy Lafleur, who suffered from a bad case of "diarrhea of the mouth" in the mind of the managing director.

Lafleur went through a frustrating season and this led to several tirades. After missing the previous playoffs with the knee injury, he worked hard to be in condition for training camp, only to be stricken with a hamstring injury. He missed 29 games during the season, scoring 27

goals and 43 assists in 51 games. The ultimate embarrassment came in the playoffs, after Richard Sevigny had
announced to the world that the Flower would put
Wayne Gretzky in his back pocket in any confrontation.
Sevigny, of course, was dead wrong, but it was Lafleur
who had to eat his words.

That summer, Lafleur worked very hard in preparation for Canada Cup II, and found himself playing on a
line with Gretzky and Gilbert Perreault. Perreault, it
turned out, was the best of the three before an ankle
injury sidelined him for the final against the Soviet Union, an 8-1 loss. The experience, and the Edmonton and
Calgary fans chanting "Guy, Guy" every time the Flower
touched the puck, seemed to rejuvenate him and he
reported to camp ready to play hard in 1981-82.

Little did Lafleur know how close he came to playing
for Buffalo a year later. Tired of his public complaints,
stories of his overnight escapades and lack of on-ice
production, Grundman discreetly shopped him around.

"At the time, Buffalo was having a very hard time
renegotiating Gilbert Perreault's contract and it looked
like they weren't ever going to agree. I met their vice-
president and lawyer Bob Swados, who was also their
alternate governor, at a governor's meeting and we
started talking. We had several conversations over a two-
week period but the whole thing fell through when the
Perreault contract was straightened out.

"Who knows? That deal might have turned things
around for both clubs. The only thing I know is that
Perreault was probably the only player Montreal fans
would accept in a Lafleur trade."

Berry's appointment came a week before the draft and
it was a quiet, almost timid contingent that sat at the
Canadiens' table June 10. In the previous thirteen
months, four men had called themselves Coach of the
Montreal Canadiens, and other bodies had been shuffled
hither and yon after a decade of almost boring but very
successful sameness. The Canadiens had three draft
picks of the 21 in the first round and another two in the
second round, or five of the top 42. If Ron Caron's scouts
had done their jobs, some talent would be found.

Drafting seventh, the Canadiens went for bloodlines and claimed Mark Hunter from the Brantford Alexanders of the Ontario junior league. The younger brother of Edmonton's Dave and Quebec's Dale, he was known as a tough, good skater with a very good shot. With choices 18 and 19 overall, the Canadiens went for Chicoutimi defenceman Gilbert Delorme and a Swedish forward named Jan Ingman.

However, the talent pool was already thinning out. Whereas 33 of 42 first and second round choices from the 1980 crop went on to play in the NHL, only 26 of the 1981 players would stick with an NHL team for longer than one season. Montreal went back to Sweden for choice number 32, drafting Lars Eriksson from Brynas, and turned to the University of Wisconsin for a defenceman named Chris Chelios as pick number 40.

Hunter and Delorme were in the lineup when Montreal opened the new season and would make decent contributions. Joining them was Craig Laughlin, a Toronto native who had been drafted four years before and who chose to finish his education at Colgate before reporting to the Voyageurs, where he played two seasons. The left winger showed promising qualities and scored 12 goals and added 11 assists in 36 games alongside Mario Tremblay and Pierre Mondou.

The team of the '70s was officially terminated during the 1981-82 season. First, Serge Savard retired, disgusted with the shabby treatment afforded him by Montreal fans during the last season. Savard may have lost a step, but he still had plenty of experience and could play on that alone. He proved it by anchoring the Winnipeg Jets defence and helping to break in Dave Babych and a bunch of fuzzy-cheeked reaguards after John Ferguson coaxed him out of retirement.

During the Edmonton series, Savard was booed mercilessly by Montreal's so-called class fans. A player who suffered two broken legs early in his career, who won the Conn Smythe and Bill Masterton trophies and probably should have been awarded the Norris Trophy at least once in his career, Savard had been a pillar on defence. He did not deserve this slap in the face.

After Edmonton humbled Montreal 6-2 to sweep the Canadiens 3-0, the veteran defenceman was in tears in the dressing room. He knew then that he had worn the Canadiens uniform for the last time, and retired in August.

Gone also was Yvon Lambert, for nine seasons the Canadiens' Gary Dornhoefer, a fearless player who would plant his rear end in a goalie's face and absorb what Danny Gallivan would call a "plethora of slashes and high sticks" so that the fleeter members of the Canadiens' power play could manoeuvre for goals. Lambert was yet another product of the rural Quebec work ethic, starting to skate in his teens and playing his first organized hockey game when he was fourteen. He would never have made it in the 1980s Quebec amateur hockey, where the so-called "Elite system" tells kids at seven and eight years of age that they are not good enough.

With the continued improvement of second-year players like Keith Acton, some rookies (Wickenheiser) and some veterans (Larouche) were being pressed. Both players experienced difficulties adapting to the defensive side of their roles. Wickenheiser took it well, but Larouche did not. As a result, he spent a lot of time on the bench, when he was allowed to wear the uniform.

Dressed for only 22 of Montreal's first 33 games, Lucky Pierre had 9 goals and 12 assists for 21 points and he was chafing at the bit. The crisis came on a New England swing just before Christmas. The Canadiens played a game in Hartford and then settled down for the 90-minute bus ride to Boston. Larouche had been benched for five straight games and spent most of his free time hollering loud and long for a trade.

Larouche became involved in a long and beery condemnation of management and coaching during the ride, even though Grundman, who was sitting up front, said he heard little of it.

"A lot has been made of the bus ride, but that was not what was wrong. Most clubs have a standard policy: players cannot drink in the bar of the hotel where they are staying. That's reserved for the coaches and management and avoids any run-ins. When we got to Boston, there was Pierre in the bar at the Sheraton." Larouche was asked to leave and refused. A little more than a week later, he was a Hartford Whaler and the happy-go-Lucky Pierre of old, scoring 25 goals and 25 assists in the 45 games remaining in the season. They loved him in Hartford, until about halfway through the next season.

They loved him in Montreal, especially when it was learned that Irving Grundman had shown a flash of Pollock brilliance in arranging the deal with Whalers' GM Larry Pleau. Larouche went to Hartford for the Whalers' number one pick in 1984, and if by some miracle Hartford would rise to the top of the rankings, thus inversely affecting the quality of that pick, Montreal had the option of flipping picks with Hartford.

"When I came here and saw that one, I almost fainted," says Emile Francis, the current Whalers' President and General Manager.

Irving Grundman and his chief hockey man, Ron Caron, were looking ahead three years. There was a tall rangy centre playing for Laval Nationals who looked very good and might be available in 1984 if the Whalers could remain near the lower echelons of the league for a few more years. His name: Mario Lemieux.

Buried in the everyday goings-on of the 1981-82 NHL season was a February 11 contest at Montreal against the Pittsburgh Penguins, a longtime league doormat. Montreal won 4-2 on goals by Gaston Gingras, Mario Tremblay, Steve Shutt (his 350th) and Doug Jarvis (into the empty net) to win their tenth straight, the first time in 14 years a Canadiens' team had accomplished this feat. More importantly, however, it was the Canadiens' 2,000th win in regular-season — a first for any NHL team.

Another event which was to have great bearing on the immediate future of the teams also took place during the 1981-82 season. The league realigned its divisions. Montreal, leader of the Norris Division which comprised Los

Angeles, Pittsburgh, Hartford and Detroit, now joined the Adams Division with Boston, Buffalo, Quebec and Hartford.

Moving from such a weak division to the league's most competitive was the tonic for the Canadiens. Whereas the Canadiens had fought the surprising Kings for the Norris championship in 1980-81, finishing with 103 points to the Kings 99, there were too many easy games with Pittsburgh, Hartford and Detroit on the schedule.

Adams Division competition with the hated Nordiques, the perennially competitive Bruins and the Scotty Bowman-led Sabres got the club going and the Canadiens finished the season with 46 wins, 17 losses and 17 ties for 109 points, third overall.

The new playoff format would have them playing the Quebec Nordiques, fourth-place finishers in the Adams with an excellent 82 points on 33 wins, 31 losses and 16 ties. The Canadiens were looking good going into the playoffs. They were getting scoring from two lines and defence was strong with the Jarvis-Gainey-Hunter line bottling up the opposition forwards and Robinson-Langway-Engblom-Picard-Delorme keeping the crease clear in front of rookie goalie Rick Wamsley.

The first series was eagerly anticipated and game one went according to form, an easy 5-1 win for the home team. Then things went sour. Quebec, led by the Stastny brothers, a scrappy centre named Dale Hunter and a born-again Dan Bouchard in goal, stunned the Canadiens 2-1 in the second and won the series' third game in Quebec.

Montreal stormed back to win the fourth game and both teams left Quebec City feeling that the Canadiens would correct things in game five. Quebec's defence was notoriously weak and the Nordiques lost two defencemen, Pierre Lacroix and Jean Hamel, to injury in the second period. However, the Nordiques entered the third period with a 2-0 lead, even though the Canadiens had carried the play from the start.

The normally reserved Forum crowd, whipped to a frenzy by this emotional confrontation with the country cousins from *la Vieille Capitale*, "oohed" and "aahed" every shot on net.

Finally, Bouchard caved in under the onslaught. Mario Tremblay, his eyes laser beams all evening, scored at 10:49 and the crowd erupted. Almost a half period remained and Montreal was coming on.

It didn't take long for the tying goal as the Canadiens pressed and Robert Picard scored at 12:14.

But Bouchard got right back up and held against the wave, stopping Mondou, Lafleur, Tremblay (twice) and Shutt as Montreal outshot the Nordiques 15-5 in the third period and the game went into overtime.

Bob Berry reminded his team that anything could happen in overtime. "We've got two jobs. We stop them, and we make sure we stop them, and then we exploit the opportunities."

With that in mind, he started a defensive alignment; Gainey, Jarvis and Hunter up front, Engblom and Langway on the blueline. And the defensive line went on the offence.

Right from the faceoff, Mark Hunter, Gainey and Jarvis carried the puck into the Nordiques zone and Engblom pitched in to trap it on the boards with Jarvis and gain a faceoff.

"Dougie and I were playing soccer with it along the boards and he yelled that it was still at my feet. I looked down, and I think it was Michel Goulet who kicked it up the boards."

The puck bounced to Dale Hunter and he sped off on a 2-on-1 break with sniper Réal Cloutier. Rod Langway was the only player back and he made the perfect play, preventing a clear pass and a clear shot. Hunter passed to Cloutier but the angle was bad and the puck rolled off Cloutier's stick and behind the net. Then it was just Dale Hunter and the puck behind the net in a mini time warp.

With everyone else in the building seemingly operating in slow motion, Hunter picked up the puck and tried to come around the goal to Wamsley's right side. The goalie slid across and the Nordiques centre tried to stuff it into the net. And then nothing ... the crowd relaxed, Wamsley had it under him.

Still in slow motion, Dale Hunter raised his stick, the referee skated leisurely to the net and pointed to the puck and then at Hunter, the red light went on and the Nordiques were streaming off their bench. Outshot 35-19, outplayed by a large margin and with a defence that couldn't stop a good midget team, the Quebec Nordiques had defeated the Montreal Canadiens and NHL hockey in the province would never be the same again.

For the second straight year, the Canadiens had failed to emerge from the first round of the playoffs.

Fingers began pointing at Grundman, Caron, Ruel and the Canadiens' brain trust. The celebrated number one pick of 1980, Doug Wickenheiser, did not play in the Quebec series, just as he had sat out the Edmonton playoff debacle of the previous year. Worse still, his spot had been taken in the lineup by Jeff Brubaker, a tough winger who had been unable to crack the Hartford starting twenty.

Other draft choices were put on glass slides and examined under the microscope. Montreal's first pick in 1978 was Danny Geoffrion, Boomer's son, and he did not make it. Dave Hunter, picked later in the same draft, was allowed to go to Edmonton and responded by shutting down Guy Lafleur in the 1981 playoffs. Gaston Gingras, picked 27th overall in 1979, was the Canadiens' top pick and was in and out of the lineup in 1981-82. Dale Hunter, whose winning goal eliminated the Canadiens, was picked 41st the same year.

Some diehards went even farther back. Mike Bossy was selected 15th in 1977, five spots after Mark Napier of the Canadiens.

And then there was Wickenheiser. In two seasons of NHL play, Dave Babych anchored the Winnipeg defence and Denis Savard had scored 194 points on 60 goals and 134 assists. Wickenheiser's numbers were 19 goals and 31 assists in 97 games.

Where is *la relève*? The torch has been dropped! The Quebec Nordiques went on to defeat the Boston Bruins in the Adams Division final and eventually lost to the New York Islanders. Every game they played that May was a festering wound for Canadiens supporters and management.

The most persistent complaint, however, was the hardest to refute. The Nordiques' all-Québécois (read French-speaking) front office and coaching staff had proven they were as good as any English-speaking front office out there, especially the English-speaking head office at the Forum. They had gone out and found good Quebec-bred hockey players and turned an expansion team into a winner in two short years. Their hockey people were better, period.

As an indictment against the entire NHL, it was a fair criticism. For too many years, French-Canadian coaches and managers were effectively shut out of the highest echelons of professional hockey by an Old Boys Network that did not look kindly on non-English Canadians. They tended to justify their condescending attitude by explaining, "Some of those French boys can really play, but I doubt they can add two and two."

However, laying that rap at the doorstep of the Canadiens was unfair. No team had gone further in hiring French-Canadians at all levels over the almost three-quarters of a century of the club's existence. Owners with names like Letourneau, Dandurand, Raymond and coaches named Lepine, Lalonde, Mantha and Ruel were ample proof of that. Nevertheless, the complainers were unforgiving.

"We caught it all that summer," said Grundman. "Everything we had done was at fault. Ron Caron was taken to task because the French media didn't like him. He was an Ottawa boy and wasn't buddy-buddy with the writers, so he was fair game. All through this he kept his cool and did his work."

Caron and Grundman, ever mindful of the criticism, then proceeded to supervise Montreal's worst draft in years. The Canadiens had accumulated five choices in the first two rounds, their regular pick in the first round, number 19, and picks number 31, 32, 33 and 40 in the second round. The 1982 crop was notoriously thin after the top 10 picks, but even here the Canadiens went wrong.

The Canadiens were determined to shut up the critics and selected Quebec junior players with their first two picks—Alain Héroux of Chicoutimi and Jocelyn Gauvreau of Granby. Neither player would make it and Héroux was selected two spots ahead of Pat Flatley of the New York Islanders, a quality forward who would star for the Canadian Olympic team in 1984. The remaining three selections by Montreal came from the United States: defenceman Kent Carlson of St. Lawrence University, David Maley of Edina High School (University of Wisconsin) and Scott Sandelin of Hibbing High School (U. of North Dakota).

Quebec, on the other hand, completely free of any language stigma, was free to make its two selections in Ontario, for David Shaw of the Kitchener Rangers and Paul Gillis of the Niagara Falls Flyers. By the 1985-86 season, Gauvreau and Héroux were out of hockey, Carlson had played a few games with Montreal and then been traded to St. Louis, and Maley and Sandelin, both highly heralded in university play, were graduating. Gillis and Shaw were regulars with the Nordiques.

Montreal may still "win" the 1982 draft if Maley and Sandelin show well in coming seasons. But the Gauvreau-Héroux and Shaw-Gillis comparison serves to prove just how much influence one playoff win by Quebec had on the Montreal Canadiens, even four seasons later.

The short-term influence also proved staggering. The Canadiens returned to training camp that fall with question marks hanging above the team like the proverbial Sword of Damocles.

If Doug Wickenheiser had not yet panned out, Keith Acton had. The diminutive centreman from Stouffville, Ontario had scored 36 goals and 52 assists in 1981-82 to lead the Canadiens in scoring. Two quality centremen were due to move up from the Nova Scotia Voyageurs: Dan Daoust (25-40—65) and Guy Carbonneau (27-67—

94). Doug Jarvis was his regular steady self at the position and Pierre Mondou, a delightful free-form scooter, had shown well the year before with 35 goals and 33 assists in 73 games alongside veterans Mario Tremblay and Rejean Houle. There was also Doug Risebrough, who had struggled through an injury-ridden season the year before and looked ready to return.

The Canadiens were rich in centres and fairly deep in forwards and defencemen. The major problem, however, was still that the Canadiens forwards were small as a group and the club had been unable to fill the void with some board-pounding skaters up front. Montreal could afford to trade a centre or two, and maybe a defenceman, to obtain a larger forward. Names mentioned included Ryan Walter of Washington, Brent Ashton of Colorado (now New Jersey) and Curt Fraser of Vancouver Canucks.

It took no time at all to clear the logjam as Grundman pulled off the largest Canadiens' trade in a decade. Montreal obtained Ryan Walter and defenceman Rick Green from the Washington Capitals in return for Rod Langway, Brian Engblom, Craig Laughlin and Doug Jarvis.

The trade registered 7.0 on the open-ended Richter Scale, and the aftershocks were in the 5 to 5.5 range. Within seconds of the announcement, the Montreal media went to work. Engblom and Langway? Together? The best defensive pairing in the league last year? You can't be serious!

Most observers had expected some movement for Langway because the New Hampshire graduate had long been unhappy with his contract and wanted to play in the United States where a dollar is a dollar and not Canadian monopoly money.

"Rod made it clear to us that if he was not traded to an American team, he was going to retire," Grundman said. "There was no doubt in my mind that he would. Rod is the sole provider for his family and he was very concerned about his family's welfare. There never would have been a question of trading him if he hadn't been so adamant."

In the wake of Langway's consecutive Norris Trophy selections in 1983 and 1984 as the league's top defenceman, it is easy to forget that the Montreal criticism centred on the trade of Engblom, a Second Team All-Star in 1981-82, and the only Canadien to crack the elite squads that season. Few people mourned the losses of the fairly anonymous Laughlin, or Jarvis, a top-notch defensive centre.

Shortly after that deal was announced, the club dealt Risebrough to Calgary Flames.

"Mr. Grundman felt that I was not going to make the team that year because they were bringing up several young centres and couldn't leave them in Nova Scotia any more," Risebrough recalled. "He was very fair to me and arranged a move to a team I approved. He didn't have to do that."

Still, trading four Canadiens to any team in one deal and a fifth shortly afterwards was a shock that reverberated throughout the dressing room for the whole season. It did not help that the "Washington Canadiens" instantly transformed that franchise into a contender and that Risebrough became the team leader in Calgary, enjoying his best scoring year since 1976.

The shock of the trade was blunted because a young Swedish player named Mats Naslund strode into the training camp, took Reggie Houle's job away from him alongside Mondou and Tremblay and proceeded to make Montreal fans forget about Craig Laughlin. At the same time, Guy Carbonneau was playing on the defensive line and scoring a respectable 47 points on 18 goals and 29 assists and Walter scored 29 goals and played an aggressive game in the corners.

Rick Green, a very strong defensive defenceman who had been the number one pick overall in the 1976 draft, proved to be deceptively fragile, missing 18 games during the regular season, and only playing 7 games the following year. Larry Robinson, exhausted by mid-March because of the time logged earlier in the season, was not himself, and Gilbert Delorme, although scoring 12 goals, tended to sacrifice position to deliver thundering bodychecks and his defensive partners were exhausted by a steady stream of 2-on-1s and 3-on-2s.

Before the trade, Montreal had the "defence of the 1980s". After it, they struggled behind their own blue-line, giving up 63 more goals (almost one a game) in 1982-83 than in the previous year.

Montreal slipped to second place in the Adams Division that season with 98 points, 12 behind the Boston Bruins, and lined up against the Buffalo Sabres in the division semi-final.

Robert Sauvé, a goaltender from Ste. Genevieve, a village on the westernmost tip of Montreal Island across from Ile Bizard, came home and posted back-to-back shutouts over the Canadiens. Montreal managed two goals in the third game in Buffalo, but they were not enough to prolong the series. The team had been swept three straight and, worse still, Montreal had not escaped the first round of the playoffs in three years.

This time the house-clearing operation would take place on the Second Floor, not in the players' dressing room. Irving Grundman and Ron Caron were forewarned of the coming changes. The first sign had come the previous November when Morgan McCammon announced that Molson's had reached into the Carling O'Keefe-Nordiques empire and come up with Ronald Corey, a marketing and beer man who had once had a tryout with the Junior Canadiens.

The message? If the Canadiens could no longer be French downstairs, they were going to be French upstairs.

14

The New Order

We were sitting in the stands, Section 36 in the west-side whites, and the oldtimer had tears in his eyes.

There below, wearing the road reds, were the original Lions in Winter, the Class of 1959, skating onto the ice surface with the familiar CH in the middle, for one more ovation.

Claude Mouton was at the microphone. *"Mesdames et messieurs: Le Rocket ... Maurice Richard!"*

As the portly Rocket skated gingerly in on Jacques Plante, the Forum ovation rose to a crescendo. Standing at centre ice with their sticks raised in acknowledgement was a group of middle-aged athletes—Tom Johnson, Bob Turner, Jean-Guy Talbot, Doug Harvey—a defensive corps as hard to penetrate as the Wall of China. Don Marshall, Claude Provost, Dickie Moore: tough wingers who could shut you down at one end and cut you open at the other.

Finally, the Scoring Machines—Henri Richard, Boom Boom Geoffrion, Jean Beliveau and of course, the Rocket.

This was a night for older fans, the veterans of the 1950s and '60s who saw eleven Stanley Cup Champion teams in twenty years. It was also a night for *les Anciens*, the men who had hung the banners high in the Forum rafters. A team which had taken greatness in stride was beginning to publicly acknowledge a longstanding debt.

A special team luncheon the day before had left the 1984-85 edition in awe.

"These guys are an inspiration to us all," said Ottawa's Bobby Smith, transformed into a fan for a day. One of the older players on the current team, he was born in the "middle of it—February, 1958—"and thus had never seen many of *les Anciens* play. But he had heard the stories.

"They were true champions, my Dad tells me. When you see these guys, you know what the uniform means to us. It's like wearing Yankee pinstripes."

Back in the stands, the greying fan took a handkerchief from a jacket pocket and wiped away the excess moisture. He pointed to the Canadiens' bench where the current team players banged their sticks against the ice or along the boards.

"What makes it so sad is the fact that those guys don't seem to know what this all means. We wouldn't be having all of these ceremonies if those guys would win once in a while."

It was the best of times, it was the worst of times and, as the fan surmised, it was time for regular journeys down memory lane, because the 1983-84 Canadiens were living a nightmare.

Suffice it to say, the worst season in memory made everybody work harder, from management to the promotions department to the players. The new season had begun four days after the Sabres put the Canadiens away in the first round of the previous year's playoffs. Ronald Corey had given the regime a year to deliver, and then cleaned house.

Gone were Irving Grundman, Ron Caron and Bob Berry. It was the biggest corporate blood-letting ever in management ranks and an embarrassment to a once-proud organization.

"Corey met with me on Tuesday afternoon, said he wasn't renewing my contract, and said I could remain with the organization for two or three weeks," Grundman recalled.

The man Pierre Larouche had contemptuously called a "glorified bowling alley manager" did not linger. He cleared out his desk and departed the building three hours later. Few people realize that Grundman would have left of his own accord. The handwriting was on the wall when Corey was hired five months before. Hockey committee or no, you could not have two bosses and that was the situation when Corey joined the team. It left both men in an impossible situation.

"I was the managing director and that meant that I was in charge of the hockey operation. Mr. Corey came on board and persistently asked to attend our hockey decision meetings. I kept telling him: 'If you want to attend meetings, call your own.' Before his appointment, the club presidency was basically a ceremonial office and not tied in with the day-to-day operations. It was an impossible situation for both of us because Mr. Corey's mandate was unclear, officially, that is."

Unofficially, the mandate was crystal clear. Clean house. Get the fans and the players believing in the Second Floor again. Better still, let's make the Canadiens Quebec's favourite beer, oops, team.

When Corey was hired, his new bosses at Molson's spoke of his personality, his drive, his leadership and his strong attachment to Montreal and Quebec. The latter reference was a slap at Grundman, who had acquired a reputation for locking himself in a corporate ivory tower, far from the maddening crowds. It was also an indication that Quebec's internecine beer wars were in high gear. Molson's Quebec subsidiary had recently undergone a major management shakeup, an advertising agency had been dismissed, and Molson's stranglehold on beer sales had slipped. Part of the reason was a sports-led resurgence of the Carling-O'Keefe Nordiques.

When the reality of the situation dawned on Molson's, they went looking for O'Keefe president Corey, a graduate in marketing from the University of Western Ontario. After graduation and before joining O'Keefe, he had covered sports for several French-language newspapers, produced hockey telecasts for the Canadian Broadcasting Corporation, worked as public relations manager for Molson's and become executive vice-president of a small company.

Corey was a firm believer in the Global Village. The

Canadiens' management style of Frank Selke and Sam Pollock and their philosophy of "listen attentively to the fans and then go right ahead and do what you were going to in the first place" was for another time. The new Canadiens would become very familiar with the medium and the message.

One message was that Canadiens' management had become estranged from the people who paid the shot, the fans. That was patently absurd, of course. Canadiens' management had always maintained a healthy distance from the people who lived and died with each win.

"A good businessman cannot be a cheerleader," Sam Pollock once said. "Cheerleaders don't win anything."

The real changes, of course, lay in the great political and social upheavals that were affecting Montreal and Quebec. In every aspect of Québécois life, people at the top were beginning to heed the masses. Previously anonymous business moguls and politicos alike welcomed the new unveiling and cultivated the new image.

A similar transformation would have to be effected by the Canadiens. With the major league public relations effort launched by the Nordiques, and that team's recent success on the ice, the Canadiens were being challenged like never before.

The new Montreal Canadiens would be run like any other major corporation. Organized under vice-presidents of finance, marketing, hockey operations; monitored in weekly management committee meetings and evaluated according to a five-year plan, the team would also become fully computerized. The Canadiens would be actively marketed like any other company, and a young man named Francois-Xavier Seigneur was hired to do the job.

"No more cathedral, no more shrine at the Forum," Corey said. "We want the fans to feel that they are part of the team, not people going to Mass. We want them to have fun at hockey games."

That request posed some problems, however. The players who wore the uniform could no longer be called the Flying Frenchmen—they had not done much flying in recent years, and a majority were non-francophones. A realistic appraisal of the situation by Canadiens' management and Molson's, showed clearly that Montreal no longer would be able to guarantee a majority French-speaking presence on the team. Even the Nordiques, who had actively pursued French players to the detriment of team strength in their first three NHL years, had discovered that the only way to success was to assemble the best team possible without language constraints.

If the Flying Frenchmen were to become the French Foreign Legion, a polyglot aggregation of mercenaries, their legacy at least could be kept alive in the front office.

On the day Grundman was dismissed, Corey fielded the question. "If you're asking whether I'm primarily looking for French-Canadian names to fill these positions, the answer is no. I want the best people available."

Nobody believed that for an instant.

Serge Savard became the automatic front-runner for the managing director's job, even though he still was a player and had an option year left with Winnipeg. That tidbit was published immediately, after some very broad hints were dropped by Canadiens' management.

Jacques Lemaire, who had returned from Switzerland to coach in American college ranks as an assistant at Plattsburgh, N.Y. and in the Quebec junior league with the Longueuil Chevaliers, was the front-runner for the coaching job. Another name mentioned was that of Orval Tessier, the coach of the Chicago Black Hawks. These rumours also arose after some name-dropping in high places.

Two weeks later, the thirty-five year old Savard was the Canadiens' managing director and the financially strapped Winnipeg Jets were richer by a third round draft choice and 50,000 dollars.

Grundman had complained that Corey wanted to run the team and was always underfoot in the hockey operations side of the front office. Would that be the case with Savard?

"Serge is in charge, complete charge," Corey told the press conference announcing Savard's appointment. "I feel he will be one of the great general managers in the NHL. Naturally, I would expect him to discuss his decisions with me, but he will make them. I have my own work, he has his."

Three weeks later, after Savard and Corey failed to convince Lemaire to take the top job, and thirty-eight days after he was fired, Berry was back as head coach of the Canadiens. Joining him as assistant coaches were Lemaire and Laperriere. It would prove to be an impossible situation for Berry.

The players were all in favour of the changes and Guy Lafleur was so moved that he promised a major concession in the coming season. "With the appointments that have taken place since the end of the season, I don't have to worry about management any more. I'm going to start a new career . . . I'm going to keep my mouth shut." Little did he know how wrong he would be.

Savard's second order of business was the June draft at the Forum. There was no opportunity for Montreal to improve its drafting position, number 17, in the first round, because a lot of teams were watching the Canadiens' 1984 drafting position (Hartford's first-round pick) with a wary eye.

"There were quite a few good young hockey players available in the 1983 draft," said Savard. "Montrealers had watched Pat Lafontaine play for the Verdun Junior Canadiens all year and hoped he might still be around, but we didn't have a prayer." Lafontaine, a Detroit native, set records with 104 goals, 130 assists and 234 points in 70 games. He was selected third in the draft by the New York Islanders. Another top Quebec junior, Sylvain Turgeon of Hull Olympiques, was a Bossy-like sniper, and had parlayed quick hands into 54 goals and 109 assists in 67 games. He was selected second overall by Hartford, behind Minnesota schoolboy Brian Lawton.

When Montreal's turn came up, Alfie Turcotte, a blue chip centre and former team-mate of Lafontaine with

Detroit CompuWare midgets, was still available. He had been the MVP of the Memorial Cup championships, won by his Portland Winter Hawks team.

"We were lucky he was still around," Savard said.

In the second round, Montreal had three picks and went to the Quebec junior ranks twice. Claude Lemieux, a combative right winger with Trois-Rivières Draveurs, was pick number 26 and Sergio Momesso, a large left-winger with Shawinigan Cataractes was 27th. Eight picks later, Todd Francis of the OHA's Brantford Alexanders, Mark Hunter's former team, was selected. Later in the draft, Montreal selected Turcotte's team-mate John Kordic, a bruising right winger, Arto Javanainen, a right winger from Finland and Thomas Rundquist, a Swedish centreman. They also continued the practice begun by Caron and Ruel of drafting high school players who would go on to American colleges for four years. These included Rob Bryden, a left winger with Toronto's Henry Carr High School, Dan Wurst, and Jeff Perpick, Minnesota defenceman with Edina High School and Hibbing High School respectively.

The loudest cheer of the session came with pick number 143 in the seventh round. "Montreal Canadiens select, from the Central Red Army Team of Moscow, goaltender Vladislav Tretiak." Savard wasn't joking. "You never know what might happen. I would rather have him on my list than on someone else's."

The rest of the summer went quickly. Savard settled into his office and was very active, as were F.X. Seigneur and others. The managing director spent most of the off-season sounding out his NHL counterparts for possible deals, and ran into the Pollock Curse.

"So many of those guys want too much for what we want because they have been burned in Montreal deals before and don't want to repeat the mistake," Savard moaned, the sleepless nights beginning.

Irving Grundman returned to his bowling business and admitted he was sleeping better, and in August, Ron Caron bounced back as the new director for hockey operations with the St. Louis Blues. The only down note sounded during the dog days was the announcement by Rejean Houle that he was retiring after ten years with Montreal sandwiched around three in the World Hockey Association with Quebec Nordiques.

When training camp began in September, a larger-than-usual rookie crop was in attendance and there were some splendid specimens. Kent Carlson, Turcotte, Kordic, Momesso, Lemieux and Francis were recent draftees and were joined by a large contingent of Nova Scotia Voyageurs, among them John Newberry, Mike McPhee, Greg Paslawski and goalie Mark Holden. On the second day of camp, the boys showed their intensity with no fewer than six fights in scrimmage.

Doug Wickenheiser and Newberry got involved in the first preliminary and moments later, defenceman Bill Kitchen fought with John Lavers, a junior player from Newfoundland. Then Chris Nilan and Jeff Brubaker indulged in their fourth bout in two days. It got so that Berry had to intervene. Normally that would have been a good sign, an indication that the team was tired of complacency.

However, the exuberance of training camp was dampened ten days later when league president-in-absentia John Ziegler came out of the closet and dealt the Canadiens a blow. Young defenceman Ric Nattress, another former member of the Brantford Alexanders, had shown well in 40 games during the previous season. Montreal's second pick in the 1980 entry draft, he had dished out impressive open-ice bodychecks and was reliable in the tough going, as was fellow rookie Craig Ludwig.

In August, 1982, while still a member of the Brantford juniors, Nattress had been arrested for smoking marijuana and fined 150 dollars. On September 23, 1983, 13 months after the incident, Ziegler stepped in and suspended Nattress for the entire 1983-84 season, ostensibly after a "month-long investigation." Nattress had met with Ziegler for a grand total of fifteen minutes September 16. A week later, the boom was lowered.

"For many years, it has been a clear policy that no employee of the league is to be involved with illegal drugs. If you choose to be involved with illegal drugs, you will not be involved with the National Hockey League."

Then in a display of pomposity belying his stature, Ziegler continued: "I would hope that Mr. Nattress will seek to straighten out his character and self-discipline so that he realizes both on and off the ice the pride and achievement that have been the hallmark of the Montreal Canadiens." If Nattress could tread the straight and narrow during the first half of the season, Ziegler added, the suspension could be reviewed and set aside after 30 games.

Savard admitted that the suspension was unduly harsh and that the team might appeal. As it turned out, the club did nothing. Any good lawyer could have invoked the Canadian Charter of Rights and Freedoms and done a lot of damage to Ziegler's overly zealous ruling. For once, Lafleur's reaction was right on.

"What's he trying to prove? It's ridiculous. The kid isn't a pusher. All he did was smoke a joint"—before he joined the Montreal Canadiens. In 1977, when Don Murdoch of the New York Rangers was caught with 4.8 grams of cocaine in his luggage during a routine check at Toronto International Airport and suspended for 40 games, he already was in the NHL.

"Murder", a valuable addition to the Rangers as a rookie in 1976-77, was never the same after that. When Nattress returned to play in December, he too, was a much more tentative hockey player. Worse still was Savard's missed opportunity to make a gesture that would show his players he had their best interests at heart.

The scrappy camp was subdued by the Nattress suspension and the Canadiens got off to a bad start in the regular season. They were short on the blueline as Rick Green came down with a serious wrist injury that would sideline him for 73 regular-season games. The injury forced the Canadiens to claim Jean Hamel when he was left unprotected by Quebec Nordiques in the waiver draft. As well, Kent Carlson, a terrific scrapper but slow of foot, found himself as a regular on defence which comprised veterans Robinson, Picard and Hamel, third-year man Gilbert Delorme, and sophomores Bill Root and Ludwig.

It was not going to be a banner year back of the blue-line and the American-born defenceman everyone talked about, Chris Chelios, was touring Canada and the United States with the American Olympic team. He would not be available before late February or early March.

There were changes up front, too. Paslawski cracked the line-up after a good training camp, as did John Chabot, a slick-passing rookie centreman. The biggest disappointment was Turcotte, who showed up for camp grossly overweight after a summer of "pizza and ice cream" and would split the season between Portland and the Canadiens.

Doug Wickenheiser, who had started out the previous season so well alongside Lafleur and Walter, and then had been inexplicably taken off the line, was finished as a Montreal Canadien. The mind games and the pressure were too much for him to handle, even though the popular player had the full support of his team-mates. It got so bad that his parents visited Serge Savard on the sly.

"They came to me and begged me to trade him," Savard said. "The Montreal experience was hurting him deeply and he was being unjustly blamed for something he had no control over, being selected number one in the draft. I said I would do my best and hoped it would be the best for all concerned. I still don't know if Doug ever found out about his parents' visit."

The Wickenheiser family's wish would come true three days before Christmas when he was moved to St. Louis with Paslawski and Delorme for big winger Perry Turnbull.

However, that was not the major deal of the season for the Canadiens. As the team set out on the new schedule, there were problems. Mark Napier, a 40-goal scorer a year before, Wickenheiser, Chabot and Picard were not dressed for an early October game against Quebec. Two weeks later, Napier and Keith Acton were en route to Minnesota and lanky Bobby Smith, whose pass had ended the Canadiens' hopes of a fifth-straight Cup in 1980, was coming to Montreal.

Smith provided immediate dividends, 15 goals in his first 20 games with the Canadiens, but could not do it all himself. Lafleur was hot in the first half of the season, scoring the majority of his 30 goals before January, but Steve Shutt was not producing, and neither were many other forwards.

When Savard obtained Turnbull from St. Louis, it was expected that his addition would turn things around, make the club more aggressive in the corners. It never worked out; the number two choice in the 1979 draft and the Canadiens' system proved incompatible and he would score only 6 goals and 7 assists in 40 games.

Berry, a coach who was trying anything and everything to inspire his charges, was reduced to a chain-smoking wreck between periods. It was a common sight after games for reporters to happen upon the coach, his head down in a cloud of smoke, wondering where it all had gone wrong. It was becoming increasingly obvious that he would have to pay for the inadequacies of the Canadiens' system and his players.

That was the situation when the Montreal oldtimers skated out onto the Forum ice December 17, 1983 for their special ceremony. It had become a standard press box joke that the number of official ceremonies and tributes before Canadiens' games was inversely proportional to the number of victories won by the team. The oldtimer who had wiped the tears from his eyes that night cried for two teams, nostalgically for the team of the '50s and with sadness for the 1983-84 Canadiens.

Nine weeks later came the fourth coaching change in four years for Montreal. A thousand or so Montrealers will never forget that Bob Berry was fired February 24, 1984. They wear that date on the T-shirts they were given at a special CFCF-Radio 1960s bash at the Château Champlain. While they boogied to the Beatles, Rolling Stones and Wilson Pickett, Berry learned of his dismissal.

Most of the people milling around Berry at the hotel

that Friday night had not yet heard of the latest events and were still wishing him and the team luck. Berry spent a long time on a public telephone just off the main lobby and then did something he had probably ached to do on many nights during this nightmarish season—he went out and got sloshed. The Canadiens' record was 28 wins, 30 losses and 5 ties. They were in fourth place in the Adams Division, 9 points better than Hartford.

With the playoffs beckoning, Savard had been forced to act. "All season long I was hoping the team would get going but I couldn't wait any longer. We made deals to strengthen the team and it didn't happen. I don't hold Bob Berry personally responsible for everything that has gone wrong. I just hope Jacques Lemaire can turn it around."

It worked—for exactly two games, with wins over New York Rangers (7-4) and Detroit Red Wings (3-1). The Canadiens ended the season 7-10 under Lemaire for a final standing of 35 wins, 40 losses, 5 ties and 75 points in 80 games. It was Montreal's worst showing since 1950-51's 25-30-15 record. (In 1969-70 when the club failed to make the playoffs, they were 38-22-16 for 92 points.)

The last 17 games were deceptive, however. While *Gazette* columnist Tim Burke correctly described the fans' diminished expectations when he wrote on the eve of the playoffs that the "Canadiens stir a feeling of pity," three major changes that would transform the team had quietly taken place during the season's home stretch.

First, Rick Wamsley was injured and goalie Steve Penney was called up from Nova Scotia late in the season. He got into four games and lost all four but played well, especially in a 5-2 home loss to the Nordiques in the last week of the season.

The second change was in strategy. Lemaire worked hard at building a new system, defensively oriented, which had all five skaters controlling the neutral and defensive zones. A scoring centre like Bobby Smith suddenly became a soccer-style sweeper, covering the neutral zone like a vacuum cleaner while his linemates scrambled for position. Only then could he launch them on a counterattack.

In the Canadiens' end, the team began playing a modified zone defence, clogging up the middle in front of the net in a bid to nullify point shots and passes crossing through the slot.

The third major change was in personnel. Chris Chelios and Rick Green joined the team for the last 12 and 7 season games respectively. They represented an automatic forty percent improvement at the blueline. Although Chelios would post only two assists in his dozen games because he was nursing an injured ankle, he provided the Canadiens with something they had lacked all season, a rushing defenceman. Green was rock steady in front of the Montreal net, policing the area with grim determination. Robinson and Ludwig, tired due to the constant pounding they absorbed during the year, were rejuvenated. Suddenly, the Canadiens defence had regained its traditional concrete hardness.

Burke's "pity" column appeared March 29. On April 9, his column was titled: "Wins over Bruins revive a tradition." Boston had finished first in the Adams Division with 104 points, one more than Buffalo and 29 ahead of Montreal. But the Bruins had to go down to the final Sunday of the season to take first place. And in their 79th game, a Saturday afternoon contest against Montreal, they barely eked out a 2-1 victory in a fight-filled contest. The game was a preview of the playoffs.

Montreal had managed to rest a few veterans in the last week of the season and they were fresh when the playoffs began on Wednesday, April 4. The plan was simple: bottle up Bruin forwards Barry Pederson and Rick Middleton and have a skater in front of defenceman Ray Bourque at every turn. Match the Bruins hit for hit.

Terry O'Reilly, a splendid player whose courage and work ethic formed the heart of the Bruins lunchpail brigade, was called on to explain why, again, the Canadiens had eliminated the Bruins.

"We had a terrific streak at the end of the season but a

lot of those wins were against some pretty bad teams. So, we deluded ourselves a bit about how good we really were. On the other hand, the Canadiens' points total in no way reflected their true quality as a team. We depended too much on Middleton, Pederson and Bourque and the Canadiens knew it. Our guys were dead tired from playing 45 minutes a game and the Canadiens made sure they hit them every chance they got."

If there was any justice in the NHL, Terence Joseph James O'Reilly would have won at least one Stanley Cup in his 13-year NHL career. Less skilled than many of his counterparts, he worked and worked throughout his career and became the heart of the Bruins. Unfortunately, he joined Boston a year too late (although he played one game and scored a goal in the 1971-72 season, the last time Boston won the Cup). Four times in his career the Bruins came up against the Canadiens in post-season play; four times the Bruins were eliminated.

"He was my hero," Chris Nilan will unabashedly admit. "If I can improve my game to the point that I'm as valuable to my team as Terry was to the Bruins, I will consider my career a success."

While Montreal swept the Bruins, clinching the series with a 5-0 win at the Forum, Quebec Nordiques were turning the tables on the second-place Buffalo Sabres.

A second Quebec-Montreal confrontation loomed, this one with a difference. This time the Canadiens were the underdogs and the pressure was on the Nordiques.

Quebec responded well in the first game, peppering Penney with 32 shots en route to a 4-2 win. The second game at the Colisée was an entirely different matter. Montreal took a 1-0 lead on a Pierre Mondou goal in the second period and Penney held the fort against waves of Nordiques for the first 40 minutes of play. However, the third period was only 36 seconds old when Anton Statsny tied it up. The stage was set for a collapse by the Canadiens; after all, the strain of protecting such a fragile lead must have worn them down physically and psychologically.

Except that it was Quebec which collapsed.

Ryan Walter and Mats Naslund took a leaf from the Bruins' book and stormed the Nordiques net as John Chabot let fly. Naslund deflected the puck past Dan Bouchard and it was 2-1. Steve Shutt and then Perry Turnbull, who had struck two goalposts earlier in the game, finished off a 4-1 win and the Colisée fans went home grumbling.

The Canadiens won the third game and appeared ready to blow Quebec out of the Forum in game four when they took a 3-1 lead into the third period. That evaporated quickly and Quebec returned home with the series tied 2-2, on the strength of an overtime goal by Bo Berglund. Montreal was given yet another opportunity to collapse and return to the bad habits of the regular season.

Game five was a replay of game two. Pierre Mondou, once again, scored halfway through the second period to give the Canadiens a 1-0 lead which they nursed into the third period. Quebec pressed but a stonewall defence and the imperturbable Penney parried every thrust. Four minutes into the final period, Guy Carbonneau forced Bouchard to make a big save and the puck came to Mario Tremblay in the slot. Bouchard was down and out of the net when Tremblay directed his shot past defenceman Pat Price for a 2-0 Montreal lead.

It was a 3-0 eighty seconds later when Bouchard lost a race with Bobby Smith for a loose puck at the blueline. Steve Shutt kept the puck onside and picked the corner with a wrist shot. Barely 90 more seconds had elapsed when Naslund skated in on a rink-long breakaway and put the puck through Bouchard's legs. At the other end, Penney stopped all 24 shots directed at him.

The events of the final game of the series, the so-called Good Friday massacre, are described elsewhere in this book. Suffice it to say that Montreal won a fight-filled sixth game 5-3, after trailing 2-0 early in the third period.

The Canadiens followed that up with a pair of victories

over the New York Islanders before injuries and momentum caught up to them and they dropped the series 4-2 to the defending Stanley Cup champions.

It didn't matter, however, because the playoffs had rescued a season and the team was back. This was the first summer in four years that the players could return home with their heads high. The Nordiques' climb in popularity was arrested and *les Glorieux* were Number One in the hearts of most Quebec, and even most Canadian hockey fans. It didn't even hurt much when the team was shut out in post-season awards and all-star nominations.

A larger turnout than usual greeted the home team at the next Forum function, the 1984 entry draft, and management did not disappoint. Irving Grundman's gift to the new management, the Hartford first-round draft choice, number 5 overall, would not be good enough to secure Mario Lemieux, the tall centre the Canadiens had coveted for four years. Leading up to the draft, Savard tried desperately to arrange a deal with Pittsburgh's Eddie Johnston to no avail. Lemieux was going to be the Penguins' franchise and Johnston knew it.

Just before the draft began, Savard completed a deal with the man who was rapidly becoming his favourite trading partner, Ron Caron. Rick Wamsley went to St. Louis in return for the Blues first-round choice, number 8 overall, and other switched choices in later rounds.

After Lemieux, Kirk Muller, Ed Olczyk and Al Iafrate had been selected in the first four spots, Savard unveiled his draft secret.

"Montreal selects, from Czechoslovakia, Petr Svoboda," he announced. Moments later, a skinny kid who could speak neither English nor French was trotted out in a Canadiens' sweater that was ten sizes too large. Everywhere he went, an interpreter followed.

Nine short months later, a gifted Svoboda would demonstrate his mercurial temper and linguistic talents during the playoffs against Boston, standing at centre ice and screaming "Fuck you, Linseman, fuck you!" over the heads of two linesmen, the referee and several players, with the conviction and inflection of a native-born Canadien while Larry Robinson hid his laughter in his gloves. On this day however, he was a little boy lost, confused by foreign languages and customs.

He spent the summer with the Savard family in St. Bruno, learning to speak English.

"Hey, don't blame that on me," Savard smiled. "We taught him nice words like 'pass the bread'. We're a polite family."

Three spots later, Montreal reached for yet another Brantford Alexanders' player when rugged forward Shayne Corson was selected. Tall centreman Stéphane Richer of Granby was next, picked number 29, and his best friend, goalie Patrick Roy, followed as number 51.

By 1985-86, Svoboda, Richer and Roy would be regulars and Corson would be banging on the door. Management was back on track.

Under Jacques Lemaire, the 1984-85 Canadiens finished first in the Adams Division, eliminated Boston in the best-of-five opening round, and then fell to the Nordiques on an overtime goal by Peter Stastny in the seventh game of the Adams Division final.

That result hurt but the organization was strong enough to stand up to it, especially in this, its 75th anniversary year, and the 60th birthday of the Forum. During the season, Steve Shutt was traded to Los Angeles Kings, a team of his own choosing, and Guy Lafleur retired when he grew tired of riding the bench. John Chabot went to Pittsburgh in a trade for Ron Flockhart, and yet another American defenceman, Tom Kurvers, made the team with a display of pinpoint passing rarely seen in the Forum. In an exhibition game against Edmonton Oilers, won 5-4 by Montreal in overtime, Kurvers' passes led to four Canadiens' breakaways and two goals.

Mats Naslund became the new Guy Lafleur and the most popular Canadien. Stars like Guy Carbonneau and Chris Chelios were not far behind.

During the late fall, the team launched an "all-time dream team" contest, in which fans could select the very best players to ever wear the *bleu-blanc-rouge*. On January 13, 1985, more than 1,800 fans and members of the Canadiens' family gathered at the Queen Elizabeth Hotel.

In the presence of the Prime Minister of Canada and the Mayor of Montreal, the Fabulous Six took the stage: goalie Jacques Plante, defencemen Doug Harvey and Larry Robinson, left winger Dickie Moore, centre Jean Beliveau and right winger Maurice Richard.

It was the highlight of the hockey year. All of those in attendance were given a unique program, the cover of which was a reproduction of a very special painting commissioned from artist Michel Lapensée that captured 75 years of hockey history.

There, in living *bleu-blanc-rouge*, they were: Howie Morenz, Aurele Joliat, Harvey, Moore, Beliveau, Claude Provost, The Pocket, Guy, Bill Durnan, Elmer Lach, Toe, Serge, Fergy, Reggie, Jake the Snake, Ken Dryden (leaning on his stick), the Rocket, The Road Runner, Coco Lemaire, Shutty, Bob Gainey, Jacques Laperriere, Scotty, Butch Bouchard, the Boomer, Dick Irvin, Irving Grundman, Frank Selke, Tommy Gorman and Sam Pollock.

The picture said 75 years. The picture said class. The picture said dynasty. The Torch had been passed. And accepted.

15

The Young Lions

Not *really* knowing has a delicious sense of anticipation to it, probably not too dissimilar from that delicate sensitivity one feels when a rap on the noggin is forthcoming. All the nerve endings seem to congregate in one place and, if the blow does not arrive, there is almost a palpable sense of disappointment.

For anyone closely watching the Montreal Canadiens, and especially for the Second Floor, the 1985-86 season was going to be a watershed. During the previous year, reports had come in from all over North America that the Kids Are All Right. Stéphane Richer, drafted from Granby in 1984, was traded to Chicoutimi and was leading the Sagueneens in scoring; Claude Lemieux and Sergio Momesso, the Class of '83, were the stars of the Verdun Junior Canadiens and the Shawinigan Cataractes respectively, two teams which would compete in the four-team Memorial Cup round-robin championship. The Ontario representative would be the Sault Ste. Marie Greyhounds, and their leading scorer, Graeme Bonar, belonged to guess who? Another top forward in the Ontario league was Shayne Corson of Brantford Alexanders, a forward who was a "Gainey who can score", the reports said.

In the American Hockey League, defenceman Mike Lalor and scrappy centreman Brian Skrudland valiantly struggled to inspire a Sherbrooke Canadiens team that would make the league playoffs on the last night of the regular season.

Back home in Quebec, Patrick Roy, the goalie who had looked so good against the Oilers in NHL exhibition, was being bombarded every night with the weak Granby Bisons and showed well, even though his goals-against average was high.

A sign that the near future was promising for the Canadiens came in September, 1984, when a special training camp was held to select the team that would represent Canada at the 1985 World Junior Championships during the Christmas holidays. No fewer than seven Montreal draft choices attended the selection camp and three, Richer, Corson and Lemieux, made the team that would return with the gold medal.

In the American college ranks, Canadiens' scouts were keeping a close eye on two players, Dave Maley, a rugged forward with the Wisconsin Badgers, and defenceman Scott Sandelin of the University of North Dakota Fighting Sioux, Craig Ludwig's alma mater. Sandelin's coach Gino Gasparidi let the world know how he felt about his defenceman when he said he was even better offensively than another UND alumnus named James Patrick, the top defenceman on Canada's 1984 Olympic team and a stalwart with the New York Rangers.

What it came down to was what scouts all over the hockey world were talking about: Everywhere you looked, Montreal had some good kids. If only half of them panned out, the Canadiens would be substantially improved over the coming years. The Canadiens were in year three of Ronald Corey's Five-Year Plan, and everything seemed to be on schedule.

While the Canadiens were losing in game seven overtime to the Quebec Nordiques in the 1985 playoffs, Bonar, Lemieux and Momesso were gathering in Shawinigan and Drummondville to show their stuff in the Memorial Cup. Lemieux's Verdun team had blitzed through the Quebec league playoffs, wiping out Hull, Shawinigan and Chicoutimi, the latter a series in which Richer had played poorly and fought often, spending more time in the penalty box than on the ice leading his teammates. His team eliminated, Richer joined his former Granby buddy Roy in Sherbrooke for the Calder Cup playoffs. He wasn't very pleased with his exit from the junior ranks and was thankful for the opportunity the American Hockey League playoffs represented.

"I had a pretty good year with Chicoutimi but the playoffs were different. I was not quite myself, I don't know what got into my head. I was dropping the gloves against everybody."

Richer, like Lemieux and Momesso before him, had discovered the new status of being a Montreal draftee in the Quebec Major Junior Hockey League.

"Players in the league seemed to be more interested in stopping me, so they could prove that they were good enough to stop a Montreal player. If they did that, maybe it would help their draft chances. I also noticed Lemieux and Momesso a lot and I'd watch them a lot more because I knew they were going through a lot of what was happening to me."

While Lemieux and Richer were born in western Quebec—the same area that had produced Guy Lafleur—they did not know each other well because Lemieux had moved north to Mont Laurier at a young age. However, they renewed acquaintances in junior, *à la* Beliveau-Moore.

"Stéphane and I had our run-ins in junior, maybe because we were probably both trying to prove that one of us was the best from our area. We're both very competitive. After I was drafted in 1983, I remember watching Momesso during games and wondering if we would both make the Canadiens. When Richer was drafted a year after us with Patrick Roy, I wondered the same about him. And I would try extra hard against Patrick when he was in nets for Granby," said Lemieux.

In the 1980s, Montreal's eighteen year old draftees more often than not were sent back to their respective junior teams for another season, or even two, of maturing.

This system, while far removed from the Selke junior hockey sponsorship era of the 1950s and '60s, where large numbers of seventeen and eighteen year olds congregated at a Montreal junior camp and were then shipped out to various teams in groups, had the same reasoning behind it.

"Unless an eighteen year old has something very special to offer the Montreal Canadiens, we are not going to put that player through the pressure-cooker of the Forum," said Serge Savard, whose son Serge Jr. played in the same league as Richer, Lemieux and Roy. "This is especially true for our junior selections from the Quebec league."

In the sociological terms introduced earlier in the book, therefore, the occupational culture for Richer, Roy, Lemieux and Momesso was quite similar to that of their many illustrious predecessors like Moore, Beliveau, Geoffrion and Plante, even though many operational changes had taken place in the Canadiens' hierarchy.

Whether they played on a team full of Montreal-sponsored junior players as in the 1950s, or as individual draft choices on an independent junior team of the 1980s, the young players grew to understand very quickly what the Montreal Canadiens meant to their lives and what the "big team" expected from them. In a 21-team league, and despite the universal draft, Montreal has managed to retain the positive aspects of the perceived familial obligations of another age: loyalty, dedication, purpose and sense of common direction.

In this way, people like Serge Savard, André Boudrias, Jacques Lemaire and Carol Vadnais passed on lessons they, themselves, had learned as juniors in Montreal and, later, as pros in such far-off places as Houston.

"After one Montreal rookie camp, you got a pretty good idea what to expect," said Lemieux. "You knew that they did not approach hockey like most organizations, and that they were looking for some specific type of individual. You also realized that they would probably make more demands on you, and could, simply because they were the Montreal Canadiens. I also got that message when I played almost a full season in Sherbrooke in the American Hockey League."

Like Steve Penney, the incumbent netminder when he

was drafted, Patrick Roy was a native of the upper-middle-class Quebec City suburb of Ste. Foy, the son of a high-ranking civil servant. His was no romantic story of a poor farm kid wearing Eaton's catalogues for shin pads and hand-me-down skates. However, the significance of making it with either the Canadiens or the Nordiques was not lost on him.

"I think you can say that once you became a Canadiens' draft pick, you had special status when you went back for another year of Quebec junior hockey. After the 1984 training camp, I thought I had done very well and might get invited to stay up. But Penney was still the number one goalie and when they got Doug Soetaert from Winnipeg, I knew they wanted me to go down to junior for one more season. After the experience of wearing the *bleu-blanc-rouge* even in training camp, it was hard to get my head into wearing the Granby uniform again. But I think Montreal Canadiens counted on that, they wanted to see how I reacted to returning to junior. It was like a test. We were a weaker team than most and I sometimes had a hard time staying in the game. I had to keep reminding myself that *they* were watching."

There was a lot more significance to the fact that the Canadiens suddenly had so many all-star draft selections in the Quebec Major Junior Hockey League. The league itself, for several years, had taken a back seat to the other two major junior leagues in Canada, the Ontario Hockey League and the Western Hockey League. Scouts and NHL general managers had fallen into the habit of routinely downgrading the Quebec league. The two most common complaints were that the league could not play defence and that the players were too small.

A detailed breakdown of the drafting practices of the National Hockey League teams shows clearly that the professional teams were not enamoured with the Quebec league and that this disaffection had festered over a long period of time.

Since the entry draft was instituted in 1969, up to the 1985 selection some 3,198 players were selected by the NHL teams. The majority, 903 or 28.2 percent came from the OHL; 699 or 21.9 percent from the WHL; 491 or 15.4 percent from U.S. colleges; 382 or 12 percent from the QMJHL; 232 or 7.2 percent from International teams; 198 or 6.2 percent from U.S. high schools and 293 or 9.1 percent "others".

Even those figures are flattering to the Quebec league because the first American high school player wasn't drafted until 1980 and international draft selections were in small handfuls until that same year. Since 1980, 198 players were drafted from American high schools, 184 from international hockey and 124 from Quebec. (The OHL had 363, the Western League 254 and American colleges 139 in the same period, the latter drop-off attributed to the increased activity in drafting eighteen year olds out of high school, before they went to college, giving them four " free", years to develop, so to speak.)

A majority of those players drafted in American college ranks after 1980 were Canadians; the good U.S. players were generally spotted in high school. A lot of those Canadians were Tier Two junior or high school players who earned hockey scholarships at sixteen or seventeen and then developed south of the border, such as Minnesota-Duluth's Brett Hull (the son of the Golden Jet) and Joe Nieuwendyck of Cornell, both drafted by Calgary Flames.

The defunct Quebec Remparts led their own league with 47 players drafted in the 1969-85 period, two ahead of Cornwall and three ahead of Sherbrooke. (The Sherbrooke Beavers moved to St. Jean in 1983 and Cornwall Royals joined the OHL a year before.)

However, the Remparts' performance would only be good for ninth place in the OHL, tied with the Kingston Canadians, who had five fewer years to provide players to the pros. The Peterborough Petes, once a Montreal-sponsored team, led the OHL with 92 players drafted in the same period, just ahead of the Toronto Marlboros with 88 and Kitchener Rangers and Ottawa 67s, both tied with 81.

The top source of WHL talent was Calgary (Centennials and Wranglers) with 64, two ahead of another former Montreal-sponsored team, the Regina Pats.

The draft pattern angered many Québécois hockey fans, to say nothing of the hockey writers who covered both the QMJHL and the Canadiens. What frustrated them most, however, was that their two teams, the Canadiens and the Nordiques, had begun to draft the same way as the other 19 teams; indeed the Canadiens seemed to do a majority of their scouting south of the border.

There were several reasons for this.

First, Sam Pollock was one of the first to enjoy success in drafting from American college ranks in the 1970s. In 1972, Bill Nyrop was found at Notre Dame and picked number 66; in 1975 Brian Engblom (Wisconsin) and Pat Hughes (Michigan) turned up. The list grew in the late '70s: Bill Baker of Minnesota ('76), Rod Langway of New Hampshire, Mark Holden of Brown and Craig Laughlin of Clarkson College ('77), Larry Landon of RPI, Chris Nilan of Northeastern and Rick Wilson of St. Lawrence ('78). Irving Grundman and Ron Caron followed up and picked Craig Ludwig of North Dakota and Mike McPhee of RPI in 1980.

Second, the college players were generally larger and better; larger—especially after the league began drafting eighteen year olds—because they were older, usually twenty-one or twenty-two when they graduated; better because the colleges might play 40 games a year and practise three times to every game played.

Chris Chelios, a notorious rink rat, played two years of Tier Two junior hockey with Moose Jaw from 1979-81 and then went to the University of Wisconsin for two more years, before joining the U.S. Olympic team in 1983.

"The major difference was that you had much more ice time at college to work on things," he said. "At Wisconsin, it was basically our rink and we didn't have to share it with many people. If you wanted to take the time, you could be on the ice working on parts of your game three or four hours a day. And the coaching staff, people like Bob Johnson, were always there to help."

In junior hockey, where small town businessmen were more concerned with their investment and the bottom line, nobody bought tickets to practice so the players slogged their way through 80-game seasons, travelling huge distances from town to town in what Dave "Tiger" Williams called The Iron Lung, subsisting on pizzas, McDonald's Quarter Pounders and beer. When they were home for a week or so, they often had to share the rink with everybody from figure skaters to nine-year-old ringette players and peewee hockey leagues.

Said one NHL general manager whose team had drafted college players almost exclusively: "At least you don't have to teach these kids how to eat, damn it! We had to bring in a nutritionist one year because we were losing a lot of games late in the third period. A number of our young guys were running out of gas and we finally figured out why—they didn't know how to eat. Guess who were the biggest culprits? That's right, the Juniors. It'd bad enough they don't get the book learning in junior, but when they can't develop common dietary sense on how to take care of their bodies. . ."

He had a point. During the 1985-86 season, the Canadiens also brought in a nutritionist to wean Richer and Roy (among others) of their hamburger road habit and teach them all about the wonderful world of pasta and complex carbohydrates. Patrick was so bad with his addiction to french fries and potato chips that his teammates nicknamed him Humpty Dumpty after a well-known potato chip brand or "casseau", after the French-Canadian word for the cardboard containers french fries come in.

When Pollock left Montreal, Ron Caron expanded the team's American scouting base, Ken Dryden was enlisted to help build a European network, and both delivered. Another factor that hurt the Quebec league was that many of the players drafted from there by Montreal could not make it with the talent-rich Canadiens, no matter where they were selected in the draft order. They might have been successful with weaker NHL teams, but could not crack the strong line-up at the Forum.

From 1975 to 1980, Montreal drafted 24 players from the Quebec League. Only seven went on to play in the

NHL: Pierre Mondou, Normand Dupont, Richard Sevigny, Alain Côté, Louis Sleigher, John Chabot, Robbie Holland and Guy Carbonneau. Of these, only Mondou, Chabot and Carbonneau played for Montreal for any length of time. The only Quebec league player drafted in the top 10, Danny Geoffrion, the number 8 pick in 1978, never made it.

With the arrival of the Nordiques and their "draft French" policy (which was immediately revoked once the Nordiques began winning and felt they had a chance to challenge for the top), Montreal was forced to look at the Quebec league in a new light. The Nordiques took Canadiens drafts like Alain Côté and Louis Sleigher and gave them a chance to prove they belonged in the NHL. The Nordiques found Normand Rochefort, a steady defensive defenceman, in the Quebec league. They turned up a scoring jewel in Michel Goulet and a quality goaltender in Mario Gosselin, who backstopped Canada at the 1984 Olympic Games. Players like André Savard and Jacques Richard, former Remparts, were reclamation projects from other teams and became successful with Quebec, if only for a season or two. All of this left the Canadiens behind the eight ball in their own backyard.

It did not help the "shop in Quebec" cause when the Canadiens' first two choices in 1982, Jocelyn Gauvreau and Alain Héroux, did not make the grade.

When Serge Savard took over, and brought in people like André Boudrias as Director of Scouting, the drafting policy remained the same as in Sam Pollock's prime: go for the character player.

"But if we could find two players of equal ability and size and one who was from Quebec, there certainly was nothing wrong with leaning to the Quebec player," Savard said.

"The funny thing is, it's only here that this can sometimes be taken the wrong way. Anywhere else in hockey, it is considered a terrific idea to go for a hometown boy if possible. Calgary and Edmonton would love to have more Albertans playing for them and Boston and Hartford love to draft boys from New England. Here we often get criticized, even in the French press, for drafting local boys or French players, and it is the dumbest criticism I have ever heard."

The Canadiens redoubled their efforts in scouting Quebec and superscout Claude Ruel, one of the best judges of hockey talent in the NHL, paid special attention to the QMJHL.

In 1983, Claude Lemieux and Sergio Momesso were drafted and Stéphane Richer and Patrick Roy came along a year later. In all cases, the so-called reputation of the Quebec league worked in favour of the Canadiens: all four players were still available after other choices were made. In 1983, Montreal drafted centre Alfie Turcotte in the first round and was able to claim both Momesso and Lemieux in the second round. In 1984, Richer was Montreal's third pick behind Petr Svoboda and Shayne Corson and number 29 overall. Roy was even more of a find in the third round, number 51 overall.

Montreal's scouting tentacles also found other players whom the universal draft ignored.

In late 1983, Jean Perron was an assistant to Coach Dave King with the Calgary-based Canadian Olympic Team. One of the team's last cuts before it headed to Sarajevo for the Winter Games was an Alberta-born centre named Brian Skrudland.

"Dave thought he was too slow, but I liked him," said Perron, who joined the Canadiens the following year. Shortly thereafter, Skrudland was signed as a free agent and sent to Nova Scotia in the AHL where he joined another free agent, Mike Lalor.

By late 1984 and early 1985, a large number of young future Canadiens were scattered throughout junior hockey and collegiate ranks. As mentioned earlier in this chapter, when the Team Canada juniors met in a special training/tryout camp in late summer 1984, seven Canadiens draftees were invited and three, Corson, Richer and Lemieux played on a line on the team that won the world championship that December.

The Memorial Cup was another indication that the 1985 Canadiens' training camp would be something special, with Lemieux, Momesso and Bonar lining up against each other. It did not help Lemieux's cause when he and his Verdun teammates showed poorly at the Memorial Cup tournament. Momesso, on the other hand, shone and his stock rose accordingly while Bonar was somewhere in the middle, playing well in some spots, and not so well in others.

The revelations of the spring were Richer and Roy, longtime friends, who found themselves in the thick of the American Hockey League playoffs with Sherbrooke. There they joined Skrudland, Lalor and Serge Boisvert, yet another free agent signing, who had ended the Montreal season in the NHL before returning to the AHL.

After the third game of the playoffs, first-string goalie Paul Pageau returned home to be with his wife who was about to deliver a child and Greg Moffett, his backup, had equipment problems.

"We put Patrick in nets and he immediately showed that he was a money player," said coach Pierre Creamer. "And Stéphane gave us a quality play-making centre who could score. Both of these players made all the difference in the world to our team."

The Sherbrooke Canadiens, a joint Montreal Canadiens-Winnipeg Jets enterprise, won the Calder Cup. Better still, they won it in front of the entire Canadiens' hierarchy. With Montreal eliminated by the Nordiques, people like Corey, Savard, and Boudrias began making the 90-minute drive to Sherbrooke to watch the American Hockey League playoffs.

The stock of Richer, Roy, Skrudland and Lalor soared.

"When I saw Patrick play in the Calder Cup playoffs, I knew he would be good enough to play for Montreal the next year," said then assistant coach Jean Perron.

Montreal had every reason to look forward to 1985-86. The team had played well and captured first place in the 1984-85 season—despite the departures of Steve Shutt and Guy Lafleur—only to lose to Quebec in overtime of a seventh game. Rookies like Chris Chelios, Tom Kurvers and Svoboda showed they belonged and mixed well with veterans like Rick Green, Ryan Walter, Larry Robinson and Guy Carbonneau. The rookie crop coming up was a winner, in junior hockey and in the AHL. If only half of the eight to ten blue chippers could crack the Canadiens' lineup, the team would be a solid challenger.

With that in mind, and any trepidation felt by managing director Savard (and Boudrias) moderated by sheer numbers, the Canadiens went to Toronto in June, 1985 for the NHL draft. There they quickly manufactured a deal with Ron Caron that sent Mark Hunter to St. Louis in exchange for St. Louis's first-round pick, number 12 and other later-round considerations. The advanced drafting position allowed Montreal to pick ahead of (number 15) Quebec Nordiques and they selected José Charbonneau, a six-foot, 195-pound right winger with Drummondville, the highest-rated Quebec junior in the draft. The Canadiens also retained their regular number 16 position and opted for Tom Chorske, a Minnesota high schooler.

By the end of the 1985-86 season, it looked like Savard had gotten too cute with that particular draft manoeuvre, especially since Hunter scored 44 goals for the Blues. The younger brother of the Oilers' Dave and the Nordiques' Dale, Mark had been an oft-injured but very popular member of the Canadiens whom Larry Robinson described as possessing the three prime requisites of an NHL hockey player: "head, heart and balls." His opinion was shared by many team veterans.

However, Charbonneau showed well on offence with Drummondville in 1985-86 and is considered a serious candidate for a regular spot on the club in the late '80s.

The questions began to be answered at training camp in September, 1985, baptized by one veteran as "The Invasion of the Killer Tomato Cheeks."

Everywhere there were good young players and many surprises. The positives included Momesso, Richer, Lalor, Skrudland and Roy, all of whom made the team on the effort they showed in camp. Other young players like John Kordic, a bruiser picked from the same Memorial Cup-winning Portland Winter Hawks team that supplied Alfie Turcotte, and Domenic Campedelli, plus Kjell Dahlin, from Mats Naslund's hometown of Timra, Sweden, all showed promise as good role players. Dahlin stayed with the team, inheriting Mark Hunter's Number 20 while Campedelli and Kordic were late cuts and went to Sherbrooke.

The negatives were Lemieux, Bonar, Corson (to a lesser degree) Steve Rooney and Charbonneau. Lemieux went through the motions in camp and was quickly despatched to Sherbrooke. Bonar, Corson and Charbonneau returned to their junior teams for another year of seasoning while Rooney, playing with a shoulder injury that would necessitate surgery in mid-season, remained with the parent club.

There was, of course, one more rookie of note. On Monday, July 29, the authors spent most of the morning interviewing Canadiens' president Corey in his Forum office. At the same time, right next door in Savard's office, F.X. Seigneur, Savard and others were hard at work on a press release and plans for an early afternoon press conference.

Several times during the interview, the team president excused himself to take "important" telephone calls. He wasn't kidding. While Corey was describing his team's makeup, Jacques Lemaire had quietly resigned as coach of the Montreal Canadiens. Always an intensely private individual who valued highly his family's privacy, he was not comfortable with life under the media microscope.

"It was a good time for me to make this decision," he said. "I felt very confident that Jean Perron could do the job; he is an excellent coach with a good background and he is well known to the players after a year as my assistant."

When the new season got under way at Pittsburgh on October 10, Perron was behind the bench. Just five days over thirty-nine years of age, he now would be the most second-guessed sports coach in Quebec.

"If I knew then that I would be starting my season with injuries to Mario Tremblay, Lucien Deblois, Ryan Walter and Steve Penney, and that Chris Nilan would get a 10-game suspension, I would have turned down the job right then and there," he said half-jokingly the following May while basking in the afterglow of the Stanley Cup.

During the 1985-86 season, Jean Perron would have many occasions to make that same remark, with a lot less levity.

The season got underway with a whimper in Montreal. With as many as eight rookies in the lineup for games, the Canadiens lurched through October and early November. The team started with a victory in Pittsburgh and a home opener win over Chicago Black Hawks before travelling to Boston on the season's first Sunday.

It is not necessary to describe in detail the emotional state of affairs that exists between the Bruins and the Canadiens. Suffice it to say the teams do not like each other. Montreal and Quebec fight a war for their province every winter, but the players respect each other. There is little admiration or respect for the Bruins, a feud whose origins go back a long, long way.

Thus, when Chris Nilan butt-ended Boston's Rick Middleton in the mouth on that October Sunday, earning an extremely rare 10-minute deliberate injury penalty (a 10-minute power play), and a subsequent 10-game suspension, those feelings were exacerbated.

Nilan was not openly apologetic about the incident, but he quietly regretted it. One reason was that 1985-86 was finally going to be the season where the ebullient right winger from West Roxbury, Massachusetts, shed his goon image and received credit for his hockey skills. In 1984, the *Boston Globe Magazine* published a long feature on Nilan titled "Toughing it Out."

Writer Charles Kenney was bang on when he began:

> It is amazing, really. Nobody ever thought Chris Nilan was anything special when he played hockey at Catholic Memorial High School in West Roxbury, nor were there great expectations when Nilan went off to play at Northeastern. And certainly nobody—but nobody—ever could have believed Nilan would make it in professional hockey.

But looking back on the years of turbulence—the times when it seemed Nilan defied the odds almost daily—looking back, the absolute craziest thing about it all is that after his first full professional hockey season with the Montreal Canadiens, Chris Nilan returned home to West Roxbury with all of his teeth.

Nilan was a gregarious kid who grew up in the Boston area in the age of Bobby Orr and the Big Bad Bruins. He idolized the Bruins and a young forward named Terry O'Reilly who came along in 1972, because he saw something of himself in both.

"Chris was never a natural hockey player," said his father, Henry Nilan, during the first period intermission at a Bruins-Canadiens game at the Garden. "He always had to fight for what he got, in all meanings of the word. He always seemed to be willing to work harder, fight more and push more for what he wanted. He came to me when he was about sixteen years old and announced he was going to play in the National Hockey League someday. I told him not to put all of his eggs in one basket, especially since I didn't think he was all that good. We always were able to talk with each other like that. Chris has always respected people who aren't afraid to say what they think."

When Nilan graduated from high school, he was neither the athlete nor the scholar to advance to collegiate ranks and he applied to a prep school, Northwood School in Lake Placid, New York for the 1975-76 school year. There he bettered his grades and worked hard on his hockey, garnering the school's award for most improved player, and was rewarded with a scholarship to Northeastern University where former Bruin Fern Flaman coached. He played rarely in his freshman year but saw a lot more ice time as a sophomore, "trying to knock everybody all over the ice." He was still the farthest thing from a star and when Chris told his father that he was going to be drafted by an NHL team, even he knew that chance was remote.

On May 25, 1978, Nilan mourned as his beloved

Bruins went down 4-1 to Montreal Canadiens in the sixth, and last, game of the Stanley Cup final.

Two weeks later his lifelong allegiance changed; he was the fourth-last pick (number 231) of the NHL draft, all by the Canadiens who used their thorough scouting system to advantage, picking numbers 229 through 234. Nilan and Louis Sleigher, number 233, both made the NHL. Ironically, the top two draft choices of that year, Bobby Smith (Minnesota) and Ryan Walter (Washington), would team up with Nilan in Montreal. The Canadiens had four picks in the first two rounds in 1978. Only one player, Dave Hunter, number 17 in the first round, made it to the NHL with the Edmonton Oilers. Danny Geoffrion, number 8, Dale Yakiwchuk, number 30 and Ron Carter, number 36 were less fortunate and only Keith Acton, number 103, made the Canadiens from the 1978 draft above Nilan.

"I always knew I would make it," Nilan says in his seventh NHL season. "I didn't know *how*. I just knew I would. I was going to do anything to get there, anything at all."

Making it meant a return to Northeastern for his junior year and continuation of his studies in criminal law. The following summer, however, Nilan decided to leave school. In August, 1979, a scant three months after the Canadiens had won their fourth straight Stanley Cup, the brash young kid from West Roxbury attended his first professional training camp.

"No matter what kind of self-confidence you have, or how you motivate yourself, that first camp is one of the scariest things in your life. Here I was trying to skate with Guy Lafleur, Larry Robinson and players like that. I threw my weight around but in a lot of cases I just bounced off guys.

"I found out what the pros and the Montreal Canadiens were all about. The players up here were bigger, faster and stronger, a lot stronger. They did not seem at all impressed by a college kid from Boston who liked to throw his weight around."

Nilan was clearly deficient in skating and offensive skills, but people like Claude Ruel and Ron Caron saw something they liked. He was assigned to the Nova Scotia Voyageurs of the American Hockey League. In the first minute of his first game with the Voyageurs, he "pulled a John Ferguson", getting into a fight with Glen Cochrane, a tough defenceman with Maine Mariners, a Philadelphia Flyers' farm team. After 49 AHL games and 307 minutes in penalties, Nilan was called up to Montreal temporarily as the Canadiens underwent a rash of injuries. He never returned to the AHL.

In his second NHL game, Nilan and Philadelphia's Bob "Hound Dog" Kelly—an original Broad Street Bully—went into a corner after the puck and the sticks went up. The gloves went off and Kelly went down, the victim of a couple of crisp right hands. The next year, Nilan became the first Montreal Canadien ever to eclipse the 200-minute mark in penalties for a season. He has never fallen below that mark since, and has outlasted a phalanx of right wingers at that position on the club, including the immortal Guy Lafleur.

"The Chris Nilan who has been my teammate has been two different players," says Larry Robinson. "The Chris Nilan who was up here his first three seasons did not play regularly and nowhere near as well as he does now. He wasn't a bad skater but it took him a long time to get going, and he had no confidence with the puck.

"The Chris Nilan who is playing with us now is very different. He is one of the best checking right wingers in the league and plays on the best checking line in hockey with Guy Carbonneau and Bob Gainey. He is a much better skater and a much better stickhandler and that shows in the statistics. A checking winger who can score more than 20 goals a year is a valuable commodity. He accomplished that with years of extra work up here. There were times when he might not have been as good as a lot of other players with Montreal, but the coaches kept him around because he worked so hard and improved every day."

When the Year of the Rookie rolled around in Montreal, Nilan was an even more valuable commodity to the Canadiens, a veteran who was not afraid to shake up some rookies. He was the catalyst in an incident that started to bring the club together in mid-season.

When the season started, several of the newcomers were greeted with the traditional "rookies haircut", although one veteran complained that "these kids are so green, they don't have hair to shave." Where illustrious names like Lafleur and Shutt had worn the familiar Numbers 10 and 22 just a short time before, unfamiliar rookies like Skrudland, Momesso, Lalor and Richer wore numbers in the 30s and 40s. Instead of being weaned slowly, a game here, a game there, in traditional Canadiens style, seven or eight of these kids were pouring over the boards every night. The man patting them on the back and telling them to go was a rookie, too.

The loss in Boston started an October tailspin that left the club in last place in the Adams Division. Never did the club look worse than in an 11-6 thrashing in Hartford where the Whalers led 7-2 after one period. The principal architect for that debacle was 1984 playoff hero Steve Penney who let in five goals on three shots (the other two goals went in after Hartford forwards actually lost the puck on their own stickhandle and it trickled under a goalie who was flopping worse than a walrus in mating season) before he was replaced by Roy halfway through the initial period.

Then something strange started to happen. Even in the Hartford game, you could see that some of the kids could play. Richer scored a goal after beating five Whalers inside their own blueline. Momesso popped one from in-close when the defencemen could not move his bulk from the crease. And Kjell Dahlin scored on the prettiest breakaway goal never seen by Montreal fans (a power failure interrupted the Saturday night telecast) in the second period.

As the rookies gained confidence, the team began to win and move up in the standings. Richer led all rookie scorers with ten goals when an ankle injury put him on the disabled list in November. The first sign of his fragile mental condition came the next day when he worried openly about getting back into the lineup. To that point, he had been one of the top four or five Canadiens forwards.

Momesso and Dahlin settled in very well and both showed a good touch around the net, to the point that for the greater part of the season the Canadiens would be the second highest scoring team in the entire league, trailing only the Edmonton Oilers.

However, Momesso did not stay past December, suffering what doctors at first feared was a career-ending knee injury and was out for the season. His loss loomed larger than just that of a big, tough scoring rookie. On a team rapidly polarizing into two major groups—not cliques—an unusually large rookie class and a solid core of veterans, Momesso was popular with both.

"The veterans all liked Sergio," said Larry Robinson. "He is a quiet, hard-working player who does his job without a whole lot of fanfare. We miss him."

His loss was offset by the performance of Kjell Dahlin, a wraithlike right winger who settled in comfortably on the right wing with Bobby Smith and fellow compatriot Mats Naslund and ran away with the rookie scoring race in the first half of the season. A left-handed shot with good speed and a deft stickhandler, Dahlin fit in well with Smith and Naslund and the three anchored the league's best powerplay throughout the season, working the puck skillfully.

"Kjell's contribution to that line and the powerplay is his ability to work the puck around with the other two," said Jean Perron. "Other teams are afraid to pressure those three because of their stickhandling and passing ability; make one mistake and it's in the net. The major reason is Kjell Dahlin. He has brought an added dimension to the line and makes it even more dangerous than it was before."

As the season moved into the second half, the Canadiens were in first place, trying to hold off the Nordiques. While the kids were playing well, and veterans like Carbonneau, Gainey, Robinson and Nilan were at peak form, the club could never show the kind of consistency that would make it a solid contender in the post-season tournament.

The major problem was goaltending. Steve Penney reported to camp overweight and immediately developed a serious groin injury. Patrick Roy would play some of the best 58 or 59 minutes of hockey seen at the Forum since the heyday of Ken Dryden. But the other one or two minutes would be a horror show, shots going in from terrible angles outside the blueline, rebounds the size of beach balls and uncertainty when clearing the puck in front and behind the net.

Doug Soetaert, the most consistent of the three goalies, rarely got to play. Before the season, Savard took a long time to sign the former Ranger and Jet while he courted Gilles Meloche, who had been traded late the previous season to Edmonton. Oilers' GM Glen Sather was adamant: "Give us Brian Skrudland for Meloche straight up." Savard had also seen the AHL playoffs and refused point blank. A week later, Soetaert was signed to another contract by Montreal.

The three-goalie system caused problems for the principals until they took time to sort out their emotional baggage themselves.

"It was so silly in practice that we were almost fighting each other to get in and out of goal," says Penney, who was traded to Winnipeg in the off-season.

"Normally, with two goalies one would take a goal at either end of the rink and that's that. With three we had to rotate, and quite often a goalie didn't want to leave the cage so the other guy could go in. The other players noticed this and, although they thought it was quite funny, they knew it was a serious situation, too."

The netminders had a heart-to-heart just before Christmas and sorted out their misunderstandings. It wasn't quite the Three Musketeers, but they saw that they shared the same predicament and it was best to talk out their problems.

Things were not that simple for the rest of the team.

Roy's inconsistency, the Momesso injury, the benching of Brian Skrudland and Dahlin's sudden slump all brought matters to a head during a West Coast swing in late February.

After a poor Forum performance against Hartford on Saturday, February 22, the Canadiens headed west for a week and games against Edmonton, Vancouver and Los Angeles, with a stop in Long Island before returning to Montreal for a four-game homestand. The team that flew west was playing strange hockey, losing a pair of Monday night home games in overtime to the Los Angeles Kings (and Soetaert to injury) and Minnesota North Stars and to the hapless New Jersey Devils at the Meadowlands, before reviving and thumping the Philadelphia Flyers and tying Washington Capitals in two of their best efforts of the year.

Montreal dropped their first game 3-2 to Edmonton in a lacklustre effort by both teams, then flew on to Vancouver for a Wednesday game with the Canucks. On Tuesday, the team held a full-scale workout at the Pacific Coliseum. On Wednesday, the Montreal papers were full of headlines about a Nilan-Richer fight in practice.

The two players came together during a drill, exchanged words, and Nilan connected with a few punches before other teammates intervened. Six weeks later, as the post-season playoffs got under way, Larry Robinson remarked that "there is no such thing as rookie and veteran in the dressing room. We're all in this together as players. We all wear the same shirt."

Another six weeks after that, the cheers of a half million Stanley Cup-happy Montrealers numbing his ears, Bob Gainey was asked by a reporter for a community TV channel how "the rookies and veterans managed to resolve their differences and come together as a team."

"There was no dissension or rookie-veteran split," he replied, very mindful of the new harmony that had guided the team to Montreal's 23rd Stanley Cup.

There was some division. Coach Jean Perron is the first to admit that the Nilan-Richer fight started the reunification of the team. "The bubble burst between the youngsters and the veterans. That's where the guys began to realize that they better pull together before it was too late."

It also helped a rookie coach deal with his own differences with veterans. Perron decided that the best strategy was to play it cool, and let the players sort it out among themselves. He knew he could not be caught favouring one side or the other. Some veterans admitted afterwards that they had expected an overreaction, especially after the French papers in Montreal played up the incident, and began to see their coach in a new light when he let the players sort out their differences among themselves.

With Soetaert hurt and Roy blowing hot and cold, Steve Penney was pressed into action in the next two games with Vancouver and Los Angeles. He acquitted himself well as the team won both, the second on a three-goal explosion in the last three minutes of play. Trailing L.A. 4-3, Montreal tied it when Nilan set up Richer with a perfect pass at 16:46 and won it on goals by Dahlin and Gainey.

Nilan and Richer made such a show of public emotion after the tying goal that a teammate on the bench quipped: "They better knock that off. This is a family arena!"

The team flew back east in a better frame of mind, and promptly got thumped by the resurgent Islanders. St. Louis Blues, also known as Montreal West or "The B Team" because of the nine former Canadiens in their lineup, waltzed into the Forum two nights later and thrashed "The A Team" 7-4 on Thursday as very little went right for the Canadiens. Boston followed and Montreal took out its frustrations on the hated black-and-gold with an 8-3 bashing Saturday night and then went flat again the following Monday and lost 5-2 to Hartford, that club's first-ever win at the Forum.

Vancouver Canucks were the next visitors and the Canadiens were hard-pressed to win 3-2. The following night the team travelled to Boston where they lost 3-2.

The slump was on again. First Calgary, then Quebec, skated away with Forum wins and Montreal slunk out of town with its tail wrapped firmly around a collective hind leg.

For four of the previous five months, the Canadiens had been the league's second-best scoring team and featured its best power play. Lately, however, the offence had ground to a halt and the power play was a poor comedy of Alphonse and Gaston indecision. Where short, sharp passes to the open man and multiple shots on goal had characterized the power play before, it was now an exhibition of uncertainty—bad passes, bad shots, blocked point drives and missed open nets.

On the team's top scoring line, Bobby Smith found himself alone more often than not . . . and for his trouble got the lion's share of the blame from the hometown faithful.

During one three-week stretch, neither Naslund nor Dahlin were skating well and Smith would often break into the offensive zone and have to pull up because his wingers were nowhere to be found. His ability earned him the Peter Mahovlich treatment from some fans. On many occasions during his career, Big Peter was castigated for passing too late or not getting the puck to swift linemates like Steve Shutt and Guy Lafleur. Strangely enough, he still holds the club's assists record with 82.

"*Maudit mangeur de puck* (puck eater)!" the fans would rail at Peter as he headed up-ice, cradling the vulcanized rubber disk on his stick.

Bobby Smith started hearing "*mangeur de puck*" too, as the fans blamed his reticence to pass on him rather than his nonexistent linemates. At six-feet five-inches, he was a large target. In early February, it appeared that Naslund and Dahlin would score 100 goals between them, but those predictions went out the window by mid-March. Naslund finished with 42, Dahlin with 31. In a 5-3 win over Philadelphia on February 16, Naslund and Dahlin scored their 37th and 27th goals respectively. In the remaining 22 games, they scored 5 and 4 goals.

To add to the team's problems, the defence was spotty.

Chris Chelios and Rick Green, one-third of the starting blue-line corps, were injured so long that everyone seemed to forget that they were still on the team. Gaston Gingras, a major reclamation project of Pierre Creamer in Sherbrooke, was called up in mid-season for spot duty on the power play. The possessor of one of the hardest slapshots in the league, he immediately paid off with several booming goals, including a howitzer that almost decapitated Philadelphia goalie Bob Froese.

Gingras' quick insertion into the lineup and the immediate dividends provide a classic example of the benefits of employing identical coaching methods and playing style on the farm team as on the big club. During a season where the Canadiens lost many players to injury, Alfie Turcotte, Randy Bucyk, John Kordic, Kent Carlson, Serge Boisvert and Gingras could move up without suffering culture shock.

"We may not have had a great many high-quality players in Sherbrooke this season," said Creamer, "but they were coached to play the same way as the Montreal Canadiens. When Gaston moved up to Montreal, he went on a power play that worked exactly the same as ours, so he fit in right away and was comfortable."

In the post-draft era, most NHL teams feature a full roster of 30 to 35 players, 22 with the big club and 10 to 13 playing for a minor league team that is operated jointly with another NHL team. For example, the Fredericton Express of the American Hockey League was stocked with players belonging to the Quebec Nordiques and the Vancouver Canucks. What system of play did coach André Savard employ? Did the former Nordiques players hockey strategies meet with Tom Watt's approval in Vancouver? Were the players who were called up to Quebec City able to fit in comfortably and quickly with the style of coach Michel Bergeron?

In Montreal, in 1986, these questions were being considered. Was it worth the extra investment for Montreal to operate under the old farm system concept? Would it be impossible to put into practice any lessons learned in the days of Father Frank and Trader Sam? "Not at all," said Savard.

Although it is almost economically impossible for a National Hockey League team to afford a full farm team these days, the Montreal Canadiens feel strongly that their community includes the AHL roster, and that players there must learn the Montreal Canadiens way of doing things. Savard is a strong believer in "Selkeism".

"We know that the main word is farm. That word means you eventually get back what you put into the ground. The harder you work on cultivating, the better the produce will be when it comes time to harvest. It was worth the money and the time invested."

Thus, Gingras paid instant dividends when he drove up the Eastern Townships Autoroute and reported to the Forum.

However, the absence of Chelios and Green, a later injury to Tom Kurvers and the erratic play of Petr Svoboda, meant that Gingras played more than the Canadiens had originally intended. On some nights, he was a major contributor; on others, he had problems.

Svoboda was a more worrisome case for the team. Young Petr, who when drafted less than 700 days earlier could not speak English or French and was munching on his very first hot dog, sparkled during his rookie season and won many admirers for his skating ability and the pounding he took from opposition forwards. He spent his first Montreal summer in the suburbs living with the Savard family and the first season boarding with another family.

In his second year he lived in his own apartment a short distance from the Forum. As a rookie, Svoboda was the team's unofficial mascot, and was taken under wing by Larry Robinson. Like many teenagers, he occasionally slept in and was late for practice and would receive a gentle slap on the wrist.

In his second year, the tardiness became a disease and when Svoboda announced that he had bought a house in the far suburbs to share with his newfound love, a stunning Parisienne, his teammates immediately took bets on how soon it would be before he would erase the legendary tardiness exploits of Rick Chartraw from the club record books.

"Jeez, he was always late when he lived up the street. Now he has to get up 90 minutes earlier just to be as late as he used to," said one player. "This might be awesome."

Sure enough, Petr was late for practice and this time there were no slaps on the wrist. Instead he was benched and he brooded.

Other problems surfaced on the ice. Over the previous year, Svoboda had put on 12 pounds and now weighed a respectable 172. He felt a little cockier at the higher weight and began to show signs of temper. When opponents crashed into him with the same enthusiasm as they had during his rookie season, he began to lose his cool and developed the bad habit of taking retaliation penalties.

The whole affair reached a head March 10 in the 5-2 loss to Hartford. In the third period, with the game still up for grabs and the Canadiens pressing in the Whalers zone, Svoboda was caught up-ice as Hartford broke away 2-on-1. He coasted back to the Canadiens' zone, a third Whaler forward sped by him into the play and scored and the Canadiens lost the game.

His fellow players, management and the fans were upset: one never quits on the play in the Forum. Ever. He saw very little ice time for the rest of the year. A month later, when announcer Claude Mouton would read out the list of Canadiens not dressed for a playoff game, a large cheer would go up when he read: "Number 25, Petr Svoboda."

When the Canadiens embarked on their last major road trip of the season, which included stops in Winnipeg and St. Louis, three days off in Montreal, and then back-to-back encounters at Hartford and Boston, the team was down. Blueline Fever had struck most members of the defensive corps and that was never better highlighted than in a 6-4 loss to the Jets. Doug Soetaert returned from a double knee injury to face his former team and played strongly for the first two periods as Montreal took a 3-1 first period lead and led 3-2 going into the third period. But his knees were still fragile.

The best player on the ice for Montreal was Chelios,

who also was recovering from a knee injury that had sidelined him since December.

The third period was a comedy of errors. Just 19 seconds into the period, Rick Green chased Winnipeg's Brian Mullen behind the Montreal net and the latter flipped the puck into the goal crease. It hit Gingras' skate and deflected into the goal.

A minute and three seconds after that, Thomas Steen directed an off-balance shot towards the Montreal net. This time Craig Ludwig redirected the puck past Soetaert. In just under ninety seconds, the Canadiens had scored two goals and found themselves trailing in the game for the first time. The Jets got two more without assistance from the Montreal defence and coasted.

That was it, as far as Perron was concerned. The team returned to boot camp drills. The Canadiens flew into St. Louis and were put through strenuous skating drills for ninety-minute sessions on Thursday and Friday.

It was time for the coach to deliver a message, one that many of the players didn't much care to hear. "The first message was simple. 'I'm the boss and you are going to do it my way.' Nobody was going to argue with that part of it."

Part two of the message was that the team had no intensity and that was unforgivable. Perron reminded his charges that the designation Flying Frenchmen belonged to history; this team was decidedly less spectacular, which is not to say less talented in its own way.

"I told them that all you need to inspire you when you play in Montreal is to look down at your chest and look at the crest. I also said that the work ethic had been set aside and that the only way this team was going to win was with a concerted team effort. We didn't have the superstars who were capable of doing it by themselves."

Some of the veterans were not pleased and Larry Robinson told Red Fisher of the *Gazette*:

> If he skated the hell out of us because he was unhappy with our performance against Winnipeg, why didn't he start doing it after St. Louis beat us in Montreal? Or after Hartford beat us in Montreal? Or a month and a half ago? Is he telling us we're out of condition after the 73rd game of the regular season?

In 11 games, the Canadiens had gone from first place in the Adams Division, four points ahead of Quebec, to fighting for their playoff lives with Boston, Buffalo and Hartford.

"Losing games is a problem," Robinson told the *Gazette*.

> We've got lots of problems. And the only way of solving problems is to get some discipline on the ice. Discipline is not to give up three-on-twos or two-on-ones to the other team—and making the most of ours. I don't know how many of them we've had in the last few games, and each time the pucks seem to be going into our net. On the other hand, I don't know how many times we had them on the other teams with nothing happening.

This outburst was a departure for the normally placid Robinson. His remarks and others by Guy Carbonneau caused many journalists to speculate that Perron's days behind the Canadiens' bench were numbered.

The first in a series of team meetings was called and it was attended by the managing director. His message was simple. "Jean Perron is the coach of this team. What he says, goes. End of story."

That Saturday, the Canadiens played a solid game, only to be undone by a couple of players who wore the CH on their hearts, even though their jerseys said Blues. Rick Wamsley stoned his former teammates and Doug Wickenheiser scored the game winner in a 3-2 victory.

Although they were sluggish on offence, the Canadiens enjoyed a good effort, especially from Steve Penney in nets. The constant criticism about Montreal's season had everyone in the league maligning the goaltending, sometimes with justification. Patrick Roy was too adventurous and tended to fall asleep in games and give away bad goals. Doug Soetaert was a journeyman. Steve Penney was poor technically. Yet both Penney and Soetaert were outstanding in what turned out to be their last appearances of the season.

Despite the criticism, Montreal was in the chase for the Jennings and Vezina trophies most of the season. Soetaert did not remotely resemble a journeyman when

Perron let him play, contributing three shutouts and a very steady presence in goal. Many team veterans openly questioned Perron's underutilization of the former Ranger and Jet, especially during Roy's more erratic periods.

Penney was terrible at the beginning of the year and had only himself to blame. He reported to camp overweight, suffered a bad groin injury, and managed to misplace the steely confidence that had made him such a formidable competitor during the 1983-84 playoffs. Nonetheless, the St. Louis game was his best of the season and followed solid performances in Vancouver and Los Angeles. He appeared ready to make the goaltending position a three-man fight again until sidelined by a sprained knee.

After the St. Louis loss, the Canadiens returned home for two days of workouts before they embarked on their last road trip of the year. The practice pattern was repeated with painful monotony—90 minutes of skate, skate, skate.

Here were no more complaints, private or public. Instead, the players began to admit their shortcomings. "Sometimes we're the last to know that we aren't doing it as individuals or a group," said defenceman Craig Ludwig.

"You don't have a meter that tells you when you're not going all out. You might think you are, except that there's no bounce in your legs and you're not taking out other players like you should. And our team is eighty percent work ethic—we beat the other guys because we outwork them. We aren't going to improve our game skills by skating like this, but our attitude will improve." Ludwig would be prophetic, although events would unwind slowly.

On Wednesday, the Canadiens met the Hartford Whalers. All day long the players prowled the Hartford Sheraton like caged tigers. Perron made the pre-game skate optional and only Randy Bucyk and Soetaert took advantage, skating alongside assistant coach Jacques Laperriere and assistant trainer Gaetan Lefebvre. The players attended a meeting in the morning, slept in the afternoon, and walked across the street to the Civic Center at 5 p.m.

Going into the contest, Montreal was in second place with 80 points, two better than Boston, four up on Buffalo and five up on Hartford. Whereas the Canadiens had been fighting the Nordiques for first place two weeks before, they now cast nervous glances in the rearview mirror.

Before the contest, Chris Nilan paced quietly outside the Canadiens' dressing room in his underwear, quietly putting on his game face and chatting amiably with Canadiens' equipment manager Eddy Pelchak and some of his Hartford counterparts. Not so popular on the ice, he is an off-ice favourite around the league, always ready with an autograph or conversation for fans and hockey hangers-on.

Just around the corner, Whalers Ulf Samuelsson and Kevin Dineen were also in their underwear, enjoying a game of basketball one-on-one in the cavernous Civic Center garage area. Samuelsson was in a particularly frisky mood, it was his 22nd birthday and he had enjoyed a good season with the Whalers, a team clearly heading for the upper echelons of the NHL.

Hartford was loose. Montreal wasn't. After the game, the standings read:

	GP	W	L	T	Pts.
Quebec	75	41	29	5	87
Montreal	75	37	32	6	80
Boston	74	34	30	10	78
Hartford	75	37	35	3	77
Buffalo	74	35	33	6	76

The Canadiens played well but could not get untracked on offence. Dahlin, Walter, Smith and Richer missed glittering scoring opportunities early in the game as Mike Liut turned in a solid performance behind a stingy Whalers defence.

There is a special dynamic to a slump—or prolonged negative performance—in sports. Once acknowledged, and players and coaches will go out of their way to deny its existence, the slump takes on a life of its own. Everything negative is magnified a thousand times while even positive efforts and results are doubted.

Pete Rose, who has known more success than adversity in his long baseball career, says a slump can get a player believing in a malevolent supernatural force.

"You might not be concentrating as well as you normally would because you are always thinking about how things are going. And even when you can win the battle inside your head and regain your confidence and concentration, you bang line drives right at people. You want to throw your bat at the sky and yell: 'Why are you doing this to me?' That is exactly the wrong attitude, but you can't help it."

Rose's point is that a slump is more of a mental condition than a physical one. When athletes are performing well, they don't think about what they are doing, they just do it. Conversely, when it seems that adversity is overwhelming them, it is all they can do *not* to think about it.

"When we are going well and a goalie stops me on a breakaway, I skate away thinking, 'All right, I'll get him next time'," Bobby Smith said after the game, reflecting on his confrontation with Liut. "When we're in a slump, I skate away thinking, 'How could I blow that?' In one case, your mind is where it should be directed, forward, because that is what you can do something about. In the other case, all you think about is the past, which you can do nothing about."

The game was scoreless late in the second period when the Canadiens made a poor line change. With four Canadiens racing desperately off their bench to head him off, Dineen picked up the puck along the left-wing boards and skated in on Roy. Gainey made a superhuman effort to overtake him and hooked the winger's stick as Dineen was about to shoot. Somehow, Dineen mustered the strength for a second effort, freed his stick and lifted a one-handed shot past a startled Roy.

The game was over early in the third period. Hartford pressed quickly and scored at 15 and 47 seconds to put the game out of reach. The first was a blueline "seeing-eye" dribbler off the stick of defenceman Scot Kleinendorst which took most of the period's first 15 seconds to skitter through a forest of skates and sticks and into the corner past a thoroughly screened Roy. The second was a flip shot by Ron Francis from a scramble just outside the crease.

The Canadiens' defence played well in front of Roy, despite missing both Robinson who had been left home with a sinus condition and Svoboda who was not dressed because of yet another tardy arrival at practice two days before.

"We played well and we weren't very nervous," said Mats Naslund. "The most important thing for us to remember is that we shouldn't panic; if we continue to work hard, this will turn around."

That night, the team bused to Boston, while Savard drove in a rented car. When he arrived, Lemaire, Savard and Perron burned the midnight oil in the coach's hotel room at the Boston Sheraton.

At 7:30 the same morning, the telephone rang in Sherbrooke and Claude Lemieux picked it up.

"Claude, it's Pierre Creamer. You've been called up. You have to report to Boston for the game tonight." Six months after his poor training camp relegated him to the minors, and three months after he finally accepted that fact and began to play like he could, Lemieux was a Montreal Canadien again.

Boston, like the rest of the Northeast, was enjoying an early spring heat wave, but leadbelly clouds threatened thunderstorms. The players and Montreal media prowled the spacious lobby, their moods matching the elements. Savard and Lemaire seemed to be everywhere while Perron stayed out of sight, fuelling speculation that his job was in jeopardy. The scene recalled the situation two years earlier when Bob Berry was struggling through the team's most difficult regular season in 30 years. Everybody noted the presence of assistant coach Jacques Lemaire and predicted "any time now."

In Perron's case, Lemaire was above him, not below, on the corporate ladder, but the speculation was the same. Nobody believed Savard when he said that Perron was his coach, no matter what.

Savard meant it.

"This team had five coaches in forty years and now we've had five in six years," he said. "We have had a different coach at the last three training camps. When I hired Jean Perron, I had the long term in mind. And don't forget, we set up a five-year plan for this club; this is only Year Three."

Perron, not as shy around the press as Lemaire had been, but also not a coach who courted publicity like Scotty Bowman, kept his own counsel. He was, however, feeling the frustrations.

"It is very, very hard to be head coach of the Montreal Canadiens. You can't begin to understand the pressures that go with this job. I was assistant coach for a year and thought I had a good line on how it would be to coach Montreal, but even I underestimated it. In this town, as the joke goes, the media and the fans are with you win or tie, but don't tie too often."

Downstairs in the lobby on this steamy Thursday, Richer, Gingras and Roy were the only players in sight as Bertrand Raymond and Yvon Pedneault of *Le Journal de Montréal* prowled, looking for material to fill their daily four pages. The next day was Good Friday and only *Le Journal* was publishing. The rest of Team Tandy, nicknamed for the portable computers used by the press, had the day off. "They've gone from a zone defence to a man-to-man," quipped another reporter, as Pedneault and Raymond squeezed Gingras and the two rookies for every last drop of copy.

And then Lemieux walked into the lobby, nattily attired in a blue velvet sports jacket and flannel trousers and carrying his equipment bag and hockey sticks. Both Raymond and Pedneault were seen looking skyward and mouthing a silent *"merci"* as they converged on the rookie and the official greeting committee of Lemaire and Savard.

That night, Lemieux played on a line with Walter and Richer and the trio was the team's best against the

Bruins in a 3-3 tie. In the dressing room after the game, Naslund summed up the performance for all concerned: "Big win."

The tie pretty much ensured Montreal's participation in the playoffs and the Canadiens went on to win three of their last four games, although not as convincingly as they might have hoped, particularly against Pittsburgh and Detroit.

In the team's last regular-season game against Buffalo at the Forum, a victory, Roy played well overall but let in two long shots, one from outside the blueline when he went down on his knees for no discernible reason while trying to catch an eye-high puck. He received a chorus of boos for the faux pas.

The playoffs and the hated Bruins beckoned and the Canadiens were still not firing on all cylinders. A team with eight rookies might be fodder for an aroused team from Beantown.

There was one piece of good news, however. Chelios and Green were back from long injury layoffs and both were playing inspired hockey. Robinson was enjoying his best season in a long while and Ludwig was steady as well. Better still, rookie Mike Lalor had proved that he belonged and Gingras was doing everything asked of him by scaring goalies to death with his shot.

With a five-day layoff, the defence rested. After all, didn't all the experts say during the season that it was defence that decided the Stanley Cup playoffs?

Cherchez le gardien. . . .

16

The Lions Fly

"If two stand shoulder to shoulder against the gods,
Happy together, the gods themselves are helpless,
Against them while they stand so."
Maxwell Anderson, *Elizabeth the Queen*

Unity of purpose, they say, is everything. It can defeat armies, spread ideas and philosophies, and stir the placid and sedentary to heroic action. Rare is the leader who does not try to promote this unity by any and all means at his disposal.

In Jean Perron's case, the process of uniting the Montreal Canadiens into a cohesive unit began in late season on the Winnipeg-St. Louis road trip and ended sometime during the Adams Division final against the Hartford Whalers.

Little did he know that this process would have a distinctly avian theme . . .

The Birdman of Alcatraz, Part Two

(A struggle in four acts)

Species represented

Patrick Roy (*Rouahis nervosus*)—A long-legged non-flyer with a wide wingspan; what it doesn't knock down with its wings, it falls on.

Claude Lemieux (*Tombus constantus*)—A notorious ocean diver which keeps coming up with pearls. Gets nasty when provoked.

Brian Skrudland (*Yappus scrappus*)—A combative cousin of the myna, pecks away constantly at enemies and can strike with lightning speed.

Larry Robinson (*Aquila chrysaetos*)—The illustrious Golden Eagle, once said to be battling extinction.

Bob Gainey (*Buteo jamaicensis*)—The classic Canadian red-tailed hawk, swoops down on anything that dares move in its territory. An older relative of the Mike McPhee, is known to favour the left wing.

Chris Chelios (*Sterna paradisaea*)—Also known as the Arctic Turn, for his manoeuverability in heavy traffic.

Chris Nilan, John Kordic, Steve Rooney and David Maley (*Pestus controlus*)-The Harriers, the reasons why most teams prefer to exhibit their most dove-like nature when confronting this quartet in their natural habitat.

Craig Ludwig, Rick Green, Mike Lalor and Gaston Gingras (*Katyus Doorbarrus*)—The reason why, as the play moves into its fourth act, Patrick Roy became *Rouahis* less *nervosus*.

Bobby Smith, Mats Naslund and Kjell Dahlin (*Snipus offensis*)—Given room to display their manoeuverability by the presence of the *Pestus controlis* quartet, proven dangerous to enemies.

Jean Perron as the Birdman.

And a cast of various other contributors.

If anything characterized the difference between the two teams that were the Montreal Canadiens during the 1985-86 regular season and then during the playoffs, it was unity. The team that blew hot and cold during the regular season bore little resemblance to that which suffocated all opposition during the playoffs en route to the franchise's twenty-third Stanley Cup championship.

As we mentioned in the previous chapter, there was friction in the ranks during the regular season. Not out-and-out dissension, that the coaching staff and upper management could quell with a series of concrete actions, but rather a lack of closeness that was hard to identify and harder to deal with.

The most obvious reason for the disunity was the onslaught of rookies: eight made the team and several others almost joined them. Veteran players became nervous when close friends were in danger of losing their jobs, a fairly standard group reaction anywhere in sports. On their side, the rookies hung together for mutual support.

Another difference was cultural, but not in the sense of language or ethnic background. Several veterans, Chris Nilan, Mario Tremblay and Guy Carbonneau, were convinced that some rookies simply did not believe in the kind of full commitment they had been reared to expect. The occupational culture was threatened, they felt, if the next generation of torch bearers could not understand that the Montreal Canadiens were not just another hockey team.

As well, the Five Year Plan hung over the heads of the veterans like a black cloud. When team management speaks of a long-term strategy to rejuvenate the team and bring it back to the league's upper echelons, veterans, quite rightfully, feel threatened. Many feel that "long-term" excludes them, especially as they see a steady stream of teammates come and go.

It took a long time for the Canadiens to coalesce. Isolation was the key factor.

For the members of the Montreal media brigade, the appearance of the Canadiens in the Stanley Cup final can most easily be described as incredible. For local fans, it might be most accurate to say that they willingly suspended their disbelief. Yet, by the time the team got there, it was a logical extension or conclusion of the natural order of things for the players whose playoff road was characterized by an intense commitment to both hard work and team discipline.

When does a working team finally come together to function as a winning team? For many social scientists, a team is best understood as a group of individuals who cooperate in the staging and execution of a set of routines. To perform efficiently, that group must exhibit such characteristics as enthusiasm, high group solidarity, unanimity of purpose and a strong shared set of beliefs and attitudes which highlight common goals.

The theory looks great on paper, but in reality we know little about exactly how and when players transform teams into united entities prepared to sacrifice for one another to achieve common goals. We have seen the cohesion manifested in a variety of winning combinations: Vince Lombardi's Green Bay Packers, the family atmosphere fostered for decades by the Los Angeles Dodgers and especially in the 1973 and 1974 editions of the Philadelphia Flyers.

Everyone remembers the brawling from coast-to-coast of the Broad Street Bullies but they forget that the Flyers were by far the most cohesive unit in the league in those two seasons. Fred Shero and team captain Bobby Clarke made sure that every player knew his place and responsibilities in the organization, even, as Dave Schultz says, to the exclusion of the players' wives and families on certain occasions.

Fight one Flyer, you fought them all, a philosophy right out of Dumas' *The Three Musketeers*. The Montreal Canadiens, and especially Scotty Bowman, knew that the only chink in the Flyers' suit of armour was the fighting side of the Philadelphia game. That is why a simple exhibition hockey game in late-September 1975 (described earlier) took on such importance.

"When that game was over, they had beaten us on the scoreboard and in the fights," said Schultz. "I sat in the dressing room and I said, 'Oh-oh! They know they can beat us at this game too.' You got the feeling that they were as together as we were." That game launched the Montreal powerhouse of the 1970s and Shultz would be out of hockey before Montreal lost another Stanley Cup.

E. Wright Bakke describes the team unification process as follows:

The agents acting for the formal organization ... and the individual acting for himself will simultaneously seek to make agents out of each other for the self-actualization of the formal organization ... and the individual himself ... The tendency of any individual toward co-operation or conflict with other participants in the organization ... will be proportional to his estimate of how much they help him or hinder him (to achieve his goals) ... The effectiveness of this *fusion* process is a function of the degree of compatibility of behaviour demanded and expected of the individual by the agents of the organization ... and by himself ...

This analysis of group integration helps explain the emergence of the *Club de Hockey Canadien* during the latter half of the 1985-86 season and in the playoffs. In discussions, the agents of formal organization impose their expectations and values on the young athletes and the set of strong commitments begins to appear within the ranks. The Canadiens spent a lot of time in group meetings during this period.

How does this influence emerge? It is everywhere at the Forum, and epitomized by people like Toe Blake, Jean Beliveau, Serge Savard, Jacques Lemaire and Jacques Laperriere.

The belief in a meaningful and constructive occupational culture, developed by Frank Selke Sr. and nurtured by Sam Pollock, provides the Montreal Canadiens with a special framework on which to build their expectations and values. It is quite similar to the process of acculturation undergone by a young recruit to a major corporation like IBM, Exxon or Xerox, or even the U.S. Marine Corps —recruits must learn to think, act, sleep and walk like "IBM people" or "Marines". They must find personal definition within the definition of group.

As Orville Brim and Stanton Wheeler explain:

A primary feature of the work setting that may aid the recruit in developing a meaningful definition of it is the extent to which others in the setting are or have been in his position and can aid his adaptation ... much adult socialization is organized so that a large number of persons are

introduced to the new setting simultaneously . . . adaptation
is likely to proceed much differently from the case where
one person enters alone, since the recruits can arrive at a
collective solution to the problems they face.

So while many teams faced with the rookie-veteran
division might have been unable to deal with such a rift,
real or perceived, Montreal had the wherewithal to use
the rookies' group dynamic to reach each individual
within that subgroup, and teach him about the benefits
of contributing as part of a larger group—the whole
team.

People who had "been there before", the veterans,
were made to understand that it was in everyone's interest to develop unity. The rookies, at the same time, were
made to see the benefits of learning from those who had
experienced what they were going through. The process
all came together in group isolation.

In past years, especially during the Pollock era, the
"playoff" Canadiens were sequestered in hotels in downtown Montreal or the nearby Laurentians. The reasoning was fairly straightforward: playoff pressures are
such that players need all of their physical and mental
energy directed to the task at hand. This focus might not
be possible if the players are at home, constantly
harassed by friends for tickets and gossip while trying to
maintain domestic harmony in homes that usually include several small children. In the case of young
bachelors, it was a good idea to get them away from the
temptations of Montreal's renowned night life.

The team attended meetings and practice as a group,
ate meals as a group and spent spare time quietly watching television, reading, or playing backgammon and
cards. It was forced socialization and players got to know
their teammates better at this late date in the season.

Another school of thought believed that the players
were being overly regimented and deprived of family and
home for an unduly long period—up to two months if
the club advanced to the Stanley Cup final series. The
frustrations of wives and girlfriends became keen late in

the playoffs and some domestic telephone calls were fraught with tension on both sides.

The case against domestic deprivation was made most clearly by Chris Nilan on the Saturday night the Canadiens won the Cup in Calgary. Injured in the third game of the series with damaged ankle ligaments suffered during a fight with burly Tim Hunter, Nilan was out of the series, even if it went seven games, so his conjugal rights were restored.

During the second intermission of the final game, he was interviewed (and kissed) by The Coach, Don Cherry, on the CBC broadcast. Later that evening, a journalist prodded him. "So what was your biggest thrill today, Chris? Winning the Cup or getting kissed on national TV by Don Cherry?"

"Neither. It was Mrs. Nilan showing up on the 11th floor of the Westin Hotel this afternoon after two months on Alcatraz!"

Alcatraz, in the real world, is a rock in the middle of San Francisco Bay. It was originally fortified by the Spanish, and then used by the U.S. as a military prison after 1859 and a federal penitentiary between 1933 and 1963. Also known as The Rock, the prison was home to some of the most incorrigible criminals in the United States and Robert Stroud, the legendary Birdman who made a name for himself as an ornithologist during his almost 60 years of incarceration there.

Alcatraz, 1986, was where the Canadiens found themselves in early April as the playoffs beckoned. In this case the surroundings were a touch less spartan than Stroud's —the Sheraton Hotel on Ile Charron, an island in the St. Lawrence River between Montreal and south shore Boucherville. The team stayed there for the duration.

It was here that the team dynamic really developed for the Canadiens. There might be two schools of thought about team isolation during the playoffs but for the Canadiens' brain trust there was no doubt. Perron was adamant. "There was no question with our team. There was one way to go and that was the hotel. With the large group of youngsters on our team, we had to bring everybody together. They don't know what it takes to win—things like concentration, relaxation ... away from the traffic. Montreal is not like any other hockey city. There is no other place in the National Hockey League where you would get that kind of attention and we had to make sure that the only thing in their minds was hockey."

What the Sheraton Ile Charron did for the 1986 Canadiens was evoke the train travel of the 1950s and the close-knit unity of the 1970s teams. Jean Beliveau and his team-mates would spend long hours discussing games, situations and individuals on eighteen-hour train rides to Chicago; Guy Lafleur, Steve Shutt and their cronies would get together in a bar and do the same as a team, and, suddenly, so did the 1986 Canadiens.

It was not only management deciding, "Let's put them all together in isolation and hope something good comes out of it." There was, as Jacques Lemaire explained, an evolutionary process involved. "Winning in team sports is a process. You just don't draft the best talent and leave it to their creativity. You have to build up a team identity and work ethic where every individual knows his role and what is expected of him.

"The first step of the process was to get the rookies to work together with the rest of the team. Once these people believe in each other, they begin to make sacrifices. They will do a little more whenever possible. That couldn't and didn't happen overnight; it was a season-long process.

"The next step was to get them to work well together and that came about in late season. That was when you got the feeling they could become a winner. I saw it during the last six to eight games of the year." This statement might amaze outsiders who only noticed one thing during that time: the slump that threatened the team's presence in the playoffs.

But Lemaire saw more during this period. "The players were doing more for each other, supporting one another on and off the ice and beginning to believe in the team's potential. The final step was to get everybody to win together and that happened during the playoffs. It was an A-B-C progression and the Stanley Cup was the result."

Two of the biggest role players were Bob Gainey and Larry Robinson, and had he not been injured, Mario Tremblay would have joined them. They were the three survivors of the previous Stanley Cup teams of the '70s and, as the team drew together during April and May, were a source of inspiration for the younger players.

Reading constantly during the two months of playoffs that the Canadiens had no superstars, that they were a generic version of the once-fabled teams who swept all before them, was a persistent thorn in the sides of many Montreal players. To a man they looked to veterans like Bob Gainey and Larry Robinson for leadership and inspiration. "When you are in the room between periods of a very tough game and you look up and Larry and Bob are sitting across from you, it builds up your confidence," said Skrudland.

"When we'd get too hyper, Larry and Bob could calm us down. When we got a little low, they'd get us up. And it didn't take a lot of talking on their part to do it. Best of all, though, was the fact that when we were out on the ice, Bob Gainey and Larry Robinson were on our side. We might have been in awe of them in the room; the other teams were in awe of them on the ice."

Other veterans helped as well, among them the three players who came in the "big trades", Bobby Smith, Ryan Walter (although out with a broken ankle until the final series) and Rick Green, not to mention Nilan.

The atmosphere was 100 percent hockey. In early April, with playoff games on television every night, the Canadiens would get together as a team to watch other series when they were not playing themselves. Perron watched the team come together.

"We had a TV set, coffee, milk or soft drinks and the guys could watch the games together. Other nights we brought in video cassettes of movies for entertainment. I didn't hear the guys talking about how boring it was, or what a sentence they were suffering through."

None of this means, though, that natural instincts were totally suppressed. "When we won the fifth game against New York on a Friday night and the guys found out we were going right back to the hotel, some of them didn't like it. We knew that there would be a layoff of at least five days because of the way the Calgary-St. Louis series was going, and some of the players thought they might get a day or two off. I said no way. We've got to win and that's it. We aren't doing this to punish anybody . . . we just wanted to make sure that we kept the guys under control."

As the playoff series went on, the players drew closer and closer together. One of them nicknamed their hotel Alcatraz, and the name spread from there. It was an in-joke that was originally kept very quiet, and only surfaced during the final series.

On road trips during the season, the Canadiens are models of decorum. Each player must wear a jacket and tie and be clean-shaven, alien behaviour for San Diego-bred beach boys like Chelios, but the rule nonetheless. In fact, the club not so gently insists that the travelling media respect this rule and it is not unusual to see writers and broadcasters quickly slapping on ties in airports as they prepare to board the team flight.

Ile Charron was off limits to the media horde that swelled with each series but a large number of press people were aboard the team charter that flew back to Montreal on Monday morning, May 19, with the series tied 1-1. The plane had hardly finished its banking ascent when off came the jackets and ties and out came the Alcatraz '86 shirts, the shorts and sandals. The white jerseys with Beach Boy cutoff sleeves, and accessories such as shades and sandals gave the Air Canada flight a definitely laid-back look as the Canadiens flew home for games three and four of the final.

On the front in bold black letters was the word Alcatraz and the small S symbol of Sheraton hotels, compliments of the staff of the team's home away from home. On the back, a stark black 86. The statement was "Us Against The World"; no media, hangers-on or team management need apply.

Rookies and veterans wore them proudly and tried to maintain an air of high nonchalance. Unity of purpose had been achieved and, better still, the team believed in it. One writer turned to another and said, "They've won it. They aren't going to lose another game and they know it."

Up front, team management knew it too, but they contented themselves with thin smiles. "I knew the guys were getting closer and I knew they were getting more demanding towards their teammates," said Perron.

"They didn't like a guy not doing his share. They wanted to win at all costs. They wanted to go home after the third game against Calgary and I wasn't sure. Then I decided that we'd return to the hotel and there was some grumbling." Bob Gainey stood up and said, "If we're going to win, we'll have to pay the price." At that point the Canadiens led Calgary 2-1, but a loss in the upcoming fourth game would have evened the series and returned home-ice advantage to the Flames.

"When the captain stands up and says these things, especially when the players know that he's got four Stanley Cup rings, they shut up and listen. Bob Gainey's got a lot of respect in the room and he did what a captain's supposed to do: he took charge," noted Perron.

The twenty-third Stanley Cup was a genuine team effort for Montreal, which is not to say that individuals were not outstanding. By the final series, many Habs were being touted for the Conn Smythe Trophy, given to the best performer in the playoff season.

Patrick Roy and Claude Lemieux emerged as the front-runners—Roy for his spectacular goaltending and Lemieux for his four game-winning goals and two overtime tallies.

Most importantly, the defensive players who shut down the opposition (Montreal would allow their opponents 30 or more shots only four times in 19 games, an amazing statistic in this so-called era of free-flow "Europeanized" hockey) began to receive their due as well. Guy Carbonneau and Bob Gainey on the first checking line, and Brian Skrudland and Mike McPhee of the second defensive trio, had done such a thorough job in Montreal's full-court press that even occasional hockey viewers sat up and took notice.

If the Bruins, Whalers, Rangers or Flames got past those four players, they ran into "the forest" as one NHL GM described the Montreal defence. Larry Robinson, Rick Green and Craig Ludwig, giants all, dealt out punishment to smaller opposition forwards and were strong enough to move the bigger bruisers out of the slot when necessary. Mike Lalor, a stay-at-home defenceman who played several inches bigger than his 6 feet, 195 pounds, and the fleet-footed duo of Chris Chelios and Gaston Gingras, gave opposition coaches fits.

"Nobody in the league has the combination of size, strength and mobility that the Canadiens have behind their blueline," said a discouraged Bob Johnson in a subdued Calgary dressing room while the Canadiens celebrated 40 feet away. "Some teams are big and slow back there and you dump the puck in and beat their defencemen to it or skate it past them. Others are smaller and more mobile and you can body them off the puck or crowd the net with big forwards. We tried both against the Canadiens and they were ready. Ludwig, Robinson and Green were quite prepared to use their bodies if we tried skating it in and Chelios and Gingras did an excellent job skating to the puck when we threw it in."

The best way for the Flames to defeat the Canadiens, beyond outscoring them in every game, of course, would be to overwhelm them physically and psychologically. Had they met the Canadiens team of mid-season, they might have been successful. After all, Calgary was the team that had slain Wayne Gretzky and the defending champion Oilers; if that wasn't good for a few psychological points, nothing was. They had a big team, powered by veterans like Doug Risebrough, Lanny McDonald (and even in Montreal they sympathized with the fact that likeable Lanny had never won the Stanley Cup in his thirteen-year career) and John Tonelli, the workaholic former New York Islander who led Team Canada to the Canada Cup win in 1984.

But by the time Calgary faced off against the Canadiens in the Saddledome, Friday, May 16, they were up against a team that was equal parts folklore, tradition and hard work.

They could not psyche out the Canadiens with tales of the fabulous exploits of rookie goalie Mike Vernon because Patrick Roy was on another planet in post-season play. And Claude Lemieux had come out of nowhere and played a Rocket Richard-like right wing, with the notable exception of his propensity for diving at the least provocation.

The playoff road had many important milestones. It all started in the first period of the first playoff game against Boston at the Forum, Wednesday, April 9.

You could sense something was going to happen in the game because the pre-game skate was somewhat unusual. Normally teams ignore each other in the warm-up, content to work out quietly and limber up for the contest that will follow in about 30 minutes. In the past, the pre-game warm-up would see NHL players blasting slapshots at their goalies and practising breakaways.

The modern day warm-up is much more elaborate. After an initial skate to get the muscles working, teams work on 2-on-1 and 3-on-2 drills inside the bluelines and players who are not involved stay out of the way by skating lazily in the rectangle between the blue and centre red lines.

The only people usually watching the pre-game warm-up are the standing room customers and a few early birds. The writers and broadcasters are having dinner in the press lounge upstairs and trading notes on players and coaches. So few witnessed the "pinball ballet" in warm-up that set the tone for Game 1. While their teammates went through their drills, Chris Nilan and Ken Linseman started "talking". Nilan, skating clockwise, and Linseman, counterclockwise, timed their rectangular skate so that they were side-by-side along the centre red line.

It went like this: Nilan and Linseman both made their turns in unison to find each other shoulder-to-shoulder along the redline. Yap yap yap, turn (skate along one's blueline) turn, yap yap yap, turn, skate, turn, yap yap yap. This intriguing little tableau played for approximately ten minutes, a good half of the pre-game skate.

After the game, Nilan was asked what they were discussing. "He kept telling me how I was going to eat his stick and I kept calling him a little faggot," replied West Roxbury's finest.

However, when the game got underway, Nilan and Linseman were not the main card. That was provided by a Bruin who was no stranger to playoff rumbles in the Forum and a Canadiens defenceman who hadn't been called upon to drop the gloves in a very long time.

Boston reported for work early in the first period and the Canadiens were nowhere to be seen. The Bruins had the better of the play and Roy was forced into good saves on Linseman and Simmer early on. There were a few roughing minors, not unusual when these teams meet, and Boston was much better than the 11-7 shots on goal totals indicated when the teams went to their dressing rooms at intermission, tied 0-0.

The second period started much the same way, quietly aggressive, when Boston's Louis Sleigher pulled what commentator Don Cherry called the "dumbest play I've seen in a long time." The puck was loose in front of the Boston bench and Larry Robinson was trying to play it with his skate when Sleigher charged the big defenceman, elbow raised high. This was the same Sleigher who had set off the Good Friday brawl with the Nordiques in 1984 when he sucker-punched defenceman Jean Hamel.

Fortunately or unfortunately, depending on your point of view, Robinson saw Sleigher out of the corner of his eye and was able to avoid most of the elbow. Sleigher, on the other hand, was unable to avoid an aroused Robinson who hammered him to the ice and fell on him, flailing away.

"The stupidest thing in the world when you play Montreal is to wake up Larry Robinson," said Cherry. "I used to tell my players not to wake him up because, if you do, he'll kill you."

After the dust had settled, Robinson and Sleigher were in the penalty box with majors and Sleigher's minor for elbowing gave Montreal a power play. By the time the pair emerged, the Canadiens led 2-0 on a pair of goals by Bobby Smith. Mike McPhee made it 3-0, tipping in a Robinson shot before the period ended.

Montreal was ready to be challenged on that night, and Boston would have to win a game in the Forum if they wanted their first post-season triumph over the Canadiens in 20 tries. Almost as if Sleigher refused to absorb the lesson he should have learned in the second period, the Bruins winger smashed into Roy behind the Canadiens net at 13:22 of the final period, Robinson immediately raced after him and thumped him once more.

Shortly thereafter, a typical Montreal-Boston melée broke out and several players squared off. McPhee and Stéphane Richer showed it would be a long series for Boston if they wanted to fight, winning clear-cut victories over Keith Crowder and Mike Milbury while Nilan and Linseman flirted with each other for 10 minutes, with a linesman hanging onto Nilan all the way. In all, 207 minutes in penalties were assessed by referee Bryan Lewis, and Jean Perron came close to thanking his counterpart, Butch Goring, for waking up the Canadiens.

Montreal would need no further wake-up calls in the series.

Game two was a strange game, especially when compared with the previous contest. Fans were still talking about the Jay Miller-John Kordic confrontation weeks later, giving the impression that the contest was as brawl-filled as its predecessor, but this was not the case.

The pre-game warm-up was as spirited as that of the first game and this time the hockey writers were in their seats, pens in hand. Nilan and Miller, then Nilan and Brian Curren, the king-sized Boston defenceman, spent a long time talking during the skate. Nilan and Miller were smiling ferociously during the badinage and all in attendance expected a fight-filled rematch.

Referee Bob Myers had other ideas, and quickly despatched players for any infraction. Defenceman Gord Kluzak was whistled down for hooking at 6:13 and when he and Nilan began yapping, joined the Montreal right winger for a ten-minute rest.

The teams once again emerged from the first period in a scoreless draw but Montreal drew first blood midway through the second period when Stéphane Richer beat rookie goalie Bill Ranford in close. With a little less than four minutes remaining in the period, Goring sent Jay Miller onto the ice for a faceoff. As Miller was skating to the Boston zone, Goring called him back and said a few words to him. Miller nodded and skated to the play.

Jean Perron tapped John Kordic on the shoulder and the Montreal rookie lined up beside Miller, a bruiser who was called up after Nilan butt-ended Rick Middleton in the mouth in October and who had participated in several confrontations with Nilan during the season.

Miller and Kordic had flirted during the first game but little else happened. "So, you here to play hockey or go?" Kordic asked as both players leaned forward for the face-off.

Miller grunted something unintelligible and Kordic turned to watch the linesman drop the puck. At that precise moment, Miller yelled, "Go!" and began flailing away at Kordic. The attack drove the Montreal winger back a few feet and he stumbled. However, he regained his balance and unleashed a barrage of devastating left hands that hammered Miller to the ice. Once again, the Bruins lost the fight, and to add insult to injury, Montreal scored a powerplay goal on the extra minor assessed Miller for instigating the fight.

Miller was not through, however. He brought thousands of Canadiens supporters to their feet when he stormed into the Bruins' dressing room and attacked the door. With everyone in the upper blues and many fans in the whites watching on extra-large TV screens installed to show replays, Miller was KO'd by the folding door.

That was the only fight that night and a theory of some hockey observers was proven right during the third period. During the 1985-86 season, and in previous years, whenever the Bruins discarded their so-called Big Bad Bruins roughhouse tactics, they beat the Canadiens.

One Montreal broadcaster said they suffered from the "Harry Sinden-Boston Garden" disease. The theory had it that Boston drafted big bruisers because of the small size of the Boston rink, euphemistically called an "arena with character" by supporters and "urban blight" by its detractors. Small players would get killed in the Garden and wouldn't have the room to put their skating skills to advantage on a rink with the smallest neutral zone in pro hockey.

When Sinden took over the coaching reins in Boston in 1966, the Bruins went for big players. The trouble was, big often also meant slow, and those players were at a disadvantage against good skating teams in the regulation-size rinks (200 feet long by 85 feet wide).

Thus for years, the Bruins would skate into the Forum and suffer defeat at the hands of better skating teams. Even during the fabulous Bobby Orr-Phil Esposito era, the Bruins could never beat Montreal in post-season play. When they tried intimidation, the Canadiens found bigger, rougher players who could skate. John Ferguson neutralized Ted Green; Rick Chartraw, Gilles Lupien and Pierre Bouchard cancelled out Stan Jonathan, Terry O'Reilly and John Wensink (despite a Jonathan-Wensink tag-team win over Lupien-Bouchard at Boston in the 1978 playoffs) and Mario Tremblay, Chris Nilan and John Kordic nullified the likes of Bobby Schmautz, Jay Miller and Brian Curren in the 1970s and 1980s.

One of the most enduring pictures of Boston playoff frustration against the Canadians is a montage of the team's last four coaches (Don Cherry, Gerry Cheevers, Harry Sinden and Butch Goring) standing on the visitor's bench at the Forum and screaming at the referee while dejected Bruins skate around listlessly, their moods blacker than their uniforms.

The repeated intimation that the Bruins could always count on being cheated out of a game by a combination of bad refereeing and the Forum crowd has been a standard Sinden complaint for almost two decades. He even has an ironic phrase for it: "The Ghosts of the Forum."

A psychologist would call this complaining negative reinforcement. Unintentional or not, Boston management has given the players an out, a subconscious excuse for losing their games in Montreal. In 1985-86, the Canadiens beat Boston six straight at the Forum—four during the season and twice during the playoffs.

Boston could easily have won two of those games: a 2-1 setback on February 1 in which they held the Canadiens to 14 shots in the whole game, and the first game of the Adams Division semi-final.

As it was, they came pretty close to winning the second contest, a game in which the Canadiens played much better than the first and held a seemingly insurmountable 2-0 lead with less than half a period to go. After the Kordic-Miller confrontation at 16:06 of the second, the teams settled down to play serious and clean hockey. At 12:15, Barry Pederson struck, converting a pass from Linseman and the Bruins were back in the game. The Canadiens sagged and 41 seconds later Crowder tied it from a scramble in front of the net.

Patrick Roy and Claude Lemieux chose this game to begin their climb to prominence. Roy was forced to make several good saves as Boston roared to life and his favourite conversational companions, his two goalposts, saved him late in the period. With five minutes remaining in the game, defenceman Ray Bourque sped out of his zone and over the Canadiens' blueline and unleashed a blistering slapshot from the face-off circle to Roy's right. The goalie was beaten cleanly, but the puck struck the post dead-on.

Less than a minute later, Lemieux suckered Boston winger Kraig Nienhuis into doing what the Bruins do best at the Forum, taking a stupid penalty.

A desultory scrum took place to the right of the Boston goal at 15:44 and Lemieux prolonged it just enough so that Nienhuis could skate up to him and crosscheck him to the ice, right in front of Myers. The Bruin winger was still in the penalty box when Lemieux rubbed salt in the wound with the game-winning goal at 17:33.

The teams travelled to Boston and this time the pre-game skate got serious, as Kluzak and Nilan almost came to blows. Alternate referee Terry Gregson and Serge Savard got in between the belligerents and were reinforced when game referee Don Koharski and his two linesmen came running out of their dressing room in their underwear.

Although there was a spate of minor penalties and misconducts in the first period, there were no fights and the Bruins led 1-0 when the teams skated off for intermission. Lemieux and Mats Naslund gave Montreal a 2-1 lead by the halfway point of the second period but goals 14 seconds apart by Reed Larson and Crowder gave Boston a 3-2 lead with one period remaining.

If the theory that the Bruins have better success against Montreal when there is less fighting is valid, so is another. The second theory says a strong skating winger who can hit will do well in the Garden.

This idea was proven barely a minute into the third period when Guy Carbonneau sped into the Bruins' zone and dropped a pass to Bob Gainey. The latter whipped it by Ranford before the Boston goalie could move.

Seven minutes later, Rick Green was whistled off for tripping and the Bruins pressed on the powerplay. Forty seconds into his penalty-killing shift, Gainey picked up the puck along the right boards in his own zone, avoided a Boston checker and sped away into the Boston zone with defenceman Craig Ludwig to his left and Bruins rearguard Ray Bourque trying to head him off.

About thirty feet away from the Boston net, Gainey, on his off-wing, looked across to Ludwig and simultaneously fired a wrist shot in the opposite direction past a surprised Ranford. The series was over and Montreal would face Hartford in the division final, following that team's rout of the Quebec Nordiques.

If the Montreal-Boston series was characterized by barely concealed hostility and pugnacity, the Canadiens-Whalers confrontation was just the opposite. Both teams had four days off to prepare and the truce period gave them plenty of time to throw bouquets at each other.

Nilan had been particularly rough on the Bruins, telling all who would listen that Boston coach Butch Goring was "yellow" and that the Bruins were cheap-shot artists and cement-footed goons. Now he was all flowers—the Whalers were a good team and even their tough guy, winger Torrie Robertson, was a quality player, he purred.

"He really said that?" glowed Robertson when Nilan's compliment was delivered. "Tell him thanks for me."

Robertson and his mates also said thanks three nights later as they skated off the Forum ice with a 4-1 win over the Canadiens. Robertson had a confrontation with Kordic and came out second best, but Hartford won the war, breaking the game wide open with goals by Stewart Gavin, Sylvain Turgeon and John Anderson in the second period.

The Canadiens and Whalers went on to play a defensive series that was characterized by hard and clean bodychecks in every zone and goaltending that scaled new heights. When Patrick Roy wasn't stoning superlative forwards like Kevin Dineen, Ron Francis, Ray Ferraro, Anderson and Dean Evason, Mike Liut was picking the pockets of Bobby Smith, Mats Naslund, Lemieux and Richer.

The Hartford Whalers, quietly assembled through a series of astute regular-season moves that earned Emile Francis the admiration of his peers, would prove to be the best team the Canadiens faced in the playoffs. "I am not putting down the Rangers or the Flames but the Whalers were a lot better team than anyone gave them credit for," said Jean Perron. "And Jack Evans coached them beautifully. They played within their system the whole way and it showed; it took an overtime goal by Claude Lemieux in the seventh game for us to beat them. They could easily have won and gone all the way like we did."

The undisputed leaders of the Whalers were the forward line of Dineen, Francis and Anderson, goalie Liut and defenceman Duane Babych. Defensively, Doug Jarvis and Stewart Gavin pressed the Canadiens forwards at every opportunity.

Anderson was a late-season acquisition from Quebec, in a trade for Risto Siltanen, and had played very well for the Nordiques during the first six months of the season. After the Nordiques bowed out in three straight, observers said that GM Maurice Filion had outsmarted himself with the Anderson-Siltanen trade.

Babych was acquired early in the season from Winnipeg for forward Ray Neufeld, a deal only John Ferguson thinks went the Jets' way and Gavin was a steal from Toronto Maple Leafs in a swap for defenceman Chris Kotsopoulos. Last but not least, Jarvis, Gainey's linemate in Montreal for seven years and four Stanley Cups, came over from Washington for Jorgen Petterson in mid-season, a trade that helped both teams despite commentator Howie Meeker's low opinion of Jarvis.

"That team took us right down to the wire," said Larry Robinson. "They deserve all the credit in the world for what they accomplished. Players like Scot Kleinendorst, Joel Quenneville and Ulf Samuelsson did a hell of a job in their zone and even when Liut was out for two games, Steve Weeks played very well in nets."

The series was tied 3-3 when the teams returned to the Forum for game seven on Tuesday, April 29. At 1:19 of the first period, Guy Carbonneau stole the puck at the Hartford blueline and walked in on Liut. The Hartford goalie slammed the door and set the pattern for 66 minutes of heart-stopping hockey. Six minutes in, Liut stopped Skrudland and McPhee on a 2-on-1 and 30 seconds after that, Roy stopped Gavin on his doorstep. Then Richer and Lemieux combined for a stellar scoring opportunity, only to be foiled by Liut yet again.

This scenario played over and over until late in the first period with Montreal killing a penalty. Mike McPhee rushed Francis, playing the right point for the Whalers, when the puck got trapped in the latter's skates. The left-winger muscled Francis off the puck and sped away on a breakaway. He beat Liut low to the stick side.

The score remained 1-0 very late in the game and it appeared the Canadiens would win their second straight series on a short-handed goal. But late in the third, Dean Evason raced up the left-wing boards with a defenceman in front of him. Babych, who had not been pressing offensively because a bad groin injury hampered his skating, was trailing. Evason crossed the Montreal line and dropped the puck to Babych who "first-timed" it past a partially screened and very surprised Roy with 2:48 remaining. The Forum went deathly quiet. The Canadiens should have been leading by several goals by then and instead were deadlocked when the siren sounded, simultaneously announcing the end of regulation play and the onset of sudden death overtime.

A year before, the Montreal Canadiens had blown game six in Quebec and then lost game seven at the forum on an overtime goal by Peter Stastny. During the regular season, the Canadiens turned in one of the worst overtime records in the league while Hartford already had two overtime victories in the 1986 playoffs, against Quebec and Montreal in game one and game four of their respective series.

How would the Canadiens react this time?

They stormed the Hartford net with little result for the first five minutes of play. At 5:12, Nilan and Kleinendorst got their sticks up in the Hartford zone and, after belabouring the issue, were assessed misconducts by referee Andy Van Hellemond.

Montreal gained a face-off to Liut's left shortly thereafter and the puck skittered behind the Whaler net. Skrudland mucked furiously along the boards and kicked it to Lemieux who moved out in front of the goal and lifted a sharply angled backhand over a surprised Liut's shoulder as he skated by. The Forum exploded.

Lemieux, meanwhile, skated towards the Canadiens bench and saw his teammates storming towards him. He did what came naturally—he took a dive and covered his head. "I scored a goal like that in junior last year and my teammates almost killed me," he explained afterward. "I don't want to get hurt by my own guys."

Three eventful weeks into the playoffs, Lemieux and Roy were folk heroes in Quebec, and their fellow inmates on Alcatraz were starting to believe. Roy admitted that he spoke with his goalposts before every game and there he was, shortly after the national anthems, about 40 feet away from his net and bent over in deep conversation.

"I started in the last regular-season game in Hartford

and I do it every night," he explained to a growing media throng. His words and delightful flakiness were the stuff of headlines all over North America and he received prominent play in *Time, Sports Illustrated* and *The Sporting News*.

Lemieux wasn't far behind when he confessed to "going off quietly in a corner "and having a private conversation with his teenaged brother Serge, who is severely retarded and has spent his life in institutions. "Whenever I am in a tight spot I talk to him," Lemieux said.

The press gobbled it up. In an age of terse "how-I-did-it" quotes, usually blamed on "dumb hockey players" but really the result of stupid and lazy post-game questions by a large number of hockey reporters, Roy and Lemieux were deemed more colourful than anyone around. When one night later, the Calgary Flames eliminated the Edmonton Oilers, everyone began to believe.

If anything, the five-game series with the New York Rangers propelled the two young players even more into prominence. The Canadiens and Rangers slept through the first game, a 2-1 win by Montreal, and the Habs bombed John Vanbiesbrouck for four goals in the middle period of the second game to take a 2-0 series lead going into Madison Square Garden.

The Rangers had 27 shots in the first game and 21 in the second and winger Wilf Paiement was not convinced by Roy. "I'd like to see how he would play if he had to face 35 or 40 shots a game. We'll try to do that back home." Other Rangers concurred.

Paiement and his teammates would get their answer the very next game.

Before the Monday night contest started, the New York faithful began chanting derisively, "Roo-Ah! Roo-Ah! Roo-Ah!", a Manhattan distortion of Roy's name. His name had been explained to them by ESPN broadcasters who couldn't even come close to the real French pronunciation "Rwah". (They, and their English Canadian counterparts were even further off on Lemieux, in the best tradition of mangled French surnames perfected by that master of foreign elocution, Foster Hewitt.)

Little did they know Roy loved the special attention

and he showed it by turning in what Jean Beliveau later described as "the best playoff game I've ever seen a goalie play."

The Rangers took the lead early in the first but Richer tied it at 6:00 when his clearing pass banked in off Vanbiesbrouck's skate. After one period it was still 1-1, despite a 16-7 New York advantage in shots on goal and a dozen clear scoring chances.

In the middle period, it was the Ranger goalie's turn to shine as Montreal outshot New York 15-6. Nevertheless, the Rangers scored the only goal. Mats Naslund tied the game at 5:06 of the third, but it looked like New York had the victory wrapped up when Bob Brooke climaxed a furious siege in Montreal territory with a shot along the ice that beat Roy at 12:54 and made the score 3-2.

It was not to be for the Blueshirts. Brian MacLellan, who was acquired early in the season to add muscle to the diminutive Rangers, took a bad late penalty at 16:04, *à la* Boston's Nienhuis, and Bobby Smith tied the game on a backhand from the slot at 17:56.

It was Montreal's third overtime of the playoff season. The question again was, how would they perform?

The answer? Spectators and the players watched in amazement as Roy kicked out thirteen New York shots, including an incredible four in a row after New York won a face-off in the Canadiens' end. In all, the Rangers took 47 shots on goal during the game, or about two games' worth for Montreal, and Roy stopped 44.

For nine-and-a-half minutes, Roy robbed the Rangers blind. With 9:30 gone in the overtime period, the teams faced off in Montreal territory. The puck was passed to the right point. Defenceman Willie Huber fanned on his attempted shot and Mike McPhee broke away down the left wing. Across the ice, Huber's defence partner James Patrick was far out of position, almost against the left point boards when McPhee broke out and Lemieux streaked up the middle. As he went to turn and head off Lemieux, Patrick tripped over linesman Ray Scapinello's skate and fell to the ice.

McPhee and Lemieux raced in alone on Vanbiesbrouck and the left winger passed to the rookie who lifted it into the Rangers net over Vanbiesbrouck's shoulder. The New York papers were full of Roy and Ray (Scapinello) the next day. TV replays show that Patrick was too far removed from the play to catch Lemieux, a good skater. Still, even the Canadiens admitted that the old intangible, luck, was on their side so far this playoff year.

After all, this was the team that had entered the playoffs with a 24-square foot question mark in goal. "Everybody else might have been worried about our goaltending but Jean Perron wasn't and neither was I," said Francois Allaire, the former Quebec university coach and the team's goaltending coach. "People said Patrick had technical weaknesses but there weren't very many. He came to the organization as a very sound goalie whose special strengths were his incredible quickness and a very good glove. He worked hard at Sherbrooke a year ago and did most of his learning there."

Allaire admitted that Roy improved his concentration during the playoffs, and that the Canadiens worked many special drills to help him improve his positioning in the crease, cutting down angles on shooters and taking away the strengths of other teams.

"By the time the playoffs came around, our work with Patrick was about the book we had on each team. For instance, Boston was very good at getting the puck in from the boards into the crease and slot so Jean improvised drills that had Patrick and the defenceman working on this.

"Hartford, on the other hand, took a lot of shots from far out so we had our players doing the same thing. New York tried a lot of European-type motion and weaves so we had him drill with our forwards a lot. Finally, Calgary liked jamming the crease with big forwards so our defencemen did the same thing in practice, forcing Patrick up against the screening player to cut down the possibility of deflections." The latter drill paid dividends in the second game of the final series when Roy got his left leg on a close-in deflection by the Flames' Tim Hunter.

If this chapter has given the impression that a set Montreal line-up played so well that all Jean Perron had to do was open and shut the doors at the team bench, nothing could be further from the truth. With the early elimination of the Sherbrooke Canadiens—they did not make the AHL playoffs—Kordic, Serge Boisvert and Scott Sandelin (who played for the U.S. national team in the World Championships) joined the team. Goalie Vincent Riendeau and forward Shayne Corson, who was still nursing an injury, also moved up after their junior seasons.

The additional players meant Montreal was carrying some thirty hockey players and Perron divided the practice sessions in two. The A group comprised those players who could be called upon for playoff action and the B group was made up of those players who probably would not play unless an injury or illness felled a regular. Several players moved from A to B, and back again, as a result of their game performances, among them Lucien Deblois, Petr Svoboda, Steve Rooney and David Maley.

Maley joined the Canadiens in late March after Wisconsin was eliminated from the NCAA championships and spent most of what remained of the regular season trying to shed a few pounds and find a place on the team. A rugged 6' 2" forward, he skated well and possessed good hockey sense. He was finally dressed for the Pittsburgh game on the penultimate Saturday of the season and played all of two shifts. He played another couple of shifts against Detroit four days later and then was relegated to the B team for what appeared to be the duration.

But as was the case with all players in the organization, people were watching him closely, whether he sensed it or not. Coach Perron was one who paid special attention to the youngster. "I could see in practice that he didn't like other players taking the body against him and that he was really anxious to get playing. He is a big boy and he showed me some very good skills and soon we decided he was ready."

New York blanked the Canadiens 2-0 in the fourth game of their series and the teams returned to Montreal for game five. Midway through the third period, with the Canadiens leading 2-1, Maley, the big Minnesotan, knocked down a clearing pass at the Ranger blueline and shot at the net. Vanbiesbrouck made the save but lost the rebound. Gainey scored an insurance goal and Montreal was in its first final in seven years.

Maley's first playoff point was a big one, and he would loom large against the Calgary Flames.

Montreal had to wait a week for Calgary to finally eliminate the stubborn St. Louis Blues as Jacques Demers' unlikely alliance of former Canadiens, Flames, and a few Blues left over from the 1983 near-move to Saskatoon took Calgary to the wire, rebounding from a three-goal deficit late in the third period of game six to score an overtime win and force a seventh game.

Calgary finally subdued the Blues 2-1 in the seventh game, and the question going into the final series was, "Would fatigue bother the Flames more than the week-long layoff would affect Montreal?"

Late in the first period of the first game, the teams were tied 1-1 when Calgary defenceman Paul Baxter flipped a puck high into the Canadiens' end. Jim Peplinski flicked it out of the air with a high stick and scored. Referee Kerry Fraser conferred with his linesmen and the goal stood, enraging Roy. He slashed Ron Finn across the back of his legs to earn a 10-minute misconduct, and then gave Ray Scapinello a two-handed shove, something which should have earned him an early shower and a date with NHL vice-president Brian O'Neill.

But this is the era of the instant replay and Fraser, like any of his counterparts faced with the situation, pretended not to see the second infraction. Imagine the uproar if, first, the goal proved to be an integral part of the final result (it was), second, he kicked out the Montreal goalie who had the hockey world abuzz, and third, the videotape showed the goal was no good (which it did).

Calgary went onto win 5-2, becoming the first team to score four goals against Roy in one game (Hartford had scored an empty-net goal in their 4-1 series opener) and five against the Canadiens (another empty net tally).

But that victory was it for the Flames. Two nights later Calgary took a 2-0 lead at 0:15 of the second period but the Flames would score only seven more goals in the next

11 periods, two of these coming with a little more than three minutes remaining in the third period of the fifth and final game.

The Canadiens won game two with three improbable heroes all scoring their first goals of the playoffs—Gingras, Maley and Skrudland—and the latter set a play-off record for fastest overtime goal, 0:09.

From then on, Montreal methodically shut down the Flames, stifling them at every opportunity. In the 1-0 Forum victory that gave Montreal an insurmountable 3-1 lead heading back west, the Flames were held to 15 shots over all, including only two in the second period and six in the third. Lemieux scored his fourth game-winner of the playoffs, pouncing on an errant clearing pass by Doug Risebrough and blasting it through a surprised Vernon at 11:10 of the third period.

Gingras and Skrudland also scored in the Cup-clincher while Maley set up Rick Green for the third-period goal that made it 3-1 and dashed Calgary's hopes. At 10:30 of the final period, 19 seconds after Green beat Vernon with a wrist shot, Naslund fed Bobby Smith for Montreal's fourth goal. It was delicious irony that the tall centre whose pass had ended Montreal's hopes of a second Drive for Five on a brisk April Sunday in 1980, scored the goal that won the Canadiens' twenty-third Cup in 1986.

Smith's Cup winner was his seventh of the series and his strong two-way play was important to the team's success. His linemate Naslund ended the playoffs with eight goals, including a pair in Montreal's 5-3 win in game three in which the Canadiens blitzed the Flames for three goals in 68 seconds late in the first period.

Larry Robinson and Bob Gainey led both on the ice and in the dressing room. Gainey scored five goals and added five assists while shutting down the best forwards the opposition could muster. His linemate Guy Carbonneau scored seven goals while Skrudland and McPhee combined for another five goals between them.

Green, Lalor and Ludwig played strong physical games in front of the Canadiens' net while Chelios and Gingras moved the puck quickly out of danger with their good skating and stickhandling.

Forgotten in the shuffle because they rarely played (one not at all) were two former Winnipeg teammates, Soetaert and Deblois. The former could have infected his team with complaints about his lot, but chose instead to show full support for his goalkeeping partner. Soetaert and Deblois accepted their lot with grace and aplomb and, as a result, showed the non-playing rookies how to behave. Their contribution was an important one.

All that said, the 1986 playoffs belonged to Patrick Roy and Claude Lemieux and it was Roy who was awarded the Conn Smythe for top playoff performer after the last siren had sounded.

Cherchez le gardien, trouvez la Coupe Stanley!

Montreal Canadiens found both in the spring of 1986. The Torch had been passed, taken up and held firmly aloft.

In a year where Jack Nicklaus won the Masters, Willie Shoemaker the Kentucky Derby and the Boston Celtics the NBA Championship, it appeared that order had returned to the universe of sports.

The Montreal Canadiens could return to their mausoleum the following September and look the Forum ghosts right in the eye.

Epilogue

"More wine?"

Francois-Xavier Seigneur is positively beaming as he solicitously reaches for the carafe of *rouge maison*.

A 26-month-old question is reversed. "So F.X., how do you market a winning hockey team?"

"The same way you market a loser, or any team," he laughs.

Early June, 1986 has been much kinder to the Montreal Canadiens' vice-president of marketing than was April, 1984, when the question referred to a once-proud franchise that looked down nervously at the maelstrom roiling below. Today, the glow of the recent Stanley Cup is still showing.

In April, 1984, two handsome French Canadians in their early thirties personified the upstairs-downstairs dichotomy of the Montreal Canadiens. The first was Guy Lafleur, thirty-two and rapidly aging in a world where the rewards are astronomical but time is compressed cruelly. The other, of course, was F.X., nineteen months older than the hockey player but considered a bright young man with a promising future in a world with a different calendar.

Montreal Canadiens emerged Phoenix-like from the ashes of their worst season in living memory that April two years ago. They showed some promise for the immediate future by winning playoffs against Boston and Quebec before succumbing to the New York Islanders. It would be Guy Lafleur's last hurrah; some thirty weeks later he would tearfully tell a hastily called press confer-

411

ence that his playing days were over. There would be no close monitoring of F.X. and the Flower as both went their separate ways. One thing became clear in the 1984-86 period, however. The importance of front office quality was recognized by just about everyone.

The results of applying a long-term marketing policy to the Montreal Canadiens, F.X.'s job, became especially apparent during this time. In fact, the situation recalled "Tay Pay" Gorman's arrival in Montreal in 1934. Gorman revived the incidentals, advertising, concessions and the game program, and put the Forum back on the road to financial respectability. Seigneur's job was to take a club that had become too staid and distant from its fans, and return it to the people who paid the shot by upgrading and updating those same areas.

"No more comparisons of the Forum with the Vatican," Ronald Corey told Seigneur when he joined the team. "This isn't a church. People are allowed to make noise and enjoy themselves." The team president immediately went out and practised what he preached, and set an unofficial club record (Most Involved Team President —Modern Era) one game during the 1986 playoffs when he was seen to lean over in his ice-level box, gesticulating wildly and yelling at the referee. Until his arrival, the team president's position was largely ceremonial and entailed sitting quietly behind the Canadiens' bench, sedately observing the goings-on while everyone around went crazy.

One way to make the team more accessible to the fans was to bring the players to the people. The Canadiens had kept their faithful on starvation rations in the past, deigning only to help distribute Molson Brewery calendars and mini-schedules, and to sign the occasional deal with a corn syrup manufacturer for coupon redemption of player pictures.

The New Canadiens were all marketing oriented, from Corey down, as the *Club de Hockey Canadien* joined the world of sports promotion. Team T-shirts, jerseys, singlets, and sweaters (each in several models) went on sale in a newly revamped souvenir shop just off the main lobby. Strategically placed mini-stands throughout the building hawked pennants, banners, crests, mini-sticks in wood and plastic, and player cards. Deals were negotiated with large companies such as Kraft, a local supermarket giant and Coca-Cola for special shirts, collector buttons and place mats.

The money changers invaded the Temple and the Temple was no more—except when it suited the purpose of the New Canadiens to recall its exalted status, that is. Corey reasoned that if people from all over the world would travel far to visit such famous Quebec shrines as St. Joseph's Oratory in Montreal and Ste. Anne de Beaupré just outside Quebec City, that the Forum could have the same draw. So the Canadiens found themselves practising before 17,000 screaming kids (a joint promotion with a potato chip manufacturer) and the museum-cum-dressing room was opened to special tours.

The team magazine in the past basically had been a hockey pictorial, with action pictures on the cover and the inside woefully thin on editorial material. Today's covers are "compositions". On one, Mats Naslund is bedecked in horned helmet and Viking furs and on another, Bob Gainey is ripping off his white shirt to reveal a Canadiens shirt underneath, *à la* Superman.

Gainey received excellent coaching for the role. When Christopher Reeve, the star of the Superman movies, was filming in Montreal, he was invited to the games. The Old Canadiens would have merely grunted in acknowledgement. The New Canadiens put him on the scoreboard and make sure the TV networks know where to find him.

"That's what it's all about in the modern world," Seigneur said. "I remember telling you two years ago that we compete with everybody for the entertainment dollar, from wrestling to the Expos to the Alouettes and pay TV, and we have to make sure that our presence is everywhere in the marketplace. Win or lose, we have to be certain that our fans do not feel that we are too far above them."

A new clock/scoreboard went up in the summer of 1985 and fans returning for the new season were greeted with a Snoopy-like dog leading cheers from his perch inside the revered CH, an animated "wave" that is synchronized with the Forum organist, and penalty-call cartoons. And if the Forum is a little too quiet, the board and organist try to stir the crowd up with upbeat music and the exhortation of *"Bruit! Noise!"*.

Mon dieu, is nothing sacred? Will they turn the Forum into a rink in Pittsburgh? The purists hate it, of course. One of the reasons the Forum was so imposing in the past was that poor play by the hometown would often be greeted by glacial silence, a big chill that was more intimidating than 10,000 boos.

These are new times. Late in one game, the Canadiens are ahead by one goal when the scoreboard and organist start a wave. The mindless thousands stand up and wave their arms on cue for a dozen passes around the stands; the noise reaches a crescendo totally inconsistent with the lack of action on the ice.

"Goddamn it!" swears one longtime regular and diehard Montreal fan in Section 32 of the white seats. "I hope the other guys score just to stop this shit." The words are hardly out of his mouth when the puck is in the Canadiens' net. The goal has the desired effect; the fans eschew bread and circuses and return to the game at hand. Quietly.

"That's more like it," he smirks.

During another game, the organist begins the ubiquitous "Hey, Hey, Goodbye", played in every rink in the league when the home team is leading late in a game. The trouble is, he starts the tune with about eight minutes left in the contest. When the other team scores, the chorus is silenced.

"He doesn't lead that song any more," Seigneur says later. New marketing and a jazzed-up presentation of Forum games does not include poor sportsmanship is his implication.

Seigneur has heard the complaints of the oldtimers and dismisses them. "We have given the team and the Forum back to the fans. This was not done as a spur-of-the-moment thing. We work on a long-term basis and everything we have done so far has been researched carefully."

When the Canadiens travelled to Calgary late on the Thursday before the Saturday night win that would clinch their twenty-third Stanley Cup, F.X. wasn't on the team charter, a rarity. He was back home co-ordinating the victory celebration and flew to Calgary the next day.

Moments after the team won, Seigneur announced a special victory celebration, one quite different from its predecessors. In the past, all the fans would get was a parade that began at the west-end Forum and ended at City Hall in Old Montreal. "This year we decided to start at the City Hall, and have the team ride to the Forum where a special mini-rock concert would culminate with the players being introduced on stage," he said.

The players struggled through crowds estimated to be between 500,000 and one million during the five-hour affair and returned to the Forum to find another 17,000 fans as well as several top Quebec performers waiting for them. Those in attendance paid a two dollar admission fee which was donated to children's charities. The players took their last hurrahs and everyone went home for the summer. Two weeks after the victory, half of the playing Canadiens were in the Bahamas, on a company-paid group holiday.

F.X. Seigneur is eating lunch and smiling a lot, the ever-congenial host. Occasionally we are interrupted as someone comes up to shake his hand.

The Forum and the Canadiens are different these days. They march to the tunes of the 1980s and will continue the process of updating and modernization as long as Corey, Seigneur and company are around.

"We're into long-term plans and corporate objectives now," said Seigneur. "For sure we will enjoy this summer, but we are already hard at work on next year and the year after."

They know they are a corporation and operate not unlike others at the top of the heap. How corporate are they? The Montreal Canadiens are cited in a book titled *The 100 Best Corporations to Work For in Canada*.

The Lions in Winter Company Limited.

Because winter is never far away in Montreal.

FUTURE POSTSCRIPT

On a crisp October Saturday in 1985, the Canadiens of the Pierrefonds Novice Minor House League come together in a room full of hockey equipment in Montreal's West Island. It is a scene repeated in thousands of rinks across North America and Europe.

Coach Ron Abbondanza hands out the familiar *bleu-blanc-rouge* sweaters and socks to a veritable United Nations of fifteen excited young boys, aged seven and eight. During the next six months, these boys will do battle in their seven-team league and they know they are the lucky ones. Only they are the Canadiens.

Jon Goyens returns to his seat caressing his new sweater and innocently asks, "Dad, did anyone ever wear Number 9 for the Canadiens?" His query brings smiles to the faces of a lot of parents in the room. His linemate Peter Murphy asks the same question about his Number 7. In the corner, goalie Darryl Boloten is struggling to fit Number 19 over his extra equipment.

"We should change that to Number 29 like Ken Dryden," says his father.

"Who's Ken Dryden, Dad?" *Tempus fugit.*

Throughout the long Montreal winter, boys with names like Castonguay, Gagnon, Gervais, Crites, Alexandre, Khatri, Baronian and Vanasse learn what it is to wear the red, white and blue with quiet pride. All the other teams are gunning for them because they are wearing the special uniform. Knowing this, they respond to the extra pressure and play like their "big brothers", never quitting, never willing to be outworked.

The March playoffs are single-game elimination. True to form, the Canadiens win all three games by scores of 1-0, 2-1 and 3-2. The championship game goes into overtime and victory comes when Number 16, a centre, steals the puck at centre ice and races in on a breakaway, beating the goalie with a low shot to the corner.

His name?

Beliveau.

Index

Credits

Every reasonable effort has been made to find copyright holders of the excerpted material. The publishers would be pleased to have any errors or omissions brought to their attention.

Excerpts on pages 26 and 43 are from *The Mad Men of Hockey* by Trent Frayne. New York: Dodd, Mead and Co., Inc., 1979. Reprinted by permission of the publisher. Excerpts on pages 34, 36, 37, 39 and 56 are from *The Hockey Book*, W.V. Roche, ed. Used by permission of the Canadian Publishers, McClelland and Stewart. Excerpt on page 51 is from "The Great Gorman" by Jim Coleman, *Maclean's*, March 1, 1946. Reprinted by permission of the author and publisher. Excerpt on page 74 is from *Ring Lardner's "You Know Me Al"*, copyright © 1979 by Bruccoli Clark Publishers and Harcourt, Brace, Jovanovich, Inc. Reprinted by permission of Harcourt, Brace, Jovanovich, Inc. Excerpt on page 102 is from *Conn Smythe: If You Can't Beat 'em in the Alley* by Conn Smythe with Scott Young. Used by permission of the Canadian Publishers, McClelland and Stewart. Excerpt on page 116 is from *Behind the Cheering* by Frank Selke with H. Gordon Green. Used by permission of the Canadian Publishers, McClelland and Stewart. Excerpt on page 135 is from "He's Hockey's Most-Wanted" by Andy O'Brien, retired sports editor, *Weekend Magazine*, October 1952. Reprinted by permission of the author. Excerpt on page 199 is from *The Canadian Encyclopedia*. Edmonton: Hurtig Publishers Ltd., 1985. Reprinted by permission of the publisher. Excerpt on page 206 is from *I've Got to Be Me* by Derek Sanderson with Stan Fischler. New York: Dodd, Mead and Co., Inc., 1970. Reprinted by permission of the publisher. Excerpt on page 238 is from an article in *Weekend Magazine* by Caspar Dzeguze. Excerpt on page 239 is from an article by Ted Blackman in *The Gazette*. Excerpt on page 360 is from "Toughing it Out" in *The Boston Globe Magazine* by Charles Kenney, March 25, 1984. Reprinted by permission of *The Boston Globe*. Excerpt on page 373 is from an article in *The Gazette* by Red Fisher, March 1986. Reprinted by permission of the author. Excerpt on page 385 is from *The Fusion Process* by E. Wright Bakke. New Haven: Yale Labor and Management Center, 1955. Excerpt on pages 385–6 is from *Socialization After Childhood: Two Essays* by Orville Brim and Stanton Wheeler. Melbourne, Fla. Robert E. Krieger Publishing Co., Inc., 1976. Reprinted by permission of the publisher.